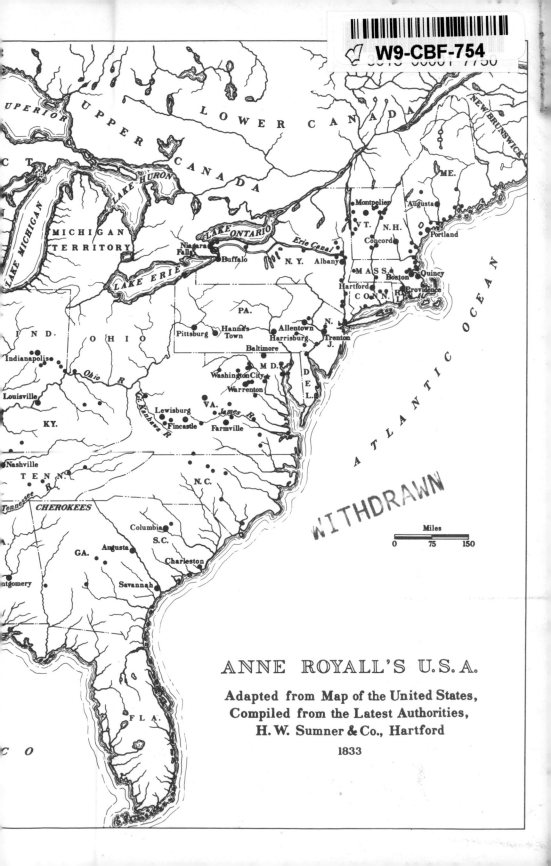

ANNE ROYALL'S U.S.A.

Adapted from Map of the United States,
Compiled from the Latest Authorities,
H. W. Sumner & Co., Hartford

1833

BOOKS BY BESSIE ROWLAND JAMES

FOR GOD, FOR COUNTRY, FOR HOME, *The Story of the National League for Woman's Service*

THE HAPPY ANIMALS OF ATA-GA-HI, *Cherokee Myths Adapted for Young Folks*

SIX CAME BACK (with David L. Brainerd)

ADLAI'S ALMANAC (with Mary Waterstreet)

BOOKS BY MARQUIS AND BESSIE R. JAMES

SIX FEET SIX

THE COURAGEOUS HEART

BIOGRAPHY OF A BANK, *The Story of Bank of America N. T. & S. A.*

ANNE ROYALL'S U.S.A.

BESSIE ROWLAND JAMES

 RUTGERS UNIVERSITY PRESS
New Brunswick, New Jersey

Copyright © 1972
By Rutgers University, the State University of New Jersey

Library of Congress Cataloging in Publication Data

James, Bessie (Rowland) 1895–
  Anne Royall's U.S.A.

  Includes bibliographical references.
  1. Royall, Anne (Newport) 1769–1854. I. Title.
E340.R88J3   070.5′092′4 [B]   72–1796
ISBN 0–8135–0732–4

Manufactured in the United States of America by Quinn & Boden Company, Inc.
  Rahway, New Jersey

CONTENTS

AN INTRODUCTION TO
ANNE ROYALL

From an interview with ex-President Harry S Truman:

Old J. Q. Adams, when he was President, used to go for early morning walks. . . . He'd walk down by the Potomac and some mornings
. . . he'd slip off his clothes and take a dip in the river. Well, there
was a shrew of a newspaperwoman—Anne Royall was her name—and
she'd been trying for a long time to interview old J.Q., and he wouldn't
see her. So one day she tracked him on his early-morning walk, and
when he took his dip, she sat herself down on his clothes. She wouldn't
let him out of the river until he answered her questions. Anne Royall
was quite a customer. She was later tried in a court here in Washington,
and caught a big fine as a common scold.
                                    —John Hersey in *The New Yorker*

Yes, indeed, Anne Royall was quite a customer, but I have to
spoil that tale about her sitting on President Adams's clothes while
she interviewed him. It's simply not true, though it crops up more
frequently than any other anecdote about Mrs. Royall. Feature
writers love it and, of course, do not bother to scratch beneath the
surface for historical flaws. I've found the story credited to every
President from Adams to Tyler, always without documentation.
Mrs. Royall was quite capable of keeping a man swimming while
she got her interview, but he would not have been the President of
the United States. Especially he would not have been John Quincy
Adams who was her good friend until the day he died.

Anne Royall's writing career began when she was fifty-five years
old. Her first travel book was published two years later, in 1826.
By 1831, when she became a newspaper publisher, she had turned
out seven travel books and was preparing two more volumes for
the printer. She dashed about—in heat and snow—in stagecoaches,
afoot and on horseback, collecting material for her books, "sub-
scriptioneered" to pay expenses, and personally delivered the fin-

ished volumes to the purchasers. Between times she wrote a play and a novel; a very bad one.

Instead of calling her a "shrew of a newspaper woman," I prefer the description of John Quincy Adams, "a virago errant in enchanted armor." During her writing career she crusaded against many evils, in and out of government; she exposed graft in federal departments and incompetency among employees, of high and low station; she campaigned against whipping in the Navy and for Sunday mail transportation. But her life-long crusade was against the Protestant churches which had pooled their strength with some notion of creating a church and state party. The church battles got her charged with being a common scold. The fine was ten dollars, a "big" one for Anne Royall who rarely had that much cash at any one time. Before President Andrew Jackson could get the money down to the courthouse, two newspapermen paid the fine. To them and to Anne Royall the issue was freedom of the press.

Half a dozen months before the common scold trial, an irate Congregationalist had broken her leg in Burlington, Vermont. In Pittsburgh a young man horsewhipped her, but she blamed the anti-Masons for that episode. She got out of Virginia with a furious mob of students yapping at her heels. Many taverns refused to accommodate her because they were on the side of the churches.

"I do not work for money," she wrote. "I work for the benefit of my country." And that she did. She was twelve years old when victory at Yorktown gave her a country and she lived until 1854, long enough for her heart to break at the sight of her beloved Republic falling apart.

Her books and newspapers hold a wealth of material for the student of American history. In her time she traveled through all the states between the Atlantic Ocean and the Mississippi Valley. There was hardly a town of importance that she did not visit and describe. She knew and interviewed every President from John Adams to Franklin Pierce. Her "pen portraits" of the great and near-great number around two thousand.

B. R. J.

San Miguel Allende, Gto.
Mexico
April, 1972

ANNE ROYALL'S U.S.A.

CHAPTER I

PIONEERS IN RETREAT

1

In July, 1782, the Court of Quarter Sessions convened at Hanna's Town on the second Tuesday of the month. The jurisdiction of this tribunal was the extensive county of Westmoreland, westernmost of organized governments on the Pennsylvania border. The attending justices tackled a crowded calendar. Five women were among the twelve tavernkeepers who applied for and received licenses "to sell spiritous liquors in small measure." That would have meant rye whiskey of local manufacture, for which western Pennsylvania was beginning to get a favorable name.[1]

The opening of twelve additional ordinaries in Westmoreland, which stretched thirty miles beyond the county seat to take in Pittsburgh, might suggest that this section of the frontier was booming. The assumption would have been dispelled by a closer inspection of the migrants who overflowed Hanna's Town and surrounded it with wagon camps. These people were no newcomers, fresh settlers from the East buoyant with plans. Their worn clothing, their lean looks, their restlessness, were the marks of frontier folk. Their presence in Hanna's Town with all their transportable gear constituted a reversal of the westward tide. These were pioneers in retreat.

A recurrence of Indian forays had driven them from their isolated clearings—"the blood of many a family had sprinkled their

3

own fields." The attraction in Hanna's Town was the palisaded log fort which adjoined the tavern of Robert Hanna, founder of the Westmoreland County seat. The report of scouts who said that white renegades were present among the red intruders was disturbing. Recent bloody events seemed to indicate that Tories had not given up the fight, though Cornwallis had laid down his sword nine months before.

Scouts brought in more bad news. Previous happenings appeared to be only preliminaries to a bigger stroke. A war party was gathering to the north, across the New York State line on the shore of Lake Chautauqua. This was too close for comfort. The leader was rumored to be Doctor John Connolly of whom the Pennsylvania border had some unpleasant recollections. He had once seized Fort Pitt (as Pittsburgh was called by those who did not still speak of it as The Forks) for Lord Dunmore, His Majesty's Governor of Virginia, and then turned loose his Indian allies to forage for their reward.

At the start of the Revolution, Connolly had gone over to the British. Rounding up western Tories, he put them into Indian dress and sent them along the frontier to stir up trouble. Their mission was not difficult. The red men had many grievances against trespassing pioneers and conjectured that if they scalped enough of them the rest would be scared away.

The defeat at Yorktown had come as a surprise to Connolly. Thanks to his strategy, he was winning his war in the West and had plans underway for another expedition to seize "Fort Pitt and all the adjacent posts." The armistice had not caused him to change his mind. Tories in his ranks had nothing to lose, and perhaps much to gain. Further, there was no stopping the Indians; they were making headway clearing out the border.[2]

As the raiders pressed nearer, each day driving more refugees into Hanna's Town, an atmosphere of doom hung over the ten-year-old settlement. Its fate appeared inevitable, though unworthy of a town which had beat out older Pittsburgh in the county seat race. In the face of danger, judges, attendants, witnesses and spectators came to the scheduled Quarter Sessions armed to the teeth.

Court was held in the largest room in town—the main room of

Robert Hanna's tavern, a two-story log house with a cockloft window poking through the roof. The few hickory chairs available were given over to the magistrates out of respect for their duties. As usual these were as routine as the granting of licenses to ordinaries, a demand which had cluttered the docket increasingly as the war went on. Opening a tavern offered destitute wives the only means of acquiring a little ready cash, which had practically disappeared from the frontier during the Revolution.

On Friday afternoon, July 12, those who had sat through the sultry session were rewarded with a little excitement. The only indictment of the term for felony was handed down in the case of "Republica [*sic*] vs. Patrick Butler." The crime was "larceny." The court ordered the prisoner "to be taken to the Public Whipping Post between the Hours of eight and twelve of the clock tomorrow morning and there to receive thirty one lashes on his back well laid on." [3]

Probably at the earliest hour his sentence specified, Patrick Butler was hustled from the round-log jail, his hands tied above his head at the whipping post, and the lashing inflicted. With two big harvesting parties scheduled that day, little time could be spared for a felon.

One party of reapers set forth to help the widow of Captain Samuel Miller, whose place was two and a half miles southeast of Hanna's Town. In peaceful times, after the work was done, they could have looked forward to an all-night celebration, with Sunday to rest up. Miller's Station, like Hanna's tavern, was a "mansion house" of two stories, with a puncheon floor worn smooth by Saturday night dances. This particular harvest would have been a double-barreled festival. A few days before, Mrs. Miller had taken a second husband in the person of Andrew Cruickshank.

The other harvesters went the other way—to Judge Michael Huffnagle's whose clearing was a mile and a half north of the town. Having made good progress, at noontime they knocked off to eat cold potatoes and hard biscuits in the shade of a tree. When they went back to work, one of the reapers began mowing along the edge of a field next the woodland. His glance strayed into the shadows of the trees and picked up a flash of movement. The

steady rhythm of his scythe did not waver. Mowing his way back
to his companions, he quietly reported that Judge Huffnagle's
woods were alive with Indians. With studied casualness the harvesters worked their way off the field.

Untying their horses and wagons, they sped from the scene to
spread the alarm. The trails leading to Hanna's Fort were soon
choked with people in flight. Captain Matthew Jack, the sheriff,
stood before the stockade urging young and old through the gate.
His dependable wife unlocked the jail and ordered the prisoners
to carry the records into the fort. As the line of fugitives dwindled,
the big gate was slowly swung almost shut. Jack cocked his head
and listened. The town's inhabitants were all accounted for, but
families living at a distance had not shown up. The sheriff said he'd
ride out and try to bring in the missing. Two young men, James
Brison and David Shaw, veteran Indian fighters, joined him. It was
said of them they would rather fight than eat. Captain Jack had
been no different in his boyhood, and Westmoreland adored him.
His feats of horsemanship were a part of backwoods lore. The
sheriff sent off his youthful aides in one direction and he himself
rode toward Huffnagle's, curious as to what was delaying the
Indians.

Jack found them holding a pow-wow in the newly mown field.
As he turned his horse toward the stockade, the savages saw him
and rushed at him brandishing tomahawks. Abruptly the sheriff
changed his course going away from Hanna's Town in order to
keep the path safe a while longer for tardy fugitives.

As Jack circled back toward the county seat, he came upon the
Love family stumbling through the brush. The sheriff hoisted Mrs.
Love and her baby onto his horse and raced them to the fort.
Brison and Shaw arrived moments later with the Indians close
behind them.

It was then two o'clock. The anxious settlers estimated that the
attackers numbered about a hundred, including their white colleagues, poorly disguised as red men. When the Indians discovered
their quarry had eluded them, they filled the air with angry
whoops. Had they but known! The fort had been stripped during

the war. Only nine old guns and a scanty supply of powder remained. Women and children outnumbered the men—mostly old men—four to one.

The disappointed savages started ransacking the abandoned cabins. Through chinks in the logs, owners saw their precious possessions thrown through doors and windows. The looting took on a more disorderly turn after the whiskey jugs were found. One brave staggered from a doorway wearing a woman's dress. Carried away with his performance he got too close to the fort. A shot finished him.

Throughout the afternoon the enemy led away horses and cattle. Hogs and poultry were slaughtered on the spot. About dusk a disturbing quiet fell upon the littered town. Another pow-wow, guessed the watchers within the fort. Scouts crept away to find out.

Meantime the besieged settlers busied themselves with a stratagem that old fighters like Captain Jack had known to work to the advantage of an outnumbered garrison. As soon as the night was black the stockade gate was opened. Horsemen began trotting back and forth across the corduroy bridge that spanned the narrow entrance. The clatter carried far and the drum rolling out the assembly sounded as if reinforcements had come. The make-believe was convincing, though at a price.

Suddenly a volley of shots rained on Fort Hanna. Only Peggy Shaw, the sixteen year-old sister of David Shaw, was hit. At this inappropriate moment she dashed to the rescue of a child who had toddled through the open gate. Poor Peggy lingered for days before she died, submitting frequently to the pain of a silk handkerchief drawn through her wound, a frontier remedy for blood poisoning. The next thing flames burst from half a dozen cabins. Men and women looked on with breaking hearts remembering hardships endured to build their wilderness homes.

By dawn the fire no longer glowed. Except for the fort and tavern, which stood apart from the settlement, only ashes remained of the town whose ambition had been to be bigger than Pittsburgh. The Indians and their white companions appeared to have departed but, to make sure, the stockade gate remained closed.

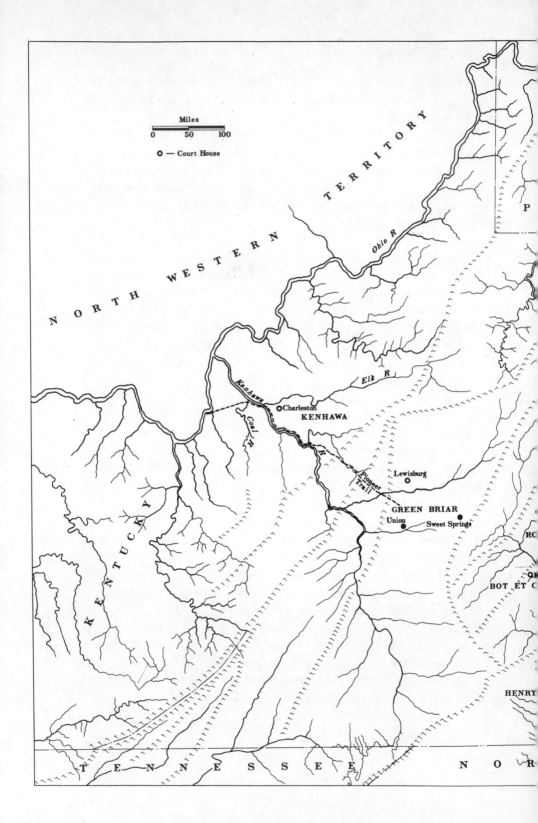

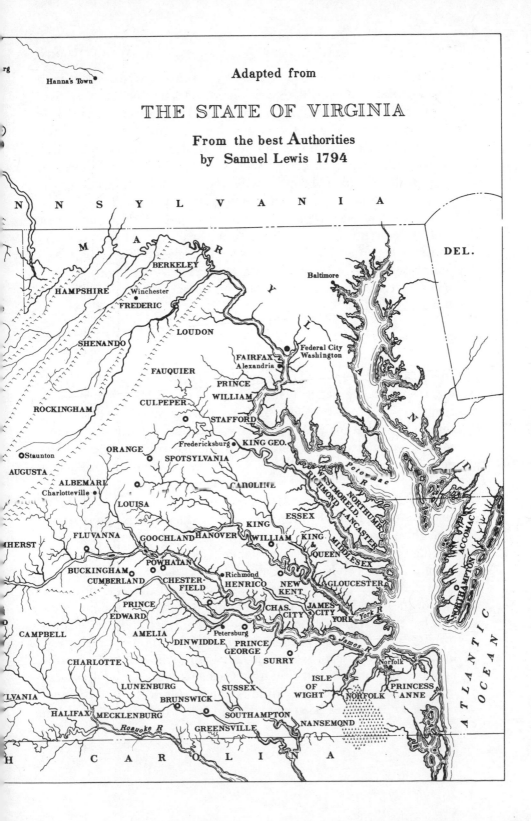

Adapted from

THE STATE OF VIRGINIA

From the best Authorities
by Samuel Lewis 1794

It was opened to an excited man on horseback who arrived with news of the fate of Miller's Station—too distant for warning. Retreating from Hanna's Town, the raiders had surprised the little frolic celebrating the Miller-Cruickshank nuptials. The bride and groom had managed to escape into the Miller blockhouse, but half a dozen men who had helped with the crop during the afternoon were scalped. Robert Hanna's wife and two girls were among the captives the Indians led off on a long march north.

The settlers dug dispiritedly into the ruins of the county seat and brought up evidence of the identity of the white men who had attacked them. The attackers had carelessly left behind garments cast aside in favor of some finery from the cabins. Among them were several jackets with buttons bearing the legend: "King's Eighth Regiment." [4]

2

In the ruins of Hanna's Town perished the ambition of one family to prosper on the Pennsylvania border. Ten years earlier William Newport, his rosy-cheeked, blue-eyed wife, and two daughters, three-year-old Anne and baby Mary, had traveled from Baltimore to take up land on the frontier. For the hard life of the wilderness they had left an orderly city where fashionable ladies had the leisure to promenade of an afternoon along locust-lined Market (now Baltimore) Street. The men sat at the inns debating the chances of war with England. Most Marylanders, prosperous enough to get along without economic mothering, were for throwing off the royal yoke. The province had suffered its share of indignities at the hands of the Calvert family. The last incivility had been the worst. The sixth Lord Baltimore, dead the year previous, had bequeathed his New World colony to a natural son.[5]

It has been suggested that William Newport, too, was an illegitimate Calvert. Calvert bastards were plentiful and one of them was, indeed, named Newport—Caecilius Newport, who was well-remembered in his father's will. But this Caecilius was not, as has been intimated, the father of our Anne Newport. He was a boy of fourteen, who had never been out of England, when Anne was born in Baltimore in 1769. She was "called after Queen Anne," and to the end of her days resented the spelling of her name without the final "e." [6]

Another suggestion is that William Newport, because of his noble lineage, was a Tory and went to western Pennsylvania to get closer to the British base of operations at Detroit. Possibly a reasonable conclusion is that Newport was one of the host of Scotch-Irish immigrants who braved the twisting mountain trails in 1772 and '73 to be on hand for the opening of the new county of Westmoreland in Pennsylvania where good land was offered cheap. [7]

Little more is known about the antecedents of Anne Newport's mother. Mary Newport was born in Annapolis, Maryland, in 1748, if we accept one report; or it may have been 1751 or 1752, if her eldest daughter remembered correctly. She was a cheerful, hard-working, illiterate woman of superior native intelligence who was the best of neighbors on whatever frontier she lived. [8]

William Newport brought his family from Baltimore by way of Taneytown, picking up Braddock's Road at Fort Cumberland on the Potomac. One of the few recollections little Anne had of the journey was the snow on the trees, indicating that perhaps they crossed the mountains in early spring, before the thaw. Having reached the promised land, they did not tarry in Robert Hanna's settlement, but continued eight miles north to Mount Pisgah, a bluff overlooking the forks of three rivers. "The handsomest situation in West Pennsylvania," Anne described it. "The Loyalhanna, as straight as a line, runs along the base of the Mount, turns suddenly and empties into the Conemaugh." Both rivers emerged into the broad, smooth Kiskiminetis.

The cabin the Newports moved into had been built by an earlier pioneer. The goods they brought filled the eight-by-ten room: a bedstead, "four wooden stools, with legs stuck in them through augur holes, half a dozen tin cups, and the like number of pewter plates, knives, forks, and spoons, a tray and frying pan, a camp-kettle, and a pot." They soon acquired a puncheon table, "a tree split in half, graced with four substantial legs of rough hewed white oak." Skins were thrown on the floor to accommodate travelers passing the night. The pewterware and bedstead, relics of their Baltimore days, gave the Newports a reputation for having the best outfitted cabin on the Loyalhanna, but the distinction was short-lived. Lacking toys, baby Mary played with the tableware. She broke some and lost the rest and the family was reduced to eating from musselshells like other frontier folk.

Though beautifully endowed by nature, the solitary situation had had no appeal for permanent habitation. The cabin was the last, except one, on a trail leading to The Forks. The nearest neighbors in the direction of Hanna's Town were the Peerys, but not handy for visiting because they were on the other side of the winding Conemaugh. On the opposite bank of the Loyalhanna, concealed by trees and brush, was a worn Indian trail older than memory. Over it padded the messengers of the western New York and Ohio Valley tribes, though the settlements rarely got a glimpse of them.

Some ten miles farther in the boundless wilderness to the west stood the cabin of Stephen Rybolt, a swarthy German with twinkling eyes and a pleasant face. He had lived there longer than anyone knew. A bent old man, walking with a staff, Stephen came out of retirement several times a year to trade in Hanna's Town, and no one received a heartier welcome at the cabins along his way. The women were especially glad to see the hermit, as Stephen was spoken of, because he always brought them gifts of lard and salt, which he carried in gourds hanging from his stooped figure. The old German had already stumbled onto the salt wells which, in a couple of decades, were to bring a rush of speculators to the Conemaugh valley.

Soon Stephen Rybolt was climbing the slope of Pisgah to pass the time of day with the new folks from Maryland. The little girls ran to meet him, squealing with delight. It was a treat to have a visitor and the miscalled hermit, in truth, was a garrulous old man with a fund of stories packed in a long memory. Anne and Mary liked the one about his dog who kept the Indians away. The dog was named Wasser, the German word for water. Nobody could stop water from running and, if Indians came near his cabin, Wasser ran barking to warn his master.

The land atop the bluff brought the Newports poor returns,

perhaps because the father spent so much time away from home on other business. The family's greatest asset seems to have been the character of Mrs. Newport. In the summer heat she tilled the fields; through the long winter spun and sewed. In the early spring she earned the family's sugar tending the kettles at a nearby camp where sap from the small sugar maples was boiled into syrup. If William Newport was absent, Mrs. Newport left her little girls locked in the cabin, cautioning them not to unbolt the door to strangers.

Once when they were alone the children had a good scare. The Revolutionary War had begun. Rumors filled the wilderness with British spies bent on destruction, which called for special caution. After their mother went off to the sugar camp, they usually ran through their chores collecting eggs, bringing in water and wood, picking up thorns to pin their clothes. (Anne did not see a real pin until she was nearly grown.) Bolting the door, the sisters prepared for another long day cooped up in their tiny home.

This time spring was new and beautiful outside. Mary, the little one, could not resist opening the door to play in the sunshine. Late in the afternoon a man on horseback suddenly rode up over the bluff and asked for a night's lodging. After the lonesome winter, Anne's curiosity and sociability got the best of her. She forgot her mother's instructions, invited the stranger inside and began to babble of a thousand things observed in the solitary months. She pointed out the big nest eagles were building in a treetop across the Loyalhanna. The birds flew up there carrying sticks "as stout as a man's arm." They would swoop down to the river and snatch a wriggling fish in their talons. One lucky fish had dropped back into the water and the little girls cheered.

The stranger told them what he knew about eagles and then asked, "Have you a stable to put my horse in?"

Anne did not let on that she had never before heard the word stable. Guessing at its meaning she led the way to the pen where old Bonny, the Newport mare, was kept, and then to the corncrib. She watched the visitor pile corn before his hungry animal and apprehensively asked whether he knew anything about feeding a horse. Bonny never got that much to eat and looked it.

Back at the cabin, however, Anne did not stint on supper. She brought out jerked venison from the chimney and baked eggs in the fireplace ashes. Her guest contributed his own salt and biscuits. While they sat around the puncheon table, he entertained them with stories of his travels in Pennsylvania. The sisters listened in silent wonder and, after the supper things were put away, Anne was disappointed to hear him say that, having ridden from The Forks, he was tired and wished to sleep. Hospitably she offered the man the Newport bedstead, but he threw one of the bearskin rugs before the fire and put his saddle at one end for a head rest. The weary horseman was asleep in an instant. Anne thoughtfully covered him with a quilt.

Not until sometime later, when she heard Mrs. Newport and Aunt Molly Carrahan, a friend from the sugar camp, coming up the path, did it occur to Anne that she had disobeyed her mother. She ran out to confess. On tiptoe the two women entered the cabin. Aunt Molly peeped at the sleeping man.

"I don't like his looks," she whispered. He looked like an Englishman. "I'll warrant he's come to spy out the land."

Though worried about what might happen, the tired young hostess dropped off to sleep. In the morning she opened her eyes on a placid scene. The visitor was pulling on his boots and Mrs. Newport was talking and smiling as if they were old friends. Aunt Molly beamed good will. Anne noted how pleased her mother was to hear what a sensible daughter she had. Before he rode off the stranger gave Anne a Spanish silver dollar. It was the first time she had seen "eight bits," as the British colonies called this currency. Their guest was no spy, they learned, but a resident of The Forks. He was William Findley, better known to the Pennsylvania backwoods as "The Walking Library," because of his knowledge of books. Later Anne would hear of him as the leader of the Whiskey Rebellion.

3

As the Revolutionary War wore on and Indian depredations increased, the Newports were often forced to desert their unprotected hilltop and take refuge at the Blane farm which had a block-house. Anne did not like it there. The Blanes had no children and Hannah Blane drank to excess. When her parents stole back in the daytime to work their field, Anne had to look after the cooking at the Blane cabin because the mistress could not stand on her feet. It was a big job for a girl not yet seven years old; too big, in fact, when Mrs. Blane got out of hand. Then Anne asked help from Patton, the eighteen-year-old bound boy who "cooked, washed, milked, churned, reaped, mowed, plowed and hoed." He was the only one who could handle Mrs. Blane. On the farmhouse wall hung a dilapidated wig, an heirloom which once had been the aristocratic adornment of a Blane ancestor. Somehow Patton dis-covered that if he put the wig on the head of the drunken woman, she would quiet down.

Anne found the bound boy "good-natured." Only once did she see him "in a passion." This was when Hannah Blane gave Anne spoiled beef to cook for the field hands. Patton got a whiff of the stew "and pitched the whole of it out of doors." From the well-stocked springhouse, he fed the hungry workers rich milk, cream and butter and "plenty of bread and onions."

Mr. Blane, a little man who stuttered, does not seem to have done anything to remove temptation from his wife's path. On his farm he operated a profitable distillery. He kept the keys locked up, but Mrs. Blane was sly and managed to get at them. Many years later Anne visited the site of the Blane farm. "Poor old Mr. Blane," she wrote, "after weathering many a storm was at last killed by the Indians a few yards from his door."

The Newports, sensing the danger, moved several miles up the Loyalhanna to the Moore farm which lay close to John Shields' Fort where a handful of troops were stationed. Beneath a small sugar maple outside the door of their new home, William New-port taught his daughter the alphabet, using the Bible as textbook. Like many frontier women, his wife could neither read nor write. As the county filled up, Westmorelanders began to fret about "advantages" for the younger generation. A mile from Moore's a school had been opened in a one-room log house. About twenty boys and girls attended. Grown youths sat on benches with the youngest students learning their "letters" from the New England primer. Mr. Newport had taken such pains with his daughter that by the time Anne entered the school she was ready for a class that used the readers.

At noontime the pupils gathered outside around a fire to cook their dinner, mostly "jerk," in a frying pan. Afterwards they sang and played games. Noisy, tumbling playmates were a happy change from the seclusion of Mount Pisgah. *The Juniper Tree* was the school's favorite game. Boys and girls joined hands, forming a ring around whomever they had chosen to be "Sister Phoebe." They walked about her singing:

> O, sister Phoebe, how happy were we,
> When we sat under yon juniper tree, heighho!
> Take this hat on your head, to keep head warm,
> Take a sweet kiss, it will do you no harm, I know.

Whereupon the holder of the hat put it on "Sister Phoebe" with a "sweet kiss." It was great fun to get hold of a new girl who had never played the game and call her "Sister Phoebe." When a tall boy kissed Anne, she was so ashamed she cried.

Presently William Newport disappeared or died and his wife hired out at housework. The frontier settlement treated the bereaved little family with sympathy and kindness. Mary Newport was not made to feel like a servant. Anne's best friend was Jane, or Jinsey Denniston, the daughter of Arthur Denniston, who owned a large farm on the Loyalhanna. Arthur Denniston came from New Jersey about the same time the Newports arrived from Maryland. In a short while, he had prospered in western Pennsylvania as earlier he had prospered in the East. A grist mill, a sawmill, a store, and the schoolhouse made up the settlement known as Denniston's Town. A patriarchal type, Arthur Denniston was head of a large family which he kept around him even after his sons and daughters married, delighting in the flock of grandchildren beginning to overrun the household. A penniless widow had nothing to fear while she lived near Arthur Denniston. When she went any distance to work, Mary Newport felt free to leave her daughters at the Dennistons, even as long as a week at a time.

Indian alarms continued. Denniston's Town was well prepared for them. Sometimes the Newports huddled with friends in the Parr blockhouse, other times at the Irvins. The Parr family was mostly menfolk, and among them Anne encountered her first bachelors, rarities on the frontier. The Irvins were always a source of amusement. Larry Irvin was a small man with a wife nearly twice his height. Already wealthy when they migrated from New Jersey with the Dennistons, the Irvins had a fine large house overlooking the river.

One day lame Mrs. Freeman came clopping into the settlement astride a horse and shouting that Indians were not far behind. Her estimate of their numbers sent everybody flying across the river to Fort Shields. The fort's garrison drove off the raiders and Denniston's Town was saved. Refugees who moments before had feared for their lives recrossed the Loyalhanna laughing for all they were worth. In her excitement Mrs. Freeman had grabbed the nearest object at hand to whip up her mount—the steelyard of her scales.

On peaceful days Anne and Jinsey Denniston romped through the meadows tending sheep, gathering walnuts, and shooing stray chickens. Fame brushed the alert, fatherless little girl for the first time. She was known as the best hen hussy on the Loyalhanna.

Knowing Jinsey had broadened Anne's small world in other ways. There were the exciting times when John Denniston, the eldest son, returned from trading trips to New Jersey and opened his packs to reveal wares purchased on the effete seaboard. Anne was on hand the day John surprised his wife with a present of lump sugar. Nancy Denniston put the cubes in a glass bowl on her father-in-law's large dinner table for family and friends to admire. For days afterwards Anne haunted the farmhouse at mealtimes, hoping the sugar would be passed around so she could sample it. But the sugar remained untouched. Anne confided her disappointment to Mrs. Newport and her mother said she was wasting her time. The Dennistons were from New Jersey and Jersey people, as everybody knew, took their tea *without* sugar.[9]

4

Frontier widowhoods were usually brief. Mary Newport's proved no exception. She married a man named Butler, about whom as little is known as William Newport. His name may have been Patrick Butler. At any rate, during the Revolutionary War, a Patrick Butler served in the immediate neighborhood as a frontier ranger, one of a group of daring spirits on whom Westmoreland County relied for protection because of insufficient militia and uniformed Continentals.[10]

If Ranger Patrick Butler was Mary Newport's second husband, then his military duties could account for the family's removal to Hanna's Town at the beginning of the '80s. Hanna's Town was the base of ranger operation in the county, and, in the seven or eight years since the Newports had first seen it, had grown by leaps and bounds. This had been Robert Hanna's doing. The tavernkeeper never missed a chance to boost his namesake. The most important benefit he had gained for it was the county court. Pittsburghers said Hanna had stolen the court, which was a slightly envious way of putting the actual occurrence. The Forks had complacently rested its case on the claim that it had more taverns than Hanna's Town, and therefore could better accommodate the visits of the court. With an Irishman's talent for politics, Hanna had made a secret trip to Philadelphia and came home with the court literally tucked in his pocket. Hanna's Town became the county seat and thereafter bloomed as an attraction for new business and more inhabitants. Though the Revolutionary War halted its development, still upwards of thirty log houses had been built after the frontier fashion, with huge mud chimneys running up one side.

In Hanna's Town, the Butlers occupied a cabin on the Forbes Road, a first-rate observation post for activity due to the war. A screen of dust, raised by the steady shuffle of men and beasts, hung over the narrow packhorse trail which wove between the "monster trees of the ancient forest" to connect with the road to Philadelphia. The Newport children spent a lot of time waiting for the pack trains loaded with cannon balls from the furnaces at

The Forks. When the drivers stopped to rest their animals, the little girls got a chance to ask questions about the distant places they were bound. The men were a rough lot, but obliging enough to let them play with the harness bells whose tinkle they were used to hearing in the night before falling asleep.

Another familiar sound was the thumping hooves beneath hard-pressed riders. It was a sound terrifying to waken to, with Indians on the rampage. Mrs. Butler was not long in her new home before she soothed her children with the same tale on which neighboring mothers relied. That was Captain Samuel Brady and his rangers pounding off after redskins. As everyone knew, when Captain Brady rode the savages took cover. They had murdered his family. Standing beside the fresh graves, the Captain had sworn that "he would revenge the death of these, and never while he lived be at peace with the Indians of any tribe." [11]

Soldiers in threadbare clothing straggled by continuously. Their bright red flag with the coiled serpent that hissed "Don't tread on me!" flapped listlessly. One day a spritely column with drums beating marched from the direction of Pittsburgh. All Hanna's Town gathered along the Forbes Road to cheer. At the head of the troops, snapping challengingly in the breeze, was a banner the backwoods had never seen—"a brilliant striped flag." Mrs. Butler explained to her daughters that the war had been won and this was the flag of their country. Anne never afterwards beheld the colors of the U.S.A. that she did not choke up and remember the first time she saw them. If her father was a Tory she certainly was not.[12]

War's end wrought no changes in Hanna's Town. Victims of the latest raids continued to pile into the county seat. Some gave up and headed back east. Robert Hanna could think of no subterfuge to hold them for his town. Actually he was glad to see them go. Food ran low.

The news of Washington's victory was followed by word of the fate of Colonel Archibald Lochry's expedition against the Indians beyond the Ohio. The maneuver had been conceived in a desperate attempt to keep hostile savages away from the Pennsylvania border. Most of Colonel Lochry's militiamen had been drained from West-

moreland County. They numbered only 106, not counting the colonel. He was among the first to die in the enemy's ambush. The
casualties were forty-two killed, sixty-five taken prisoner.

Emboldened by their victory, the Indians intensified their attacks. Official reports kept Philadelphia informed of their progress.
"The savages have struck us in four different places, have taken
and killed thirteen persons with a number of horses . . . two of
the unhappy people were killed one mile from Hanna's Town.
Our country is worse depopulated than ever it has been."

"This morning a small garrison at Peter Clingensmith's four or
five miles from Hanna's Town, consisting of between twenty and
thirty women and children, was destroyed."

"The enemy are almost constantly in our country, killing and
captivating the inhabitants." [13]

The coming of winter brought a lull in the raids. In February,
four months after Yorktown, Colonel William Crawford, with
nearly five hundred volunteers from southwestern Pennsylvania,
marched west to continue the campaign that had ended so disas-
trously for Lochry. In the same month, the mild winter having
ended early, the Indians renewed their forays. Westmoreland de-
duced that Colonel Crawford was not doing so well. No one, however, dreamed how badly he was doing. In early June he decided
to retreat. The savages trapped his expedition as they had Lochry's.
Colonel Crawford was not lucky enough to be killed in the fight.
His captors burned him alive.

After that there was nobody to stop the Indians. On they came,
until on Saturday afternoon, July 13, 1782, they reached Hanna's
Town.

In the house on Forbes Road, Mrs. Butler heard the alarm barely
in time to pick up her baby son, James Butler, and run to the fort
with Anne and Mary behind her. Years later Anne was to write:

On that day my heart first learned the nature of care. The whole re-
passes again before me, and with it all the sufferings of those times.
[Seaboard people had] little idea of what poor frontier settlers suffered
[with] the Indians pursuing and shooting at us. At other times concealed

in brushwood, exposed to rain and snakes, for days and nights [we were] without food [and] half the time without salt or bread.[14]

Anne said that it was her mother who led the children into the fort. Her stepfather Butler was not mentioned. Yet one chronicler of Hanna's Town raid declared that Patrick Butler, the ranger, was killed on Sunday, the day following the sacking of Hanna's Town, in a raid on Freeman's settlement. The Freeman family never made it to nearby Fort Shields, a familiar sanctuary to Patrick. The Indians killed a Freeman son and made captives of two Freeman daughters. However it may have been with Ranger Butler during the siege, we do know of an occurrence earlier in the day which would explain why his stepdaughter never wrote a line about him. This was the thirty lashes Patrick Butler had been sentenced by the Court of Quarter Sessions to receive at the whipping post.[15]

Whether or not Mary Newport Butler lost her husband subsequent to the Hanna's Town attack, it is plain that she lost him somehow and so became a widow for the second time. Moreover, she was finished with the Pennsylvania frontier. Joining a band of disillusioned Westmoreland refugees she set out for Virginia, taking baby James and Anne, who was just entering her teens. Her younger daughter Mary remained behind with a family who had decided to stick it out in Pennsylvania. The two sisters who had lived in such close companionship in the wilderness were to meet only twice in the next forty years.

CHAPTER II

A SERVANT'S DAUGHTER

1

Eight miles north of Staunton, Virginia, where the Valley turnpike crosses Middle River, the Anderson farm bordered the highway. The farm possessed some local fame because of a massacre of friendly Indians which had taken place in the barn on a July evening in 1754. The Upper Valley of the Shenandoah had turned against the white murderers, denying them privilege of attendance at Stone Church, five years older than Augusta County in which it was situated. The stern punishment had driven the offenders from the Valley for, without benefit of the Presbyterian preacher's Sunday sermon, they believed their heavenly future in doubt.[1]

As John Anderson, who had patented 747 acres on Middle River, had no part in the bloody event in his barn, he remained a respected communicant of the little house of worship which nestled in the shadow of the mountain a mile above his farm. When he died he had willed the farm to his son Andrew, likewise reared to endure all-day Sabbath services at Stone Church. The Revolutionary War had interrupted Andrew Anderson's pursuit of godliness and agriculture. Volunteering at once, he had left to his wife management of the farm and his nine children.

A second wife, Mrs. Anderson was not the mother of the Anderson brood and so brought vitality to her task. Still, with so much to do, the mistress of the Anderson acres was glad to take as a

22

helper a woman from a passing band of Pennsylvania refugees. And Mary Butler was glad to find shelter for herself and children. It is impossible to say just how they came to end the long march from the ruins of Hanna's Town at Colonel Andrew Anderson's in the late summer of 1782. It is not improbable that the colonel himself brought them there. He had been in command of a regiment at Fort Pitt and had marched it home to the Valley of Virginia by way of the pike that passed the farm. Mrs. Butler may have tagged along. As a cook she would have been no burden.[2]

Mary was soon cheerfully adapted to the life of her new home. With the house full of children she proved particularly useful. In Westmoreland County she had learned to concoct medicines from herbs and, in no time, the fame of her cures spread along Middle River. A patient, unselfish soul, "always reckoned sensible" with ample knowledge of misfortune, Mrs. Butler was content to be useful.

Her daughter Anne, however, found no contentment in their new situation. After a couple of generations of peace and prosperity, the Upper Valley had begun to shed the crudities of its pioneer period, adopting the social refinements of Virginia Tidewater. Family became the prime consideration. Wealth, too, was important, but what made Anne Newport unhappy was the distinction between master and servant. The Valley was well supplied with indentured servants and the sensitive young girl found herself relegated to their society. It was a blow to someone who had had the run of the Denniston place.

The remainder of her life was colored by what happened to her at the Anderson farm. Here was nurtured the aggressive nature, so easily offended into angry defense. Here began the posturings and pretenses which later, when she was the notorious Anne Royall, would send her sweeping through one town with a regal air, only to lapse at the next stage stop into the rough idiom of the frontier, splashed with raffish terms imported from the slums of England. Some people found the name-calling amusing; others were scared and ran away to hide, though retreat was never a guarantee of escape from the scratch of Anne Royall's pen.

At the moment, however, Anne's miserable plight moved her to tears rather than anger. Sunday attendance at Stone Church was an ordeal. Custom required her to sit with the servants. She never felt more humiliated than during those moments after the service had ended and she stood apart, a looker-on while church members fell into little groups to greet each other and chatter of Valley happenings. No one reached out a friendly hand to make Anne feel that Christians considered her one of them.

These weekly exposures to long sermons worked out badly—at least, for the Presbyterians. They were the chief targets of Anne Royall when she later launched her crusade against the Protestant churches.

The girl's life became almost as solitary as it had been on Mount Pisgah and she spent a good deal of her time reading. Mrs. Butler, who could not read, sought to cheer her moody daughter with the gift of a collection of books entitled Little Histories. Among the individual volumes were *Seven Wise Masters*, *Moll Flanders* and *Paddy from Cork*. Anne ran through the histories in no time. But books could not take the place of playmates, and of these she had none, not even in school.[3]

Not without envy, she watched the comings and goings of the gay daughters of Colonel Robert Grattan who lived on the farm north of the Andersons. They had wealth, beauty and enviable family connections. The Grattan girls' father was a curious sort. The youngest of seven children he had been pampered by a strong-minded, strong-bodied mother who used to ride horseback over the mountains with her husband on trading trips to Philadelphia. Once she had brought her son a violin from the East. Robert practiced on his fiddle, instead of learning to run the family farm and his father's store in Staunton. When he inherited these properties, Robert Grattan had willingly turned them over to a brother-in-law to manage.

With time on his hands Robert often walked down to the Valley pike to hail the new settlers streaming by to Carolina. There Anne Newport encountered him. He spoke to her. The smile and friendly words warmed the girl's heart, but the next time she saw the colonel he passed her as if in a trance, without a sign of recognition. She took it for a snub, which it wasn't, and it cut deeply.[4]

2

Presently, though, Anne Newport won a friend among the quality, who rode out from Staunton on Sundays and sometimes stopped after church service to visit at the Andersons. Though a kinswoman of the English poet, James Thomson, Mrs. William Lewis's Valley renown rested on her marriage into the Lewis family. Her father-in-law was John Lewis "who slew the Irish Lord," as the huge limestone slab which marks his grave near Staunton proclaims. Sir Mingo Campbell, of Campbell's Manor, County Donegal, had met his fate when he brought an armed force to evict Lewis for nonpayment of an increase in rent. With his wife, four sons and two daughters, the slayer had escaped to Virginia, settling in 1732 beside a beautiful spring near Staunton. He called his new home Bellefonte.

A fifth son was born at Bellefonte. In time Lewis descendants were plentiful in the Shenandoah Valley, although four sons had spent the better part of a score of years serving in the border campaigns known by the general title of the French and Indian Wars. It is hardly to be wondered that the Indians, after having fought a generation of Lewis giants—not one of them was under six feet tall—suspiciously regarded red clover, introduced into the country by old John, as stained with the blood of their warriors.

Between wars the sons of Bellefonte crossed the Alleghenies and took up land on the frontier they had helped to conquer. Anne seldom saw the "tall, robust, handsome" husband of Mrs. William Lewis in Staunton. He was "over the mountain" clearing the 100,000-acre grant in which his father and his brothers owned a third interest. Old John had surveyed the grant and thought the land better than Bellefonte. Colonel William Lewis thought so too and, when his father died, had bought out his brothers' shares. The heart of the grant was the Sweet Springs whose waters, long before the coming of white men, were celebrated among the Indians as a cure for skin troubles. While soldiering, Colonel Lewis had dreamed of turning the Springs into a health resort.[5]

Anne Newport's meeting with Mrs. William Lewis had a touch

of fate. From the older woman she first heard of Captain William Royall of illustrious Tidewater ancestry who lived, by choice, on the frontier. The Lewises and the captain had been friends of long standing when the latter hurried to Staunton during the Revolutionary War to attend the session of the General Assembly which had been run out of Charlottesville by Tarleton's dragoons. The captain was a delegate from Amelia County, not quite Tidewater but a dumping ground for younger sons of the so-called aristocratic families who were not entitled to inherit the plantation seats of their fathers. Like the mother country, Virginia subscribed to the dynastic laws of entail and primogeniture. When the Assembly legislators arrived in June, 1781, Staunton people accommodated them in their homes. One jittery Sunday night the Lewis household was awakened by the roll of drums, the signal that the dragoons were approaching. Tarleton had made a bloody sweep up from the South. People trembled at mere mention of his name. Thinking the legislators would rush off to Rockfish Gap to fight the English, the Lewises gave them all assistance. Instead, the delegates tried to save their skins by retreating farther westward. That had been unnecessary; it was a false alarm. After Charlottesville, the dragoons had moved eastward to renew the attack on Richmond.

"Next morning," Mrs. Lewis told Anne Newport, "the streets of Staunton were strewed with portmanteaus, saddlebags, and bundles of clothes, which the affrighted tuckahoes had dropped in their hurry to escape. Meantime, the cohees repaired, to a man, old and young, to the place of danger." [6]

Cohee was the name snobbish eastern Virginia had given Valley folk who, instead of saying "said he," used the expression of their Scotch-Irish ancestors "quoth he," or "quo' he," as they pronounced it. In retaliation the Valley derisively called the easterners tuckahoes, an Indian word for a species of large mushroom growing underground. [7]

Mrs. Lewis was, of course, a cohee partisan. She said that an exception to the general behavior of the tuckahoe members had been that of Captain William Royall who joined the defenders at Rockfish Gap. "The sight of gray-headed men and little boys, with their guns and shot pouches on their shoulders," so impressed the captain that he made a vow to sever his tuckahoe ties at the end of the war and come to live among the courageous cohees. The gallant tuckahoe's respect for bravery was in keeping with the patriotic temper of his own Amelia County. Early in the war the young ladies of Amelia had pledged themselves "not to permit the address of any person—unless he has served in the American armies long enough to prove by his valor that he is deserving of their love." [8]

All too soon Anne Newport lost her only Valley friend. William Lewis sent word that the log house he had built at the Sweet Springs was ready to receive his wife. Anne Montgomery Lewis, several times a grandmother, set out on horseback to cross the Allegheny Mountains to a wilderness home.

3

Her departure may have had something to do with Mary Butler's decision to leave the Valley. Not many months afterwards, Mrs. Butler and her daughter traversed the same mountain road, though not on horseback. They walked the hundred and fifteen miles to the Sweet Springs. Eighteen years old by this time, and two inches under five feet tall, the thin girl at her mother's side was stronger than she appeared. Anne had none of her mother's blonde good looks. Her face was lean, hair drab, and mouth a narrow line that curled with a mocking smile rather than with joy or amusement. Her chief attractions were her vitality and an intellect which she had fallen into the trick of exhibiting. [9]

Their first night on the road the two wayfarers stayed in Staunton, probably at Mrs. Burns' tavern, with Mrs. Butler giving her services in return for lodgings. She had left the Andersons as empty-handed as she had come half a dozen years earlier. When Anne became famous, a woman of eighty-seven years professed to recall the couple who had slept one night at her grandfather's place on Middle Mountain. She remembered that "the poor woman was much afflicted with sores . . . and had a child with her," a natural mistake if describing the under-sized Anne Newport. The Virginia lady did not mention James Butler. He would have been about seven years old. Left behind, probably, though not for long. The "sores" were an old complaint of Mrs. Butler's. She hoped the Sweet Springs would cure the eczema.[10]

Some eighty miles from Staunton mother and daughter reached the splendid new hostelry that Dennis Callaghan had put up at the junction of four mountain roads. The derivation of the arresting tavern sign—"a red cow painted as large as life"—was not lost on pioneers bound for Tennessee and Kentucky at the close of the eighteenth century. It was right out of *John Bull, or An Englishman's Fireside*, a play which had kept the frontier laughing for half a century. The gnome-like Dennis tricked himself out in the costume of Dennis Brulgruddery, the bumbling innkeeper of the comedy, and no one could have looked more ridiculous in the "long swing-tailed coat with buttons about the size of pewter plates; a pair of breeches made very loose . . . ornamented with knee buckles." Anne Newport preserved a vivid recollection of the handsome Mrs. Callaghan—"a tall, elegant figure with a blooming countenance," but she did not remember Mr. Callaghan, which leads one to surmise that she and her mother were back in the kitchen and not treated to the entertainment that Dennis put on for paying customers.[11]

Half a dozen miles from their destination they turned off the main road onto a trail which skirted a creek between two tall mountains. Suddenly the weary travelers emerged "upon a pastoral vale." This was the site of the Sweet Springs. Anne paid little heed to the scenery. She looked forward to reunion with her good friend Mrs. Lewis. They found her at The Wigwam, as her husband called the new six-room log house.

They rested a day or so and then climbed Peters Mountain where Major (promoted at end of war) William Royall had built a manor house of Tidewater elegance. The major, still a bachelor, hired Mary Butler as housekeeper. One suspects the hand of Mrs. Lewis in this arrangement, perhaps agreed upon before the Anderson farm was forsaken.

4

Colonel Lewis planned to surround the Sweet Springs with a group of log cabins for the accommodation of health-seeking guests. A short distance south of the resort he envisioned the rise of a model town. Each house there, he stipulated, must be at least sixteen feet square and topped by a stone chimney. Stores, tanneries, a distillery, and the like might establish themselves at the Sweet Springs, but no commercial enterprise would be permitted to enter Fontville, the name the colonel had chosen for his Allegheny arcadia. Fontville never got beyond a pencil sketch. For a time building activity was no further along at the Springs, the trickle of visitors being accommodated at The Wigwam. The few settlers who wandered off the Buffalo Trail, the main pathway to the Ohio River which passed some ten miles north of the Springs, quickly ran up unpretentious shelters and got on with the business of finding a living.[12]

So far the only encouragement given Colonel Lewis in efforts to boom his real estate had come from Major Royall who held the patent for 846 acres on Potts Creek, a couple of miles east of the Springs. Still the colonel was displeased. Here was the house of his dreams, which could have been an inspiration to Fontville home-seekers, but it was a mile and a half off the principal approach to the Lewis land and hidden from view part way up the mountain.[13]

As his neighbors soon learned, William Royall was never one to follow a beaten track. Of independent means, he was a kind man and devoted his time freely to tasks intended to lessen frontier hardships, such as locating roads and, in this, his judgment was excellent, thanks to military experience. The major often served on the circuit court grand jury, when other men would seize any excuse to avoid the duty. The trouble lay, in part, with the situation of Botetourt County, the Sweet Springs county, which straddled the Alleghenies. Fincastle, then as now the Botetourt county seat, is east of the mountains, while the Springs is clear over west. Sessions alternated between Fincastle and Lewisburg, the Greenbrier County seat twenty miles beyond the Springs. It was a hazardous journey to attend court in either place. In the spring, talesmen risked drowning in swollen streams and, in winter, they suffered frostbite. One victim put in the court record that he "had both ears bitten off" while crossing the mountain. His loss did not save him from caustic comment by a neighbor woman who observed that "the Almighty did that which ought to have been done long before." [14]

But perils of the road never daunted the master of Peters Mountain. Ever a patriot, he loved his country above everything. With more leisure, more money, and more education than any of his neighbors, his duty was to set a good example. A sentimental follower of Rousseau, the major believed in the essential goodness of mankind. Given time, he was convinced, these new Americans would recognize their political responsibilities.

The neighbors were probably more impressed by the many petitions William Royall composed and sent to distant Richmond asking for public improvements. Sometimes, when a piece of patronage was hard to get, he would travel east at his own expense and, often as not, bring it off. Both his legislative experience and Tidewater family connections helped in these matters.

Royall kith and kin had been accumulating on the James River since 1622, when Joseph Royall brought twenty colonists from England in a wispy little craft solicitously named the *Charitie*. For his trouble Joseph was paid in headrights. All told Joseph received a grant of eleven hundred acres on the north side of the river west of "Ye Neck of Land at Charles Citie." As the clan multiplied, successive generations of Royalls pushed farther up the river highway until halted by the "falls," a barrier as well for the sailing vessels that crossed the sea to trade. William Royall was born within sight of the "falls" at the Hundred Neck, the plantation which his grandfather, the third Joseph Royall, had built on the west bank of the Appomattox, near where it mingles with the James. The fourth Joseph Royall died young and the Hundred Neck became the inheritance of his younger brother, Richard Royall. In the tradition Richard had named his first-born Joseph. William was his second son and so not in line to inherit his father's considerable estate.[15]

"Richard Royall, Gent.," as the father signed his name, was one of a quartet of gentlemen justices who, for long, presided over sessions of the Chesterfield County Court. He was "cousin" to the other three—John Bolling, William Kennon and Richard Eppes. His wife's brother Peter Eppes who lived across the Appomattox at City Point, the busy harbor of the Upper James, was sheriff. Richard himself had been sheriff for a time. He was also a vestryman of the Curle's Episcopal Church, further securing the supremacy of the ruling clique of cousinry as a self-perpetuating closed shop.[16]

Coming of age in the decade before the outbreak of the War for Independence, William Royall read Rousseau and Voltaire and was outspoken in his disapproval of the high-handed reign of the colonial upper crust. In his day William would have been considered a "radical," and probably his parents wondered what the younger generation was coming to. Among their son's contemporaries, studying at the College of William and Mary, there were many who espoused the views of liberal French writers. William studied for the law, but did not graduate. When he came of age, Justice Royall settled his second son on a tobacco plantation of four hundred acres in Amelia County, some six miles beyond Amelia Courthouse. The land had been the father's first "western" patent. Like neighboring planters, Richard did not bother to re-enrich the soil, but moved on to virgin fields, farther and still farther away from his Tidewater plantation which, however, remained his true home. The new resident of Amelia County had scarcely settled in when the colonies lost the argument with England over taxation without representation. William Royall joined the militia and started drilling.[17]

Then suddenly the life mapped out for the second son of Richard Royall took an unexpected turning. Early in 1774, his older brother, the fifth Joseph Royall, and his wife Rebecca (née Eppes) died, probably in a fever epidemic which the swamps of Tidewater regularly bred. Their daughter, Elizabeth, survived them. Because she was female, Elizabeth had no claim on the estate her father was heir to. Before the year was out Justice Richard Royall was dead. His will gave all his lands to "my loving son William" together with the "Residue of my Estate, both real and personal." When his widow passed on in a couple of years she bequeathed to William "my claim of Dower in the lands formerly belonging to my late husband." [18]

The heir promptly dipped into his fortune to charter a sloop which he loaded with wheat and staples and sent as a gift to Massachusetts, feeling the pinch of England's blockade of the Port of Boston. Apprehensive of an outbreak in Virginia, Lord Dunmore, the royal governor, surreptitiously removed the colony's gunpowder from the public magazine at Williamsburg to a schooner anchored in the James. Calling for volunteers, Patrick Henry started for the little colonial capital to demand return of the ammunition. "Independents" came on the double from all directions to join the march. Lieutenant William Royall's militia company afterwards claimed the distinction of "first" to reach Henry's side. Sixteen miles from Williamsburg, the governor's messenger met the marchers and paid up handsomely.[19]

When hostilities started, Lieutenant Royall was sent south where he fought in some of the bloodiest engagements of the Revolution —Charleston, Camden, Guilford Courthouse, Cowpens, Eutaw Springs. Most of these were defeats, or retreats executed under the command of the wily Nathanael Greene to delay the northward advance of the enemy on Virginia.

For seven and a half years of war service, Captain (promotion) Royall "never drew a dollar of pay"; nor did he once claim his daily ration. The captain found for himself, contributed horses and, in the retreat from Camden, "brought the Virginia line to Guilford Court House, North Carolina, at his own expense." William Royall was "undoubtedly a self-denying patriot," concluded a Virginia historian.[20]

The enthusiasm of the self-denying patriot floundered in disillusionment after the Revolution. The war changed almost nothing among the hereditary ruling class of Virginia. Governor Thomas Jefferson managed to abolish the laws of entail and primogeniture, but his plan for a public school system was rejected. Six years after Yorktown a man still could not vote in the Old Dominion unless he owned a piece of land and had a little schooling. Schools were wanting. The rich families had tutors. As protection against the growing influence of western counties, Tidewater imposed a system of district apportionment under which one thousand Piedmont and trans-Allegheny votes had as much representation as one hundred Low Country ballots. Another disillusionment for Major Royall was the continued acceptance of the Established Church, prime ally of the status quo.[21]

Thus the excursions William Royall made back East in behalf of improvements at the Sweet Springs served to remind him of youthful dreams gone astray. Returning to Peters Mountain he would sit late evenings in his library sipping Madeira and brooding over what had not come to pass. The land of the cohees had also disappointed him. The rugged westerners who, in the darkness of Rockfish Gap had seemed like Rousseau material, were as ambitious for wealth as any tuckahoe. Once they had it, they would live no differently from the easterners they presently made fun of.

On their part, the cohees had given up trying to understand Major Royall. They esteemed him for his education and fine house, and listened respectfully when he instructed them in how to run their farms. But the major's ideas were impractical. He could afford to try them out on his plantation because he had money to make up losses. But not his neighbors. They lived uncertainly from crop to crop. In private, the practical farmers chuckled over some of Major Royall's theories. One had come from a French book he read to them. Anyone could tell that Frenchmen knew next to nothing about livestock. Yet the major had decided that henceforth he would not tamper with the natural state of his farm animals. Neither geldings nor steers roamed his fields.[22]

5

Anne Newport was content in her new home. She hurried through chores and then dashed into the library. What an array of books! Nothing could have pleased Major Royall more than to come upon the daughter of a servant woman reading his books. He introduced Anne to his favorite authors and so discovered the girl's quick mind and eagerness to learn. That was all he needed to assume the role of teacher. In his hands, Anne Newport received more education than most men of her generation. Education of women was still considered unnecessary except, in a limited way, for females pertaining to the upper class. Judging by results, Anne's education was somewhat lopsided. William Royall spent little time on dull drills in spelling and grammar but devoted himself to ideas and subjects which most interested him. The major's special interests were literature and history, particularly the history of his country, little of which had been written.

A lot could be told by relating the history of the Royall family. Anne enjoyed accounts of the teacher's youth, lived among peace and plenty behind the brick walls of the plantation on the Appomattox River. It sounded like a fairy tale compared with her precarious childhood. On the other hand, the major was stimulated by the tales of the people who fought for survival on the Loyalhanna. Arthur Denniston—there was a man he thought he would like to know.

Stories of Indian raids in western Pennsylvania led to discourses on the War for Independence. With firsthand knowledge, Major Royall led his pupil through the military strategy of the war and then took her behind the scenes to examine the international intrigue, a classic of cold-blooded cunning. The effect was to soften Anne's dislike of the red men and to increase her distrust of the English.

With meager aid from the limp, little newspapers that arrived each week from Philadelphia, teacher and pupil kept up with current history. It was a day of jubilation when news reached William Royall that Thomas Jefferson's "Bill for Establishing Religious Freedom" had been enacted. At last, the monopoly of the Anglican Church had been broken. While governor, Jefferson had made potent enemies through his persistent onslaughts on the domination of the all-powerful Tidewater families, in order to give his "country," as he called Virginia, "the foundation of a government truly republican." The landed gentry naturally fought off all threats to its ascendancy. Knowing little of military matters and not a man to impose authority, Jefferson was not at his best as a wartime executive, but he was not a coward or a traitor or guilty of malfeasance in office, as his bitterest opponents charged in the Assembly.

Hastily summoned from South Carolina to participate in the defense of Richmond, William Royall had sat in the Assembly, for the first time, as delegate from Amelia. He was horrified by the criticism. This was the session thrown into panic by the arrival of Tarleton's dragoons. When it reconvened in Staunton, the legislators left Mr. Jefferson to be dealt with by the "following session" of the Assembly.

Less than two months after Yorktown, the following session was called to order. Delegate Royall was again in his seat, impatient to clear Jefferson's good name. William was immensely proud to call the older man "cousin." Tom Jefferson had married Martha Wayles, whose mother, as was William's mother, had been an Eppes. After much oratory, laced with innuendo, the legislators, eager to get back to neglected plantations, passed a wishy-washy resolution giving "thanks . . . to our former governor," saying not a word to refute the contemptible accusations against Jefferson. These would linger in people's minds ever afterwards.[23]

Disgusted with the ambiguous outcome of the inquiry, William Royall walked out, though his term had several months to run. Late in December, his colleagues ordered the sergeant-at-arms to "take into custody . . . the member from the county of Amelia." Some thirty-odd members having "failed to appear," the session was having quorum trouble. The sergeant-at-arms rounded up a handful of delinquents, but the Amelia delegate was not among them.[24]

6

So the days passed companionably on Peters Mountain with two lonely individuals quickly transformed by contentment found in sharing thoughts, confidences, studies, and daydreams. With neighborly intuition, the Sweet Springs remarked the change that came over William Royall. His step was brisk, his countenance beamed and he had no time for long talks with his neighbors. The sly old bachelor! It was Mary Butler's daughter, of course. Lucky girl! No dowry and not much to look at, even in the bloom of youth. Well, with all the money the major had, there should be quite a wedding celebration.

Time passed, but there was no wedding; only more gossip. Of significance was an indicated break in the friendship with the

Lewises. It had become the custom of Major Royall and Anne, after an afternoon gallop, to tie up their horses at The Wigwam and visit with the Lewises. But the horses were seen no more standing in front of the log house. John Lewis, the eldest son, was a veteran of the Revolution. He had often climbed Peters Mountain to reminisce with William Royall. But John had stopped going to the mountain. His explanation was forthcoming later when, under oath, he declared in court: "Major William Royall . . . lived with her [Anne] some years or kept her as a concubine." [25]

It could have been true. Though callers at the plantation were few, curious neighbors managed to keep informed about activities on Peters Mountain. Word sifted down that the middle-aged William Royall sometimes drank more than was good for him and neglected his fields. Thank goodness he kept his mill in repair and all were welcome to use it. They knew that James Butler had arrived from the Valley and the major sent him to school for a "good English education." If James attended the academy of the Reverend G. M. Devenish at the Springs, he was submitted to a rigorous program—six hours daily, six days a week and "no vacation that can possibly be avoided." Anne thought her stepbrother had "talents, but no ambition." After a few years at the academy, his practical mother took James out and apprenticed him to a saddler.[26]

A berrypicker who came to the door one Sunday morning had lots to tell when she raced down the mountain. Anne was reading a book by the French naturalist Buffon which she put down to go to look for Mrs. Butler. Returning, she found the woman examining the colorful biological illustrations.

"La!" exclaimed the berrypicker. "Do you read such books today?"

"Why what's the matter with it?" asked Anne.

"It an't a good book. I would not read such a book on the Sabbath." [27]

The Protestant Sabbath, a day of inactivity except for the worship of the Lord, was strictly observed at the Springs though the town boasted no church building. Faith was nurtured by services conducted in one of the larger cabins a couple of times a month

by itinerant preachers and missionaries. Mostly they were Methodist circuit riders. No church-goer himself, William Royall was
not without reverence. In his youth, disapproving of the Established Church, he had found expression for his religious needs in
Freemasonry, "one of the greatest institutions in the world," he
told his young pupil. The Masons "lived" Christianity, while organized churchdom was so busy collecting money and filling minds
with intolerant dogmas it neglected to practice the simple teachings
of Christ. So it was that Anne Newport learned to idolize Masonry
and to formulate a personal religion: "Principle is the thing, and
not creed." [28]

7

The growth of the Springs continued to lag. Colonel Lewis had
further worries with competition from nearby springs. He replaced
The Wigwam with a hotel and launched into an inspired scheme
to fill it with paying guests. Much grumbling was still heard over
the inconvenience of getting to court. In 1788, in the reorganiza-
tion of Virginia's judicial system, circuit courts were superseded
by district courts. The new title brought no relief to Springs litigants whose choice remained faraway Fincastle or the hazardous
ride to Lewisburg. For the justices and their entourage the enlarged
westernmost district of the state presented the longest and roughest
riding of their tour. The district comprised the four mountain counties of Montgomery, Botetourt, Greenbrier, and Kanawha whose
limits stretched to the Ohio River. With an eye to promoting his
resort, Colonel Lewis suggested that the court break the journey
between the Botetourt County seat and Lewisburg with a sitting
at the Sweet Springs. The colonel offered to donate the land and
build a courthouse and jail.[29]

"Court Days" brought crowds and excitement, much as do
county fairs of the present. If Lewis's proposition was accepted,
he would acquire a ready-made clientele and entertainment to boot.
It was the custom of courts to sit at county seats. Colonel Lewis
tried to avoid stepping on any toes when he refrained from asking
that the Springs be made a county seat. His proposal fairly crushed

the foot of Colonel John Stuart, county clerk of Greenbrier and jealous guardian of everything pertaining to his territory. Having nursed Lewisburg through the stockade period when it was called Fort Union until it became a town in 1782, Stuart had no wish to share the bonanza of the court sessions with a rival town. He put up a good fight, but lost. Lewis's proposition was practical and moreover the justices welcomed the opportunity to interrupt their trip amid the pleasures of the Springs. Despite the rift in his friendship with the Lewis family, William Royall was named "to view" the new courthouse when completed and determine whether it was "sufficient for the purpose intended."

The first court was held in the Lewis courthouse on October 18, 1796. John Tyler, father of a future President, was one of the two presiding justices. He was an old friend from Charles City County, and also a devoted Jeffersonian. His assignment to the western district was juridical demotion inflicted by Tidewater bigwigs whom he had displeased. William Royall served as juror at the initial session of the court. The following year he sat on the grand jury. In 1799 and in 1800 he was foreman of the grand jury at all four terms. His last service appears to have been in October, 1802, when he was a member of the grand jury of which John Lewis was foreman.[30]

During visits of the court, lights burned late into the night on Peters Mountain. William Royall kept open house for Tidewater friends and barristers. Guests had every reason to congratulate themselves on their luck in finding such hospitality in the backwoods. Evenings the gentlemen sat long at table, relishing the dishes of mountain game prepared by Mary Butler and savoring the excellent wines of the host. After giving her mother a hand in the kitchen, Anne Newport posted herself outside a half-closed door and eavesdropped. She hoped to hear some good talk; about the French Revolution, perhaps, for which she and the major were enthusiastic. They had named the new hound Citizen. But the talk was gossipy, rather than weighty, as Major Royall had warned it would be.

Next morning, riding down the mountain to court, the visitors no doubt discussed William Royall and the young woman who lived in his house, as frankly as the major and Anne discussed them. They were sure to hear the gossip from the Lewises. After court adjourned tuckahoe attorneys returned to Tidewater to spread the tidings of Major Royall's romance. The news must have been disturbing to James Roane who had married Elizabeth Royall, only child of William's deceased older brother. Uncle William had always been most generous with his orphaned niece, and later with her husband whose money-making schemes were seldom crowned with success. One time the major had met the salvage bill incident to the foundering of the ship *Nancy*, in which Uncle William had purchased a one-eighth interest for his nephew-in-law. Since 1787 he had held a mortgage for two thousand pounds—accumulated interest raised the value to three thousand pounds—on land Roane had invested in not far from the Springs. Moreover, William Royall permitted the young couple to live rent free at The Forest, the ancestral family plantation in Charles City County. The Roanes needed the large house because Elizabeth was well into a career of motherhood. She named her first son William Royall Roane. Uncle William was delighted and promised to make the namesake his heir.[31]

The glittering prospects of the young man were shattered a year after the first sitting of the Sweet Springs court. When the winter's snows melted from the mountain a circuit-riding preacher crossed over to the courthouse at Fincastle and recorded the following:

"Married in the county of Botetourt by the Revd. Wm. P. Martin on the 18th day of November 1797 William Royall to Anne Newport as per certificate of said Martin dated 4th of May 1798."

The bride was twenty-eight years old. The groom was in his middle fifties.[32]

CHAPTER III

THE WIFE OF A DREAMER

1

The Lewises remained unforgiving, though doors at the Sweet Springs gradually opened to the wife of Major William Royall. Good will was rewarded. Peters Mountain added a sawmill, filling a need in the booming resort town. Because his wife was competent, more and more the major let slip into her hands the running of the plantation. The steep land was not the best for farming, about one acre in six being tillable, and eventually Anne Royall added sheep which did not need much looking after.[1]

One morning early, husband and wife rode off to Lewisburg where Major Royall had business. The coolness of the influential Lewis family probably made Anne a little nervous about her reception, but she got off to a good start, making a friend of Mrs. Alexander Welch, first lady of the Greenbrier County seat. Such were the hazards of border existence that this handsome, gray-haired pioneer had been widowed three times. Anne spent a good part of her visit sitting with Frances Welch in her garden, cultivated on the site of Fort Union, as Lewisburg was earlier known, and listening to tales of the Virginia frontier. They had a familiar ring to the refugee from the Pennsylvania frontier, a circumstance which may have helped Mrs. Royall to remember them and later put them into her first published book.

Mrs. Welch had known Jacob Marlin, the long hunter who, with his partner Stephen Sewell, stumbled onto the buffalo trail which opened the great pioneer pathway through western Virginia to the Ohio River. In the fall of 1750 the hunters had reached the Greenbrier River, a treacherous, swift stream beyond which white men did not venture. Having taken little game, Marlin and Sewell plunged in, risking their lives for a winter's supply of meat. The swirling current carried them to the far bank at a point where, since time immemorial, herds of buffalo had entered or emerged from the river on their seasonal trek to and from the plains. The hunters made camp in a cave, but cramped quarters soon had them quarreling. Sewell moved into the hollow of a nearby tree. He did not dare go farther for, by then, the adventurers knew they were camped, at the height of the hunting season, on the favorite preserve of the Shawnee Indians, ever foes of the whites. The disputes between Marlin and Sewell worsened. When no red men were near, they would shout angry remarks and, then in distrust of each other, sat up all night "with their guns cocked ready to fire." The Shawnees, and not Marlin, killed Sewell.

"What did you quarrel about?" Mrs. Welch had asked Marlin.

"Why, about rela-gin!" One was a Presbyterian, a "dissenter" from the Church of England of which the other was a dedicated communicant. Who was who Anne Royall neglected to say.[2]

The first white guide to hack his way through the tangled mountainous length of the buffalo trail had been Mathew Arbuckle, a Scottish giant who planted his hunting shack where the town of Lewisburg was to grow. Twice the hostile Shawnees wiped out the little settlement. In 1774, returning for a third try, Arbuckle brought his bride, a pretty twenty-four-year-old widow from the Shenandoah Valley. He deposited her at Fort Union and went down the buffalo trail with the army of Colonel Andrew Lewis, brother of the Sweet Springs proprietor, to defeat the Shawnees at the Battle of Point Pleasant. After seven years of marriage the captain was killed in 1781 before the door of his log house when a tree fell on him.[3]

In the second year of the Revolution, the Shawnees, primed by the British, had returned and laid siege to Donnally's blockhouse, eight miles west of Lewisburg. With one shot, Dick Pointer, a

Negro slave, had saved the blockhouse. Learning that the hero was
still living, Anne Royall hurried off to talk to him. She found
"a shabby creature with a head as white as wool" whose "principal
support is derived from donations."

The able-bodied males from the neighborhood of Donnally's
had all gone off to fight for independence, Dick related. Some
had started for the Ohio to hold off the Indians; others had marched
six hundred miles to join Washington at Boston. Only the slave
and four old men were left behind to defend some fifty women
and children who crowded into the blockhouse after Fort Union
sent a warning. Dick spent the night ramming a muzzle "with old
nails, pieces of iron, buckshot" and any other material which
might prove suitably fatal. He could barely lift his musket when
the Shawnees dug their tomahawks into the stockade at dawn.
By the time Dick Pointer was in position to fire, they had broken
through. The discharge knocked out Dick. When he came to,
troops from the fort had arrived and the Indians had fled, save
three dead ones. "Several persons" told Mrs. Royall that "had it
not been for Dick Pointer's well-timed shot, every soul in the fort
must have been massacred." As a reward, Colonel Donnally gave
Dick his freedom.[4]

Lewisburg's classic tale of heroism, however, belonged to Mrs.
Archibald Clendenin whose husband was scalped before her eyes.
After destroying the ill-starred settlement (first destruction), the
Shawnees started back to the Ohio shepherding a band of captives,
mostly women, among them Mrs. Clendenin, her three children,
and her sixteen-year-old brother John Ewing, visiting from east
of the mountains. They had been two days on the trail when Mrs.
Clendenin resolved to escape. She jumped down a steep precipice
and crept under a large rock. Missing her after a time, the Indians
laid her baby on the ground, thinking its cries would induce her
to return. "Make the calf bawl and the cow will come," they
reasoned. At length they killed the baby and went on.

"Mrs. Clendenin remained under the rock till dark. The second
night she reached her desolate habitation and found the body of
her husband. She threw a buffalo hide over it, and continued
toward the settled part of the country. In nine days she arrived

[at her mother's house] on the Cowpasture River." The distance was not great, probably sixty miles, but the distraught Mrs. Clendenin, traveling only at night, had crossed the Allegheny Mountains alone.

After four years, a treaty having been made with the Shawnees, John Ewing, too, came home to the Cowpasture, bringing the sad news that, early in their captivity, his nephew had been killed. Mrs. Clendenin's daughter, however, had grown fond of life with the savages and elected to remain.

While captive, John Ewing had learned the Shawnee language and made himself useful to Chief Thobqueh. For all his wisdom Thobqueh had been perplexed by many statements in a white man's Bible that his braves had brought back from a raid. The old chief listened intently as John Ewing translated. "And the Lord God formed man out of the dust of the earth. . . ." Yes, that was credible; Thobqueh had always been suspicious of the lowly origin of white men. Then came the deluge. The best the translator could do with the ark was to say it was a big canoe. After John had enumerated all the passengers taken aboard the ark, Thobqueh angrily snapped the Bible closed.

"That's a lie!" he exclaimed. "There never was a tree on the Scioto Bottoms big enough to make such a canoe."

Anne Royall heard the story of Mrs. Clendenin from her daughter, Mrs. Maiz, born of her mother's second marriage. Mrs. Clendenin had come back to Lewisburg with a new husband and made her home where Archibald Clendenin had been savagely murdered.[5]

2

Lewisburg was not a pleasure resort but a real town, reflecting the sturdy character of the people who lived there. The Royalls left it reluctantly to return to the inanities of the Sweet Springs. Since the advent of the court, visitors arrive in droves to drink the sour waters and turned night into day in pursuit of pleasure. They set a pace more apt to wreck their health than to restore it. Anne Royall deplored the effect of Colonel Lewis's high-toned guests on the townspeople.

The young men must have ruffled shirts of the finest linen cambric, because the gentlemen at the Springs have them so. They must have fine boots and spurs, whip and gloves. And as for Miss, she must have a fine crepe dress; it must be in the fashion; it must be tucked and corded, trimmed with some twelve or fourteen yards of satin ribbon; she must have a fine ruff [and] a hat, trimmed in bon ton style; she must have the "nicest, nicest" sort of shoes, they must be "prunella" [cloth uppers]; silk hose, and silk gloves; horse and saddle, a whip too.[6]

The pace picked up considerably when Robert Bailey blew into town, one step ahead of the Augusta County sheriff, with his faro bank. Bailey had fled Staunton after a court found him guilty of operating an "unlawful gaming table." The punishment was degrading for a man who prided himself on the drawing-room atmosphere with which he surrounded his games. "My order to my dealers always was to suffer no person to bet but gentlemen and to exclude all common persons."

Bailey called himself a "sportsman." "The name gambler was always loathsome to me." The sportsman made a deal with Colonel Lewis to rent the courtroom between sessions. By the time the court was due, the faro bank had become so popular that the "gentlemen" were unwilling to vacate for the justices. Bailey proposed that the court make use of the room during the daytime and that he move his tables in for the evening. Lewis refused; in the season, the ladies took over the courtroom at night for their balls. Bailey persuaded the proprietor to set a midnight curfew on dancing. He ran his bank thereafter until eight o'clock in the morning when the sessions of the court resumed.[7]

3

In 1799 the county of Monroe was whittled from Greenbrier County, despite the agonized protests of Colonel Stuart. The new county was the handiwork of John Hutchinson, a former member of the Virginia Assembly and wise in the ways of lobbying, though not yet called by that word. Hutchinson took the job of Monroe

County clerk and, as soon as he had built a courthouse and created Union, the county seat—"a poor little village," according to Anne Royall—he set out to dress his backwoods district with greater importance. After three years Hutchinson succeeded in moving his county line eastward to take in the misplaced transmontane reaches of Botetourt County. Colonel Stuart railed.

Hutchinson now launched his main drive, agitating for the removal of the district court from the Springs to Union. He flooded Richmond with petitions and engaged in adroit wire-pulling. The two colonels, Lewis and Stuart, patched up their differences to oppose the wicked design of the Monroe County clerk. But Lewis played into the hands of Hutchinson when he let Robert Bailey take over the courtroom for his faro bank. Petitions to Richmond charged that the Springs courthouse was "never in the custody of the jailor," but "used in vacation [of the court] as a boarding house . . . and now is in ill repair. The jail is totally insufficient and several escapes have been made." Furthermore, declared Hutchinson, through his hotel Colonel Lewis enjoyed a "monopoly" which enabled him to charge high prices for accommodations. The expense of a witness, said the clerk, was "equal to the fine for his absence."

The proprietor of the Springs dispatched to Richmond an angry denial of Hutchinson's charges. His prices were no loftier than those levied at the "public houses" in Union, and, moreover, his tavern accommodated two hundred guests, "all the people who come to the court," whereas Union had shelter for only fifty. The courthouse Lewis had built "is of stone, much larger than the one at Union, and has walls two feet thick. The jail has two rooms, whereas the jail at Union has a single room 18 feet square. Only two felons have escaped from the Springs jail."

The grasping Mr. Hutchinson had his way. The district court sat for the last time at the Sweet Springs in 1807, after which the records were taken to the Monroe County Courthouse. By then, Colonel Lewis could have felt no pain over parting. In the eleven years he was host to the court, he had acquired a steadfast clientele that readily fell in with the fashionable routine of annual visits.[8]

4

William Royall took no part in the squabble for possession of the
court; nor did he and his wife join the gay society that frequented
the Lewis hostelry. In the midst of the row, Major Royall went
off to view 4,889 acres awarded him in the Virginia Military Re-
serve for his services as "a captain of the continental line for seven
years and four months." Though the warrant for bounty land
came from the state, the major could not take title until the Federal Government issued the patent. This might take several years.
The government insisted on resurvey and detailed inspection of
papers offered as proof of service. Veterans grumbled over the
snarl of red tape. To obtain ready cash, many sold their warrants
to land speculators who made a business of knocking on doors.
Sellers got no bargain. When Benjamin Ladd, one of the most
active speculators, made him an offer, Major Royall assigned Ladd
half of his acreage, an exorbitant commission, to rescue the patent
from official hands and sell the half that William Royall retained.

"You'll get nothing for your pains," the major warned the specu-
lator. "The land has been picked [of lumber]." [9]

Ohio was a disappointment, but William Royall returned to the
Sweet Springs enthusiastic over a bustling Virginia settlement where
the Elk River meets the Great Kanawha. George Clendenin, a
nephew of Archibald whom the Shawnees scalped, had built a
two-story log stockade there in 1788. The following year, when
Kanawha County was laid off, Clendenin's Station was designated
the county seat and the name changed to Charleston, honoring
Clendenin's father. In no time fertile farms spread over the rich
bottom lands. Daniel Boone hunted and lived at Clendenin's, but
was crowded out when the population reached fifty. William
Royall saw Charleston as an unspoiled, robust town, a refuge for
which he had long scanned the American horizon. The county
seat would grow, but not nearly so large as Alexander Welch (he
was the third husband of the Lewisburg widow) had anticipated
in his survey of the town site. Welch had imaginatively laid off
Front Street sixty feet wide. Sight unseen, for a score of years,

William Royall had been patenting land in and around Charleston and profitably leasing timber rights. He told his wife he would sell Peters Mountain and go to live in the Kanawha county seat. They would build their house on Front Street which ran along the bluff overlooking the beautiful Kanawha River where more traffic glided by than on Mr. Welch's broad thoroughfare.[10]

Anne Royall was all for the move. The years were passing and she longed to see something of the world.

"I have learned mankind only in theory," she said wistfully.[11]

Time passed and no buyer claimed the plantation, a large and expensive holding for western Virginia. The year wore on and the Royalls still had not left for Charleston. William Royall consoled himself with brandy. One afternoon he stumbled out of the house and rolled down a steep incline. With the help of Davy, a slave, Anne led her bruised husband indoors and put him to bed. Suddenly Major Royall turned on his wife and blamed her for his misfortunes. He thundered for whiskey to ease his pain. Davy held him fast until he fell into drunken slumber. In a few days the major was himself once more—pleasant, reasonable, considerate, affectionate, and busy with plans for their new home. As the months dragged by and still no purchaser appeared, the scene was repeated. Peters Mountain became a prison for both husband and wife.[12]

5

"I have little partiality for mountains," Anne Royall wrote. "They are splendid objects to look at, but nothing wears worse than mountains, when you take up your abode among them." The splendid objects were at their worst during long winters. "The cold blasts killed lambs and calves by the dozens, chilled vegetation, overwhelming everything with snow." [13]

William Royall usually managed to make the best of the winter's inactivity and, though sorely distressed by the prolonged delay in getting off to Charleston, he could still pass the time comfortably when a blizzard confined him to the house. He would settle down in a big chair before a log fire with a book and decanter on a

table beside him. By nightfall, if he did not drink too much, he
would feel mellow and talkative and bent on cheering up his restless
wife, with a story or two of his younger days in Tidewater. "During our winter evenings he used to relate many of those ancient
tales of his dogs and guns."

Hunting held little interest for Anne, but one ancient tale
amused her. It was about Spad, the major's favorite spaniel, re-
nowned in Tidewater for his feats of retrieving. Once Spad came
with a duck in his mouth, which he had pursued about four miles,
as appeared from evidence of neighbors. But Spad, though the best
of his kind when in a good mood, would sometimes get in the
pouts and run home as fast as his legs could carry him, "leaving
his master to get the ducks out of the water. Whenever I got in the
pouts, my husband uniformly called me 'Spad,' which never failed
to restore me to a good humor." [14]

Peters Mountain took on a sunnier tone when, in 1806, a nine-
year-old girl came to live at the plantation. She was Anna Malvina
Cowan, eldest daughter of Anne Royall's sister Mary who had
married Patrick Cowan, a farmer of Westmoreland County, Pennsylvania. Mary had borne half a dozen children and so had not been
difficult to persuade to send her sister's namesake to make her home
with the childless Royalls. William Royall adored Anna Malvina,
and arranged for her to attend the Ann Smith Academy at Sweet
Springs.[15]

Not long after the arrival of his stepniece, James Butler, grown
to manhood, went off to try his luck in Kentucky. Mary Butler
followed her son in 1808, to housekeep on her third frontier. That
same year Mrs. William Lewis died. Though no longer friends,
Anne Royall felt keenly the passing of the woman who was a
bright memory of her girlhood. Another event of the busy year
was the visit of John Bradbury, an entertaining Englishman, who
spent a week at the plantation. Fresh from a sojourn at Monticello,
Bradbury was on his way to St. Louis to begin a study of plant
life in the Mississippi Valley. Eventually more than a thousand of
his specimens survived the Atlantic crossing to be potted by the
Botanic Garden at Liverpool.[16]

In the fall William Royall felt a yearning to see his old home once more. It would be his first trip to Tidewater in four years. Before undertaking the journey, he penned a new will with which he was not altogether satisfied. He told Anna Malvina that "if he lived till he returned he would get some person to write it over . . . in a fairer hand." Major Royall said he "did not wish so bad a wrote will to appear after his death." He shoved the document into his desk—into the "prospect drawer," as he and his wife had named it—and asked Anna Malvina "to put him in mind" to have it witnessed by the first person who came to the house. Next morning James Wiley, a rifle slung over his shoulder, knocked at the door offering to sell a quarter of a deer he had killed. Uncle William invited the hunter indoors and had him attest the will. Then he "went to the cupboard and brought a silver ladle and laid it on the table and told . . . Wiley that if he should not return, that the ladle was Anna Malvina's." [17]

As usual, the visit to the Low Country was disillusioning. A weary old man returned to the mountain fretting over the shortcomings of his kinsmen. He disapproved especially of his great nephew and namesake, William Royall Roane. The young man was "unsteady and too fond of dancing." As for Roane's parents, William Royall declared he had done enough for them. After canceling James Roane's note for three thousand pounds, he had signed over to him and his niece Elizabeth title to the remaining four hundred acres of Joseph Royall's original plantation in Charles City County. Included with the gift were twenty-four slaves, most of whom had been born on the plantation.[18]

Weighed down by countless farm tasks and by this time used to her husband's inconstant moods, Anne Royall paid small attention to alterations William Royall made in his will. Some years earlier they had talked over the matter of her inheritance and it had been her husband's idea to set aside her dower, the third she was legally entitled to as wife, and give her use of the income from the remainder of the estate. After her death, the residuary legatee, whomever her husband settled upon, would receive his inheritance.

Major Royall still had faith in one relative. While he recuperated from the fatigue of his journey, Anna Malvina prepared his trays and sat beside his bed, entertained by the same reminiscences that had once cast a spell over her aunt. Up and around again, Uncle William informed the young girl that he had added some bequests for her to his will: land, furniture, two slaves, a mare and saddle, and a cow. Anna Malvina must have a substantial dowry if she was to attract a suitable husband.[19]

6

The last visit of Uncle William to Charles City must have dashed the hopes of niece Elizabeth and her husband James Roane for betterment of their dwindling finances. The rich uncle to whom they had long looked for ultimate relief had taken leave of them in a huff. Colonel Roane was, of course, a planter, though the worn shell of the emigrant Joseph Royall's old plantation could hardly have produced adequate support for his large family. In business ventures beyond his tobacco fields the colonel complained of his luck. The records of several Tidewater counties indicate that the Roanes eked out their income, now and again, by disposing of a piece of land which they had had the good fortune to inherit. In 1798, for instance, Colonel Roane obtained $500 for one thousand acres in Ohio in the Virginia Military Reserve which had been granted to his deceased brother Christopher for services in the Revolutionary War. Three years later husband and wife sold some three hundred acres in Chesterfield County for £900. This acreage, which adjoined the Hundred Neck, may possibly have been part of Elizabeth Royall's dowry, a present from Uncle William at the time of her marriage to James Roane.[20]

The Roanes were, therefore, at their wits' end to reestablish themselves in the good graces of Uncle William, particularly since his irritability was clearly a manifestation of the onset of old age. They had made little headway after a couple of years when they received word that William Royall was in poor health. Frantically they grasped at a straw. In the summer of 1811, the Royalls were surprised to receive a letter saying William R. Roane, the major's namesake, would visit them. Anne was pleased. The grandnephew would be the first member of the family to set foot on the plantation since her marriage.

William Roane arrived at the height of the Springs season and cut quite a dash among the fashionable guests. Uncle William complained of the frivolous bent of Roane and his flashy clothes. Anne defended him; he was young and fond of a good time. The nephew got along fine with his youthful aunt.

Still, Anne Royall could see a big difference between William Roane and a boy of the same age who came often to the plantation. Her husband would have been proud of a nephew like Matthew Dunbar. The son of Scottish immigrants who had settled at Sink's Grove, about sixteen miles west of the Springs, Matt had borrowed and read most of the books in the Royall library. He was a rare companion with whom the Royalls could share their enthusiasm for literature.[21]

Nephew William frittered away none of his time in the library. He admired the horses though, and, prompted by Mrs. Royall, Uncle William gave the young man a brood mare valued at two hundred dollars. Almost immediately the major regretted his generosity, suffering more pain than the mare as Roane charged up and down the mountain at a furious pace.

"That Roane is a great rascal!" Major Royall proclaimed and brought out his will for a rereading.[22]

William Roane went often to the Lewis tavern where he picked up talk about his uncle and his young wife. Opinion was general that too much alcohol was to blame for the decline in William Royall's health. Sometimes he was so "deranged as to endanger the safety of those around him." Charles Dew who was often at the plantation in the course of some twenty years believed that "having company" made Major Royall want "to be in a state of intoxication." Mornings he was usually sober and "sound of mind," but "in the after part of the day," having entertained friends, the major would wind up in a "fitt of frenzy."[23]

This was the sort of gossip the nephew chose to store up for future use. Without much trouble he found other helpful sources. None was more helpful than the two Lewis brothers. While confirming rumors of William Royall's alcoholism, Doctor Charles Lewis said that Anne Royall's treatment of her husband was "highly cruel and barbarous." Only recently the physician had

been summoned to Peters Mountain where he found the husband
with a "badly injured" eye inflicted, so the patient stated, by
"that damned Irish bitch." Moreover, Major Royall continued, "his
wife made the servants drag him out of his chamber into an adjoining room and throw cold water on him."

John Lewis contributed little firsthand information because "for
some years past . . . I declined visiting" William Royall. Yet he
could tell of a visit to the mountain one day when he saw Major
Royall run out of his manor house. "He was pursued and overtaken
by his wife and niece and two or three negroes and forcibly taken
back." Later the major had limped into the tavern with a "very
sore leg occasioned," so the husband claimed, "by a blow from his
wife."

The Lewises introduced William Roane to a neighbor who had
seen "Mrs. Royall catch her husband by the nose and squeeze it
severely several times." This source said he had "heard that Mrs.
Royall made the negroes hold Royall on the ground and while in
that position she threw hot ashes in his face." John Shawver, an
old friend, repeated a conversation in which Major Royall complained that his wife "confined him in a gaol." The major also told
Shawver that Mrs. Royall "made the negroes strip him and carry
him in his shirt tail out into the rain, saying she would by that means
bring him to his senses." [24]

7

Though William Roane remained a month at the plantation he appears not once to have seen his uncle in a "fitt of intoxication," an
almost daily occurrence in the last four years of the major's existence, as intimates declared under oath. It would not have been to
nephew William's advantage to admit that his uncle was a raging
drunkard most of the time. But he did jog his memory, later before
a court, to bring forth one tale which, if it was not soaked in
alcohol, at least did most to undermine the reputation of Anne
Royall.

According to young Roane, he had returned to the mountain
one afternoon to find his uncle with "a contussion of the arm"

which, as the suffering old man claimed, had been "inflicted by a stroke from his wife." The elfin, one-hundred-pound villainess stood silently at the foot of the bed while her husband accused her of having "endeavored several times to kill him." Mrs. Royall offered no denial, Roane said. What, Uncle William asked, could his kinsman do "to arrest her in her cruel and wicked course, as he considered his life in danger?"

Apparently nephew Roane had no answer. Next day he started home on the gray mare, well satisfied with the outcome of his visit. William Royall had let him read his "last will." After payment of the wife's dower and "token bequests to Anna Malvina and William S. Archer," a cousin several times removed who lived in Amelia County, William R. Roane was named heir to "all the balance of his estate." The heir thought he had a pretty good idea of the size of the estate. One time, when Uncle William was laid up, he requested his namesake "to take a schedule of his property." Among other possessions, Roane remembered listing "6,696 acres of land, seven likely negroes and a good stock of cattle, sheep and hogs." [25]

After several months, William Royall received a letter from his nephew. James Wiley, the hunter, was at the plantation when it arrived and so witnessed the temper Major Royall got in over the missive. It was a "scurrilous letter," the major said, "containing a great deal of abuse against his wife." Certainly, now, his namesake would receive no part of his estate, and so out came the will for changes. [26]

William Royall was still worked up when Charles Dew stopped by. Dew was surprised to hear the major say that he "had altered his mind as to his nephew [Roane] being heir. . . . I asked him the reason, to which he answered that William R. Roane had been prematurely endeavoring to get his estate in his hands before his death. He said he had destroyed the Will in favor of William R. Roane and wanted to make another." And, Dew added, "it was early in the day and he [Royall] appeared to be in his right mind except . . . a great deal irritated." [27]

After receipt of the "scurrilous letter," neighbors, as well as members of the household, overheard William Royall say that Wil-

liam S. Archer, "a relation and a worthy gentleman," had replaced
William R. Roane as residuary legatee of his estate. Having destroyed his last will and testament, it was unnecessary to make a
new one. The document Major Royall had written in his own
hand in 1808 named Archer as his principal heir. The reinstated
favorite was the son of Major John Archer with whom William
Royall had served during the Revolution.[28]

8

Such was the state of Major Royall's displeasure with his great-
nephew when the United States declared war on England in 1812.
Though married and father of a couple of children, James Butler
marched with Kentucky militia under the command of Major General William Henry Harrison to relieve the siege of Detroit. Mary
Butler came back to Peters Mountain. Anne welcomed the serene
presence of her mother in a house no longer at peace with itself.
As all knew, William Royall's days were numbered. The family
conspired to keep drink from him and the major conspired to outwit his guardians. When he took too much, about all that could
be done was to protect him from injury. The house slaves—Davy,
Aggy, and Stepney—always followed the reeling man as he stumbled about out-of-doors. When William Royall became "outrageous and violent," Davy, the strongest slave, would maneuver
him to bed and hold him there until he fell asleep.

Such scenes went hard with the wife who had loved him. "It
was out of her power oftentimes . . . to treat him with that tenderness and manifestation of affection which it was her wish to
have done. . . . It was difficult to restrain him from the commission of very improper acts, but . . . she never performed an
intentional act of cruelty toward him in her life."

During a rational interval, Uncle William asked Anna Malvina
to bring his will from the "prospect drawer." He looked the document over and noted it was not in order. James Wiley was the
sole testator; the law required two. In her son-in-law's literate
household Mary Butler had learned to write her name. It seems
fitting that her wavering signature should have affirmed his final

testament on earth. On another day Major Royall sold some land and bought a carriage to take him and his wife to their future home in Charleston. Even as death approached, the romanticist clung to his dream of Utopia beyond the horizon and, to keep his spirits up, his wife encouraged the dream. He was more like his old self as he lay in bed planning a new life.

But the lucid moments were only flickerings among the ashes of a burned-out fire. Somewhere in the mountain mists—in the comforts of his featherbed, in the heady fumes of brandy, among the books that immobilized too many of his hours—William Royall had lost his way. He knew as well as anyone that he had failed and the knowledge tortured him. After a week of derangement, he died on December 12, 1812.[29]

CHAPTER IV

A WOMAN OF PROPERTY

1

The widow of William Royall notified William S. Archer, at his plantation in Amelia County, that he had been named residuary devisee of her husband's estate as well as coexecutor of the will. Assuming that Mr. Archer would communicate with the Roanes, Mrs. Royall did not inform them of the passing of Uncle William. Mr. Archer did promptly communicate with William R. Roane who hurried to Amelia where his "cousin" told him that his uncle's estate "was given to Mrs. Royall for her life [and] the remainder to him [Archer]."

"I shall disclaim all interest," said William Archer. "Your mother is entitled to [the estate]." [1]

On March 16, 1813, three months after the death of William Royall, having heard nothing from Tidewater, the widow-executrix initiated legal formalities to probate her husband's last testament. Accompanied by an attorney, Mary Butler, and James Wiley, Anne Royall rode to Union to present the document for recording at the Monroe County Courthouse. By then, rumor was current that the Roanes planned to contest the will. Accordingly, Isaac Hutchinson, who had succeeded his politicking father as county clerk, declined to receive the papers offered him. He changed his mind after listening to the attorney's argument. Hutchinson then put Mary Butler and James Wiley under oath and both affirmed their signatures as witnesses of the will.[2]

The document, dated November 4, 1808, a day or so before William Royall had trotted away from Peters Mountain on his final visit to Tidewater, disposed of his estate in the manner William Archer had explained to William R. Roane, except for one tract of land. The major had bequeathed some 190 acres "lying at the mouth of Elk River in the County of Kennahway . . . unto Anna Malvina Cowan when she comes of age eighteen." Mrs. Royall and her niece had known about the bequest for several years. William Royall had told them when he returned from a trip to Charleston that he had recorded the deed conveying ownership of the land to Anna Malvina. However, his will stated that "if she chuses," Anna Malvina should have "four hundred pounds in lieu of the land on Elk River." The English pound was then worth $2.60, which put the cash value of Anna Malvina's legacy at above one thousand dollars. Listed also were a couple more bequests to the young girl, though the silver ladle was not specifically mentioned.

A week later the executrix filed an inventory of the personal estate of William Royall. A complete inventory of his real estate does not appear in this record. Only the land owned in Monroe County, estimated to be worth $806.20, was scheduled. Young Roane's schedule of land holdings appears to have been low; William Royall had owned nearer eight thousand acres. Isaac Hutchinson required the executrix to post a bond for $9,000 which may have been the clerk's rough evaluation of the estate.[3]

Legal procedure having been satisfied, the heiress to a fortune which should permit her to live in comfort the rest of her days, made ready to quit forever the melancholy scene of her recent ordeal. She was forty-three years old, an age at which women of her day might expect that life held little more for them. But not Anne Royall. She was eager to explore the unfamiliar world.

"One cannot live shut up in a closet," she decided.[4]

She further decided that failure to make a quick sale of the plantation would not hold her longer at the Sweet Springs. Her husband had died waiting for a buyer; she might do the same. The sure way out was to turn the key in the front door and leave. Anne arranged for an auction of the plantation on the steps of the courthouse at Union and delegated Andrew Beirne, whose general store was owed a bill of $135.62, to attend the sale and prevent the property from going for a song. Mr. Beirne seemed like just the man for the job. He had a reputation for shrewd trading.[5]

And so, on a spring morning in 1813, when the bare red earth began to turn green and new leaves twirled on the trees, Anne Royall stepped into her carriage and, with Anna Malvina, rode down the mountain for the last time. Stepney, the slave who suffered from "weak spells," was probably perched on the driver's seat with Aggy at his side. Davy, the strong slave, brought up the rear with several pack horses loaded with the most treasured possessions from the plantation. Two young Negresses, Lucinda and Betsey, completed the little cavalcade. At Lewisburg the travelers entered the main stream of traffic on the Kanawha Turnpike. Anne Royall was bound for Charleston—Clendenin's Station that was— the destination for which her husband had bought the carriage.

2

The salt boom had been raging four years when Mrs. Royall bumped over the ruts of Front Street. The hardy, simple folk whom William Royall had admired were scarcely evident among the speculators and riff-raff who swarmed in the West's new mecca. Older settlers would remember them as "men of bad morals," given to "rioting and drunkenness," "quarrelling and fighting," "gambling and cheating." The fighting bore no relation to the current war with England, which presumably was pushed into the background in the delirium of the get-rich-quick fever. Prices skyrocketed, as demand outraced supply. Rooms were at a premium. Anne Royall seems to have found accommodations. At least, she did not join the throng that slept each night in the public square of which the Kanawha County Courthouse was the center.

The boom had been touched off by the War of 1812 which cut off the New York salt market, and by the timely invention of David Ruffner who had found a way to bring up the strongest brine from below bedrock. Mrs. Royall had hardly stepped from her carriage when, "with high-wrought enthusiasm," she hurried down to the Kanawha River to see the salt works. She pushed her way through a file of wagons hitched to oxen "ill-used and beat," and pack horses waiting in a quagmire to take the loads of "strong red salt." Keelboats jammed the river also waiting for cargoes, their crews drinking and dancing away the tedious hours to the scraping of fiddles. For all the excitement, Anne found the salt works "dismal looking," twelve miles of "long, low sheds [which] abound on both sides of the river." Adding to the gloom was a "bare, rugged, inhospitable mountain, from which all the timber had been cut."

Ruffner's crude invention was called a gum. It was a fat, giant tree whose hollowed-out center was broad enough to admit a man and his tools. The gum was suspended in shallow water where a seepage of brine indicated salt deposits.

A man is let down into the gum by a windlass and digs around the edge. When he fills a bucket with sand and earth, the bucket is immediately drawn up, emptied and let down again, and so on till the gum descends to rock. All the while water is pumped out of the gum. No man can remain below longer than twenty minutes, owing to the excessive cold at the bottom. To bore through the rock where the best salt is, a long auger is let down and handled by a man outside the gum on a lofty scaffold. On the ground a mule team, rigged to the auger, walks round and round working the pointed instrument deeper. The moment the auger passes through the rock, the water sprouts up to a great height through the gum.

About the time Anne Royall came to Charleston, David Ruffner was trying to convince rival salt works, which had been quick to appropriate his invention, that their furnaces should be adjusted to burn coal, as his were doing. The black "stones" could be picked up almost anywhere round about. "Fire-wood in the course of time must become scarce," warned Ruffner, as the bare mountain that cast its shadow over the salt works was a reminder. Woodchopping had become a prosperous sideline of the salt industry. David Ruffner's warning went unheeded.[6]

Inevitably Anne Royall took a flyer in salt. Another newcomer to Charleston was William Hensley, a blacksmith from Augusta County, Virginia. Jointly with Anna Malvina, Mrs. Royall signed a contract giving Hensley rights for three years to "experiment for salt water at his own expense" on the Elk River land which her niece might "chuse" on her eighteenth birthday. If salt was found, the two Annes agreed to go into partnership with the blacksmith, sharing expenses and profits.[7]

Salt was also behind the efforts of Mrs. Royall to conclude a complicated legal action begun by her husband. After leasing fifteen hundred acres on Coal River to Joseph Brown for ten years, William Royall had changed his mind and instituted ejectment proceedings against the tenant. Burying himself deep in the wilderness, Brown had managed to live out a couple of years of his lease before the sheriff caught up with him. Anne promptly leased the land to three partners, one of whom was Colonel Andrew Donnally, junior, whose father's blockhouse had been saved by the slave Dick Pointer. While the salt boom lasted, the younger Donnally bought up leases right and left.[8]

3

Meantime, profits were being made from a rapid turnover in town lots. Anne Royall got a toehold on Lot Number 11, at the corner of Front Street and First, in partnership with Colonel John Reynolds and his wife Miriam. The Reynolds were substantial citizens, the colonel having represented Kanawha County in the Virginia legislature for four years. The partners gave Patrick Keenan, seller of the lot, five hundred dollars down and contracted to pay two more installments of one thousand dollars each. The final payment was due in August 1815, two years after purchase.[9]

Whatever the arrangement with Reynolds, Anne Royall began construction of a tavern on the lot. This looked like a good proposition because of the shortage of rooms in the booming county seat. Logs were cut and hauled from the Elk River land and pretty soon the new hostelry, with the services of the five slaves brought from the Springs, was catering to a hustling clientele. The owner of the tavern would have liked nothing better than to spend more time with her guests, but instead she was kept galloping between county courthouses to defend lawsuits against the estate of William Royall.

There was the action, for instance, that Jacob Smith filed in Lewisburg, Greenbrier County, demanding that Mrs. Royall return "goods and money" paid for land he had bought from William Royall in 1809. In the contract, Major Royall had agreed to dig a well for the new owner and accept, in part payment for the property, two horses valued at "perhaps ninety dollars." After going down twenty feet, Smith had decided he did not need the well. Anne had disapproved of the entire transaction, believing Smith had engineered it "in a fraudulent manner, he [William Royall] being much intoxicated at the time and not knowing what he did." Smith had paid up with "very indifferent animals," which brought only "thirty-five or thirty-six dollars." The plaintiff based his claim for damages on the unfulfilled part of the contract—the uncompleted well. The case dragged on for four years before Anne won and Jacob Smith was ordered to pay costs.[10]

The Smith litigation is of interest because, in submitting evidence, Mrs. Royall for the first time publicly acknowledged her husband's addiction to alcohol. One more time, when pushed into a corner to defend her good name, she would swear to the same fact and then never again mention it. To the end of her days, in all she wrote about William Royall, there was only praise for his character, his scholarship, his ideals and his patriotism. Anne Royall herself, throughout her life, was temperate. And no wonder.

The last tie with the Sweet Springs seemed to have been cut when Mrs. Royall received word that Peters Mountain had been sold. The auction had been poorly attended and the plantation brought a disappointing five hundred dollars. Though Andrew Beirne had replied to her reminder that he had promised to attend the sale, "business of importance" took him elsewhere on the day of the auction. In his place he sent William Herbert. James Wiley, the new owner, believed "he had gotten a very hard bargain." Wiley said he would not "have given that price," if the plantation had not adjoined his farm. More important to him than the manor house was his need of range for his stock.

After the auction Wiley stopped by the Beirne store to arrange for terms to pay. Strapped for cash, as most people were at this stage of the war, he proposed to pay the $135.62 debt owed the storekeepers by the estate of William Royall and give his note for the balance to the widow. Andrew Beirne agreed. And why not? He pocketed the only cash to change hands in the sale of Peters Mountain.[11]

So passed the first years of widowhood. Out of the "closet," Anne had raced exuberantly to catch up with some of the living she had missed. Her greatest pleasure was the sociable Front Street tavern; it was also her most expensive. She had gone into debt for furnishings, but hopefully looked to earnings to pay for them. Expenses arising from lawsuits against her husband's estate had not been anticipated and, after spreading her income thin in investments, Anne found it difficult to keep abreast of them. But given time, she was certain she could take care of everything. Unfortunately, Anne had left her disgruntled in-laws out of her reckoning.

4

On June 20, 1814, James and Elizabeth Roane petitioned the Superior Court of Botetourt County "to annul . . . a paper purporting to be the last will and testament of William Royall." They charged that the "paper" was a "forgery made by his widow Ann Royall," for the purpose of depriving Elizabeth Roane, "next of kin and heiress," of her "just rights."

The petitioners declared that "William Royall never did intend to give his property . . . to his wife . . . a woman with whom he at first cohabited without marriage, but whom he was afterwards induced to marry. . . . Toward the latter part of his life, and at the time when this paper purports to be dated, he had no affection for her." Instead he "was remarkably attached to William R. Roane . . . and for many years before his death expressed his intention to make him his heir."

The will which the widow had recorded at the Monroe County Courthouse, said the Roanes, had never been executed by William Royall nor had it been "attested by the said Wiley and Mary Butler. . . . The paper appears to bear the date . . . of November 1808. . . . At that time Mary Butler was in the state of Kentucky, several hundred miles distant from William Royall. . . . Wiley's name is spelled wrong. He ordinarily spells it Wylie." It was "to reward Wylie for his services in proving the will" that the widow sold Peters Mountain to him for $500 when the property, the complainants claimed, "is probably worth five thousand dollars or more." Wiley and Anna Malvina were named codefendants in the suit.

To restrain Mrs. Royall "from any further waste of the estate" while the action was pending, James and Elizabeth Roane asked the court to remove it from her possession and put it in the hands of a curator. They demanded that the widow "be compelled to render a full accounting of rents, hire and profits" received under her administration; and "that the sale to Wylie be recalled." [12]

At the moment Anne Royall could not afford to be deprived of any part of her income. From the haste with which she arranged her affairs so as to exclude a curator from the management, the court presumably appointed one. She took care of her stake in Lot Number 11 by leasing the tavern to Patrick Keenan. She accepted no cash, but Mr. Keenan signed an agreement giving her a "comfortable room . . . with Kitchen in the town of Charleston for 7 years rent free." [13]

Far more important was the disposition of the five slaves. She was fond of the Negroes and concerned about turning them over to a curator to be hired out to strangers until the Roane litigation was disposed of. Looking about for a kind master, Anne Royall selected Colonel Andrew Donnally, junior, who took Davy, "a young and healthy Negro and considered very valuable," for $150 a year to work at his salt furnaces. For $110, the colonel also hired Stepney, older than Davy and "liable to occasional slight illnesses." Donnally gave Mrs. Royall an advance of $500 which Anne scattered among creditors, holding back a small sum to help pay her myriad legal expenses. As for the Negro women, she kept all three. [14]

When Patrick Keenan took over the tavern, Anne and Anna Malvina moved out to a cabin at the mouth of Elk River, hoping to make themselves less available to the demands of the curator. So began a frantic scramble to outwit the curator and hold onto the better part of her income. But that gentleman, whoever he was, was inexorable.

Her new home was the property of her Front Street partner, Colonel Reynolds, who had offered to buy Anna Malvina's adjoining 193 acres as soon as age permitted the young girl to make her choice. No matter if the estate of William Royall was tied up in litigation, aunt and niece were certain that this land, which William Royall had deeded to Anna Malvina during his lifetime, was a property which the curator could not legitimately claim. As yet Mr. Hensley had not found salt springs, but the contract with him did not preclude the sale of timber rights and these rights provided Mrs. Royall with her principal income for a couple of years. She built a log cabin on the land and rented it to hunters for twenty dollars annually, equal to the rent she paid Colonel Reynolds for his cabin. Anne picked up a little more income by renting a room to Richard Slaughter and his wife Frances. Another lodger was Newton Gardner who kept a mercantile store.[15]

Anna Malvina celebrated her eighteenth birthday by announcing her engagement to Mr. Gardner. She informed her aunt that she would take her legacy in money, rather than the land. She could get nothing at all, of course, until the contest over the will was decided.

Considering her depleted finances, Mrs. Royall's preparations for her niece's wedding were somewhat elaborate. A dressmaker was summoned from Charleston to make the bridal gown. The result did not please Anna Malvina and the rejected garment was turned into a petticoat. From Henry McFarland's store in Charleston came love ribbon, calico, sarsenet (very fine, light silk), silk gloves, silk hose, silk handkerchiefs, yellow kid shoes, tabby velvet, yellow silk, green cashmere, and many more items. The tabby velvet was for a pelisse which James Truslow, new tailor in town, fashioned with trimming of velvet riband. (Truslow was paid with timber from the land next door.) What stock Mr. McFarland did not carry was ordered from the Beirne Brothers in Union. Rarer articles were sent from the over-the-mountain store of Colonel Matthew Harvey in Fincastle, where William Royall had traded since his earliest days in the West. When he died, the major owed Harvey more than one hundred pounds, still unpaid.

On the eve of the wedding Anna Malvina developed a toothache. Her aunt took her to Doctor Coff who extracted the tooth, charging one dollar. He received cash. Mary Butler, in Cincinnati awaiting the end of the war and the return of her son (James got the "Ohio Fever" while serving under William Henry Harrison and moved his family from Kentucky), arrived on the Elk in time to attend her granddaughter's wedding on July 7, 1814.[16]

5

The newlyweds continued to live in the Reynolds cabin. Anne Royall found the new member of the family a helpful addition. It was her "good luck," she confided to Mrs. Slaughter, to have Newton Gardner bringing supplies from his store when she was pinched for money. With his wife's inheritance involved, Gardner was, of course, eager to advise Mrs. Royall in her preparations to defend against the Roanes.

On funds Gardner advanced, Anne Royall traveled to Monroe and Greenbrier counties to interview old acquaintances and gather depositions. In the days of poor roads and reluctant witnesses, the bulk of evidence was presented to the court through notorized statements. When attorneys wanted the deposition of Mary Butler, who had gone back to Cincinnati after the wedding, Gardner encouraged Anne to make the long horseback ride to procure her mother's evidence. Colonel Donnally obligingly released Davy to accompany her. Twice a year Davy also escorted Mrs. Royall to Fincastle to receive the exasperating information that the trial of the Roane suit had been put over to the next term of court.[17]

The journeying was not unpleasant. To exchange a few words with a horseman or a wagon of pioneers met on the road had a touch of adventure and, evenings in taverns where Anne put up, the talk was usually stimulating. People talked a great deal these nights about the more than twenty million acres that General Jackson had won for the U.S.A. by his victory over the Creeks. Speculation was endless as to the unplumbed wealth that should be found in this eastern extension of the Mississippi Territory. There was sure to be someone among the tavern company who had heard of a homesteader settling in northern Alabama country only a few years back and making a fortune from timber and farming. Fantastic tales were related about the rich soil which grew everything quicker than elsewhere. For old people the climate was as good as baptism in the Fountain of Youth. Jackson had stipulated in his peace terms that the defeated Indians were to be moved to new homes beyond the Mississippi River. The uprooting was underway, but the Redcoats and their intriguing Spanish allies in West Florida also had to be cleared out. Sniffing boom, some of Charleston's footloose citizenry were already headed south, gambling that Old Hickory would win against the English.

On a January night in 1815, Mrs. Royall was in her room at Patrick Keenan's when William Quarrier, the town clerk, galloped through Front Street shouting: "General Jackson has defeated the British at New Orleans. Get up, we are going to illuminate!" [18]

Anne Royall would have liked nothing better than to get up and ride away to Alabama. With peace, what a ferment of people would be on hand for the government's first public sale of land! Andrew Beirne was going. His journey could be taken as an omen of the territory's future. Where Mr. Beirne went money was sure to be made.

In the lifetime of William Royall, husband and wife had watched with fascination the rise of Andrew Beirne. The handsome young Irish immigrant had first appeared at the Sweet Springs with a pack on his back peddling from door to door. On the side he dealt in ginseng, which grew wild on the slopes of western Virginia. In China the exported weed was cherished as an aphrodisiac. As soon as he got enough money ahead, Andrew took his brother for a partner and opened his first mercantile store in Union. Profits presently gave the partners capital to venture into Lewisburg with a second store. More branches were added when the Beirnes took their operations into a third county. Thus did Andrew Beirne, early in the nineteenth century, discover the economic advantages of chain-store merchandising.

Instead of taking off for Alabama, Anne Royall found herself again shut up in a "closet" and forced by a perverse fate to keep company with an unwelcome task. The long wait for the trial to start went hard with the occupants of the cabin on Elk River. After two years Newton Gardner was in pretty deep financially. Post-ponements made him doubt whether Mrs. Royall could win. When he lost hope, he would remind Anna Malvina's aunt of her unpaid note which he held and cite his contributions to the household: the grain, for instance, that he brought from his store to feed the two cows. Anne would retort that she had bought the cows who ate Mr. Gardner's grain. Anna Malvina sided with her husband.

To complicate the situation other creditors were losing hope. The installment on Peters Mountain paid by James Wiley to cancel William Royall's indebtedness to the Beirne Brothers store had been claimed by the curator who also took the plantation away from Wiley. Before this happened Mrs. Royall had received a small loan from Andrew Beirne, in expectation of an early and favorable out-come of the Roane litigation. Including Anna Malvina's wedding finery, she owed the Union merchants more than two hundred dollars. And there was still Colonel Harvey of Fincastle; his bill had risen to more than four hundred dollars. Meanwhile, the curator relentlessly ferreted out bits and pieces of the disputed estate with the result that Anne Royall was reduced to practically no income from her husband's legacy.

In desperation in January, 1817, she quietly sold her interests in Lot Number 11 to Colonel Reynolds. She received five hundred dollars down with the promise of five hundred more within a year. Creditors, and not the curator, got practically all the money.[19]

6

The Roane suit finally came to trial on April 11, 1817, at the Bote-tourt County Courthouse. Counsel, principals, a few witnesses and bundles of depositions filled the little courtroom at Fincastle, leaving scant space for spectators come to give ear to the most scandalous lawsuit the Allegheny countryside had known. It would have been a good show just to watch the performance of Chapman Johnson, a Staunton lawyer, who had a reputation for "forensic eloquence." Johnson represented the plaintiffs. Of lesser fame was Joseph L. Fry, of Kanawha County, attorney for Anne Royall *et als*. Lending the defense a hand out of gratitude for past favors was youthful Matthew Dunbar, a law student one year away from admittance to the Charleston bar.

A jury was quickly chosen. The twelve men were a representative group—farmers, merchants, artisans. One juror owned nineteen slaves; three had none.[20]

Without a transcript of the trial (Isaac Pitman was then only four years old), it is not possible to report all that took place in the courtroom. Apparently the jury spent the better part of two days listening to the reading of depositions introduced by both principals. For the plaintiffs the longest deposition came from William R. Roane. He recited incidents of his visit to Peters Mountain, stressing the "barbarous treatment" meted out to Uncle William by his wife. Roane told, too, of the will Major Royall had shown him. He said it was not the "paper" probated by the widow. The document he had read named him residuary legatee.

Because of their history and long residence at the Springs, the Lewises had no peers in western Virginia. What the two brothers swore to—Doctor Charles and John—carried more weight than the testimony of any other witness; and both brothers were on the side of the Roanes.

In the main Doctor Lewis recounted injuries to William Royall which he had treated. He was the only witness opposed to Anne Royall who admitted that her late husband was "intemperate." But the doctor contributed one lethal statement to clinch the charge that Mrs. Royall had forged the will and the signatures of the attestors. He testified that he had seen Mary Butler in Lexington, Kentucky, in the fall of 1808, which placed her some distance from the Sweet Springs on the date of her son-in-law's will.

The defense demolished the last statement in a twinkling. Besides affidavits affirming her good character, it was shown that when Mrs. Butler went with her daughter to the Monroe County Courthouse to probate Major Royall's last testament, she told Isaac Hutchinson, the clerk, that she had signed the paper *after* her return to Peters Mountain, at a date later than appeared on the document. Hutchinson himself recalled what Mary Butler had said to him, and he was no partisan of the widow.

For some reason—perhaps his religious side was involved—John

Lewis had no use for Anne Royall. In his Presbyterian eyes, she had committed an unforgivable sin, no matter if, as Lewis testified, "it was said he [William Royall] married her twice." Most of Lewis's testimony was "it was said" or "I have heard," but as to Mrs. Royall's premarital relations with her husband, he gave positive evidence. This was a situation the plaintiffs emphasized implying, of course, that if Anne Royall had sinned before, she would have no scruples against committing forgery.

The defendant made no denial of John Lewis's accusation that she had "cohabited without marriage." But forgery was a different matter. If she had been "moved to commit fraud," she said, she would have executed a will giving her more inheritance than the one questioned by the Roanes. After all, "the will allows her but a very limited interest in the estate (during widowhood)." The charge of mistreating her late husband was a "slanderous aspersion." William Royall "being very intemperate for some time before his death . . . she was obliged to resort to measures" to restrain him, though "she never used harshness toward him, much less cruelty."

Anne vehemently denied having bribed James Wiley by selling him Peters Mountain. The charge was "base . . . false, illiberal and ungenerous." The plantation could have been purchased by anyone who bid high enough at the public auction. "The land was advertised for several months in the several adjoining counties before the sale." Moreover, "William Archer, the residuary legatee, was likewise notified of the sale." As for forging the signature of James Wiley and misspelling his name, Mrs. Royall declared that "it is a notorious fact which can be proven that he [Wiley] writes his name variously at different times. Sometimes Wiley, at other times Wilee, Wylee and Wyllee."

Wiley testified that he had written his name "exactly" as it appeared in William Royall's testament "until the year 1809 [when] Isaac Hutchinson . . . informed him that he spelled his name wrong, that the proper way of spelling it was Wylie," as his ancestors did. He brought to court a collection of affidavits from friends who had known him since boyhood. They confirmed his signature on the will and declared further that they "never knew or heard anything against his moral character."

As to the bribery charge, Wiley indignantly reiterated that he had got no bargain. The land was only good for range, less than one-tenth tillable. The Roanes, said Wiley, "placed too high a value on the place." [21]

After a long second day, the case went to the jury. Before midnight the verdict was reached:

"We the Jury find that the Writing purporting to be the last Will and Testament of William Royall deceased . . . which bears the date November 4, 1808, and attested by James Wylie and Mary Butler . . . is the last Will and Testament of William Royall decd." [22]

Chapman Johnson was on his feet immediately, demanding the verdict be set aside as contrary to the evidence. The court was without power to oblige him. Johnson announced that he would appeal to the Superior Court of Chancery at Staunton for a new trial.

If the suit was tried again, James Roane was convinced that he would fare better in a courtroom away from the cohee ambit. Accordingly, upon his return to Richmond, he went before a city magistrate and made an affidavit asking the Staunton court, in the event the appeal was granted, to assign his case to a jurisdiction other than Botetourt County where "much prejudice . . . exists in the minds of people generally" against him.

A new trial was ordered by the Superior Court to be held at Fincastle.[23]

CHAPTER V

THE LAND OF PROMISE

1

With the winter to wait out for retrial of the Roane suit, Anne Royall hoisted her small frame onto the back of a big amiable horse named Pony and, accompanied by the slave Davy on a second horse, took the muddy road that ran south of the Great Kanawha westward to the Kentucky line. At forty-eight years of age, she began a ride of some four hundred miles over a trace to see the wonders of the newly annexed territory south of the Tennessee border.

How Anne got together funds for the trip to Alabama we do not know, but there appears to have been a good bit of juggling to take care of the most pressing financial involvements. Patience exhausted, Colonel Harvey and Andrew Beirne had obtained judgments which the sheriff was prepared to execute by seizure of the slaves Aggy and Lucinda. Mrs. Royall took desperate measures to keep the Negresses from falling into the hands of strangers. She sold Aggy to Newton Gardner for four hundred dollars and, for the moment, quieted the merchants with a little on account. At the same time Anna Malvina's aunt gave Gardner a new note for $95.68 3/4, covering her indebtedness to him. She agreed to a "penalty of double that sum," if unable to pay on time.[1]

The travelers covered ten miles the first day, spending the night at Cabell Courthouse. That evening Mrs. Royall penned the first of thirty-two letters to "Dear Matt," later collected into a book

71

entitled *Letters from Alabama*. Several writers, unable to identify
Matt, have made him out a mystery man, implying that he was
Anne's lover, a relationship, wrote one, "which evidently started
before Royall's death." Matt, of course, was Matthew Dunbar, the
studious boy from Sink's Grove, who had borrowed books from
Peters Mountain. He, too, had moved to Charleston and was presently reading law in the office of Attorney James Wilson. Because
of friendship and incidentally to gain experience, he served, without
pay, as minor counsel in the contest of Major Royall's will. Also,
he was host to Tray, Anne Royall's dog, when she traveled. The
description of Matt given by a Kanawha County historian hardly
qualifies him for the role of adulterer: "One of the most distinguished, as well as most honorable lawyers of the Kanawha bar."
Mrs. Royall herself cleared up the identity of Matt in a letter she
wrote to a Philadelphia publisher: "*The Letters* [from Alabama]
were written for the sole amusement of my friend a Mr. Dunbar." [2]

A portion of the first "Alabama" letter could have come from
Matt's mother:

"Go to bed early. Cards subject you to bad company and bad
hours. Pursue something more worthy of yourself."

Snow was falling when Davy and his mistress resumed the road
next morning. Shortly they met "a gentleman riding alone. He was
thinly clad, without portmanteau or saddle bags, and even without
a great coat." The horseman asked how far it was to Charleston.
After giving directions, Anne handed him her letters.

"Will you deliver this packet to Charleston?" she said.

In a moment she "repented" the request. "The man might be a
rogue." Warily Mrs. Royall questioned him. He told her his home
was in Scotland, but he was on his way to Canada.

"You are in poor trim for a journey to Canada at this season of
the year," said Anne. "At any rate, you have the deportment of
a gentleman, and I will venture to trust you."

The "rogue" bowed solemnly, but his eyes were merry as he
replied in the stilted style of a character out of a nineteenth-century
novel: "Fear me not. I will not deceive you."

Anne Royall had proceeded only a short distance when she
encountered "three men riding with lead horses, heavy laden."

Sight of them was reassuring; perhaps they belonged with the horseman who had her letters.

Two nights later she put up at an "inn kept by Mr. Clack," where the guests were still talking about the distinguished Scot who had been in their midst. He was Thomas Douglas, fifth Earl of Selkirk, and already famous in the U.S.A. for his social reforms. At his own expense he had attempted to alleviate London's poverty and unemployment by establishing colonies in Canada. After succeeding with two pioneer transplants, Selkirk had bought up what is now approximately the province of Manitoba for a third colony. There he built homes and schools and brought over boatloads of his distressed countrymen. Their arrival was not hailed by the Hudson's Bay Company, which foresaw that the emigrants would soon be demanding higher prices for pelts than the company paid French and Indian trappers. Accordingly, a rumor was put out that the colonists had come to take away the livelihood of the Canadians. The aroused natives set fire to the model village and the settlers fled for their lives. Selkirk hurried from England. With mercenaries standing guard, he rebuilt his colony and set about winning over the misled trappers. He invited them to send their children to his schools and to use his church for their worship. After peace was assured, the Scottish lord entered the United States to study colonization of the new settlements in the Mississippi Valley. He was returning from St. Louis when Mrs. Royall gave him her letters.

"Old Mr. Clack informed us that his [Selkirk's] suite consisted of his Physician, his Secretary and his servant—the three men I passed. His Lordship ate a great many eggs, ten or fourteen at a meal; wrote to a late hour and slept under a great many blankets between his own sheets."

All of which convinced Mrs. Clack that the foreigner harbored "some bad design" against the U.S.A. "He must be a Tory," said Mrs. Clack. "He would always be axin' me how many neighbors I had, how many were in each family, and how far distant the country was inhabited around us." [3]

The ride across the state of Kentucky was, for the most part, through "gloomy, lonesome woods from which the light was excluded by lofty timber." In the neighborhood of Mount Sterling, Anne was saddened by the sight of dead "sugar trees," the small maple of her youth. "I was informed that they are killed by a worm, which attacks the leaves with avidity. Having dispatched the sugar trees, the worm has begun the same process on all others except the walnut."

Beyond Danville, "a very handsome little town in the 'Barrens,' " Anne was hailed by a farm wife who invited her to breakfast. The hospitable lady, eager for chitchat, turned out to be Mrs. Thomas Madison, nee Susanna Henry, sister of Patrick.[4]

After seventeen days on the road, during which she and Davy forded many rivers, they arrived at the "chocolate colored soil" of Tennessee, "the land of heroes." Though the New Orleans victory was nearly three years past, the military triumphs of Andrew Jackson were still the chief topic of conversation. "Next to General Jackson, General William Carroll is the idol of the people. It would be a serious matter to say anything against either general in this country."

Mrs. Royall criticized Tennesseans as a whole. "I am afraid they indulge too great a fondness for whiskey. When I was in Virginia, it was much whiskey; in Ohio too much whiskey; in Tennessee, it is too, too much whiskey!"[5]

2

A few days ahead of the New Year, "in defiance of wind and weather and bad roads," Anne Royall entered Alabama Territory jauntily at ease with two horsemen picked up on the road. One was a Tennessean and the other a Virginian, fed up with hero worship.

"By God!" he exclaimed, "I suppose you think General Jackson is God Almighty."

"By God, sir!" said the Tennessean, "I think he is next to Him!"[6]

Fortunately Anne Royall had not wearied of talk about the Tennessee idol. In Huntsville she lodged at Talbot's Tavern, favorite gathering place of Old Hickory's former comrades-in-arms who had settled on land ceded a decade earlier by the Indians. For the moment the town was host to an uncommon number of soldiers, on their way to rendezvous with Andrew Jackson, readying a march against the Seminoles. In the evening Anne joined a group seated around General John Coffee, Jackson's devoted friend and right-hand man. She had expected "a fierce warrior," but Coffee was "mild as a dewdrop." The general, she judged, "was about 200 weight, six feet in height, 35 or 36 years of age. His black hair is carelessly thrown to one side in front, and displays one of the finest foreheads in nature." [7]

In the morning Anne Royall hurried out to view the sights of the Madison County seat. Having skipped the log cabin period, Huntsville looked older than its ten years. The first settlers were well-to-do planters from the worn-out tobacco lands of Virginia, North Carolina, and Georgia. From the start they built period manors and furnished them with refinements brought from former homes. "The citizens live in great splendor," wrote Anne Royall.

Besides the military, Huntsville was overflowing with new arrivals from all parts of the U.S.A. Within a month, fifty thousand acres stretching west along the length of the Tennessee Valley would go on sale. The extensive tract had been ceded by the Cherokee Indians who were "encouraged" to move from their ancient homes to the parched amplitude bordering the Arkansas and White Rivers.

"Huntsville," Anne Royall continued, "takes its name from Captain Hunt who built the first cabin on the bluff where the Court House now stands. He spent much time waging war on the rattlesnakes lodged amongst the rocks. When they were digging the vault of the Huntsville Bank, they found a vast number of snake skeletons."

Hunt had been a squatter, like too many others who rashly tried to get a head start on the sale of public land. After wiping out the snakes, Hunt "was compelled to abandon his settlement to a rival who purchased the land at the Land Office in Nashville," as required by the government. The buyer of the Hunt land had been "Colonel Leroy Pope who is the wealthiest gentleman in the Territory. Colonel Pope tried hard to have the name changed to Twickenham, after the residence of his namesake Alexander Pope in England."

The county seat was built around a large public square. On the east side of the square, Anne Royall read a familiar name on one building: "Beirne & Patton." With a sure instinct for trade, Andrew Beirne had dispatched William Patton with a wagonload of goods from Union to open a branch in the prosperous town, even before Andrew Jackson had wound up the Creek campaign. "Mr. Patton is one of the richest men in Huntsville," Anne wrote Matt.[8]

3

After a week in Huntsville, Anne and Davy took off west for Melton's Bluff, on the south side of the Tennessee River at the head of Muscle Shoals, some seventy miles distant. The second morning they arrived at the Shoals, where the foaming river is about three miles wide. Throughout the day they followed the noisy rapids and put up in the evening at a "house of entertainment," as the territory liked to call its taverns. The place was somewhat terrifying to the lady traveler. "The landlord and a number of boatmen had been drinking freely." As Anne Royall came through the door, the Reverend Gideon Blackburn, the itinerant missionary "who civilized the Cherokees," strode out. "He crossed the river, late as it was, to seek lodging elsewhere." Mrs. Royall was disappointed not to spend an evening with the preacher, "a stout, coarse-featured man of middle age with great expression of countenance."

For the first time on her trip Anne went to her room directly after supper. Matt had requested that she write him about "every day things, common life, manners, evening-chat." This letter reported no "evening-chat." "I heard many things that would not look very seemly on paper."

Next morning Anne, Davy, and the two horses were ferried across the river to the south shore. Because they expected to pass through several villages from which the Indians had recently departed over the "Cherokee Trail of Tears to the West," Anne hired a guide. The walk through the first empty town left the survivor of the Hanna's Town raid in "pensive and melancholy mood."

"Why, these Indians have been like us—cornfields, apple trees and peach trees. Fences like ours. The house looked tight and comfortable. Poor Gourd [the owner]! Guide says he was very kind. He helped to subdue the Creeks, and made an excellent soldier."

What of government policy removing the Indians of the South to the arid Southwest—would it work? "A vain hope!" decided Anne Royall. "Distance alone will not screen the Indians from the intrusion of the whites." She knew her frontier.

Late in the afternoon Mrs. Royall arrived at the tavern of Colonel Pettis, atop Melton's Bluff. The Bluff boasted a resident population of ten white families, but the "comers and goers" made the town appear larger. "All the trade of East Tennessee passes the Bluff." Colonel Pettis was a native of Virginia, "handsome and very good-natured." He gave Mrs. Royall a room with a sweeping view of the river. Ducks, geese, and swans drifted on the stream, while thousands of paroquets perched in trees draped with "bunches of moss like Hannah Blane's wig."

All was excitement next morning when a pilot brought news that eleven boatloads of Cherokees, bound for Arkansas, had tied up a couple of miles downriver to permit the braves to hunt and the squaws to do the washing. Anne Royall leaped into a crowded canoe and went splashing to the encampment. The migration consisted of three hundred men, women, and children. They had been divided into thirty camps which had thirty fires with thirty pots of venison stewing. "The smell was nauseating!"

The sightseer was disappointed in the looks of the Cherokees. "There is nothing majestic about them." Though the women were "ugly lumps, their hands and feet were exceedingly small and beautiful." All the women were "well dressed with fine cotton shawls on their shoulders and men's hats on their heads. No bonnets seen amongst them." In the camp, "not the least noise was heard. The poor dogs! They were nothing but skin and bones."

The Indians ignored the white visitors. "Not one word could I get from them," Anne reported, "though I was told that nearly all were taught our language in the schools that the Reverend Gideon Blackburn established for the tribes. Having walked about and made a number of inquiries, I sat myself down and made signs to an old Indian woman that I wanted to smoke. She very courteously handed me her pipe, but did not speak." [10]

People at Melton's Bluff were more talkative and Anne Royall picked up something of the history of the place which she wrote out for Matt. It was a helpful thing to have done. The town has long since vanished and local history books have little to say about it. The founder was John Melton, a river pirate who died perhaps two years before Mrs. Royall arrived.

Melton was an Irishman; became displeased with the white people; attached himself to the Cherokee Indians; married a squaw, and settled at this place many years ago. With the assistance of the Indians, he used to rob the boats that passed down the river and murder the crews. By these means he became immensely rich. He continued his piracies until the treaty between the United States and the Cherokees (1791), after which Melton cultivated his cotton plantation and kept an excellent house of entertainment. His table was furnished with the best liquors, meat, coffee and tea, and all prepared in the best manner.

I saw and conversed with many of Melton's slaves; amongst whom was a superior cook he had purchased in Baltimore. She said that Mrs. Melton would sometimes take it into her head to go into the kitchen, particularly when she took a dram. Mrs. M. wanted the cooking Indian fashion. She, the cook, being responsible to her master would go to him. The old man would sally forth, and the horsewhip always restored order.

From a window of her room at the Pettis tavern, Anne Royall looked across snowy cotton fields to "orchards, gardens, mansion and Negro town." All this had once been Melton's plantation. Andrew Jackson was the present owner. One afternoon, with several tavern guests, Anne climbed the road that led from the river's edge up to the mansion house.

We entered the courtyard by a stile; and the first thing we met was a large scaffold overspread with cotton. Damp from dew and often rain, the cotton must be dried in this manner. The mansion was large, built with logs and with shingled roof. General Jackson's overseer, who joined us here, said he lived in the lower story, the upper being filled with cotton.

[The field was] about one hundred acres, white with cotton and alive with Negroes. They have great patience, and seem to be cut out for the endless business of picking each individual pod. Here are from 40 to 50, who scarcely seem to move out of one place; nor can you tell which way they are going. It requires practice to be a good picker; an expert hand will pick about 100 weight per day. Children of twelve years of age, and often under, make 75 cents per day.

From the field we sauntered along to the cotton-gin. We watched a considerable tree pulled round and round by a horse to turn a screw which pressed the bales of cotton.

On our return home, we passed two lines of Negro cabins. The cabins were warm and comfortable, and well stored with provisions, General Jackson being one of the best masters. As I lingered behind the party, thinking of my own Negro children, the little things flocked round me looking up into my face and eager to be caressed. Oh, slavery, slavery! Is there no hope? [11]

4

Several mornings later Anne Royall heard shouts rising from the river road. She rushed to the window and there came the tall, slender hero of New Orleans "walking slowly up the bluff, between two aides. He was dressed in a blue frock coat, with epaulettes, a common hat with a black cockade, and a sword by his side." Anne was disappointed when General Jackson "walked by our door to Major Wyatt's, his companion in arms," who ran a rival tavern. Old Hickory, however, was well aware of the obligations of a hero. In the evening he came to sit a while among the guests at the Pettis house. Mrs. Royall did not think him "handsome," though she found the general "easy and affable. He appears to be about 50 years of age. There is a great deal of dignity about him. He related hardships endured by his men, but never breathed a word of his own."

Long after the general had returned to Major Wyatt's, the Pettis lodgers sat talking of the "hero of the South." One guest who had served in the Creek War recalled how Old Hickory "would walk through the mud for miles, and let his sick men ride his horse." The veteran had fought in the battle of Tallushatchee where Jackson found an Indian baby boy clasped in the arms of his dead mother.

"Kill him! Kill him!" shouted the savages who believed that a baby orphan belonged in the spirit world with his dead parents to look after him.

The general took "the boy in his arms, had him fed and clothed and hired a person to take the infant to Huntsville to be nursed. General Jackson has adopted the child and calls him Lincoyer Jackson."

Previously, when a fever epidemic swept through Melton's Bluff, Old Hickory had hurried from Tennessee to his cotton plantation with a flock of aides to help relieve the stricken town. From her sick bed, the wife of a local merchant watched the Jackson party at work.

They would take buckets and go to the river for water, heat the water and bathe the afflicted. The general administered medicine with his own hands. Thus he went the whole night through, tending to the wants of all, black and white, and consoling them. When he left the Bluff, he ordered a Negro woman, one of his slaves, to wait on all those who were without servants.[12]

In the morning, following his visit to the Pettis tavern, Andrew Jackson took a turn about his plantation and then started for Spanish Florida to put the Seminole Indians in order. This successful campaign gave the U.S.A. the richest El Dorado so far annexed.

5

"There are so many pleasing objects here. I am all delight."

Reluctantly Anne Royall, the defendant, turned her back on the pleasing objects and headed back for Virginia with Davy. On April 10 she was again in the courtroom at Fincastle. The judge who had presided at the first trial of the Roane suit had been assigned to the new trial. Mrs. Royall did not like Judge James Allen. "He is an old man—walks, talks and bobs his head up and down. I do not admire old men for judges. Give me a man in the prime of life while his blood is warm." [13]

After a jury had been impaneled, the case was put over until the fall term of court. In September, when evidence had been heard for two days, one juror was withdrawn and the case continued until Spring. Anne Royall rode alone to Melton's Bluff to pass the winter.[14]

On June 8, 1819, she came once more to the courtroom at Fincastle. Judge Allen bobbed his head from the bench. Three days later the jury brought in a verdict that was a clean sweep for the Roanes. William Royall was declared to have "died intestate." Therefore the "writing purporting to be his last will and testament . . . and admitted to record in the county court of Monroe" was "cancelled and annulled." In the circumstances, his widow was entitled to only her dower while the plaintiffs would receive two-thirds of the estate. James Wiley, a defendant with Mrs. Royall, was ordered to turn over to James Roane the plantation which he had purchased for $500, together with an accounting "for the rent and profits since the time it came into his possession." Anna Malvina Gardner and her husband, also named defendants, were likewise told to "surrender . . . all the real estate in their possession which belonged to William Royall and account for the rents and profits." The widow was instructed to give up any part of her husband's estate remaining in her hands, including "slaves, goods, chattels, books and papers." The court decreed that the four defendants should share expenses incurred by James Roane to prosecute the suit.

The "iniquitous costs" of the litigation fell heaviest on Anne Royall. She denounced the decision as "unfair," and blamed the "stupidity of old Judge Allen." "He ought to have been impeached." The court appointed four commissioners to "lay off" the amount of the widow's dower. When the commissioners reported their findings, Anne Royall's dower was not even a widow's mite. "Lawyers, judges and all got the whole of my estate between them." [15]

The victory of the Roanes released an avalanche of related litigation, such as James Wiley's suit against Mrs. Royall to recover the money he had paid Beirne Brothers to settle the bill owed by William Royall. The only subsequent action necessary to tell about here had to do with Anne Royall and the Gardners. While she was on her first trip to Alabama, Newton Gardner had decided to sell the Elk River land which his wife had rejected in favor of her cash legacy of four hundred dollars. The sale of the 193 acres deeded by William Royall to Anna Malvina was conducted surreptitiously. Not until Mrs. Royall returned to Charleston from the South did she learn that Gardner had disposed of the land. The understanding with Anna Malvina was that when she collected her four hundred dollars, she was to reimburse her aunt for money laid out in her behalf since the death of Uncle William. The most costly expenditure had been for the girl's trousseau. Anne Royall promptly sued the Gardners, demanding payment for a list of expenses which she submitted to the Court. Newton Gardner retaliated by asking for an accounting of rents and receipts for timber rights that Mrs. Royall had collected on the Elk River property. Gardner held the trump card. He demanded that Anne Royall pay her note which, because it was overdue, carried the double penalty for the original loan.

A commissioner was appointed to determine expenses admissible in the two actions. He seems to have put his finger on the sore spot when he reported that "if personal altercations and animosities [had not] arisen, neither of the preceding accounts would have been exhibited." In the end the commissioner found that Mrs. Royall owed the Gardners a little over two hundred dollars, the value of her note plus interest.[16]

Annulment of William Royall's will forced Newton Gardner to return to the commissioners either the Elk River land or the sum received from the sale. Whichever way he may have complied, Gardner did not abandon relentless pursuit of the two hundred-odd dollars the commissioner had affirmed that Mrs. Royall owed him. At the Kanawha County Courthouse is an accumulation of sheriff's orders, originating with Anna Malvina's husband, for the seizure of Mrs. Royall's "goods and chattels," and "her body." At this time debtors went to prison. Anne could not pay, if she had wished to.[17]

Through all her troubles "Dear Matt" was a loyal defender. He counseled, kept up her spirits, and charged no fee. But the talks about books, religion and everyday happenings were bygone pleasures. Matt had found himself a wife—Maria L. Hutt of Charleston. Anne wrote the newlyweds: "I give you joy on your marriage and I hope you may be as happy as I wish." But the rare companionship of Matthew Dunbar was irreplaceable and evenings were long and lonely at Patrick Keenan's. Matt urged Anne to get away from the scene of her frustrations. More humiliation was in store for her if Newton Gardner succeeded in his purpose to jail her for debt. Thus it came about that Anne Royall dumped her muddled affairs into the young attorney's lap, locked her few possessions in her room, and quietly took the stage to Alabama. Yes, a stage had begun to make three trips weekly over an "improved road." [18]

6

Anne Royall spent the next four years roaming around Alabama. In that time she saw the territory acquire statehood and the boom fall apart in the Panic of 1819—a bad one. Too much bank credit had encouraged speculation, especially in land. Scene of the biggest land boom in history, Alabama was hit hard. Worse yet, the price of cotton had dropped 50 per cent.

So the dream was shattered. The crash came with unbelievable haste. New towns begun with the rosiest prospects were abandoned overnight to weeds and rats. The rats scurried off when a prankish younger generation found their fun in setting fire to empty houses. Town planning had been an unusual feature of the Alabama boom. Hitherto purchasers had looked to government sales to provide cheap farm land, but in the Tennessee Valley speculators cut up into town lots the most fertile soil the U.S.A. had ever offered at public auction.

On a small dole against her dower, Anne Royall managed to nurture her curiosity about people and places. She traveled as far south as St. Stephen's, almost to Mobile, but in the main she wandered back and forth across northern Alabama, marveling at towns lucky enough to have survived the crisis and pondering the ghostly relics of imagination gone berserk. The "ups and downs" of the miscast countryside were reminders of her own sudden descent from affluence. But Anne's mind was too preoccupied with all she was seeing to brood over what might have been.[19]

Melton's Bluff was an early casualty. Mrs. Royall caught Colonel Pettis preparing to move half a dozen miles south to Courtland, so named in expectation of becoming the seat of Lawrence County. The Pettis house was bare of guests. The Panic kept travelers home and not many pilots passed down the Tennessee with cotton for the New Orleans market. To raise a little cash, Colonel Pettis took to performing marriages. Anne witnessed the tying of one knot. "The colonel told the couple to stand forth, asked them several ludicrous questions—made them repeat the Lord's prayer, and then pronounced them man and wife." [20]

Courtland was an anomaly of the Panic. It was prospering. The first time Mrs. Royall visited the site it had been a cornfield. Eighteen months later the cornfield had been transformed into "a considerable town of fine brick houses." She ran into Colonel Beirne, down from Virginia, to choose a likely spot for a new store. The colonel's greeting to his old customer was "cold and frowning." Beirne should have looked cheerful. The Panic had taken a heavy toll among Huntsville merchants, but Beirne & Patton continued to flourish. Even when the county seat was awarded to Moulton, the Courtland branch experienced no slump.

Moulton was another postboom growth. "There were only four cabins" when Mrs. Royall paid her first visit. Two years later she saw Moulton surrounded by the finest cotton plantations west of Huntsville. Though the planters were pinched by the low price of cotton, they had not gone wild and chopped up Moulton's rich soil into town plots.[21]

York Bluff, on the south side of the Tennessee River, was the shattered dream of Andrew Jackson. The night before the general visited the Pettis house where Anne Royall saw him for the first time, he had camped with General Coffee and several intimates at

York Bluff. The group had become convinced that a great center of commerce was destined to grow up at the head of Muscle Shoals, precisely where they had pitched camp. The idea was not new. Jackson had probably heard his father-in-law, Jack Donelson, surveyor and Indian agent, talk about the potentialities of continuous navigation up and down the Tennessee which, through its tributaries, reached into the Holston, Cumberland, Kentucky, and Illinois settlements. Moreover a short portage linked the great river south with the Alabama and the gulf, a shorter route to New Orleans than by way of the winding Mississippi. At the auction in February, 1818, the Jackson hopefuls had bought all the land bordering the Tennessee from York Bluff (Sheffield today) to Cold Water (now Tuscumbia), roughly a stretch of five miles. The Panic killed off York Bluff in embryo. Moreover, Jackson and his friends had picked the wrong side of the river. Florence, laid out by the affluent Cypress Land Company on the opposite bank of the Tennessee, developed into the big city at the head of the Shoals.

Mrs. Royall arrived in Florence two years after the drive for metropolitan eminence had begun. The citizens were "bold, enterprising and industrious." They built so fast that "it is not uncommon to see a frame house begun in the morning and finished at night." The town had "many large and elegant brick buildings," a string of cotton warehouses at the river's edge, the handsome Lauderdale County Courthouse, a "boulevard," and a weekly newspaper, *The Florence Gazette*. In Florence, Anne again greeted General Coffee whose "constitution," she observed, appeared "much reduced by the hardships suffered" in Florida. The York Bluff venture had only mildly reduced the general's pocketbook. In addition to a sizable share of the Cypress Land Company, he owned a prosperous farm a few miles north of the city. Mrs. Royall was introduced to Mrs. Coffee, a niece of General Jackson's wife. Mrs. Coffee indulged in no "gadding abroad," as so many Alabama ladies appeared to do, and her tastes "were simple." "She comes to preaching in a plain bonnet and a calico dress." Odd local institutions were the "doggeries." "A Doggery is a place where spiritous liquors are sold; and where men get drunk, quarrel, and fight, as

often as they choose." Losers had no worries over medical treatment. "Every town is flooded with doctors. This would lead one
to think the country is sickly. No such thing. It appears the first
doctors who came here made great fortunes." [22]

When not traveling, Mrs. Royall resided in Huntsville at the
boardinghouse kept by Major Rose, a veteran of New Orleans.
Formerly "one of the first merchants" of the town, Major Rose
had been "overwhelmed in the general wreck." Financial ruin,
however, had not wrecked the spirit of the "merry major." He
talked of going to Texas where hopeful followers of boom and
bust were already congregating. The betting was that before long
Old Hickory would seize Mexico's fertile savannahs north of the
Rio Grande.

Two more victims of the pricked bubble boarded with Major
Rose. They were the brothers Sanona, architects imported from
Italy by the Cypress Land Company to dress the city of Florence
in classic design. "They are men of rich imagination, very gay
and lively in conversation." Andrew Jackson had contracted for
the services of the Sanonas at York Bluff. The Italians lived with
a mountain of blueprints, plans for unrealized towns with Italian
names and copies of Florentine landmarks to embellish them. Dazed
by the sudden turn in their fortunes, the Sanonas appeared not to
notice the whispers that "stigmatized them as worse than the devil."
They were Roman Catholics. It took a tornado in a nearby town
to change the Protestant sentiment of Huntsville. The architects
had proved invaluable in directing the rescue of victims trapped
beneath the wreckage of buildings.[23]

Evidences of the growing power of Presbyterians in Alabama
could be shared and understood only by Matt.

"There is a great deal of preaching here," Anne wrote him,
"and a great many ill-natured remarks pass between the Presbyterians and Methodists. It appears the Methodists have braved
every danger, and preached to the people gratis, in the settling of
the country. Now that the people have become wealthy, those sly
fellows, the Presbyterians are creeping in to reap the harvest."
Anne believed the Methodists had the advantage, "many of them
being the best orators in the country." [24]

The Presbyterians were flooding Alabama with missionaries to tell of their successes with conversions in far-off places. Anne went to hear her first missionary hold forth. "He collected a large sum to convert the Heathen." Colonel Leroy Pope, the richest man in Huntsville, "put only 25 cents in the hat," and thereby set the town wagging about his stinginess. Mrs. Royall also criticized the colonel. "It was beyond doubt the worst laid out quarter Colonel Pope ever spent!"

All of this brought to mind a subject on which she and Matt had heard William Royall discourse at his best. Her comments reflected the major's viewpoint: "Wherever I turn, I see ignorance the most besetting crime. When our reason is cultivated and our minds enlightened by education, we are enabled to strip off that disguise which knavery, bigotry, and superstition wear."

To whom else but Matt could Anne write of the books she read in the South. "Nothing gives me more pleasure than talking to you on paper." So she talked of Phillips' [Charles, a contemporary Irish orator] *Speeches* which she "devoured," and of Lady [Sidney] Morgan's *France*. "Lady Morgan's style is classical, nervous, glowing. She examines herself and bursts the chains of prejudice. I have seen several new novels which, with the exception of Walter Scott's, I do not read. Insipid, frothy nauseous stuff!"

In a Huntsville store Anne picked up a book from the rubbish heap. "I found it to be 'Salmagundi,' a humorous and well written work, by Paulding and Irving."

"Oh," said the clerk, "that is not a *good* book. Here is a *good* book."

He handed Anne Royall a copy of [Robert] Russell's *Seven Sermons*. This collection by an English divine, pointing the way to eternal salvation through prayer, had turned out to be a gold mine for English and American publishers. Brought out in the middle of the eighteenth century, the *Sermons* had reached the fiftieth edition in New York in 1766. The sixty-fifth printing was run off in Philadelphia in 1795. Anne bought the discarded copy of *Salmagundi*.

With all the "preaching and praying" in the South, Mrs. Royall "never heard a word on the subject of politics." She heard no dis-

cussion of "the two great parties, Republican and Federal—for the
reason there are no parties here. They are all Republicans [Demo-
crats of that time]. Few of the people know the meaning of the
word Federalist [more or less our latter-day Republicans]." [25]

7

Matt replied with bad news. Newton Gardner had broken the
lock on her room at Keenan's and carted away the furniture. The
residue of Peters Mountain glory, as listed by the sheriff, was a
pathetic lot: "1 bed and coverlet, 1 bolster and looking glass, two
old carpets, one hand bell and brass spice morter [sic]." The sale
enriched Gardner by "seven dollars and 87 cents."

"The wretch!" Anne commented angrily.[26]

Her temper subsided quickly for her mind was possessed of a
new idea.

"Don't laugh," she told Matt. "I have a notion of turning author."

At this point, the attorney was finding nothing to amuse him in
the affairs of Mrs. Royall. The commissioners had laid off her
dower. After deductions, the dower was nonexistent and Matt had
been unsuccessful in attempts to persuade the Roanes to give Uncle
William's widow an allowance. They insisted that Mrs. Royall was
in debt to them, having wasted a portion of their inheritance in
foolish investments.

As requested, Matt bundled up Anne Royall's letters and sent
them to Huntsville. She proposed to put them in shape for publication under the title of *Letters from Alabama.* Meanwhile Anne
began a novel which she called *The Tennessean.* The story, she
explained, was "founded upon a well-known fact—a secret expedition undertaken by a number of enterprising young men (principally Tennesseans) to the Spanish dominion some fifteen years
since. The novel is little more than a narrative of the sufferings and
difficulties encountered by the party." [27]

Before completing *The Tennessean,* the author was inspired by
a new idea. She liked to travel. Why not travel and make it pay?
She considered a journey through Pennsylvania, New York, and
New England which would give her material "to portray the East

to the western part of the United States." On the instant, she decided to return to Virginia where she believed sufficient friends
would advance funds for the eastern journey. As she packed, Anne
Royall settled on a title for the travel book—*Sketches of History,
Life and Manners in the United States.* On her final night in Huntsville the first week of July, 1823, she "accepted an invitation" from
Colonel Pope to dine at Poplar Grove, his plantation on the outskirts of the town. She had schemed for the invitation. She sent
the colonel a note saying she was writing a book and needed an
interview about cotton-growing in Alabama. Anne already knew
how she would begin the *Sketches.* So she began, not with cotton
statistics, but with gossipy revelations about the most prominent
and richest citizen of the town and his wife.

Colonel Pope lives in princely style. If any man is to be envied on
account of his wealth, it is he. His house overlooks the town from
the west. If I admired the exterior, I was amazed at the taste and
elegance displayed in every part of the interior: massy plate, cut glass,
chinaware, vases, sofas, and mahogany furniture of the newest fashion.
Mrs. Pope is one of your plain, undisguised, house-keeping looking
females; no ways elated by their vast possessions, which I am told,
are the joint acquisition of her and her husband's industry.[28]

CHAPTER VI

A CAREER BEGINS

1

Matthew Dunbar, newly named to represent Kanawha County in the Virginia legislature, did not let political duties interfere with pursuit of an income for Anne Royall. Before the Alabama stage arrived in Charleston, he had applied to Washington City for a pension for his client who, as the widow of a veteran of the Revolutionary War, appeared to qualify for the government's bounty.

The return to Virginia was kept secret. Still Charleston was a small town and, sooner or later, Newton Gardner was sure to hear that his quarry was within range of the sheaf of subpoenas ordering her arrest for debt. Accordingly, while waiting for the Pension Bureau to act, Mrs. Royall galloped off to Cincinnati to visit her mother.

In her seventy-third year Mary Butler was as lively and busy as she always had been. At sight of her oldest daughter, tears flooded her bright blue eyes. They were strong eyes, too. By contrast, her book-loving offspring wore "spectacles" pinched onto her nose and tethered round her neck to a "broad green riband."

Mary Butler lived with her son James. For the first time Anne met James's wife Sally, "a great bouncing woman, with rosy cheeks and a rolling black eye." Sally was already mother of an ample brood. "My brother was careworn and shrunk up to nothing." [1]

Poor James! The Panic had stunned him. In the decade of the

great western migration, no American city had grown as rapidly as Cincinnati. A fine port whose river reached into the heart of the nation, the Queen City of the West had been exploited to the hilt. The Second Bank of the United States had opened its coffers freely to whoop up the campaign to create a western trade center bigger than Pittsburgh. New factories and warehouses sprouted like weeds along the banks of the Ohio and steamboats, fresh from yards, jammed loading platforms to carry away goods to the clamoring population filling up the Mississippi Valley. James Butler, proprietor of a small mercantile house, was encouraged to lay in a mountain of supplies, giving as security a mortgage on his store. When the boom ran out of steam, James had run out of customers and the bank foreclosed. In a daze the bankrupt merchant wandered through the still city streets looking for work. The Queen City had no job for James, or for anyone else, and, as his rainy-day savings dwindled, the worried father thought considerably about moving farther west. Indiana was luring settlers with offers of cheap farm land on easy terms.

If James was baffled by the sudden disappearance of a livelihood, his much-traveled sister was prepared to explain the source of his misery. From Alabama to western Virginia, she had followed the trail of "corrupt banking power," observing "thousands of people living in want." Like her brother, the thousands "cannot see from whence distress comes. It is that land and money get into the hands of the few." As the stage bore her northward, Anne had noted that "the brave Tennesseans, whom no foe could conquer," were more afflicted by the oppression of "this Hydra, the Second Bank of the United States" than were Alabamians. They had "lost their liberty, their common sense, their all to this voracious monster." Far worse, the traveler concluded, was the "oppression" in Cincinnati. "The citizens have nothing left but their lives and bare walls, and the bank owns the walls.[2]

The melancholy atmosphere palled after a couple of weeks and Anne Royall, throwing caution to the winds, took the road back to Charleston. Mindful of her travel book, she stopped at Gallipolis to interview Ann Bailey, whose horseback ride is as famous in the annals of the West as is Paul Revere's in New England.

"Mad Ann," as the frontier knew her, had donned buckskin and dedicated herself to the extermination of the Shawnees who killed her husband. Armed with rifle and shot pouch, she prowled the wilderness, now and again showing up at a clearing with a collection of Indian scalps hanging from her belt. Mad Ann got to know the trails of western Virginia as well as any scout and the Continental Army was glad to use her knowledge during the Revolutionary War. As a reward, the military gave her a big white horse which she named Liverpool after the city of her birth. The war ended, the widow Bailey remarried and settled down to housekeeping at Clendenin's Station. In 1791 her wifely duties were interrupted when Ohio tribes once more went on the warpath, laying siege to the little fort, poorly stocked with ammunition and defenders. Mad Ann volunteered to ride to Lewisburg for reinforcements, through one hundred fifty miles of forests and mountains where the enemy lay in wait for the first white man reckless enough to risk the dash. Wise in the ways of Indians, Ann Bailey guided 'Pool around the trap and so saved Clendenin's.

The venerable heroine, "a low woman in height, but strongly made," was eighty-one years old when Mrs. Royall called at the cabin she had built with her own hands out of old fence rails. Mad Ann's greeting was a request for a "dram." Forewarned, the temperate Mrs. Royall produced a bottle and began the interview.

"How did you find your way to Lewisburg?"

"I had a pocket compass," said Ann Bailey.

"How did you get over the watercourses?"

Mad Ann had forded some streams, swam others and when necessary built a raft. "I halways carried a hax and a hauger and could chop as well as hany man."

Studying the "affable, pleasing countenance" of the Cockney heroine, Anne Royall wondered—had Mad Ann ever been afraid? "She replied 'no, she was not, she trusted in the Almighty.' "

"What would the general say to you, when you used to get safe to camp with the ammunition?"

"Why, he'd say you're a brave soldier, Ann, and tell some of the men to give me a dram."

A horse and a dram—that's all Soldier Bailey had ever received for risks taken. She had no complaint.

"The poor creature was almost naked," wrote Mrs. Royall. "She richly deserves more of her country than a name in history."

Little time remained to make amends. Mad Ann was dead inside a year.[3]

2

The Pension Bureau had not replied and Anne Royall retreated to Lewisburg to wait. There she completed *The Tennessean*, and mailed the manuscript to the Philadelphia publishers Carey & Lea.

"I made a bungling hand of the shipwreck," she confided to Mathew Carey. She had no "acquaintance" with the sea, the Tennessee River being the largest body of water she had seen.[4]

Mrs. Royall's choice of publisher is not difficult to figure out. Mathew Carey was the most active of a handful struggling to give the U.S.A. a book trade. Despite independence, control of America's reading taste remained with the English. One reason was the lack of an international copyright law. American publishers freely reprinted English authors without paying royalties. Moreover, "it had long been accepted as axiomatic by American publishers that it was injurious to their commercial credit to undertake the publication of an American writer unless the books be Morse's *Geographies*, Watt's *Psalms*, or something of that class." As late as the year 1840, a caller at Carey & Lea reported: "There is no disposition to publish anything but the lightest literature from England, and when something native . . . is ventured upon, it is smothered with charges and the author gains nothing—unless it can be counted gain to be 'left alone with his glory.' "[5]

Mathew Carey was an Irish emigrant who had learned to set type in Benjamin Franklin's printing office near Paris. Anne Royall had probably heard of him for the first time during the War of 1812 when he published a pamphlet called *The Olive Branch*. The U.S.A. was then near to losing the contest with England. New England merchants and shipowners, ruined by the blockade of Atlantic seaports, were ready to throw in the sponge. Western expansionists—the so-called War Hawks—preferred to fight on and drive the British from border forts which had not been ceded at the close of the Revolutionary War. "Dedicated to a beloved, but

Mr Carey   Alexandria 12th Feby 1826

Rd'd Ma 15
Ansd 18

2,697

Sir Since I wrote my first letter to you respecting the Tennessean (the name I designed the Novel) I have concluded to send you another work, a miscellaneous production, It had an in- =dex which will assist you if you wish to examine it, separately when it really is. I did intend to give it the title of Letters from Alabama, but I have been so prevailed a head it, that if I had it Ме- =dien I should throw it in the fire — In the first place I wrote it once on coarse paper, & in the second place I sent it on to my friends in Virginia to have it copied & published nearly two years since — Instead of which it was miss-sent, got to Wash- ington city & lay there until I arrived at this place, I found it the seal broke & much abused, & not having time to copy it, & wishing it published before I sent my other works to press I sent it to the only acquaintance I have in Baltimore for that pur- pose — When lo! Mr Baker my acquaintance says the Booksellers there are fearful of publishing for what reason he does not say — I think it a much better written work than the Tennessean — However I am no judge I had it reviewed in Huntsville & it was pronounced a work of some merit — I sent on with it the report of the review but it was not amongst the papers when I recd them — The hand writing is the worst perhaps you ever saw but if you have not been abused at Baltimore too much, I think perhaps with a little use to the hand you can make it out — Finally I would rather bestow it to you than it should not get out on account of my friends — This work will sell well also in the western states — But the patience of my friends is no doubt exhausted — These letters were actually written to my friends & the most of them without any design of being published un- till I was advised to it by some of my Literary acquaintance If you can make any thing of them let me know when you write respecting the other — But don't open them first if you do, I am afraid you will be discouraged from all attempts to read the Tennessean

Your Mot Obt St
Anne Royall

N B The first nine letters are not marked on their pages, all the others are beginning through mistake at 27 I believe — Letter 10 was said to be the best in it

Letter from Anne Royall to the Philadelphia publishing house of Mathew Carey. *Library of Congress*

Bleeding Country," *The Olive Branch* warned Americans against a watered-down peace. Only a decisive victory and the conspirators cleared out completely would insure against "humiliating oppression."

Carey's pamphlet won the hearts of the bibliophiles on Peters Mountain, whose viewpoint naturally was that of the West. The "powerful reasoning," documented with personal experiences inflicted by Ireland's oppressor, "had a very salutary effect on the public mind," Mrs. Royall remembered. The sale was phenomenal—ten editions—and, as most Americans know, we won a very salutary victory at the Battle of New Orleans.[6]

Besides admiration for the "giant pen" of Mathew Carey, Anne Royall had a practical reason for seeking his patronage. The pride of Carey & Lea was "Parson" Mason Locke Weems, itinerant clergyman, spellbinder and best-selling American author of the period. Before turning scribbler, Weems had been the publisher's star salesman, trumpeting his wares up and down the eastern seacoast, while "holding forth a goodly sermon in every village." He had made his literary reputation with a loosely fabricated biography entitled *The Life and Memorable Actions of George Washington*. In the fifth edition the cherry tree fable burst upon the nation. Only one other contemporary book outsold the biography—an edition of the Bible on which the Parson had persuaded Mathew Carey to gamble fifteen thousand dollars. Weems peddled the Bible.[7]

Anne Royall appears to have caught more than a glimmering of the problems of a native writer; and a lady writer, to boot. Not illogically, she concluded that if Weems's salesmanship was the key to literary success, then she must enter by the same door. The Parson's selling method dovetailed nicely with the kind of books she wished to produce. While traveling about to gather material, she would "subscriptioneer" (Weems's word) for subsequent offerings.

Early in December the Pension Bureau wrote that no record of William Royall's military service had been found. Coming on top of a long year of anxieties, the shocking information put Anne Royall in bed. Though not for long. She got back on her feet with resolve strengthened. She would go to the Federal city, put the record in order, collect her pension, and launch the tour to complete her first volume of travels.

How Anne Royall raised money to fare forth from Lewisburg, I do not know. The only contributor mentioned was Henry Erskine, brother-in-law of Hugh Caperton, Monroe County merchant and rival of Andrew Beirne. Probably there were others, such as the loyal Matt. Still, from her own account, the trip was no pleasure jaunt.[8]

The first night on the road Mrs. Royall tossed uncomfortably atop the Allegheny Mountains at the inn of Dennis Callaghan, where she and her mother had paused crossing from the Valley thirty-five years earlier. The clowning Callaghan was dead, but the "famous stand" prospered under the management of his "two stout, amiable sons."

At Staunton, Mrs. Royall stayed, probably as a guest, at the tavern of Mrs. Chambers, an old acquaintance. In a day or so she was in a stagecoach rattling over the familiar Valley Road, past the Anderson house—which "produced mingled emotions of joy and sorrow"; past the Grattan place, hardly recognizable "owing to the erection of new buildings."

Anne Royall used up ten days on the road, though half the time should have been adequate. Delays were due to breakdowns and drunken drivers. "It was well the horses were sober!" [9]

At last, at ten o'clock on the night of December 15, 1823, "the worst carriage I ever was in" clattered up to the entrance of the City Tavern in Alexandria, half a dozen miles short of Washington City across the Potomac River. Mrs. Royall had no money for lodgings, but a few words with Horatio Clagett, the proprietor, drew an invitation to enjoy his hospitality. Mr. Clagett was a Mason and very proud of his hostelry's historic association with the lodge in which George Washington had sat. He gave the destitute widow "an elegant parlor and bed chamber, and a servant to wait on me!" Horatio Clagett appears to have had a weakness for lady writers. Half a dozen years after Anne Royall, Frances Trollope was his guest. She, too, left without paying her bill.[10]

3

Anne Royall remained the winter in Alexandria, making few acquaintances. "I was not fit to appear out of my room. I had but one handkerchief in the world, and that, I was compelled to sell off my neck to redeem a letter out of the Post Office." [11]

The letter was the manuscript of *Letters from Alabama*, "seal broken and much abused." Anne promptly resealed and directed it to Philadelphia. "This work will sell well in the Western States," she assured Mathew Carey. In short order, the *Letters* was returned by the eldest son, Henry C. Carey, who had succeeded to the management of the firm. "American works do not pay the expense of publishing, owing to the rage of the American people for foreign productions," explained the new head of Carey & Lea. Nevertheless, he kept *The Tennessean* under consideration. The author disagreed. "I think the *Letters* a much better work than *The Tennessean*." [12]

She then unfolded the plan to sell the *Sketches* by subscription. The publisher had it in his power to start her off. Would Mr. Carey please "solicit" William Duane, former editor of the *Aurora*, late minister to Mexico, and friend of Thomas Jefferson, to become her patron?

Mr. Duane, no longer basking in political favor, was himself struggling with the composition of a travel book on Colombia. Carey & Lea showed no enthusiasm for the proposal and shortly returned the manuscript of *The Tennessean*.[13]

As prospects faded, Mr. Clagett exerted himself to keep up the spirits of his guest. On Washington's Birthday, when the Masons of Alexandria paid tribute to the late squire of Mount Vernon, the innkeeper laid a place for Major Royall's widow at the banquet to which trooped social and political bigwigs from across the Potomac. In her black dress, without kerchief, Anne sat down to the "most superb supper I ever beheld." She was disappointed that President Monroe did not attend. The majority of the guests were disappointed that illness confined Senator Andrew Jackson of Tennessee to his boardinghouse. With the presidential election only ten months off, the Hero of New Orleans appeared to be far out in front of the four other aspirants to the office.[14]

Despite the kindly attentions of Mr. Clagett, Anne Royall, like Parson Weems, found nothing praiseworthy to record about Alexandria. Weems had enjoyed the scenery, but thought the people "were without energy." Mrs. Royall was "shocked by a sight entirely new" to her eyes—"men and children, combining every shade of colour, from the fairest white, down to the deepest black. Such a multifarious mixture excites feelings of horror and disgust." [15]

In late March a letter from the Pension Office informed that a second search had failed to turn up the service record of Major William Royall. The government agency suggested that the papers might have been destroyed in the great fire which had swept Richmond a decade past. Other Virginia widows had run into the same dead end, but they had succeeded in substantiating their claims through affidavits of their husbands' war comrades. [16]

A trip to the Virginia capital was in order. Lacking the wherewithal for the journey, Anne Royall canvassed the riverfront and made a deal with Captain Queen of the *Mount Vernon* to take her to Potomac Creek, halfway to Richmond and as far south as the packet could navigate. She promised to pay the captain out of her first pension check.

Anne broke the news of her departure to Mr. Clagett, saying he and his ten children would trouble her conscience until she was able to settle her bill. "The friend of the friendless and the pride of mankind" was concerned for the hardships the poor widow might face once she had left his roof. On a sunless, windy afternoon in the first week of April, 1824, George, the waiter, Suckey, the chambermaid, and "my favorite little girl" escorted Mrs. Royall to the wharf and waved goodbye as the *Mount Vernon* puffed into midstream. The little group was also on her conscience; she had not a "copper" for any of them.

Down the river the *Mount Vernon* charged against a "smart gale." When everybody went to supper, Anne huddled beside the stove in the drafty ladies' parlor. Her threadbare raiment told the chambermaid why. Emma was her name and "this dear, sympathetic creature" brought the shivering traveler a meat pie from the galley. [17]

Near midnight, four hours behind schedule, the passengers debarked at Potomac Creek and piled into the stage waiting to take them the eight miles to Fredericksburg. In the chilly dawn they were put down at Joe Young's tavern to wait for the Richmond coach. The experienced eye of the proprietor quickly spotted the

penniless wayfarer. Joe Young scowled and Anne Royall kept her
distance. Later, without breakfast, she walked through the town
"imploring relief." The cold wind drove her back to Young's with
a lone contribution of twenty-five cents. She needed five dollars for
a ticket to Richmond. Again the "iron-hearted" Joe Young
"frowned, turned his back and walked off." [18]

"Faint and weary" Anne sat in the "common room" waiting for
someone "to relieve her distress." At noontime an "elderly, rough,
plain" farmer pushed through the entrance, calling to Young that
he had a wagonload of hams and bacon to sell. The newcomer noted
the old lady shivering in the corner. Mr. Grigsby introduced himself and gallantly moved Anne's chair closer to the stove. Then he
went into the saloon. Some drinks later, after collecting for his pork,
the farmer bought the old lady a ticket to Richmond. He offered
her pocket change, but Anne refused it. Between times, a "travelling gentleman" had given her a couple of dollars.[19]

The stagecoach picked her up at two o'clock in the morning. By
daylight she admired the handsome manors glimpsed through the
trees, but recalled that William Royall had complained about the
"profligacy" of his native state. The "deserted worn out fields" of
the plantations were tragic testimony that the "great and wealthy
Virginia has killed the goose that laid the golden egg. The slaves
instead of being a benefit have proved a serious injury. The planters
have secured nothing to their children but poverty. Influenced by a
foolish pride, they neglect to encourage useful arts; their lordly
souls can not brook the indignity of teaching their sons to earn their
bread by their own labor." [20]

In midafternoon the coach pulled up at the Union Tavern, Richmond's finest. Mr. Bohannon, the proprietor, declined to invest in
Mrs. Royall's career. Anne scribbled an appeal to Thomas Ritchie,
editor of the Richmond *Enquirer*. Mr. Ritchie, a Mason, instructed
Mr. Bohannon to accommodate Mrs. Royall as his guest. Even so
the *Sketches* did not eulogize the celebrated hospitality of the southern capital. "I should give it quite the contrary character."

The fact is Anne Royall had a miserable time in the city where
William Royall's numerous kinfolk remembered her as an adulteress
and forger. She "suffered more agony than I ever did before or

since." She ran up against the South's clannishness when she sought aid from "one of the nabobs, Dr. T." After the British burned Norfolk during the Revolution, William Royall had brought the homeless Trent family to his Amelia plantation and kept them for a year. True, "Dr. T." had been a boy at the time, but still Anne expected him to show some sense of obligation to the widow of his father's good friend. She asked Doctor Trent's help in locating a few of her husband's comrades-in-arms. When the physician learned her identity, "he walked off, saying, 'I wish you hadn't sent for me, maum.' "

Who ultimately facilitated the roundup of affidavits is not clear, but Mrs. Royall appears to have obtained all she believed necessary to satisfy the Pension Bureau. Then she was stuck. "Had it not been for the humanity of two Yankees, I must have perished in the city of Richmond. These gentlemen found for me on the road." [21]

4

A week after bidding goodbye to Alexandria, Anne Royall at daybreak stepped off the steamboat at Georgetown in the District of Columbia, without a penny in her pocket. Her baggage contained more papers than clothing. Besides affidavits, she carried reams of manuscript—*Letters from Alabama, The Tennessean*, the draft of a play (she had never been inside a theater), and the record thus far of her travels for the *Sketches*. Nowhere had she wasted time. At Joe Young's, for instance, while waiting for a miracle to get her out of the place, she "had beguiled the time" with composition.

Anne was as excited as a girl walking out with her first beau. It was the beginning of an enduring love affair, beset by quarrels and reconciliations, frustrations and triumphs.

The steamboat company provided a carryall to transport passengers into the city proper. From a Georgetown hill, Mrs. Royall had her first view of the "idol of America." It was disappointing. "Groups of houses, scattered over a vast surface, had more the appearance of so many villages" rather than a "mighty city" with a population of fifteen thousand.

The vehicle creaked eastward on Pennsylvania Avenue past the

Washington City, 1821, sketch by Baroness Hyde de Neuville. The White House, center, is flanked by the Treasury, left, and the War Department. In background is the Navy Department. *New York Public Library*

Six Buildings and the Seven Buildings, two lengths of two-story brick residences that had begun an architectural trend in Washington City. Though ten years had gone by since the British burned the Capitol, the city echoed to the banging and scraping of carpenters and masons, replacing clapboard and shingle with less combustible construction. Amid the rufous glut of brick, the flat-topped White House "rivalled the snow." Beyond it, Pennsylvania Avenue widened into three inviting graveled driveways, with a wall of houses bordering the two outside lanes. This populous area was known as "the city." "We are going to the city," Capital dwellers were wont to say, though they might start from just around the corner.

The company in the carryall howled protest when the driver turned off the Avenue and bumped through dusty F Street. Anne Royall had a hazy view of Judiciary Square, the City Hall and the poorhouse, an old wooden building which, she was told, was run on an annual budget of three thousand dollars. Some days later she visited the poorhouse. "The smell was insupportable." Worse yet she "found several wretched children in the comfortless asylum."

The "towering dome" of the Capitol reminded her of a huge "inverted wash-bowl," but it crowned a "handsome" building, painted a "glittering white." The stage circled the iron and stone fence enclosing the Hill, and plodded up the rise of New Jersey Avenue, scattering the pigs wallowing in mud puddles. On both sides of New Jersey stretched lines of boardinghouses which catered to members of Congress.[22]

The hospitality of the steamboat company ended as a spring shower began. Lugging her box, Anne Royall scurried to cover in the handiest vestibule. Surely Fate guided her footsteps. From a window of the home a pair of friendly eyes watched her. A tall, thin young woman opened the door and invited the dripping traveler to step inside.

Sally Dorret came of good Maryland stock. Her father had sold a prosperous farm on the Eastern Shore and moved to Washington hoping to reap a harvest in zooming land prices. Not long after losing his stake, Dorret had died in a cholera epidemic which also claimed his wife and widowed daughter. Without resources, Sally had turned her home into a boardinghouse and undertaken the rearing of her sister's four orphans. The day Anne Royall ran into her vestibule two nephews had found work in the pressroom of the *National Intelligencer* and Sally's heart was fairly brimming with thankfulness for the easing of her burden. By the time the shower was over, Mrs. Royall had found a home in Washington City; and a friendship that lasted as long as she lived.[23]

Next morning the widow of Major William Royall hastened to the Pension Bureau to present proof, through affidavits, of her husband's service to his country. Still she did not rate a pension. Under the law only widows of veterans married prior to the year 1794 were eligible. Anne had wed three years too late. It would require an amendment by Congress setting forward the limitation on the marriage date by at least four years before her claim could be recognized.

But all was not lost—perhaps. There was still the so-called commutation-of-pay resolution which, in one form or another, had from time to time caught the attention of Congress during more than two decades. It was an election year and so the resolution had been patriotically revived as a hot issue. If the bill passed, the government would pay the heirs of Major William Royall a fair-sized sum.

The history of the resolution went back to the dark year of 1780 when victory over the English was despaired of. General Washington, in an effort to hold together his discouraged troops—only four thousand at that stage—had recommended that Congress offer officers and men five years full pay or half pay for life, if they served until the end of the war.

When the obligation had fallen due in 1783, the treasury had no funds. Congress wriggled out of the situation by issuing new certificates, advancing the redemption date to the year 1791. Meanwhile the new pledges were to draw 6 per cent interest. In 1792, the U.S.A., still grappling with a deficit, refunded the I.O.U.'s, paying off at two-thirds their value, though with interest of only 3 per cent. New vouchers were distributed for the unpaid third, but the 3 per cent interest would not commence until *after* ten years. These last certificates had never been redeemed. With no pressing need for cash, William Royall had not bothered to collect from the government at any time.

The Eighteenth Congress was still in session and Anne Royall plunged into the crusade for passage of the commutation-of-pay resolution. Ranging the legislative offices in her shabby dress, she was a graphic argument for one widow's need of relief. Lawmakers received her cordially, listened sympathetically, and promised "to do what they could." Their affability encouraged the crusader to pour out the story of her literary ambitions. Interviews usually terminated when Congressmen, with a display of good will, signed the subscription list. Why not? "In 1824 I would not accept subscription money, lest some accident happen and people might lose their money." [24]

The ease with which signatures were gathered took Mrs. Royall by surprise. "For God sake dear sir," she appealed to Henry Carey, "send me a form to the subscription as I am a stranger to this business." [25]

With undeviating single-mindedness, between calls Anne Royall energetically explored the Capitol, from dome to cellar. The latter was piled high with hickory logs for the fireplaces of the legislative offices. Rising on the ashes of the edifice destroyed by the British, the new Capitol was far from finished. Two hundred workmen labored toward its completion. Setting up the columns for the east portico was "quite a frolic. They are brought by water from a quarry of freestone thirty miles below the city and weigh eighteen tons each. They are taken from the wharf, without the aid of horses, upon a strong carriage, with a hundred men pulling. Sometimes the members of Congress will turn out in the evening to assist 'the big wagon' and join in all the pleasantry to which the novelty gives rise. When the column arrives at the Capitol, it is cheered by loud huzzas." Of the "two hundred hands, there are perhaps not half a dozen sober men. They drink *scute* (as they call whiskey) on the job. When their day's work is ended, they hie to the grog shops and taverns to spend their earnings." [26]

Inside the Capitol, Congressmen had no call to hie themselves to a tavern. "Spiritous liquors" were retailed on the premises. The western sightseer blushed to report "the number of abandoned females, who swarm in every room and nook in the Capitol. Near the very door of the Representatives hall is a temple dedicated to one of these females. No matter who comes or goes, President, foreign minister, respectable citizen or stranger, this *Hortensia* commands the pass to the gallery and the hall and sits in her chair of state with a maid to attend her. What would the saviour of our country think were he to arise from the tomb to witness the daily scenes exhibited in the Capitol of the city which bears his name?" [27]

The chaos of the rotunda spilled over into the House of Representatives, "lounging place of both sexes, where acquaintance is as easily made as at public amusements." In the gallery "so little order was maintained" that Mrs. Royall had difficulty hearing the speeches. There was silence, though, when John Randolph, booted and spurred, hunting dog at his feet and waving a riding crop, obliged with one of his performances. The Virginian always attracted more attention than his colleagues. Tall, rawboned and badly proportioned, he was "neither handsome nor the contrary." His voice was "shrill," but his language was "flowing, refined and classical." Randolph's eyes, Anne decided, were his best feature. They were "black with scarcely any white" and in debate glistened with "never-to-be-forgotten fierceness." Though listeners chortled over his ironies, the speaker's expression remained "stern and immovable."

The plantation William Royall owned in Amelia County had been bought by John Randolph, but he did not make his home there. When Anne called at the office of the representative and found him out, she left a few lines to remind him that she was the widow of Major Royall. Randolph replied with "a very polite note which proved of infinite more service to me than if he had given me a hundred dollar bank note." The public had so much curiosity about the eccentric Virginian that wherever she went "Mr. Randolph's letter was sought after and read with much eagerness." After two years "it was worn out" from handling.[28]

Anne herself briefly fell under the spell of the southerner, undertaking to defend him against "ludicrous stories" of his overfondness for strong drink. After "investigation," she declared the stories were "false," including the current one published by a Washington City newspaper. The tale recounted how John Randolph had punctuated a speech before the House with requests to the doorkeeper for "more porter." Mrs. Royall decided the "slander was fabricated by the Yankees," explanation enough why "Mr. Randolph will not let his horses eat hay raised north of the Potomac." [28]

At another House session, Anne heard Representative Daniel Webster of Massachusetts make an eloquent plea for passage of the commutation-of-pay resolution. "I hope the House will not give it the go-by," said Webster. "Disguise it, evade it, the truth is that the plighted faith has never been redeemed." Mr. Webster was "a man of talent and great generosity," wrote the needy widow.[29]

The resolution got the go-by moments before Congress adjourned. Overnight Washington City lost half its population. All the earlier "bustle" of the streets disappeared. Neither "black nor white, old nor young, were seen hastening on foot nor on horseback from the Navy Yard to the Departments and from the Departments to the Navy Yard, all for some mighty nothing. The poor horses must dread the meeting of Congress." [30]

Chief mourners for the departed Congress—besides Anne Royall —were the

savage and fierce-looking females who rent rooms. Most of the boarding houses belong to the banks, in consequence of their having advanced money to erect them and builders could not pay. These houses the banks rent out to needy adventurers, who purchase a carpet, two or three dozen tables and chairs, hire a score of free negroes, and take in boarders. They live like princes during the winter, but have pinching times all summer.[31]

5

Anne Royall had not lived like a princess during the months she prowled the halls of Congress. Though she reveals nothing of her trials in the *Sketches*, the evidence of how badly off she was crops up, from time to time, in bits of memoirs scattered through later works. One such tells of the day she walked out to Georgetown College where a priest handed her a dollar.

"Madam," said the good father, "go and buy something to wear." [32]

She was wearing, as she had worn continuously since Alexandria days, the only dress she owned. Clothes, however, never bothered

Anne Royall and at this point she did not abandon the black dress. The priest's contribution probably went into the little fund she was building up for travel.

With the collapse of the dream of financial aid through the all-important resolution, Mrs. Royall lost no time in readjusting to the setback. In the summer heat she tramped through Washington City, adding to her sightseeing notes and begging for contributions. Yes, actually begging—in the name of the deceased patriot who had been her husband. Though gifts from the Masonic membership seem not to have come up to expectations, she foresightedly collected letters of introduction to lodges in eastern cities that she expected to visit. She found a valuable friend in Captain Easby, master mason employed in the reconstruction of the Navy Yard. The captain had no money himself, but passed the hat among his Irish laborers, who toiled for 75 cents per day. The captain came back with an empty hat.

"What shall I do?" asked Anne.

The captain smiled encouragingly and took a pencil from his pocket. On a scrap of paper he scribbled a note to William Prout asking "as a memento of masonic charity to let Mrs. Royall have a dollar."

The note opened a new field to solicitation. William Prout was one of the District's original landholders. He had sold his acres, not unprofitably, to the Federal government for the site of the national Capitol. Married to the daughter of Jonathan Slater, another seller, Prout had come to be rated one of the wealthy men of the city. For a brief period Mrs. Prout took Anne Royall under her wing, guiding her on a tour of the Slater homestead, "oldest house in the city" which had "stood an hundred years" near the Navy Yard. Recently Mrs. Prout had enclosed her ancestral home "with new plank, to shield it from the weather." Having gone to such pains, the heiress "stabled her favorite horse in this sacred relic." [33]

No doubt upkeep of the horse cost Mrs. Prout far more than she laid out for the relief of Mrs. Royall. Still many blessings flowed from their acquaintance. Mrs. Prout introduced Anne into the close-knit little group of original proprietors and their descendants who kept aloof from the city's transient government servants. Anne was invited to the home of Mrs. John P. Van Ness who could boast "the most elegant estate in Washington." The Van Ness "palace," situated on the bank of the Potomac at the mouth of the Tiber, had cost thirty thousand dollars to build, a huge sum for the times. The visitor was truly awed. "The gardens for taste and beauty are unrivalled." But Mrs. Van Ness was a very sad woman. Her only child, a married daughter, had suddenly died a few years before. The unhappy mother had "laid aside her sceptre and crown as queen of society," and thereafter devoted "most of her time and income to the relief of the distressed. She is at the head of every charitable and humane institution in Washington."

Like Mrs. Prout, Mrs. Van Ness, the daughter of David Burns who surrendered some of the most desirable acreage to the District, had preserved "the house in which her father lived." But no horse bedded down in the "low frame building." Mrs. Van Ness showed Mrs. Royall through the old house. "She told me with a deep sigh, that she enjoyed more real happiness in it than in her present princely edifice." [34]

Most of the proprietors and their heirs were Catholics, and for a time Anne Royall found Catholics more helpful than Masons. "How much have I heard said about these Roman Catholics! I have heard them accounted little better than heretics. But I must confess, I never was amongst people more liberal, more affable, condescending, or courteous."

One helpful Catholic gentleman was Colonel William Brent, nephew of Daniel Carroll, largest landowner in the District. That summer Sally Dorret fell in love with a young Irishman who clerked at the Navy Yard. His name was Stackpool, which he shortened to Stack. Every night Stack came courting, and Anne was forced to vacate the parlor to the young lovers and retire to her bedroom. She missed the evenings with Sally whose "simple philosophy sustained her through darkness and difficulty." Sally's philosophy was that tomorrow was another day and it was bound to be better.

The Dorret ménage had another flaw. With three boys romping through the halls, Anne Royall did not have the quiet she needed to write. Colonel Brent owned ten shares of stock in the Brick

Capitol, which patriotic stockholders had hurriedly constructed for Congress after the British had destroyed the government seat on Capitol Hill. The legislators having moved back to the Hill, the patriots attempted to realize something on their investment by renting rooms in the Brick Capitol. They had little success. Colonel Brent, who was clerk of the Supreme Court, perhaps the temporary Capitol's only paying tenant, told Mrs. Royall to take her pick and move in—rent free.

Anne Royall gave thanks for her privacy and spent long hours over her manuscript. The Brick Capitol (which occupied the present site of the Supreme Court) was the friendly, informal habitat of people who, for the most part, were as hard up as Anne. Across the hall roomed E. J. Middleton, small storekeeper by day and flute player by night. A considerate neighbor, Mr. Middleton worried lest he disturb the lady writer.

"The softness of your music beguiles me of my cares," Mrs. Royall graciously reassured him.[35]

Daytimes Anne determinedly pursued her sightseeing. A younger woman could not have covered more ground during the long humid summer. At the prison she learned of the new law exempting women from prosecution for debt in the District of Columbia. Still wanted by the Charleston sheriff, she warmly praised "this humane act in favor of the tender sex." One Sunday she joined some fishermen bound down the Potomac in a skiff. Before the day was over, she wished heartily she had not undertaken to enlighten westerners on how fish are seined. As the sun rose higher, the seiners shed their shirts and drank like the "veriest sots."

She had a disappointing interview with Attorney General William Wirt, author of *The Letters of the British Spy*, a best seller which reached nine editions in 1803. Having enjoyed the book, Mrs. Royall expected noble words from the author. Whatever their disagreement, she had nothing favorable to say about Mr. Wirt, then or later. The attorney general was "somewhat corpulent" with "vacant blue eyes," possessed "no dignity, no independence." She finished him off by quoting "a gentleman of the City" who said "that had Mr. Wirt died when he wrote *The Spy*, he would have rendered his name immortal." [36]

Anne Royall encountered her second man of letters when she dropped by the Library of Congress, recently settled in the north wing of the new Capitol. The room was "handsomely furnished with sofas, mahogany tables, desks, Brussels carpeting, spermaceti candles," the whole so comfortable that it was rapidly gaining favor over the rotunda as a popular rendezvous. Anne wandered among the stacks, reading the titles and fondling volumes that had once felt the touch of Thomas Jefferson.

Mrs. Royall struck up acquaintance with George Watterston, first librarian appointed by Congress and literary lion of the moment. His new novel, *The L Family, or a Winter in the Metropolis*, satirized in gossipy style the social doings of the Capital. Mrs. Royall did not like the book as well as *Glencairn*, an earlier work by Mr. Watterston, which she had read in Alabama. The "mannerly and modest" author "blushed deep" when she praised *Glencairn*, and began to lend her books from the government's collection.[37]

Though Congress had gone home, the summer of 1824 was an unusually lively one in Washington City. Of the five candidates for the presidency—Crawford, Jackson, Adams, Clay, and Calhoun —the last three remained in the Capital to advance their political fortunes. Anne Royall found "it impossible to learn the truth, either from the parties or the papers," as to how each aspirant stood on important questions of the day. In spite of the double shuffle dealt her by glib legislators she still clung to her ideals about the sanctity of the mission a man faced when he accepted a public office. Her great discovery that summer was her rare individuality in this respect. "It must be a matter of serious grief to all lovers of their country to witness the low means by which electioneering is conducted."

In Alexandria, Anne had talked politics with a former member of Congress. He was for William Harris Crawford. "Crawford," the gentleman proclaimed proudly, "is a Virginian although he lives in Georgia."

"What of it?" Mrs. Royall asked.

"Softly," cautioned the former representative. "Don't you know the President has many lucrative offices at his disposal?"

That wasn't how Anne Royall wanted her country governed.

"When men of the first talents and information, as we find in these party leaders, descend so low as to aid in blinding and misleading an honest and unsuspecting yeoman of his country, by fashioning him into a tool to vote as they please, it is time for the people to think for themselves."

Mrs. Royall was thinking about one curious aspect of the campaign. "From the great deal that is said of Crawford, I should suspect that all is not right." Everything was all wrong with Mr. Crawford, who lay abed in the home of a Virginia colleague, hopelessly paralyzed. His backers kept mum about the gravity of his condition, lest the truth weaken their position when it came to trading Crawford votes for patronage.[38]

The three available candidates signed Anne Royall's subscription list. She dismissed Speaker Clay quickly—"his hair is majestic"—and wrote at length about the "personal beauty" of Secretary of War Calhoun. "In Washington, Mr. Calhoun is held the model of perfection." [39]

Strange, it was the prim John Quincy Adams of Massachusetts who won her western heart. A complete stranger, she was ushered into the private office of the Secretary of State without a wait. From the "superhuman serenity of his countenance," she wondered "whether he had ever laughed in his life." Yet Anne felt she was in the presence of a "truly great man. He has the least of what is called pride, both in manners and dress. Mr. A. appears to be about fifty years of age, middling stature, robust make, with every indication of a vigorous constitution."

The Secretary listened with interest as Mrs. Royall detailed the shortcomings of the pension law and agreed that it should be revised. When she spoke about her projected tour of the Atlantic States, Mr. Adams said she would enjoy New England.

"Stop at Quincy and see my father," he suggested. The venerable second President of the U.S.A. was almost blind and therefore visitors "were one of the few pleasures left him."

Secretary Adams subscribed for *The Sketches* and *The Letters* and, over Anne's protest, insisted on paying in advance. He dropped the money into her lap.

"Go and see Mrs. Adams in F Street," he said.

At the three-story brick house near Fourteenth Street, a Negro butler guided Mrs. Royall to the Secretary's wife "in the back parlor." Mrs. Adams was "tall, slender and elegantly formed," and, after Anne came to know Louisa Adams, she described her as the "most accomplished American lady I have seen." How grateful was the battered bookseller-author for a friendly reception. "You do not have to stand and wait here. The rich and poor meet with a cordial welcome." [40]

The innuendo was directed at the White House where she had been "repulsed." "One would think that civility, at least, might be expected at the door of the first man of the nation." President Monroe received brief notice in the *Sketches*. "He looked very old."

Door-to-door bookselling had produced its quota of rebuffs. "If you are poor, you have no business in Washington; and unless you are well-dressed, you will have good luck if you be not kicked out by servants, should you attempt to enter a house." At congressional boarding houses, servants were "bullies," differing from their employers only "in colour." Anne blamed her frigid receptions on the fact that "every house has a doorbell," an inhospitable device which the West had eschewed as "an aristocratic English invention." If the servant answering the bell "finds you are not a member of Congress, head of department, or foreign minister, he thrusts his body directly in the entrance, taking all possible precaution to keep you out, and thus the general question, is the master or mistress at home? You receive the same answer ninety-nine times out of a hundred, which is 'he is not,' although he is then listening on the other side of the door." [41]

Newspaper editors were cordial. Anne Royall visited the offices of most of them, asked questions about their politics and received equivocal replies. With rare exception, they were the mouthpieces of the party that paid their bills. Anne herself left with the editors a good impression of the extensive literary work she had in mind to do. She made lifelong friends of Messrs. Gales and Seaton, editors of the *National Intelligencer*, the Capital's oldest newspaper. Her attachment to the English-born Joseph Gales, junior, was beyond prediction. Temperamentally and politically, the two were poles apart. For one thing Gales "did not believe in government by the masses." He did believe fervently, however, in freedom of the press. When a few years later, Anne began to twit him publicly for his Tory politics, hailing him as the "Henglishman," or "Jo-ee," or "Josey," the dignified Mr. Gales never lifted his pen in protest. Always "humane and kind" to his bumptious editorial assailant, he would dig into his pocket to aid her when all others had turned her away. The newspapers that she later published could not have continued without contributions of type discarded by the *National Intelligencer.*

"I should be a traitor to my country," she wrote, "if I let my gratitude for personal favors keep me from attacking the editor of the *Intelligencer* for sentiments which spell RUIN to the nation." [42]

6

By summer's end, the travel fund contained sufficient to take Anne Royall as far as Baltimore, a day's ride by stage. The would-be author confidently fixed October 13 as the date of her departure. This would be the day after Washington welcomed the Marquis de Lafayette, returned to the U.S.A. for a triumphal tour of the nation whose independence he had fought for. The reception of the hero promised to be an unforgettable affair. The Federal government had appropriated $2,700, or nine hundred dollars more than the District's annual school budget, to entertain the distinguished guest.

With the city in a tumult of preparations, the quiet of the Brick Capitol ceased to be. Across the way in Capitol Square, hammers pounded from dawn to dusk on construction of a reviewing stand. At night, heavy-footed citizens tramped round and round as they got in step to escort the hero. "Nothing was heard in the streets or in the houses, but Lafayette! Lafayette! We have Lafayette ribbons, Lafayette waistcoats, Lafayette feathers, hats, caps, etc.; even the gingercakes are impressed with his name."

At last the great day dawned. Mrs. Royall climbed to a third-floor apartment for a view of the ceremonies in the Square, already

covered with a countless multitude. Twenty-five young ladies, dressed in white, each with a flag in her hand, took their stations. Twenty-four of them represented the twenty-four states. Besides these young ladies, the pupils of the different schools formed a file through which the general was to pass.

An elegant carriage, drawn by six white horses, was dispatched to meet him, while the military, and a vast number of citizens, repaired to the toll-gate, a mile from the city. As soon as the Marquis passed through the gate, artillery saluted him and shortly afterwards a cloud of dust proclaimed the general's approach; but so great was the throng around him, that I only saw the necks of the horses that drew his carriage. The crowd pressed upon the general, to the hazard of his safety, until the marshals drew their swords and dispersed them. Lafayette was addressed by the daughter of Mr. Watterston, the Librarian, a little girl ten years old, who represented the District. The general took her affectionately by the hand, and passed on to the Capitol.

From the reviewing stand Mayor Roger C. Weightman delivered the city's welcome. After the troops had passed in review, the carriage and white horses were brought around and the "Nation's guest" rode off to take midday dinner at the President's house. He had been invited to stay at the White House, but refused when told the public disapproved because the arrangement would be "too exclusive." The people having been served, the official program called for the general to rest up before the evening banquet at the Franklin House where he was quartered.

If the repose of the aging hero was disturbed, the blame cannot be laid at the door of Mayor Weightman who had ordered stores closed and vehicles off the streets. As it was, Franklin House was located far out on Pennsylvania Avenue at Twenty-First Street in country quiet. To further insure the privacy of the visitor a guard was stationed before the door of his suite.[43]

By some stratagem Anne Royall outwitted the guard and had a long and fruitful interview with the venerable Frenchman. She reminded him that her husband had served at the siege of Richmond, and, like the Marquis, had taken no pay for soldiering. Did General Lafayette recall the retreat from Petersburg when he ordered Captain Royall "to remove some horses out of the path of the advancing enemy? The captain had delivered all but one of the animals to the quartermaster. The horse he lost cost him nearly 200 £'s." It was the property of a Mr. Ruffin who, after the war, had sued Captain Royall for reimbursement, ignoring the fact that his whole stable might have fallen to the British if William Royall had not done his job so well. Mr. Ruffin won his suit.

Richmond and Petersburg had been nightmares to Lafayette. What a headache the horses had been! Negro slaves had rounded them up and delivered them to Cornwallis. Tarleton, noting that the animals were better than those brought from England, mounted his dragoons on the blooded racehorses and dispatched them to cut down Virginians. The general gallantly congratulated Mrs. Royall on the bravery of her husband and listened patiently to her account of the shabby treatment meted out to Captain Royall's widow by a heartless government bureau.

There was not much anyone could tell the Marquis de Lafayette about the thankless rewards of patriotism. But when Mrs. Royall invaded his suite, his heart was overflowing with gratitude for the gifts showered on him since his arrival in New York two months earlier. Purses, land, jewelry, furniture, clothing—Mathew Carey had sent him a check for four hundred dollars—and this was only the beginning of the tour which was to last a year and take him into all the grateful states. Perhaps Lafayette had already heard rumor that Congress was preparing to vote him a gift of $200,000, which was the amount spent out of his personal fortune in behalf of America's independence.

So the moment was ripe to ask a favor. Mrs. Royall did not ask for money. She wanted a memorandum detailing the military service of William Royall in the Revolutionary War. With such a letter she could impress the Masonic membership—Lafayette had been a lodge member some four decades—and quickly open doors to prospective subscribers. The Marquis did not hesitate. What he wrote Mrs. Royall does not tell us, but his letter seems to have served her well.

Lafayette's letter, Randolph's letter, a subscription list, letters to sundry Masons, a stagecoach ticket to Baltimore—these were Anne Royall's assets as she ventured forth to strange cities where she knew not a soul. She had left an important item out of her calculations, it seems. A few days before leaving Washington she called at the Adams house to say goodbye. Mrs. Adams looked at the old black dress and hurried from the parlor. She returned with a shawl which she draped over Anne's shoulders. Mrs. Royall would need it on her journey, said the Secretary's wife, for northern winters were very cold.[44]

CHAPTER VII

"A STRANGER FRIENDLESS
AND PENNYLESS"

1

At midday the stage halted at the tavern out of which a few evenings earlier General Lafayette and his supperless party had charged upon learning the name was Waterloo. The innkeeper told Anne Royall that his Tory landlord had stipulated in the lease how the tavern should be called.

Mrs. Royall's brief stopover brought mine host no peace of mind. He served an excellent dinner of "ham and greens, a savoury turkey, a pair of ducks, and a variety of excellent vegetables." Anne called for her bill.

"Three quarters of a dollar," said the proprietor.

The stage passengers paid up, but not Anne Royall. "Where are your rates?" she demanded.

"We fix our own rates," said the landlord.

"Then we stand on even ground," retorted Anne. "You fix your rates; so do I."

She handed him fifty cents and took her seat in the stage. An experienced traveler, she knew the rules. The law required taverns to post their tariff where all could see.[1]

Late in the afternoon the horses struggled over the crest of a hill. "Towering spires and white monuments just appeared, and then the city"—the city where Anne Newport Royall had been born. Up and down the hilly landscape ran rows of houses, whose bright blues and yellows were in pert contrast to the massive public buildings of stone and stolid brick mansions built by fortunes made in the tobacco and the East Indies trade. All was contained between the headwaters of Chesapeake Bay and the amphitheatre of orchards and woods rising to the north and the west.

The stagecoach swayed around crooked, narrow streets with Anne sitting on edge. On Light Street the driver pulled up at a painted sign depicting a foamy erupting fountain. Anne rented the cheapest room at the famous Fountain Inn where Lafayette had been a guest the week before. Next morning she asked George Beltzhoover, the landlord, to conduct her through the suite the general had occupied. Everything remained as the Frenchman had left it. In awesome whispers Mr. Beltzhoover informed that the rooms had also served as the headquarters of General Washington.

Fountain Inn was a more citified hostelry than Clagett's and the landlord more of a businessman. He could see no profit as a patron of literature. Anne Royall moved out of the expensive inn and looked among the Masons for assistance. James Curry, "a noble Scot and master carpenter," and his wife welcomed her into their modest home on Hanover Street. "Transcendently kind," Mrs. Curry decreed the passing of the old black dress. She canvassed lodge members and wives for contributions and herself stitched up a new garment.[2]

In rustling attire Mrs. Royall called on Messrs. Warren and Wood, managers of the celebrated Holliday Theater, hoping to interest them in the play she had written. The theater's fame dated from an October evening in 1814 when "Mr. Harding [sang] a much admired new song written by a gentleman of Maryland in commemorating the gallant defense of Fort McHenry, called *The Star-Spangled Banner*."

Anne presented a letter of introduction to William Warren who, in younger days, had made a reputation as a comedian. Their meeting called out none of his talent. After a hasty glance at the letter, Mr. Warren grumbled that "he wished no concern" with the visitor. The *Sketches* describe the manager as "a surly, ill-natured dog."

William Burke Wood, the younger partner, had been a matinee idol. He received Mrs. Royall "with an air worthy of Chesterfield himself," and explained that the Holliday Theater had undergone a change of policy in recent years. "We play no American pieces at all."

She had chosen a bad time to approach the partners. They had just closed an expensive failure which had nevertheless been the work of an American playwright. He was Samuel Woodworth who shortly would acquire some fame (and not much cash) as the author of *The Old Oaken Bucket*. The title of his play was *La Fayette* and, considering the occasion, the production was expected to be a hit. After two performances, on the eve of the hero's visit to Baltimore, the curtain was rung down permanently. Far from stimulating attendance at the Holliday, Lafayette in the flesh stole the show.[3]

With heavy heart Anne hurried through the motions of sightseeing. In ten days she had completed the task and promoted a free ride to Philadelphia. The donor was General William McDonald, a Revolutionary hero who, gambling on Fulton's invention, had introduced the first line of steamers on the Chesapeake Bay. Every afternoon at five o'clock a sloop left Bowley's wharf for Frenchtown across the bay in a haven of Elk River where ten stages—"without one lamp amongst them"—raced passengers overland to Newcastle, Delaware. From thence the journey continued by boat up the Delaware River to the Quaker City. All told, the trip required about twenty-four hours, the fare four dollars.[4]

In spite of the discomfort of two transportation shifts during the night, Mrs. Royall praised the custom of the McDonald fleet of seating men and women together in the same dining room. On western steamboats they took their meals in separate rooms. Still, for "elegant furnishings," the palm went to the westerners. "I have seen no satin spreads, or gold fringe in any of them, which is common in our boats."

2

Dawn November 1, 1824, found Anne Royall sitting on the chilly deck watching the sunrise brighten the river flats. Her mood was solemn. The failure of the Baltimore conquest—two subscriptions only—had shaken her confidence. Yet, here she was entering the second largest city of the U.S.A., without a friend. Before her lay the degrading touch-and-go rounds—begging, wheedling, seeking. Anne gazed at the misty shores of New Jersey. "I thought of George Washington, I thought of his toils, his dangers, and the soul-trying scenes he underwent, whilst retreating through that state, before the enemies of his country. Matchless man!" [5]

With four pennies in her pocket, she stepped ashore at Hamilton's Wharf, near the foot of Walnut Street, in midmorning and put in the remainder of the day walking the brick sidewalks in search of aid. "I applied to none but the Masons. The Masons in Philadelphia behaved mean." [6]

In late afternoon she stumbled upon an obliging landlord—"an Irishman by the name of M'Carty," who kept the Horse and Groom in Strawberry Alley. "Had I not met this humane family (all Roman Catholics) I must have perished. Not being accustomed to the hard pavement, my feet the first day became very sore and much swelled—I was so much fatigued that I was unable to undress. Mrs. M'Carty pulled off my shoes and stockings, as I lay on the bed, and bathed my feet in gin [sic!] or some sort of spirits. The next morning, though they felt very sore at first, when warmed by walking they ceased to be painful."

Anne walked first to the house of Carey & Lea on the southeast corner of Chestnut Street and Fourth. She hoped to persuade Henry Carey to reconsider her books. She hinted of "her distress" to Carey, "being told he was a Mason." Though her work was once more rejected, the call was rewarding. "I gently reproached H. Carey for not introducing me to his father; he stepped into an adjoining room, and the elder Mr. C. soon made his appearance."

"What is your business with me?" said he.

"Only to say I have seen Mr. Carey."

"He blushed and said: 'Come this way, I have something for you.'"

Carey gave Mrs. Royall a copy of his latest book, a biography of Alexander Hamilton, and a handful of pamphlets—"addresses to the people." She had time to "exchange but a few words before Mr. Carey departed" for an appointment. She described the publisher as "upwards of fifty years of age [he was sixty-four] with black hair and eyes, countenance grim and marked with lines of deep thinking." A year later, on a second visit to Philadelphia, she noted that "Mr. Carey possesses a warmth of heart and soul, which the sight of distress blows into flame." At this meeting he told her "he was much displeased that I did not let *him* know of my distress."

Anne continued walking and succeeded in scraping up a few contributions, though no subscriptions. By sunset she was back at the *Horse and Groom* with blisters on her feet. She drank a cup of tea and went to bed "determined to finish what I had begun. I might as well walk to death, as starve to death."

Next morning her feet "were prodigiously sore and painful and swelled, but not so as to prevent wearing shoes." Resolutely she set off to sightsee. She walked to the Schuylkill bridge and thence to the Fairmount waterworks, "the glory of the city." After three years, taxpayers still grumbled over the cost of the waterworks— $350,000—though there had been a noticeable abatement in yellow fever epidemics each summer.

Anne Royall figured that she had walked eight miles before returning to the *Horse and Groom*, "with the skin of my toes bursted, my heels completely rubbed off, and both bled freely." Too weary for supper, though she did try to down, without success, the rye coffee to which Philadelphians were addicted, she threw herself on the bed without undressing. "Next morning shoes, stockings, and my feet, were all glued fast together by the blood! But it was Sunday, and I had time to devise ways and means to get them asunder," without Mrs. M'Carty's spirits which "smarted bitterly. By bathing and soaking I separated the shoes from the stockings, but to get the stockings from the raw flesh was no easy matter, and took several hours."

Monday morning Anne started off, believing that one day's respite had worked a miracle cure. She had not walked far before her shoes pinched unmercifully. "Light as my purse was I was compelled to draw upon it for the amount of a pair of shoes for which I paid seventy-five cents. These were, of course, the lowest quality. I left the bloody shoes in the store." [7]

3

The day went badly. At the moment the best-known clergyman in Philadelphia was the Reverend Doctor Ezra Stiles Ely, pastor of the Third Presbyterian Church. Doctor Ely's consuming ambition was to unite Protestant churches into an interdenominational force to spread the gospel. Once united they would wield their power to obtain legislation from the federal government which would give them more say-so in deciding evangelical matters affecting the U.S.A. To this end Ely had organized the American Tract Society, which would shortly initiate demands in Congress for an end to Sunday mail service and travel. The Session of the Third Presbyterian Church, "E. S. Ely, mod.," had gone on record against Sabbath labor when it "rebuked a prominent master of a steamboat and devoted member of the church" for operating his boat on the Lord's Day. Rather than be cut off from his church and so condemned to everlasting torment, the captain had pleaded "strong temptation" and promised "the offense would not be repeated." His repentance satisfied Doctor Ely, though perhaps not his employers who had a government mail contract.

The pastor's decisions were law in his parish. Living in fear of the "woeful eternity" promised sinners, the congregation accepted his verdicts without argument. "The Session of the Church," Doctor Ely informed a member, "require you to abstain from participating in the communion of the Lord's Supper, until further notice. . . . Common fame accused you of being a notorious scold, of ungovernable temper . . . and peculiarly abusive to your husband." The lady reformed. Ely kept watch on juvenile conduct. Discipline was the responsibility of parents. He promptly stopped the distracting squirming of children required to sit through his long Sabbath sermons. "Parents should be solemnly warned to exercise their parental authority in training the younger members of their homes to show due reverence at times of public worship." [8]

Having heard that "Dr. Ely was a pious christian, and, withal, a man of great wealth," Anne carried her subscription list to his home on Spruce Street. His name on her list should attract other subscribers because the reverend doctor had a large following in all parts of the U.S.A.

I was informed that his house stood back from the street, in a square, and on his gate I would see a silver plate with "Rev. Dr. Stiles Ely" on it in large letters. I found the gate, and the silver plate—the big letters—the big house—and the BIG man. The big door was open. The doctor appeared, but I briefly repeated my business. He turned off short and said he was engaged.[9]

One glance at the list headed by the name of the infidel John Quincy Adams may have decided the preacher that the devil himself had come to his door. Anne had no idea how Presbyterians felt about Unitarians.

In her new shoes Mrs. Royall pursued her weary course to the State House. The old brick building where the Declaration of Independence was signed might have been torn down long since had not the artist Charles Willson Peale leased it for a museum to display his collection of stuffed birds, animals, wax figures, and two hundred-odd portraits of Revolutionary leaders and contemporary government and military figures. Peale also had had troubles with the Protestant churches which complained to the city council that he kept open on Sundays. Anne had wound up her tale of woe describing the Reverend Ely as a "monster." Showman Peale was much too clever to quarrel. Tongue in cheek he posted a placard at the entrance of the State House: "Here the wonderful works of the Divinity may be contemplated with pleasure and advantage. Let no one enter with any other view." [10]

Anne Royall entered to view the skeleton of a mammoth, plowed up in 1801 on a farm in Ulster County, New York. Thanks to Peale's talent for reaping publicity, the mastodon had always been a big drawing card. Once the proprietor had seated a dinner party around a table set up within the ghoulish framework. Another time Peale moved in a piano for a concert. Women visitors often went into hysterics upon confrontation with the enormous relic. Anne came close to hysterics when she started up the staircase of the State House—"wide enough to admit a wagon and team." The second step shivered under her foot and a bell rang—a Peale invention to rouse the ticket seller. Mrs. Royall paid twenty-five cents

and continued her climb. At the top she was greeted by Franklin
Peale, son of the octogenarian artist, who led her to the mastodon.
No hysterics. "I was greatly disappointed. The skeleton had not
that formidable, dread-inspiring aspect with which I expected to
be overwhelmed."

Anne thought the Peale portraits more interesting. She especially
praised those of Commodore Perry, Doctor Rush, the architect
Latrobe, and Albert Gallatin. The life-size figures of notable Americans fashioned in wax were "marvellous." She paused before a tall
form in Indian dress and said sadly: "Poor misguided Meriweather
Lewis!" The remark, made only fifteen years after Lewis's mysterious death, would appear to indicate that Mrs. Royall believed
Lewis had died by his own hand. The manner of the explorer's
death is still debated.

Though material for *The Sketches* was conscientiously explored
on aching feet, subscriptions and contributions were not forthcoming. In desperation Anne took to waiting at night outside
Masonic Lodges for the members "to rise." The vigils brought scant
recompense.

The Quaker City was a painful disappointment, producing only
one subscriber. He was William Darby, author of the *Emigrant's
Guide to the Western Country*, who introduced himself at Letitia
Court, the "ancient dwelling of William Penn." Few pioneers
started west without a copy of the *Guide* which Darby revised each
year. His maps were reputed to be more accurate than those issued
by the government. At the Battle of New Orleans Andrew Jackson had shown a preference for them. Anne was familiar with the
guidebook and felicitated the author on his ability to make a living
from his travels. Mr. Darby was "the only gentleman in Philadelphia" who invited Mrs. Royall to visit his home. "It was not in
my power to accept the invitation." Mrs. Curry's dress was showing the effects of constant wear. Another handicap—she had no
money to hire a carriage.[11]

4

Sunday again, but no day of rest for the frustrated traveler who
hoped to be on her way to New York on Monday at 2 A.M. "I still

lacked 50 cents of the fare, which was two dollars. I walked the streets nearly the whole day, soliciting everyone I met. Some would give me a few cents, and some hundreds refused even that." The last donor was Daniel Dick who kept a tobacco shop on Front Street, near the *Horse and Groom.* Though Mr. Dick did a very small business, he had a large heart. He always had a few words of cheer for Mrs. Royall when she limped by his shop, feet aching and spirit sick with discouragement.[12]

Though two dollars had been hard to raise, Anne was fortunate that her ticket cost so little. A rate war was raging between the two Philadelphia–New York lines. Fares had been more than halved in the scramble for customers. The paddle wheels were frothing up the Delaware River when the ticket taker discovered Mrs. Royall had boarded the wrong boat. He demanded two dollars for his line. This was the last straw; Anne burst into tears. Captain Fisher stomped from the bridge to find out what the racket was about. He paid out the money for Anne Royall to continue to New York. She dried her eyes, and looked back at the fading lights of the City of Brotherly Love. "I never left a place with less regret," she wrote.

With smokestacks spewing clouds of black smoke the rivals toiled toward the landing below Trenton. Here passengers were piled into two stages for the twenty-five-mile dash overland to the Raritan River where two more steamboats awaited them at New Brunswick.

These opposition lines are certainly an advantage to travellers [Anne decided], but it is one of great hazard. We got to the Raritan first and I was almost carried to the boat by the porters, in their eagerness to conquer the other line. No sooner were we in the boats than the steam was liberally plied to the wheels, and a race between the *Legislator* and the *Olive Branch* commenced for New York. The former was our heroine. It was quite an interesting sight to see such vast machines, so near to each other that passengers were able to converse. It is well calculated to amuse them, were it not for a lurking fear that we might burst the boilers.

Six months later the *Legislator* did burst its boiler. Four persons were killed and several injured.[13]

The day was cold, the sky leaden. With only Mrs. Adams' shawl to keep her warm, Anne Royall sat out most of the journey in the "stove room," her discomfort unrelieved by a conversation in progress beside her.

"I was led to believe that your state would have supported Mr. Adams," said one gentleman. Anne assumed he was talking about New Jersey where electors had already voted in favor of Andrew Jackson for President.

"Do you think we would have voted for a man who doesn't believe in the Christian religion?" asked his companion.

"Why, how is that?"

"John Q. Adams is a Unitarian," explained New Jersey.

"What can he mean?" thought Anne. "Jew, Turk, or Algerine?"

"He may be Unitarian," retorted the first speaker, "but that doesn't prove him not a Christian. I am a Unitarian, and I believe in Christ."

"Yes," said New Jersey, "but you deny Christ is the Son of God."

There they were again—the Unitarians. On the frontier there had been only the older and better-known denominations—such as Presbyterians, Methodists, Baptists and a sprinkling of Quakers—but the farther east she traveled Anne Royall ran into more and more sects, splinters shaved from the familiar faiths after disagreement over fundamental theological interpretation. Her eavesdropping brought to mind the Philadelphian who had called gentle Mr. Dick "a heretic." Why? "Mr. Dick is a Universalist." She still did not know what the Universalists stood for. But, no doubt about it, Mr. Dick had behaved like a true Christian to her.[14]

5

Both steamboat lines advertised "to get through in one day" to New York. Beginning in Philadelphia at 2 A.M., "one day" ended at nine o'clock in the evening at the foot of Rector Street and the North River. By lamplight Anne Royall picked her way across town to the boardinghouse of Oliver Jaques on Front Street, recommended by Captain Fisher. Next morning after breakfast she hurried out to see the sights of "far famed Broadway—four miles long,

Columbia College, Park Place, New York, New York, from the *New-York Mirror, and Ladies Literary Gazette*, Dec. 6, 1828. *Courtesy of the New-York Historical Society, New York City*

The Peale Museum in Baltimore, established by Rembrandt and Raphael, sons of Charles Wilson Peale. When Anne Royall visited it in 1828, "the most abominable woman keeper" insisted that she pay twenty-five cents admission fee. She always complained about the crowded busy streets during her Baltimore visits.

and sidewalks paved with flag and distinguished for the fashionable, the gay and the idle. It is likewise the seat of much business; the lower stories of most houses being occupied by retail shops."

Afoot Anne Royall ranged the city between the rivers and from the Battery to the northern limit at Canal Street. The pavement was easier on her feet than the bricks of Philadelphia. Still, she concluded "it would require the constitution of Samson to visit all the public institutions." She tried. She viewed the City Hall—"too low for its size"; Columbia College—"one great building of gray stone near Park Place, average number of students, 200"; New York Hospital near Broadway and Duane, to which "every seaman in the merchant service pays 20 cents per month deducted from their wages for their care, if sick or disabled"; State Prison in Greenwich Street overlooking the Hudson; the Alms-House where the "paupers looked plump and hearty and most of their beds were of feathers." At Bridewell on the East River and the jail in the park near the City Hall—"two black arsenal looking buildings," she found the women prisoners "most abandoned, vicious, impudent. They saluted me with the familiarity of an old acquaintance, and asked if I came to keep them company!" [15]

The four free schools, operating under the Lancastrian system, were "by far the most interesting objects in the city. To see such a vast number of children, from four to eight hundred in one house, governed by a word, a nod, or a glance from their teacher is truly astonishing." To hold down the budget, the Public School Society of New York had adopted Joseph Lancaster's plan for educating the masses as early as 1809. For taxpayers the economy inherent in the system was the training of older scholars (monitors) to teach younger students who were drilled and disciplined as if part of a military establishment. As Mrs. Royall described a New York schoolroom:

The teacher sits upon an elevated seat, at one end of the room, the pupils facing him; these sit on long benches, one behind another, gradually ascending to the last. Each row of benches has a desk before it. The juniors, that is those learning their letters, have sand; the monitor takes hold of the forefinger of the pupil, and guides him in forming a letter. After a few lessons in this manner, the pupil by the aid of a machine which contains the letters of the alphabet in large print, proceeds alone keeping his eye on the letter before him. When he is perfect in the alphabet, he is removed to the next desk, where he has words of two letters; these are pasted on boards which hang before him. When he is perfect in this, the pupil is removed to the next desk, and so on. When students read or spell, they rise from their desks and stand within a circle marked on the floor. The teachers are gentlemen of talent, temper and ability. I spent many hours daily in these schools, which were the most pleasing of any spent in the city.[16]

6

Having inspected public institutions, Mrs. Royall turned her attention to people. "It is well known that New York has produced her share of literary men. Of these, perhaps Washington Irving is the first, but James Kirke Paulding has ever been my favorite." Maybe because Paulding had visited the Sweet Springs and written a witty little book ridiculing the "desperate monotony" of daily life there. Paulding had become known as the "people's writer," but Mrs. Royall found him at his mansion in fashionable Whitehall Street, living in "princely style." The visitor was "charmed with his appearance." The famous "raven locks fell over his neck and forehead in ringlets of ineffable beauty," and she judged Paulding "upwards of 40 years of age. Mr. P. is in height about five feet ten inches, his figure spare, but well-formed. His face oval, complexion dark, features delicate, and his black eyes uncommonly brilliant. In his manners he is frank, generous and gentle as a dove. His house is the abode of hospitality." Paulding, we assume, subscribed for the *Sketches*.[17]

Perhaps from Mr. P. she heard about Charles Wiley's bookshop at 3 Wall Street which was the rendezvous of "bookish people." Anne Royall began to appear there shortly after the interview and soon became acquainted with many of the habitués. Their club was the Den, Wiley's back room, but Anne was probably not invited into this masculine preserve. Her breezy western manner made her popular with Den members. An early acquaintance was Samuel Woodworth, "an amiable man," the very same whose play *La Fay-*

ette had failed in Baltimore. Woodworth had tried his hand at many forms of writing—poetry, journalism, novels, criticism, drama, opera—to support six children, while satisfying his urge for literary recognition. After the abrupt closing of the play, Woodworth had found himself a new job. He was editor of the *New-York Mirror and Ladies Gazette,* a sprightly review founded a year earlier by George Pope Morris with the avowed purpose of encouraging the Den's talented membership. Anne was "particularly struck" with Mr. Morris, who had made enough money from sentimental verse to launch the magazine. His most famous poem, however, belonged to the future. It was about a tree near West End Avenue and Ninety-eighth Street which he pleaded with a woodman to spare. Morris subscribed for the *Sketches* which he would later review.[18]

Another poet moderately successful was James Gordon Brooks, literary editor of the *Minerva* which described itself as a "literary, entertaining and *scientific journal.*" "Florio," Brooks' pen name, served Anne Royall handsomely as friend and abettor of her career. She described him as "a small, elegant, young man, with a fine taste for writing."

An important friendship to come out of Wiley's was with the printer-publisher himself—"a friend to the distressed and to the genius of his country." Wiley believed that the time was overdue for the U.S.A. to declare its literary independence of England, and he had backed up his idea by publishing perhaps a dozen novels by Americans. He was fortunate to have James Fenimore Cooper at the top of his list, though not all of Cooper's books were profitable. Between best sellers there were duds. In 1824 when Anne arrived on the scene Wiley had suffered a failure with *Lionel Lincoln,* Cooper's fourth novel. But the main thing was that Mrs. Royall's travels and her plan for selling them interested Wiley and he gave his promise to publish the *Sketches.*

Anne Royall had already called on one New York publisher and been turned down. To have stumbled on one other than Wiley was a surprise. Walking down Dover Street, she saw a sign: "J. & J. Harper, publishers." In a "dingy room," she met four brothers, "mere lads, commencing their careers without funds or friends.

They were more cautious than Wiley. They wanted to be publishers, but they were still printers." [19]

Dignified old-timers like Charles King, editor of the *New York American*, and Theodore Dwight of the *New York Daily Advertiser* never could abide Mrs. Royall's unfeminine behavior. But Major Mordecai M. Noah, then editor of the *National Advocate*, a Tammany-supported daily which he helped to establish in 1817, hailed Mrs. Royall as "the new literary comet." Of Portuguese-Jewish ancestry, the tall, good-looking major at forty-one already had several careers behind him—diplomat, playwright, politician, high sheriff, lawyer, and off-and-on newspaper editor. He generated excitement no matter what he undertook. Appointed New York sheriff in 1822, he had thrown open the doors of the Debtors' Jail during a yellow fever epidemic and told the inmates to save themselves. Noah was not reelected sheriff. The clergy of the city "not only denounced him, but represented to the municipal fathers that God had sent the plague to the community for having named a Jew as sheriff." Along with his editorial labors, the major was engaged in raising funds to establish a colony in America for oppressed Jews of all nations. The year after Anne met him, Noah laid the cornerstone of "Ararat, City of Refuge," on the Niagara River. The refuge never had a refugee.[20]

"He is doubtless the best, if not the ablest editor in the Union," Anne wrote. "His talents are principally devoted to instruction and amusement. His papers are free from the bitterness, too common in most party papers, and are sought after and read by all parties."

A recent addition to the *Advocate* staff was an emigrant from Scotland. "I am under infinite obligation to my friend Mr. Bennett [James Gordon, senior]," Anne acknowledged. "Mr. B. is a tall slender man, well-formed. He is a gentleman of considerable literary taste. He appears to be but little known in New York, and is not likely to rise in a city devoted to priests and shavers." New York came to know him.

Her description bears no resemblance to the portraits of the awkward, unkempt, unfriendly, sharp-tongued, ambitious young man drawn by contemporaries. Still Anne Royall made a friend of

Bennett, a friend indeed who, in trouble, used his clever pen to defend her. For the moment she seems to have been so bewitched by his personality that she failed to call attention to his most conspicuous feature. He was cross-eyed.[21]

7

The Masons of New York came through handsomely. In relieving Mrs. Royall of money worries, they gave her confidence which accounts, in large part, for her success with the variety of people she interviewed in the U.S.A.'s largest metropolis. The Mason who appears to have made her his special charge was Jonathan D. Stevenson, proprietor with Abraham Rider of Chatham Garden, a sumptious "refrectory and saloon" flanking the entrance to the New Chatham Garden Theater. The Chatham had a hit, a comic opera entitled *The Saw-Mill or a Yankee Trick.* The author was Micah Hawkins who ran a grocery and hotel near the Catherine Street Ferry where he kept a piano beneath the counter. "He played a sort of running accompaniment to the varied demands of his customers. . . . and in the interval between serving out sugar and salt . . . he composed the opera." Also a poet, Hawkins was his own librettist. The manager of Chatham Garden Theater was Hippolite Barrière, a Frenchman who had more theatrical successes to his credit than any contemporary producer. Through Mr. Stevenson, Anne Royall met Mr. Barrière, who gave her a ticket to the Hawkins opera—"the first regular play I ever saw performed." In the cast was "handsome, slim and graceful" William Rufus Blake, of Nova Scotia, twenty years old, making his debut in New York. The star was Caroline Placide Waring—Blake later became her second husband—daughter of a notable American stage family.

The scene of America's first operatic production was laid in upstate New York. The farmer had a beautiful daughter loved by a handsome youth. Papa gave the young man the gate because he was poor and owned no land. The plot spun around the trick played by the rejected suitor to relieve his future father-in-law of some acreage and win the hand of the maiden.[22]

With Tammany in the ascendancy, "bosses" held sway over the political precincts. Mr. Stevenson was a Tammany boss, benefactor of the needy, whose loyalty to the party was properly recognized with gifts that thwarted the hungry wolf sniffing at the door. As a Mason he would probably have felt duty-bound to offer Mrs. Royall a certain amount of relief, but the aid he poured upon her went beyond the bounds of duty. And so, because of all he did for her, we cannot help but entertain the suspicion that Mr. Stevenson was among the first Lodge members to perceive that Anne Royall might be a useful instrument in stemming the rising tide of anti-Masonry.

Mr. Stevenson's first step was to line up Mr. Barrière. With promises of generous Masonic patronage, the manager consented to give a benefit for Anne Royall at Chatham Garden Theater. Stevenson promptly had tickets printed and put them on sale in his saloon where he posted a sign inviting all to aid "the WIDOW of a Masonic Brother and an old Revolutionary officer." For the benefit he and Barrière, honoring the western lady, chose the play *John Bull, or the Tradesman's Fireside*, the frontier's most popular drama, thanks to the buffoonery of Dennis Brulgruddery and a love story that never failed to move the audience to tears.

Mr. Stevenson busied himself with advertising the benefit in the daily newspapers. To one lengthy notice he added a wistful poem:

> Tis charity that soothes the Poor Man's woes.
> And to the needy widow grants repose;
> Tis Masonry that prompts the sacred theme,
> And mars the troubles that would intervene.
> It knows its office, each endearing tie
> Of soft-eyed genuine Philanthropy.

Each day newspapers carried further preliminary announcements, intended to make a man downright ashamed of himself if he did not come to the aid of the WIDOW. One tear-jerker signed SEVENTY-SIX, read: "Every young soldier in our city must feel the present appeal, and if a single spark of the fire of '76 remains benevolence will surely kindle it on the present occasion into a generous flame that will warm the heart of a soldier's bride."

Mr. Barrière decided to play his best talent—William Blake and Caroline Placide. They volunteered their services, as did all the cast. In the midst of his campaign Mr. Stevenson got carried away. Why not turn Mrs. Royall's benefit into a gala Masonic celebration irresistible to all the brotherhood? Mr. Barrière agreed. They settled on the addition to the program of "a Grand Masonic Transparency, during the representation of which the celebrated *Masonic Welcome* will be sung. . . . Wm. Blake will deliver, in appropriate costume, the Masonic Monologue called *The Secret* in which he will explain why Ladies have never been admitted to that ancient and honorable Fraternity, with additional lines written by him expressly for this occasion." To complete the evening Mr. Barrière tossed in a second play *The Young Widow*. The lengthy program, they agreed, should take place on the evening of February 28, enabling Mrs. Royall to resume her travels the following morning, properly supplied with funds.[23]

Late in the afternoon of February 27, a northeast gale blew into the city bringing a blizzard. By morning drifts clogged the streets and the snow was still falling. The day was so bad that no ships ventured in or out of the harbor. It was a sad climax to the inspired labors of Jonathan Stevenson. After several inspections of the deserted streets, he debated with Mr. Barrière whether to open the theater for the evening's benefit. On the other hand, if the performance did not take place, the money collected from the advance sale of tickets would have to be returned.

In the middle of the afternoon the snow let up. Stevenson and Barrière decided to proceed with the show. Mrs. Royall should, at least, have the money already in hand, though it was too bad the weather would deprive her of box office receipts.

Anne Royall arrived on foot at Chatham Garden Theater long before "½ past 6," curtain time, walked glumly past the snow-covered fountain in the garden and entered the folding doors behind which a double flight of stairs (to the right and to the left) ascended to the first circle of boxes. The theater accommodated thirteen hundred people. How wonderful it would have been to find every seat occupied, at from fifteen to forty cents per person! But only a few early birds were on hand to study the extravagant decor of the new auditorium—fawn-color, sky blue and gilt, interior of the two tiers of boxes "crimson, with brass nails and fringe." [24]

Anne sat in a fringed box, counting Masons and members of their families as they trooped in. Suddenly there seemed a surge of them. Before the lamps were dimmed, she thought there might not be an empty seat. It was true. Mr. Stevenson and *John Bull* had brought off one of the most successful benefits of the day. Mrs. Royall was handed one hundred and eighty dollars to begin her tour of New England. [25]

CHAPTER VIII

FAILURES AND TRIUMPHS

1

The best route to Albany was by steamboat. When Anne Royall left New York for Albany at 3 A.M., after her benefit, the Hudson River was frozen solid. With nine other passengers she glided up the snow-covered Post Road in a stagecoach whose wheels had been replaced by sled runners. The trip would have been quiet, comfortable, and scenic in daylight, if "two lady travellers had not kept up such a chattering, and forsooth they must be shut up so close that one cannot enjoy the appearance of the country."

The night was passed at Poughkeepsie and another three o'clock start made the following morning. In midafternoon, as the stage drew up opposite the New York State capital, the driver, doubtful of the strength of the river ice, ordered passengers to get out and walk across the Hudson. Because she was small and slight, Anne was permitted to ride in the stage. She had the company of a man of "unwieldy size," who refused to forsake his seat.[1]

Albany had been prepared for the coming of Mrs. Royall in a lengthy newspaper announcement, most likely paid for by Masons, detailing the literary works to be published by subscription.

The letters [from Alabama] are a miscellaneous production embracing strictures on Manners, Customs, Dialects, Religion, Education,

Literature, and Females, of the United States, with Biographical sketches of the most distinguished men of Alabama and Tennessee. . . .

The "Tennessean" is a Novel founded upon a recent and well known fact, still fresh in the memory of hundreds in that part of the United States where . . . everyone remembers a secret expedition undertaken by a number of . . . enterprising young men (principally Tennesseans) to the Spanish dominions some fifteen years since. The Novel is . . . a narrative of the sufferings and difficulties encountered by the party. . . .

Sketches by a Traveller will comprise physical and moral remarks on the Eastern and Western parts of the United States, including the history of the principal cities and towns from their origin. . . .

These works are offered to the public obviously very low, viz.— (in boards) The Letters at one dollar; Tennesseans one dollar twenty-five cents, the Sketches one dollar fifty cents.

The author is a female of respectability . . . the widow of . . . an officer of the revolution. This Lady, by one of those unforseen misfortunes common in the human family, has fallen into distress, and appeals to the humane and benevolent citizens of this great and patriotic city for their patronage. These Works, we find, are patronized by the most distinguished men of the United States. . . . Subscriptions will be received at the Bookstore of Messrs. Webster and Skinner, in this city.[2]

Mrs. Royall stayed a month in Albany, lingering for the sake of an interview with Governor DeWitt Clinton who, by championing the building of the Erie Canal, had endeared himself to western hearts. Having taken office only two months before Anne arrived in the state capital, the governor's days were crowded. She received an appointment for March 15, but the meeting was put over until March 28. Both engagements are entered in Clinton's diary, little more than a record of callers and his daily constitutionals. On the day set for "Mrs. Royal's" first visit, the governor noted that he took two long walks. When he ultimately received "Mrs. Anna Royale," he had time for only one.[3]

The visitor remarked that Governor Clinton was "inclined to corpulency," which might explain the concern with his daily ramble. "Like all men of sense, he uses few words." Clinton apparently

used so few in this instance the *Sketches* had to fall back on a
parcel of adjectives to pad out the interview.

His whole deportment is dignified and commanding, with all the
ease and grace of an accomplished gentleman. He is six feet at least in
height. His face is round and full, with soft gray eyes. [Most of which
the interviewer had to take back in a later travel book.] When I first
saw him, it was in the dusk of the evening, and no light in the room.
His "face" is neither round nor oval. His high, square, firm forehead
is like no other man's. The upper part of his head retreats back more
than common and his chin is thrown out. He is a stout man, and though
he is a little lame, an active man for his age, which is about fifty. It is
well known that the Erie Canal emanated from the great head of
Governor Clinton. He is himself a canal; his mind, like a mighty river,
flows steadily on.[4]

While awaiting the initial interview, Mrs. Royall had trekked out
to the "northern extremity of Market-street," to introduce herself
to General Stephen Van Rensselaer, descendant of Dutch patroons,
Albany County's representative in Congress, and, for the moment,
an exile from Washington where henchmen of Andrew Jackson
were bitterly blaming him for the election of John Quincy
Adams to the presidency. Adams had won the vote of the New
York delegation by one ballot—Van Rensselaer's. A gentle aristocrat
who entered politics because he believed it was his obligation as a
man of wealth and social prominence, the eighth patroon of Rensselaerwych was baffled by the hue and cry of the defeated party.
He had had a difficult time deciding between two good men. Even
when the voting began in the House, he had not made up his mind.
He bowed his head over his desk and asked for Divine guidance.
An Adams ballot fluttered to his feet. Surely *this* was a sign from
heaven.[5]

It was a pleasure to dismiss politics for a day and conduct an
historically appreciative lady over the ancestral estate which was
his pride. Besides, the visitor had Masonic ties and Van Rensselaer
was Master of the Grand Lodge of the State of New York. Anne,
of course, was goggle-eyed over the extent of the patroon's domain. The West, for all its vastness, could boast no individual land

holdings as large as Rensselaerwych which bordered both sides of the upper Hudson for a distance of some dozen miles. The land had been purchased from the Indians in 1630 by Kiliaen Van Rensselaer, a wealthy diamond and gold merchant of Amsterdam who never set foot in the New World. Kiliaen colonized his patroonship with sturdy Dutch, Norwegians, Germans, and Scots, giving them perpetual leaseholds at modest rentals. "He built sawmills, gristmills, homes, and farms for them; supplied foodstuffs and cattle; set up laws regulating trade, hunting, and fishing." The last of the patroons quoted a portion of the original rental contract to Anne Royall: "He leased those lands out 'while water ran, or grass grew,' exacting the tenth sheaf of grain the land produced." Kiliaen's descendants had wisely continued to operate under the same liberal terms of the original lease, which no doubt accounted for the uninterrupted existence of Rensselaerwych, the only patroonship to have survived the colonial period.

The "tall, slender, hazel-eyed Stephen Van Rensselaer had brought more of his estate under cultivation than any of his predecessors." His home was "the finest in the vicinity," said Mrs. Royall, "and he has a great number of tenants. When he is absent, which is a great part of the year, his strict orders to his steward are to relieve the poor." [6]

Mrs. Royall commented on "the intelligence, affability, and liberality of sentiment" encountered among the first families of the state capital—old Hudson Valley families, such as "the Van Rensselaers, Taylors, Lansings, Spencers, Woodworths, Laceys, Chesters, Ludlows, and DeWitts." But she was aghast at the "bigotry of the middle and lower classes."

Most of the bigotry was directed against the "Irish bog-trotters" recruited to "claw" out the Erie Canal. They were hard-working, hard-living—and Catholic. On whiskey systematically doled out by the canal commission's own "jigger men" and generous meals of spuds (here began the *Society for the Prevention of Undersireable Diets*, according to the late Samuel Hopkins Adams), the "canawlers" were turned into Bunyans—"earth movers and stump pullers" —tough enough to withstand the malarial vapors of the Montezuma Marshes, the most fatal stretch of the 363-mile length of "Clinton's

Ditch." Yet, evidence of their prowess—they built "the longest canal in the world, in the least time, with the least experience, for the least money and the greatest public benefit"—won them no kudos among smug descendants of earlier Protestant immigrants. The mighty Irishmen were abhorred and shunned. They were "foreigners." [7]

The main topic of conversation in Albany was the Erie Canal, scheduled to open for traffic some six months after Mrs. Royall's visit. Anne scooted up to Troy, the eastern terminus of the waterway. As yet there was nothing much to view, and so she paid a call on Emma Willard who, she heard, "kept a female seminary of high repute." The interview went badly—at least for the lady who "is said to be the best qualified female teacher in the state." The Royall verdict: "There is nothing very remarkable in Mrs. Willard's appearance, excepting her masculine size." [8]

2

On April 2, Anne Royall left Albany by stage for Springfield, Massachusetts. There she spent two days "going through the shops of the United States arsenal, admiring the ingenuity of the machinery, and the skill of the workmen," and another day watching the manufacture of paper "upon a newly improved plan" at the factory of David and John Ames.

One would like to know how Mrs. Royall wormed her way into the factory. "Manufacturers throughout the country were watching the marvelous inventions at the Ames Paper Mill. Workmen sought employment in order that they might steal the inventions." As protection, employees were thoroughly investigated. If hired, they were "sworn" not to divulge the nature of their labors. Perhaps the brothers gave Mrs. Royall the run of the mill on the assumption that she was a harmless old lady who would be unable to make head or tail of the intricate operations of the machinery. She understood all right and described them in detail to her readers. [9]

Next stop was Hartford, Connecticut. Anne found the citizenry "affable and liberal." The people were "not advanced so far as to countenance a theatre, though they have a circus." Given a few more years "they will extend their national amusement to the stage which may be the means of saving them from the too frequent use of spiritous liquors. Many a man for want of amusement goes to the grog shop. Whiskey in the West, and gin in the eastern states!" Still and all, Hartford could point with pride to the first permanent school established in the U.S.A. for the education of deaf mutes.

Opened in 1817, the Asylum for the Deaf and Dumb—happily "and Dumb" was soon dropped from the title—had already been the model for similar institutions organized in New York, Philadelphia, and the State of Kentucky. The founder of the school was Thomas Hopkins Gallaudet who, as a sickly youth, became interested in the problem of the hopelessly mute. He had gone to France to study advanced methods for their education and returned to Hartford to raise funds for a school. Though himself unafflicted, Gallaudet had married one of the first young ladies to graduate from his institution. "She is very handsome, with one of the most expressive faces in creation," said Mrs. Royall. She spent an evening in the Gallaudet home, "conversing with them by signs and by means of a slate. They have a very beautiful child two or three years old, who can talk fast enough. It was amusing to see her hold communication with her parents by signs."

Anne made a tour of the school with Laurent Clerc, "a brilliant deaf teacher" whom Gallaudet had met in Paris. The Frenchman had lost his hearing when he was five years old. He, too, had married a graduate of the Hartford asylum. Charging no tuition, the school accommodated about seventy students whose progress, Anne reported, was "beyond conception." [10]

Mrs. Royall's description of Hartford's "distinguished" author, Lydia H. H. Sigourney differs from one written by a visitor who followed her. Wrote Anne: "Mrs. S. is above common height of females, hair as black as a raven, the finest black eyes." The second interviewer described Mrs. Sigourney as "short" with "flaxen curls carefully arranged."

The color of her hair had played no part in making Lydia Sigourney the most sought after writer of the day. About the time Anne Royall saw her, Mrs. Sigourney was contributing to perhaps twenty periodicals and each year publishing a volume of memoirs,

prose, history or poetry. Her sentimental verses were in demand
for framing, while her solacing maxims monopolized the greeting
card field. She was so popular that when Godey started his *Lady's
Book* in 1830, he paid Mrs. Sigourney for the privilege of merely
using her name as an editor. And, though Edgar Allan Poe always
criticized her works in the *Southern Messenger*, he continuously
solicited her popular contributions. Mrs. Royall found Mrs.
Sigourney not with pen in hand, but "engaged in the domestic con-
cerns of her family." The "family" consisted of her husband's three
children by a former marriage. All Hartford believed Lydia Hunt-
ley had made a good match when she married Charles Sigourney,
hardware merchant. At the insistence of her fiancé, Lydia had
abandoned her literary career. But Sigourney was not nearly so well
off as people assumed. In fact, his hardware business was in a bad
way. His wife picked up her pen and rescued him from bankruptcy.

"She shrinks from the homage paid her virtue," wrote Mrs.
Royall, seemingly overcome by the Sigourney style. "She received
me with cordiality, her countenance animated with a pleasant smile,
her cheek bedecked with blushes." [11]

3

"Boston rises gradually from the water's edge on all sides, and
terminates upon a lofty eminence in the centre. This gives it a fine
display from whatever point it is approached."

Mrs. Royall approached by the "middle bridge" over the Charles
River and was soon "lost in narrow streets, with houses mountain
high on each side. I was no little afraid of being dashed to pieces."

She put up at the elegant Exchange Coffee-House, from which
she did not emerge until the following afternoon, when her fears
had subsided. On first inspection, Anne Royall did not like what
she saw. "The sidewalks are narrow, and badly paved, and the town
is badly lighted." Unlike New York or Philadelphia, merchants
"shut up their shops at dark," giving the town "a gloomy appearance."

After a week, the visitor changed her mind. The "intellect of
Boston men"; ladies whose minds had been "improved by travel-

ling"; the "Unitarians and Universalists, the most humane and benevolent sects I have met with"—all combined to "dislodge the prejudice I had imbibed from infancy against the city. In Philadelphia people scarcely asked me to sit down, but in Boston I have been caressed, and loaded with favors, though a total stranger without even an introduction."

She went through her usual sightseeing routine. "Boston has struck out a new path with respect to the poor. They have attached a large farm to the Alms House, which is worked by the paupers, and by this means they are of little or no charge to the city." At the State Prison, convicts were paid for their labor. As a result "the prison-yard is in one continual roar of hammers and chisels; at work even on jewelry, printing, and engraving. Many of these convicts clear their expenses, and have money to take with them when they leave the prison."

At the Navy Yard Mrs. Royall "walked through one of the battleships of 110 guns, and five decks—the most awful, dread-inspiring machine in the universe!" She strolled on the Common beneath "the celebrated elm planted by Mr. Quincy" and took off on a pilgrimage of historical discovery. In one quest she was most persistent.

It will be recollected that Doctor Franklin was a native of Boston. Almost the first object of my curiosity was to enquire the spot where his parents resided; but to my great surprise, his family was scarcely recollected! After much heart-rending researches, I discovered where the house had stood opposite Old South Church, in Milk Street. The place is now occupied by another building.

Faneuil Hall was "kept locked up," but the "clerk of the market" produced the key and left Anne "to contemplate in silence, this sacred cradle of American Liberty." On Sunday she worshiped at "old south meeting-house." Her eyes roamed over the "superb fittings." Before the Revolution the church had been the "most richly furnished meeting-house in the colonies, the cushions being covered with red damask." The British had "stripped it of everything, converting it into a stable!" Few landmarks of the Revolution went unvisited. Anne "gloried" in the period. This was the beginning of the U.S.A., when men had fought and died because they believed in the republic they strove to create. Rightly they had faith in the superior men who led them. What a shoestring war it was! How thrilling, after fifty years, to talk to survivors of "those trying scenes"! [12]

One survivor was the widow of John Hancock, the richest man in New England before the War for Independence. The once beautiful Dorothy Quincy lived in a poor little house, a far cry from the splendid mansion on Beacon Hill over which she had once presided. "It is a reproach to Massachusetts to suffer the widow of a man to whom is owed so much to remain in her present situation," scolded the Widow Royall.

The situation seemed not to weigh heavily on a lady notable for her gayety and entertaining prattle. "She is under common size, with a light handsome figure," Anne noted. "She has what is called a laughing eye, and is as sprightly as a girl of sixteen." After the decease of Mr. Hancock, Dorothy Quincy had married Captain James Scott, who sailed a merchantman in her first husband's fleet. "He died also. Mrs. Scott is a little turned seventy, though no one would suppose her to be more than sixty; her fine yellow hair clinging in ringlets over her forehead with scarcely a gray hair to be seen. She keeps the portrait of Mr. Hancock in her parlor, which she showed me with much seeming pleasure."

Mrs. Scott needed no prodding to tell of her adventures in the early morning hours preceding the Battle of Lexington. The British having put a price on his head, John Hancock fled to Concord where by day he presided over the Provincial Congress and at night slept in Lexington at the home of the Reverend Jonas Clark. Chaperoned by Hancock's Aunt Lydia, Miss Quincy was visiting her fiancé when Paul Revere banged on the door of the parsonage to warn "The British are coming!" John Hancock strapped on his ammunition belt. Samuel Adams, also wanted by the British, attempted to persuade the president that he was more useful alive guiding the affairs of the Congress than a dead hero. Hancock was determined to fight, but he reckoned without the womenfolk. Mrs. Scott boasted to Mrs. Royall that she and "Aunt Lydia kept Mr. Hancock from facing the British that day." The two ladies had "clung round his neck so tenaciously that the president was unable to extricate himself from them." Moments before the first shot ripped the air above Lexington Green, Hancock had rushed off with Adams to hide in Woburn. Dorothy Quincy followed in a carriage, bringing a fresh salmon for their breakfast. The fugitives never tasted it. The redcoats were hot on their trail. For two nights the rebel leaders hid out in a swamp while the enchanting Miss Quincy faced the pursuers with disarming innocence.[13]

4

Dorothy Quincy's forebears had settled and given their name to a village less than ten miles south of Boston. Most Quincy descendants were in a hurry to get out of their home town and enjoy the more exciting life of the Massachusetts capital. As one writer explained their urgency: "Quincy . . . was on the wrong side of Boston's narrow-gauge social tracks." Nevertheless, the town remained the constant home of the Adams family which, by 1825, having produced two Presidents and two Signers, appeared well on its way to becoming "the most distinguished Family in American History."

As John Quincy Adams had instructed her, Anne Royall went "to pay my respects to ex-President Adams." A servant took away her letter of introduction and returned to invite her "to walk upstairs." Mr. Adams, dressed in green camblet [probably camlet, a rich fabric made of camel's or goat's hair], his venerable locks perfectly white and uncovered, was sitting up, by the fire." Anne "flew toward him," realizing that he was about to rise from his chair to greet her. The ex-President talked about his age. He was "eighty-nine years and six months old, a monstrous time for one human being to support." Anne thought him "very feeble." Mr. Adams told her "he could walk about the room, and even downstairs; his teeth were entirely gone; and his eyesight very much impaired; he could just see the window, he said, and the weather vane that stood before it, but retained his hearing perfectly. His face did not bear the marks of age in proportion to his years, but his legs were evidently much reduced."

The second President of the United States wanted to hear about

Alabama—"its trade, navigation, and productions of the soil"—and
Mrs. Royall proceeded to tell him. They talked too about "his son
(the President) and Mrs. A," whom he had not seen since his election. Anne changed the subject when she saw a tear glitter in his
eye. After taking tea with John Adams, Mrs. Royall went on a
tour of the "mansion" in company with "Mrs. Smith, a niece," who
made her home with Mr. Adams.

The house, "a large frame building, built about thirty-six years
ago," faced south, commanding "a full view of Quincy." The first
floor consisted of "three apartments [rooms], with a gallery leading to the staircase. One of these is a common room, into which
strangers are first introduced." The second room was

a parlor, the furniture of which resembled a female Quaker's dress,
rich but simple. The chairs were filled with deep satin cushions; elegant
sofas and carpets completed the furniture. The third apartment contains
the family portraits. The portraits of Mr. Adams and his lady were
made when they were young; likewise his daughter and John Quincy
Adams whose likeness has very little resemblance to the original of
this day.[14]

A distant cousin of the ex-President who delighted Anne Royall
was Hannah Adams, notable as author of *A History of the Jews*.
She "was probably the first woman in America to make writing a
profession." Her principal work, *The Dictionary of Religion*, went
into four editions and was reprinted in England. An orphan and
poor relation, Hannah had supported herself during the Revolutionary War by making lace, an occupation that was not for a
woman of her aggressive nature. When she achieved recognition
as a historian, she boldly invaded the Atheneum, a strictly masculine
preserve, to pursue her research. Miss Adams was too well-known
to draw more than mild opposition. In fact, the directors blamed
themselves. They decided it was better "to lock her in, because it
was not polite to lock her out." Even so, commented Mrs. Royall,
"it required a certain sort of heroism for one of her sex to claim
the freedom of the library alcoves and to endure the raising of eye-
brows."

Hannah Adams was seventy years old when Anne met her. Though she had been carrying on a savage pamphlet war with the Reverend Jedediah Morse for ten years, accusing him of infringing on her school book, *A Summary History of New England,* the "leading trait in her countenance is innocence."

Miss Adams was declining in health [wrote Anne], though very cheerful and walks a good deal in fine weather; her hair is perfectly white, her features regular and very delicate; her eyes a dark hazel, very small, but soft and intelligent; her teeth are decayed and disfigure her very much. She lisps in speaking. Her countenance is animated, her face being constantly lighted up with a smile. She informed me that she was upwards of three years compiling her Jewish *History*, and that at one time she must have had as many books before her, as would have filled the room we were in.[15]

There were more Adamses. Mrs. Royall attended an "exhibition" at Harvard College where she watched the eighteen-year-old Charles Francis Adams, only son of President Adams, display his scholarly attainments on the eve of graduation. "He delivered a dissertation upon the moral effect of the stage, as highly tending to improve taste, and refine manners."

The "exhibition" brought out the intellectual elite. Mrs. Royall presented herself to the Reverend John Thornton Kirkland, Harvard president. She described him as "comely," but in her opinion Edward Everett "has a more classical look." Her preference for the recently resigned editor of the *North American Review*—he had been elected to Congress—was influenced by the oration Everett delivered the previous year before the Phi Beta Kappa Society when General Lafayette had been the honored guest. His subject was "Circumstances Favorable to the Progress of Literature in America." Everett held out the promise of a rosier future for the profession of letters, thereby brightening the outlook of aspiring writers in the U.S.A.

The Marquis de Lafayette, on the last lap of his lengthy stay in the U.S.A., returned for a second visit to Boston while Anne Royall was there. The occasion was the laying of the cornerstone of the

Bunker Hill monument. Mrs. Royall attended the ceremony and afterwards called on the "Nation's guest." Both had been deeply affected by the patriotic proceedings. Later Anne told a newspaper-man that Lafayette had "dropped a tear upon a rose he presented me and which I have preserved ever since." [16]

5

"I have dealt so much with prodigies of late, that my poor stock of language is exhausted." Mrs. Royall's benefit money was also exhausted. Kindly subscribers to the *Sketches*, taking note of the worn clothing, began to tuck more than the price of a book into her pocket. One benefactor was appropriately named Miss Joy. Another was the Reverend Jared Sparks, lately arrived in Boston from a Unitarian pastorate in Baltimore, to replace Edward Everett on the *North American Review*. The former minister was "as meek as Moses." He became interested in the *Sketches* and freely gave Anne Royall editorial advice, thereby gaining her enduring friendship. She nearly came to blows with "a saucy editor [Frederic S. Hill, editor of the *Lyceum* of Boston], a young man of wealth who merely writes for the amusement it affords him. He had the presumption to criticise the Rev. Sparks." Her new-found friend "laughed" at the tale of her heated defense.

"No doubt I deserved it," said Sparks.[17]

The lesson in turning the other cheek was lost on Anne Royall. With equal fire she defended the editor of the *Monthly Western Review*, after a Boston newspaper had "published a falsehood upon my friend the Rev. Timothy Flint." She went to the newspaper office to demand a retraction.

" 'Where is the editor?' I asked.

" 'I am the editor,' said a great awkward clown.

" 'What you! Such a beef-headed fellow as you editor of a paper!' saying this I turned around and ran downstairs."

The editor published an account of the visit reporting that "after giving us a *royal* look of contempt, and threatening to cow-skin our apprentices, she proceeded downstairs with the agility of a cat." Anne agreed "the last is probably true." [18]

Again in funds, Mrs. Royall made a side trip to Salem. She found the town lovely and peaceful, showing no scars from its witch-craft past. Passing into limbo as well were memories of the days when square-rigged merchantmen jammed the harbor. Young men, who in bygone days would have sailed the seven seas, now worked in shoe factories which hummed day and night to catch up on orders for a Salem innovation. Shoes were no longer cut to be worn on either foot, but were specifically shaped to fit the right foot and the left foot.

From Boston Mrs. Royall traveled by stage to Providence, Rhode Island, where she boarded the night boat for New York. "This was the first time I ever was at sea. I slunk into my berth sick enough." A book of Byron's poetry which she borrowed from the ship's library was no antidote for her discomfort. Turning the leaves at random, she read:

"Everything now must pass through the fiery ordeal of criticism, compared with which, walking on red-hot plowshares would be recreation. A critic, like a tiger, attacks all whom he can master, and kills for the dear delight of butcherings."

"This made me quake for my *Sketches*," wrote Anne.[19]

The situation was worse than she could have imagined. Arrived in New York, Mrs. Royall learned that Charles Wiley, the printer, was dying. Meanwhile, his business was suspended. She spent the summer of 1826 tramping the hot streets in search of another printer. Betimes she wrote and edited. In the last endeavor she had a windfall. James Gordon Bennett, the young reporter on the *National Advocate* of whom she earlier had made a friend, helped her "in correcting my words for the press." Bennett particularly liked her reporting of the interview with ex-President Adams and the unembroidered account of a visit to the Misses Byles, daughters of the "celebrated Mather Byles, a great poet, a great tory, a great clergyman and a great wit." [20]

Despite his toryism, the Congregational minister had been gen-erally liked by Boston. During the war, after dismissal by his church, a court had ordered him banished from the Colony, but the sentence was never carried out. As Byles wryly sketched his punish-ment: "I have been guarded, re-guarded, and disregarded."

At the time of the father's trial, his two daughters, Mary and Catherine, were in their early twenties. While redcoats occupied Boston, the young ladies had been the recipients of "flattering attentions from Lord Howe and Earl Percy." The latter had once ordered the regimental band to serenade them. When Anne Royall found the sisters they were in their seventies. Staunch loyalists, they had lived all the years since in their father's house shut away from the republican world they disdained. Only on Sundays did these "withered roses of another age" emerge from their retreat "closely veiled" to attend Trinity Church. Survivors of their generation remembered their history, but like their father, the Misses Byles were disregarded by modern Boston.

The ever-curious Anne Royall had wondered about the "mouldering mansion" that stood at the corner of Tremont and Nassau Streets, "enclosed by a decayed wooden paling." From "the looks of the old rotten step at the door, the grass growing through it, the silence—I imagined it could be no other than a deserted house." She opened the sagging gate and knocked on the door. "An elderly female thin visaged and wrinkled" bade her enter. (She was Mary Byles; Catherine, the younger sister, was ill in bed.) Miss Byles "seemed averse to conversation and appeared to wish me away." Anne was not invited to sit in the "handsome chair, on which was carved a royal crown." The chair, brought from England by a grandfather, was a Byles treasure. The visitor persisted and "drew a few sentences" from Miss Mary.

She was a warm lover of the British government. She said the Americans had her father, herself and sister up, in the time of the Revolutionary War, treated them ill, just because her father prayed for the king. But she said they were very kind to her and her sister now, though she complained bitterly against somebody who had knocked the bark off one of their trees; it was poor spite, she said.

When she left the house which had "looked something better inside, though poverty and neglect marked it throughout," Anne inspected the tree. "I saw a few inches of the bark rubbed off, which was doubtless an accident." [21]

6

Half of September had passed and still the *Sketches* had no publisher. Anne kept going in New York on slim contributions from the Masons who had already treated her handsomely. One day she heard about a publisher in New Haven, Connecticut. Thither she proceeded by stage. "I was once more amongst strangers, without one cent of money, and without a single change of raiment."

She arrived at a bad time. "New Haven [population 10,000] had just been thrown into deep distress by the failure of the Eagle Bank, in which calamity the rich and poor alike were involved." Seemingly all the printers and publishers of the town were likewise involved for their business was at a standstill. Mrs. Royall was briefly sheltered by Morse's Tavern, at the corner of Church and Crown Streets—"the best house of public entertainment in the city." A. Morse, the proprietor, may have been a Mason. The year before he had been host to Lafayette. Anne blurted out that she could not pay. Mr. Morse said she was "welcome to stay."

Eventually she found "asylum" with the hospitable Widow Abigail Bishop. "I was so destitute I was unable to purchase a dress, sufficiently decent, to appear in company." A Massachusetts lady who boarded with Mrs. Bishop took up a collection.[22]

Though the town was commercially dead as a result of the bank failure, Anne Royall continued through the winter her quest for a publisher. Loquaciously and boastfully, she told everyone she met about her book. Talking, soliciting, or energetically interviewing professors connected with the college, and prominent citizens, she made friends and enemies. David Daggett, "a man of brilliant parts" destined in a few years to occupy the office of mayor, "with contempt" told her "you are too troublesome in this town. Go where you came from." Anne published the last word:

"Mr. D. is tall and stout and wears powder in his hair. His eye has the color and fierceness of a rattlesnake; his complexion is a dirty yellow. I enquired of those acquainted with him the cause; they said 'it was because he ate so many pumpkins.' "[23]

The interview with Noah Webster, himself in the throes of rais-

ing funds to print the first *American Dictionary* (the edition was a
flop financially), also turned out badly. Mrs. Royall's version:

I knocked at the door with more than common enthusiasm; for,
though we backwoods folks are not learned ourselves, we have a warm
liking for learned people. In a few minutes, a low chubby man with a
haughty air stepped into the room; his face was round and red and by
no means literary looking. He was dressed in black broadcloth, in
dandy style. He eyed me with ineffable scorn and scarcely deigned to
speak at all. I am sorry for his sake I ever saw the man, as it gave me
infinite pain to rescind an opinion I had long entertained of him.

What went wrong? A Webster biographer suggests that "Mrs.
Royall had touched off one of Webster's prejudices, and he chose
dignified silence as the best defensive weapon." Webster's prejudices
made him a sitting duck for Anne Royall. His biographer continues: "A Quaker-like purity of mind, and an ambition to model
his life on those of the grave biblical elders, gave Webster a strait-
laced and dour countenance. . . . His severity rose from unrelaxed
principles of noble thought and action. He winced at vulgarity
and obscenity as if he had been lashed with a blacksnake whip."
Webster, Mrs. Royall wrote Jared Sparks, "is just the pompous
blockhead I have described him." Of all the literary men encountered in New Haven, she maintained he was the "most dangerous
because most deep." She distrusted "that deep designing puritanical
conscience who has taken upon himself the responsibility of the
mighty Dictionary." [24]
From a different mold came the Reverend Jedediah Morse.

The father of American geography is a lively and genteel man, not
only polite, but sociable and condescending. Mr. M. is under six feet
in height, remarkably slender and straight. He appears a little turned
seventy. His hair is plentiful, parted from the crown to the forehead,
and drops off on each side; it is gray but not perfectly white. His head
is remarkably small, rather more than common. Our country increases
so fast that the old gentleman hardly gets one geography out before
it is out of date, and he has to commence anew.

SKETCHES

OF

HISTORY, LIFE, AND MANNERS,

IN THE

UNITED STATES.

BY A TRAVELLER.

Royall

NEW-HAVEN:
PRINTED FOR THE AUTHOR.

1826.

Title page of Anne Royall's first travel book. *Library of Congress*

The Young Ladies' Academy at the Convent of the Visitation, Georgetown, D.C., the only illustration in any of Anne Royall's travel books. *Library of Congress*

The Reverend Mr. Morse was "always so pleasant and communicative," that Anne Royall visited him frequently during the long winter when she needed cheering up. Unlike Noah Webster, Morse "did not read his Bible upside down." [25]

The turning point came at the end of winter, when she learned that Governor Oliver Wolcott was coming to New Haven. Her landlady took up a collection among the boarders to buy cloth for a new dress. "Governor Wolcott furnished me with a letter (may heaven reward him for his deed), wherein everything was said that might awaken sympathy or inspire respect." The letter of the popular executive, reelected each term since 1817, opened doors. It brought her to the attention of Thomas Green Woodward who, with John B. Carrington, was the proprietor of the *Connecticut Herald*. Mr. Woodward agreed to take a chance and print the *Sketches* on credit. "Even Yale College nobly stept forward," with a contribution which, Anne told Jared Sparks, "aided her" to publish the hapless volume. Probably Yale's gift paid the bindery bill of Durrie & Peck. In May Anne Royall held in her hands the first copies of *Sketches of History, Life, and Manners in the United States*. What a tale of adventure, suffering and sacrifice it might have told! But it didn't. The hardships seeped through later books, when she could afford to give way to bitter memories. At any rate, she wrote Jared Sparks, "the whole is stamped with truth."

Mr. Woodward, she decided, was another Mr. Wiley. "He nobly gave me up my books, and though an entire stranger to him, trusted to my honor for the payment." Anne loaded all she could carry in a market basket and boarded the stage for New York. She arranged with Durrie & Peck to ship her more books, not only to New York, but to Albany, Hartford, Boston and other stops where she had subscribers. She would see to the publicity in towns where she delivered them. This book *had* to bring her fame. She owed a lot of money.[26]

CHAPTER IX

THE FIERY ORDEAL

1

After producing a book, a lady author customarily sat quietly and awaited "discovery." Anne Royall was not content to wait; she foresaw the hazard of being passed over. She had made a concession to custom when she permitted authorship of *The Sketches* to be credited to A Traveller. Though her name did not appear on the title page, still she wanted everyone to know this was her book, the book that she had doggedly promoted and written.

Minutes after arriving in New York, she hooked a basket of books onto her arm and sailed out to exhibit her triumph to her good friends at the *National Advocate*. Major Noah greeted Anne with verbose gallantry. He tapped her basket, saying it was the "rival of the golden casket" in which Alexander the Great had guarded Aristotle's edition of Homer's *Iliad*. He called her the "Mrs. Walter Scott of America," a title which other newspaper editors took up and worked to death. Next day he wrote about *The Sketches* in his newspaper. But he stuck to custom. The "work," said the *Advocate*, was "written by an intelligent lady from the western country." Noah's star reporter Bennett thought so well of the interview with ex-President Adams that he suggested reprinting the whole in the *Advocate*. Anne was grateful for the attention. "Not wishing to take up so much of his paper for free, I sent Noah five dollars, but he returned it." [1]

Major Mordecai Manuel Noah, by J. W. Jarvis, now in the collection of Congregation Shearath Israel, New York. *Frick Art Reference Library*

Spirits buoyed by praise, A Traveller climbed the stairs to the
office of Theodore Dwight, publisher of the *New York Daily Advertiser,* the most influential newspaper in the state. The *Advertiser's*
prestige was such that out-of-town editors, of the same conservative
disposition, held off committing themselves on issues of the day
until they had read what Mr. Dwight had to say. An ultra-Feder-
alist—Dwight had been secretary of the Hartford Convention—the
publisher and Anne Royall were not likely to have much in common, except antipathy. Easy camaraderie in a female was as distaste-
ful to Theodore Dwight as the flamboyant journalism of Mordecai
M. Noah. Anne swaggered into his office and handed him a copy
of her book. Dwight's greeting was chilling and the call was short.
After two weeks the *Advertiser,* carefully veiling the name of the
lady author, noticed *The Sketches.*

A Book of Travels in the United States has lately appeared from the
pen of a lady, a native of Arkansas. . . . The book we have not seen,
and know nothing of its merits. An extract published in some of the
papers, narrating the circumstances of a visit to Mr. Adams, contains
nothing remarkable. The style is easy, and the writer is said to be frank
and well educated. It is new to us to be criticized by travellers from
that point of the compass.[2]

Mrs. Royall sold few copies of *The Sketches* in New York above
those already subscribed for. Disappointment and fear gripped her.
Snatching up her pen she angrily began a second travel volume,
calling it *The Black Book* because, she explained, it would be about
the "black deeds of evil doers." New York was told off in the first
somber entry: "The ladies of New York do *not* read. A New York
lady will not look at a book, unless it has a red cover." [3]

Anne bustled out of the city accompanied by boxes of books to
deliver in New England. To avoid seasickness, she took the stage to
Boston—fifty hours, fare ten dollars, as against twenty-four hours
by steamboat, fare five dollars.

Boston reviews were enthusiastic and A Traveller lost her anonymity. Said the *Boston Commercial Gazette:*

Here is a first view of everything—politics, literature, history,
biography, rivers, mountains, men, women and children. . . . A little

incident which happened to herself, makes in her pages as great a figure as an epoch in history, not from egotism, but from a wish to tell the whole truth. . . . She marches on speaking her mind freely, and *unpacking her heart* in words of censure or praise, as she feels. Sometimes she lets fall more truths than the interested reader would wish to hear, and at other times overwhelms her friends with flattery more appalling. At any rate, hit or miss, the sentiments she gives are undoubtedly her own, nor will it be denied that she has given some very good outlines of character.[4]

The *Columbian Centinel*, owned and edited by a Federalist, also praised the author. "She frequently notices *minutiae* which most travellers do not think worth their attention. . . . Although she has exhibited some bitterness of remark on certain of our male characters, she has almost invariably done justice to our females, and the praise bestowed will be estimated as the more valuable, coming from the pen of a lady." [5]

Orders poured in faster than Durrie & Peck could bind *The Sketches*. "In Boston, nearly the whole of the Edition was bought up." Anne Royall briefly savored success and took off westward to continue deliveries. Though she had heaped compliments on the inhabitants and handsome landmarks of Worcester, the editor of the *National Aegis* devoted two columns to denouncing *The Sketches*, out-sized space for a book review in a newspaper of only four pages. "It is so full of thorough-going absurdities . . . that it must rank with the ingenious fictions of English tourists." A few days afterward the same newspaper came out with two more columns taking to task the editor of the *Essex Register* of Salem. The *Register* editor had accused the Worcester journal of "rudeness" toward the "itinerant lady." The Worcester editor's retort jabbed at an old wound. Salem had been "bewitched by the flattery spread" by Mrs. Royall.[6]

No flattery coated the interview which originally had been Anne's purpose in stopping at Worcester. She wanted to meet Doctor Aaron Bancroft, the Unitarian minister who some years back had gained fame as leader of the schism which ripped the Unitarian Church apart. Despite a slight stroke, recently suffered, the seventy-year-old Bancroft "walks about and converses with the facility of youth," Mrs. Royall reported. She found him charming, intelligent and mannerly. "The Doctor lives in affluence, amidst an amiable family, like himself possessed of all the affability and ease common to people of the best society." The amiable family consisted of thirteen offspring. George, the future historian, was not present. He had gone off to his first teaching job at a boys' school in Northampton.

Still, Worcester bought *The Sketches,* as did Springfield, where notices were equally as scathing. The *Hampden Journal:*

We should not feel inclined to place this woman's name (or rather the title of her book) in any conspicuous place in our paper, for any other purpose than to warn our readers against a gross imposition; and even this object would not perhaps justify us, if respectable papers had not seen fit to speak commendably of Mrs. R.'s production. . . . The printer has wisely withheld his name from the title page; unwilling probably to share in the disgrace which would fall harmlessly upon the head of a poor, crazy vagrant. . . . We do assure them [the readers] they would render a more substantial service to the community by aiding to commit the wandering author to a Home of Correction, than by purchasing the book and thus directly assisting to extend her impositions still further.[7]

2

The U.S.A. was building up to one of its recurrent cycles of violent intolerance. Hatred would focus chiefly on the Freemasons who, since the time of Benjamin Franklin and George Washington, had been held in high esteem in the republic. No one can say precisely how the whispers began, but suddenly people were saying Masonry was "a select society which tended to bring within its ranks many of the wealthy, educated and influential men." In other words a rich man's club. Suspicions were soon weighing the nature of Masonry's secret rituals. Perhaps, in secret, the brotherhood was plotting the overthrow of the government; perhaps the rituals were orgies.[8]

The evangelical churches were more responsible than any single group for the flow of attacks on Masonry. The churches looked upon the lodges as competitors who stood in their way of gaining complete control over the minds and souls of masculine adherents.

As early as 1821, a decade before Anti-Masonry became a political movement, bigwigs of the Presbyterian church meeting at Pittsburgh, "condemned the Masonic institution as unfit for christians," and ordered ministers and laymen to resign from the organization. Two years later the Methodist Conference took a similar stand. In New England, the Congregationalists, beset by more and more trespassers in the religious field, "attacked at one and the same time the Unitarians, the Universalists, and the Masons." Even the modest Dutch Reformed Church felt called upon to take a stand. "We find the religion of the Association [Freemasons] to be a mixture of Paganism and Mohammedanism, with the corruption of Judaism and Christianity. . . . We also find it . . . guilty of administering illegal, profane and horrible oaths." So effective was the churches' denunciation that it came near to wrecking the brotherhood. Masonic membership in New York State, for instance, dwindled from 20,000 to 3,000. In Vermont "every lodge surrendered its charter or became dormant." [9]

The persistent harping, by the evangelical churches, on the sins of Masonry, was all part of a long-range plan leading to a great religious revival whose purpose was to establish the Protestant oligarchy as a mighty political force in the life of the nation. The first step toward putting this plan to work was to persuade the denominations "to forget their sectarian differences and join their scattered forces in a nationwide association." The first fruit of unity had been the American Bible Society, organized in 1816. Then came the powerful American Sunday School Union in 1824; and finally, in 1825, the American Tract Society. The religious press expected a great deal from the Society. "The advantages which may be expected from the distribution of religious tracts are indeed so many and so great. . . . It is a *cheap way* of diffusing the knowledge of religion." [10]

The campaign against the Masons had not approached its ultimate extreme when Anne Royall got herself embroiled by acknowledging her gratitude to the brotherhood for financial help and other favors while she was writing *The Sketches*. Reviews of her travel book in New England, outside of Boston, were not reviews *per se*, but an extension of the evangelical downgrading of Masonry. The

Salem editor who defended Anne was Warwick Palfrey, junior, and the columns of his newspaper, solid with announcements of lodge meetings, leave no doubt of the editor's dedication to Freemasonry. The Worcester newspaper printed no such announcements and from this we may assume it was against the brotherhood. Anne Royall further offended by telling of the Catholic aid she had received. Protestants despised Catholics and the Catholic Church had no love for Masonry, but it kept clear of the hate campaign to ruin the brotherhood.

Where Protestants were concerned, Anne Royall never expressed herself without bias. In *The Sketches* she had been especially careful to omit her religious views. Not until a later travel book did she tell about her interview with Doctor Ely of Philadelphia. By that time the churches' war on Masonry was in full swing. The brigades had taken to the field and were hacking and chopping and undermining everywhere. Anne Royall seldom climbed into a stagecoach without finding among the passengers several missionaries bound for their labors in the vineyard of the Lord. The sight of them annoyed her and she delivered many face-to-face sermons critical of their missions. These encounters she did not mention in *The Sketches*. And certainly she did not write a word then about all the tracts she tossed out of tavern windows and public conveyances. Reports of her antichurch conduct naturally got back to headquarters. Clearly she was not a friend, but a dangerous opponent, as long as she held a pen. The churches retaliated by belittling her and her books, in the hope of alienating readers.

The editor of the *Hampden Journal* was Frederick Adolphus Packard, very much involved in activities of the Sunday School Union. A couple of years hence he would resign from the Springfield newspaper to become editorial secretary of the Union. "During his period of editorship more than 2,000 books passed through his hands. Between forty and fifty of these were written by him." At one time Packard prepared a "Select Library" of some 120 volumes for use in public schools. Horace Mann, secretary of the Massachusetts Board of Education, found the books "patently sectarian" and refused to permit their introduction into schools under his jurisdiction. "As a result, Packard carried on for years in magazines and newspapers a persistent attack on Mann and the Board." There was no reason to expect Mr. Packard to say a kind word for *The Sketches*.[11]

3

Anne Royall rode into Albany unaware of all the to-do her travel volume had stirred up in Massachusetts. She did not know as much about what was going on behind the scenes as we have already told the reader, though she had seen enough to suspect that the evangelical churches were busy with some scheme of which she was sure not to approve. When the reviews, good and bad, caught up with her, she probably thought only of how helpful the publicity should be. "I wish to write books people will read," she said. "Nothing like hard cutting and spice to make books and papers go down, and truth most of any." [12]

Developments in the New York State capital were, to say the least, spicy. She had offended the Bucktails, the political party opposed to DeWitt Clinton, because she had not interviewed the Bucktail leader, Martin Van Buren. Resentful Bucktails had boycotted *The Sketches*. Anne made haste to call on Senator Van Buren. The interview began on an odd note. Who, asked Anne, are the Bucktails?

With the greatest good humor, Mr. Van Buren explained their political tenets and the cause of their dislike of Clinton. The Bucktails are the old republican party, and are called Bucktails from the Tammany Society. The Society, on certain days, such as anniversaries, wear Bucktails in their hats. From the word *old*, I asked if there were any *new* republicans. I thought Mr. Van Buren seemed at a loss, and at length he said that those who opposed the Bucktails, were generally esteemed Federalists (meaning Clintonians).

Anne accepted the politician's statement with a grain of salt. "Amongst the bucktails," she observed, "are to be found federalists as well as republicans, and the same [is true] of the other [Clin-

Phila^a oct^r 5th 1822

Mr Little

Su sir

10 Copies of the 2d vol Black book — Be
so kind advertise & sell for
$2.. pr copy (if any of the 1st be left)
or $1.. pr volume for either as
I wish to sell off fast — I will
send a few more in a few days
— you will see by a note at
the end of the 2^d vol there is a 3^d
volume forth coming & perhaps
you may find yourself in it for
not letting me know the result
of your success

very respectfully

Anne Royall

Mr Little
Albany bookseller

Letter from Anne Royall to her Albany, N.Y., bookseller, W. C. Little.
Library of Congress

ton's] party. In fact, if I were to judge by what I saw, I would say that many of them do not know what they are."

She had a point. A year later Clinton and Van Buren shook hands and Clinton's party helped to return Van Buren to the Senate. That brought the senator into the camp of General Jackson, whose candidacy he had spurned in the 1824 election.

Back to the interview. "Why should any man in New-York dislike DeWitt Clinton?" Mrs. Royall asked the leader of the Bucktails. "He has proved himself the greatest friend of the State."

The senator took time to duck the question. "Clinton is a man of talent," he said finally.[13]

4

In July's heat, seated in one of "E. Young's new red coaches, with spring seats," Anne Royall joined the crowd bound for Saratoga Springs. The short trip was not pleasant. The passengers were "three young fops, and one, two or three cooks and chambermaids, awkward dowdies dressed in silks." An annoyance to everybody was the "deranged missionary, his arms tied behind his back. The gentleman who attended him said he was a native of Vermont, to which place he was then conveying him to his aged mother. What a sight for a mother!"

Now that she had learned that the churches were fighting her as well as the Masons, there was no need to spare feelings in *Black Book*, I. Neither did she spare Saratoga Springs.

When we began to draw near the Springs, our carriages were beset with a host of boys and girls. Some would have a few blackberries in their hands, others wild flowers. They would run by the side of the stage, hold them up to the passengers, and cry out "give me one cent."

But these troops are nothing to those who await your arrival at the Springs. Ten or a dozen waiters were in readiness, at every public house. The moment the stages stop, two or three fly to the door of the carriage, and scarcely take time to turn the bolt, in their eagerness to get the passengers out; the residue fly to the trunks behind, and both passengers and trunks are literally torn from the coach. I put up with my friend Palmer, my old landlord at Albany, who keeps

Montgomery Hall, boarding five dollars per week, though boarding may be had for two dollars in the village. The three great Hotels, viz: Congress Hall, United States Hotel and the Pavilion, have ten dollars! No wonder they have few boarders; it is robbery. The cooking is shocking; and the flies, in swarms, covered every dish.

The Society of these springs is very different from that of the Springs of Virginia. There the people come in their own carriages, bring their own servants, come early and stay late, usually from six to eight weeks. These are people of the first respectability. But at Saratoga they come in pairs, in chaises, and bring crackers and cheese in little baskets.

Next in number are a host of thorough going cocknies, from the cities. These generally accompany females of their *own* kidney, between whom there appears to be a very pleasant understanding. Now and then a sturdy Dutch farmer and his wife come in their own chaise, walk down to Congress spring, take a drink, walk back, take tea, say nothing, go out after tea, walk up the main street to the Pavilion, return to the tavern and look out through the window.

I saw a few ladies and gentlemen from Boston and New-York. The Boston ladies were clad in the graces, the New York ladies were loaded with silk and laces (one of them asked what state Alabama was in).

It is amusing enough to observe how the Editor of the newspaper puffs the Springs in the season. "One thousand visitors are at Saratoga, and many more expected." The thousand dwindle to 60 or 70 of all sorts and sizes.

Anne Royall received two "puffs" herself from the *Saratoga Sentinel*. G. M. Davison, the editor, reprinted the *Columbian Centinel* review and then a week later published his comments. He predicted that the "original remarks on 'life and manners' give to the book an interest which can hardly fail of securing to it a favorable reception." [14]

Though Mrs. Royall accused the *Sentinel* of exaggerating the number of visitors, the Springs was more popular than usual that summer due to the presence of Joseph Bonaparte, ex-King of Spain and Naples. In exile, Joseph had dutifully followed the instructions of his illustrious brother to take up residence "somewhere between Philadelphia and New York, so that news from the old world could reach him."

Joseph had settled on an estate at Bordentown, New Jersey, but, now that Napoleon was dead, he wished to locate somewhere more to his liking. He had found what he wanted at Saratoga Springs and so came to dicker over price.

The Count de Survilliers, as Joseph chose to be known, and his retinue took rooms at the United States Hotel, the newest hostelry in town. When she heard, Anne Royall made a beeline for the resplendent hotel, determined that *The Sketches* should ride to further acclaim on the satin coattails of royalty. She gave her card, fresh token of success, to the landlord and "desired him to hand it to the count." She waited a long time before de Survilliers, attended by his nephew Prince Achille Murat, entered the parlor. The ex-king, "stout and muscular," was worth waiting for. He paid Mrs. Royall five dollars for a copy of *The Sketches*, though he neither read nor spoke English. The extravagance, however, was not likely to impoverish him. Joseph had carried into exile a fortune estimated at $2,000,000.

Prince Murat, one-time heir to the throne of Naples, was "most amiable," and spoke English like a native. He should have; he was postmaster at Tallahassee, Florida, where he had entered into the life of the community, seemingly without nostalgia for the good old days. Murat was also writing a book about the American scene. His description of the humdrum routine of the "elegant" visitors to Saratoga Springs echoes Mrs. Royall's complaints.

People rise early, go and drink . . . of the water of the fountain; return to breakfast in common; the papas and mamas are ready to die with *ennui* all the day; the young ladies play music, the young gentlemen make love to them; from time to time some excursion is made in the neighborhood; in the evening comes dancing. . . . It is at Saratoga that the lovers meet, who parted, in the winter, at Washington, and it is at Washington they promise to be found again on quitting Saratoga: these places of mutual resort, and, more than all, the public and sociable manners in which people live at the waters, present every facility of augmenting the circle of acquaintance. In short, an American has friends in every town in the Union, who wherever he may be going, ensures him, as well as those whom he may recommend, a hospitable reception.[15]

5

Anne Royall returned to Albany to begin a tour to Niagara Falls, traveling part way by the Erie Canal, which had been in operation less than a year. She did not begin her journey at Troy, the eastern terminal of the canal, but cautiously took off from Schenectady, skipping the concentration within fifteen miles of twenty-seven locks necessary to bring the canal to the level of the Hudson River. The locks scared passengers off. The day before Anne's departure a woman had drowned in one of the locks. "She was sitting in the bow of the boat in a chair reading, and the boat as it went in the lock, struck against the side and pitched her forward into the water."

[The packet was] very pleasant, fitted up inside like a steamboat, with dining room, and separate rooms for gentlemen and ladies. The fare including board is four cents per mile; without board, three cents. The freight boats take passengers for one cent and a half per mile, same price of freight. The distance to Utica is seventy-nine miles which the packet ran in twenty-four hours, drawn by three stout horses, relieved every ten miles by fresh horses and a fresh driver.

Before departing Schenectady Anne had engaged in an ominous conversation with the husband of a friend.

"Have you heard of my travels?" she inquired eagerly.

"Yes," replied the man. "I heard it would do to light pipes with." [16]

After covering less than half the length of the canal, Anne left the packet at Utica and rode the stage overland to Buffalo. A bad choice. She had plumped herself down in a hotbed of anti-Masonry where already sputtered "the spark that set off the powder magazine" known as the Morgan Affair. William Morgan, a brick-and-stone mason residing in Batavia, had been initiated into Masonry a year earlier and in the current year had become the center of attention for both Masons and Antis, when he signed a contract with David C. Miller, publisher of the Batavia *Republican Advocate* to write a book revealing the secrets of Masonry. About the time Mrs.

Royall arrived in Utica, the community heard that Morgan had registered by copyright the title of his volume as *Illustrations of Masonry.*

The coming of Mrs. Royall poured no oil on the disturbed scene. Her reputation as pro-Mason had preceded her and, with success behind her, she spoke out loudly and boldly against whatever displeased her. Her appearances on Utica streets were marked by bitter arguments on religion and on Masonry. She could out-talk anyone and she did so, in strong language. The *Utica Intelligencer* announced her visit by reprinting the unfavorable review which had appeared in Theodore Dwight's *New York Commercial Advertiser.* This was followed by reprint of a second article from the pen of Mr. Dwight who had been prodded into defending himself against Mrs. Royall's personal abuse. The incident had occurred at Ballston Spa, whither Anne made a short excursion from Saratoga Springs. Unwittingly she put up at the same boarding house where Dwight had installed himself and family. When everyone else was showering attention on the lady author, the New York editor pointedly ignored her. Moreover, he was at pains not to present her to his wife. The snub put Anne right back in the Anderson kitchen. In a fury she repaid the editor with a battery of insult. At every meal while Dwight said grace Anne muttered complaints, such as "our meals grow cold under these prayers of hypocrisy." The diners tittered. She called attention to the "venom in his eye" or to the "austere countenance heavily charged with puritanical frigidness." Above a whisper she directed attention to his "haggard and wrinkled wife; she looks much the oldest."

Mr. Dwight kept silent. Privately he composed a vengeful piece for his newspaper.

A book has been recently published by a female who calls her name Royall and who professes to be the widow of a Revolutionary officer, in which the author gives pretended sketches of the country, manners of the inhabitants, with biographical notices &c., and she is now travelling about from place to place, collecting materials for a second volume. A more contemptible book was never palmed upon any community. The author possesses no one quality of a book maker, unless it be confidence, of which she has a competent share. Her object is extremely mischievous; and nothing prevents her from accomplishing it but want of capacity and credit. She goes into families without the least ceremony, and if her reception is not such as suits her, she will threaten the master or mistress with exposure in her book. She has lately been at the Springs, and intends to proceed from thence to the western parts of the state. Many very respectable persons are grossly abused in her first volume, apparently for the sole reason they did not treat her with as much attention as she thought proper to demand; and it is probable many others will meet with the same fate in her second.

William Leete Stone, editor of the *New York Commercial Advertiser*, reprinted Dwight's paragraphs, with the addition of his opinions: "She is without exception, the most impudent and persevering *bore* that we ever saw in the shape of a woman and she ought to be discountenanced universally. . . . Search the wide world round, and the equal of Mrs. Royall cannot be found. She is herself her only parallel—and that is some consolation."

The *Utica Intelligencer* reproduced both the Dwight and the Stone comments adding, that since "the person mentioned has recently taken up her abode in this village, with the intention of remaining several weeks, we think it proper that our citizens should know something of her character before they are called upon for contributions."

Such was the publicity that welcomed Anne Royall to Utica. It was scarcely designed to make her a popular guest. The cycle was complete when Stone's *Commercial Advertiser* reprinted the remarks of the *Utica Intelligencer!* At this heated stage, Utica would have damned anyone who displayed a trace of affection for Masonry. People avoided Mrs. Royall and declined to buy her books. At King's Tavern, where she stopped, the landlord borrowed a copy of *The Sketches.* The book was returned "entirely spoiled. On almost every page, some blackguard sentence was written. I am told they [tavernkeepers] are mostly *bucktails;* let them be bucktails, or cowtails, the nether end of any animal fits well." [17]

Anne Royall retreated from Utica. On a Friday afternoon at

five o'clock she boarded the stage for Buffalo and arrived on Sunday at 1 P.M.—"upwards of two hundred miles without a stopover." The opening of the Erie Canal had transformed the western limit of the water route into "a flourishing village, with many fine brick buildings and two thousand inhabitants who do not read."

Anne did not tarry in Buffalo. Loading her trunkful of books onto a steamboat, she sailed up the Niagara River to the falls. The trip was "sublime," as were the falls. With a guide she went down "by circular stairs to the margin of the river. This is a fool-hardy undertaking, dangerous and difficult, and yields neither pleasure nor information. The rock on which you pass under the falls is slippery from the number of eels which cover it."

Four miles distant was the residence of Sir Peregrine Maitland, "Governor of Upper Canada and Lieut. Governor of all Canada." Mrs. Royall hired a carriage and with trunk presented herself at the door of the governor. Sir Peregrine received her "with great courtesy," bought several books and served her wine. A veteran of Waterloo, the governor confided that "his duties were great and engrossed the whole of his time." His nineteen-year-old son was his aide. "I was charmed with the son—the humility and profound respect which marked his deportment to his father. Sir Peregrine sent a servant to carry the trunk to the stage stop." [18]

The brief visit to Canada was a pleasant interlude in a harassing tour. The return journey eastward through New York was no picnic. Arriving in Rochester, Anne discovered that the *Monroe Republican* had published Mr. Dwight's commentary and so scotched her sales. Toward the end of August Mr. Stone informed readers of the *New York Commercial Advertiser* that "the country papers make frequent mention of this travelling virago." In Johnstown, "one gentleman to whom she applied for a subscription, speaking his mind rather freely to her, she became enraged, and challenged him to mortal combat with pistols." While she was not "popular," Mr. Stone reported, with evident sadness, "still there are those who give her letters, take her into their house, buy her books, and thus contribute to forward her impositions, and increase her audacity." [19]

Stone's continued denunciation puzzled Anne. On her first trip to New York, the editor had shown friendship. "Never will I forget, when meeting him by accident one day in Mr. Carter's office, he took his pen in hand and said, 'Come, gentlemen, let us patronize this lady.' Such an act at any time, would be generous, but at that time, it was godlike." The explanation probably lay in the fact that earlier Stone had been a "high Mason." Since the start of anti-Masonry, he had resigned from the fraternity.

So, with the tide running against her, Anne sat back in the eastward bound stage and admired the landscape. "The whole of New-York for beauty and scenery almost turns one's head." Or she jotted down bits of information gathered in conversations along the way—"the Germans of the flats [Herkimer] are much displeased with the canal, as they now have no employment for their wagons." She left the coach at Schuylerville to tramp over the battlefield where General Burgoyne had surrendered to General Gates. Her guide was a veteran of the battle. Later she called at the home of Major Philip Schuyler, namesake and grandson of New York's Revolutionary hero. The major's house was built close to the site of his grandfather's manor which the British had burned. Mrs. Philip Schuyler—"her figure is majestic, features handsome"—walked Anne to where the earlier structure had stood. Remnants of the garden remained. "The rose bushes and lilacs are still fresh and green. Four locust trees planted by General Schuyler mark the entrance to his old home." At the rear she saw the field where the general had cultivated wheat which his wife Catherine burned to keep it from falling to the enemy.

The stage in which Anne Royall rode to Albany was happier than any she had known for a month. The passengers laughed, teased and chatted. As the horses drew abreast of a typically Dutch house, a seatmate told Anne that General Simon Frazer had died there of wounds received in battle. When the driver refused to make the unscheduled stop to give Anne time to describe the interior, the passengers "persuaded" him to change his mind. One passenger bought several copies of *The Sketches* and sold them inside the coach. Mrs. Royall asked the salesman his name. He drew a pamphlet from his pocket. "The lines on this sheet were written by P. Russell, who has received *eleven* wounds under the American flag, who has endured *seven* captivities, remained two full years in iron and cold stones in a dungeon, in Morro Castle, on the Island of Cuba." Mrs. Royall thought him "authentic. He showed us the wounds."

In Albany she bought a ticket on a barge which cruised down the Hudson River in daylight to New York. Passenger boats made the trip only at night. The barge was crowded with visitors returning from Saratoga Springs. Anne found their company "irritating." The "children were the greatest pests, rattling buttons and cents, gingling [*sic*] pebbles and drumming with sticks, crying, darting in and out." Never afterwards could she stand the sight of a rocking chair. "Their motion, see-sawing backwards and forwards," came near to making her seasick.[20]

New York City was a refreshing change after western New York. She learned that several of her newspaper friends had "castigated" Colonel Stone for attacking her. She had left a packet of personal papers in the care of Major Noah and, when Stone cast doubt on her as the widow of a Revolutionary officer, the major looked through these papers for documents to prove her claim. He printed one signed by Major Royall and attested by his nephew William S. Archer which Mrs. Royall had once submitted to the Pension Bureau. He went further and published letters from some of her famous subscribers. There was not space for all and so Major Noah listed them: "We find her warmly recommended by the first gentlemen of our and other states. Amongst those of our state, we find Governor Clinton, John V. N. Yates, Esq., Dr. S. L. Mitchell, Dr. David Hosack, J. K. Paulding, Esq., and many others. . . . They speak of her in the highest terms of respect."[21]

Energetically the author made the rounds of booksellers to pump new life into sales of *The Sketches*. Publicity had brought her notoriety and the book sold better than on her previous visit. She wrote a sharp note to Durrie & Peck in New Haven: "When you send me more [copies] do dear gentlemen put none of those rat eaten ones up. Do if you please have my books packed in a box." The letter provides an accounting of the number of *Sketches* sold—

Part of a letter written by Anne Royall on January 29, 1842, in answer to an autograph hound who also requested a portion of her manuscript. She was seventy-three at the time. This is one of the six letters of Anne Royall known to exist. *Library of Congress* "between 700 and 800 copies"—and the author had sweated over nearly every sale. For the times it was a pretty good quantity for a nonfiction book.[22]

6

Anne Royall had many faults, but she never lacked sympathy for someone down on his luck. After a newspaper (Noah's probably) had published an item intended to attract purchasers for the sculpture of Henri Isaac Browere, Anne went herself to the artist's studio to see if she could help out with further publicity. She found Browere "struggling with poverty, a family of six children, and but 33 years of age." The studio was filled with his unsold creations:

. . . busts and portraits of seventy-six of the most eminent statesmen, heroes, divines, literati and distinguished characters of the United States. This extraordinary man is now engaged and contemplates finishing, the full length statues of Washington, Adams, Jefferson, Madison, Monroe, Clinton, and Hamilton, in bronze. He is one of the most singular characters of his day, alike eminent as a limner, sculptor and taker of busts. Shame on New York! Shame on my country—to suffer this genius to droop neglected!

Browere drooped. Lack of patronage prevented him from realizing his ambition for the bronze works. As a taker of life masks Browere had no peer, even down to the present. A year before Mrs. Royall interviewed him he had perfected a molding material which he used for his masks. When Browere died eight years after Anne talked to him—and by then he was the father of eight children— he left behind a large collection of life masks many of which are on view at the museum of the New York State Historical Society at Cooperstown, New York. But the secret of his molding formula was buried with him.[23]

While in New York Anne Royall received two reviews from the *Western Virginian and Kanawha Gazette* of Charleston. The first review delighted her. It was a reprint of the favorable comments of the *Boston Commercial Gazette*. A month later the editor, Mason Campbell, suffered a change of heart and wrote an account of Mrs. Royall's life as a prostitute in Charleston.

There are some parts of her "history, life and manners" which are still fresh in the recollection of many of us. . . . When she was a resident among us, her fortunes were yet humble, and far from having attained that celebrity which now enables her to command a handsome subsistence by the prostitution of her pen, she then found it a convenient mode of adding to her pecuniary resources by the prostitution of her person. . . . Such was the infamy of her character, and so notorious the prostitution of her person that during her residence in Charleston she was never admitted to the fashionable society of the place.

To strengthen his story, Campbell quoted only one selection from *The Sketches*, wherein Mrs. Royall described the "abandoned females who swarm in every room and nook of the Capitol." The editor commented: "Whether she felt her passions again kindled at the view of scenes with which she had been familiar . . . it is certain her emotions appear to have been extremely violent and with a well counterfeited indigestion, which a modest lady would have felt, but never expressed, she declaims with wonderful pathos, on the side of virtue."

This is the first and only time I came across Anne Royall published as a prostitute. As far as I know, no newspaper reprinted Mason Campbell's gossip, though her circle of enemies was not decreasing. Before marriage Anne may indeed have been William Royall's "concubine," as her in-laws insisted, but when she lost her inheritance, she was a middle-aged woman, and no beauty. As a prostitute I think she would have starved to death.

As elsewhere there was an editor who rushed to Mrs. Royall's defense and this we learn from the *Gazette* itself which obligingly published the following:

THE CLASSICAL MR. SMOOT—The Editor of the Woodstock "Sentinel of the Valley," the classical Mr. Smoot, has seen proper in his paper of the 14th instant "to pay us his respects" for some remarks we made a few weeks since upon the "history, life and manner" of Mrs. Royall. This gallant editor appears to be singularly enamoured with the character and writings of this fair authoress, whom, with rare felicity of comparison, he pronounces her the "MADAME DE STAEL of this country!" [24]

7

The U.S.A.'s Madame de Staël, having wound up her business in New York, pushed on to Philadelphia. Where once she had begged in the streets, she was welcomed with open arms.

"Is this Mrs. Royall?" inquired a tall, blond man shaking both her hands. He was Roberts Vaux, Quaker philanthropist and leader of prison reform. "I have seen thy book, I have read thy book, I love thy book, and I love thee, too." Mr. Vaux, however, had not purchased "thy book," but borrowed the copy of the French Minister. Still, it was no disadvantage to have a "man of princely fortune and a steady friend of merit" talking enthusiastically of *The Sketches*.

The Philadelphia newspapers gave Anne Royall generous praise.

She tripped into our office the other day, [reported the editor of the *Freeman's Journal*] spectacled and calashed, and introduced herself and her book, the latter of which she presented to us. "My dear man," said she, "look at my patronage." With that she threw out a roll of paper on the floor, which reached from one end of the office to the other, and which contained several hundred names, many of them the most distinguished in the country.

The *Journal* reprinted most of what she had written about Philadelphia, though finding it "full of simplicity and error." [25]

But the *National Gazette and Literary Register*, the Philadelphia daily more concerned with books than with news, completely ignored the presence of the author in the Quaker City. This was galling. The editor, Robert Walsh, junior, was the most influential critic in the U.S.A. "If a novel receives his approbation," observed the *New York Enquirer*, "it is received, read, and talked of in ecstasies." Walsh refused to receive Mrs. Royall—at his office or in his home whither she tracked him down. "Pa never speaks to anybody at all," one of the editor's twelve children told her at the front door. "He is always very much engaged." Hoping somehow to wheedle a "great and learned puff," she left a copy of *The Sketches* for "Pa." Mr. Walsh wrote no puff. Egged on by newspapermen with whom the critic was unpopular, Anne ridiculed "Robert The One," as Major Noah called him, in her new book. She wrote the major: "I shall strip him as neatly as a goose on a New England thanksgiving table." Noah gleefully published her threat and the press of the nation, scenting blood, gave Mrs. Royall's letter wide circulation.

Efforts of a friend failed to promote an armistice.

"Mrs. R. you must allow he [Walsh] is a fine writer."

"I allow no such thing," snapped Anne. "He is a prolix frothy fool, who does not wish to be understood by the common people, nor does he write for the benefit, amusement, or instruction of his country. Compare his far-fetched bombastical style with that of Doctor Franklin. Walsh's style is merely meant to show off his vanity."

At length the two came face to face in Carey's bookstore. When Henry Carey avoided an introduction, Anne introduced herself.

"You need not be afraid," she reassured the critic. "I am only the terror of evil doers."

Without a word Walsh turned and hastily ran out the back door of the store. Foolish man! "Some did say," Anne maliciously reported, "that he never stopped running until he arrived at Boston!"

Some said a lot more. By the time the press got through rehashing the story, it bore slight resemblance to what had really happened. Five years later a southern editor wrote his version, prefacing it with a poem whose authorship was credited to "Old Play."

> Lo, now the unequal conflict. See where comes
> The *royal* gladiator—in her eye
> Fixed steadfast on her enemy, there burns
> A flame that nought can conquer. Strong she bears
> A trenchant weapon, with a wiry edge,

> To equal which, all Birmingham, and him
> Europe's best knife maker, and England's boast,
> Roger's himself, would labor long in vain—
> A tongue—ye Gods! a tongue!

This delayed account had Anne Royall attacking Robert Walsh physically. The noise attracted a crowd "with the Mayor of Philadelphia in the van. With much difficulty he got the reviewer off, with the loss of a few handfuls of hair. . . . The *National Gazette* [Walsh's] appeared the next day in mourning." [26]

From Philadelphia, which was a more liberal patron than New York, Mrs. Royall moved on her native city.

> Flushed with success I expected to be worshipped in Baltimore. After landing from the steamboat I went to bed, as it was twelve o'clock at night; but next morning, with all eagerness, vanity, and security of a female authoress, I ran to E. J. Coale [his bookstore]; he was not in. I asked after the money for the books; the clerks grinned without making reply.
> "My books or my money," said I.
> "Your books," replied a grinner, "are here, all safe."
> "What, none sold?"
> "I believe there is one."

The author was crushed. She hurried to the office of her friend, Isaac Munro, editor of the *Baltimore Patriot*, who attempted to rescue the situation by printing the review of the Philadelphia *Freeman's Journal*. He also published what the "celebrated authoress" had written about Baltimore. Still, Mr. Coale could not sell *The Sketches*. Anne waited around a day or two, meanwhile looking with unappreciative eyes upon the "shoals of ladies" who filled the streets. They got rough treatment in *Black Book*, I. She was disgusted with their "great white satin Bolivars [hats], double the size of those worn in New-York and Philadelphia, covered with artificial flowers and broad red ribbon, bows and bows, hanging down to their knees. With hoyden stride they walk on shaking their heads to make the flowers shake. In no city I have ever been in do the females dress so abominably as they do in Baltimore."

U.S. Capitol in 1825, with "inverted washbowl," as Anne Royall first saw it. *New York Public Library*

Anne took the stage to Washington. When she entered Waterloo Tavern, the landlord greeted her effusively. He had read *The Sketches* and hastened to tell her "the price of dinner had been cut by twenty-five cents."

Back in the National Capital, Mrs. Royall was again the guest of Colonel William Brent in the Brick Capitol. As she strolled through former haunts, she noted that those most formidable bugbears, the boardinghouse landladies, were friendly. "Whenever I passed doors formerly shut against me, they would run out saying, 'Won't you walk in Mrs. R.? Can't you stay and dine? Won't you come and take tea?' "

Mrs. R. had no time for farce. On the whole, the Washington press gave her good notices. She emptied her trunk of *Sketches* and hurried back east to get out her novel. The public would not be allowed to forget her.[27]

CHAPTER X

THE HOLY WAR BEGINS

1

The Tennessean was published in New Haven on February 15, 1827. The author hurriedly filled her old trunk and set off to recross the frozen countryside, hoping to reach Washington in time to "catch the members of Congress before they adjourned on the 4th of March."

"I can see her now," wrote a contemporary, "tramping through the halls of the Capitol, umbrella in hand, seizing upon every passer-by, and offering her book for sale." Among buyers seized upon were the "Hon. Sam Houston of Tennessee—a giant in whatever point he may be viewed"; Senator H. Eaton, also of Tennessee —"distinguished of mean and manner"; Edward Livingston—"benevolent and intelligent, and altogether worthy of the great family to which he appertains." A free copy went to Editor Duff Green who acknowledged in the anti-Adams *United States Telegraph* that he had been "honored with a visit from the enterprising authoress." [1]

The above-named gentlemen belonged to the so-called "inner circle," plotting the strategy that should elect Andrew Jackson to the presidency in 1828. Already the "sulphurous clouds of personal abuse" hovered ominously in the political sky. Anne admired "the magnanimity with which they [Jackson backers] accept the scoffs and slanders levelled at their favorite." But she was much too smart a salesman to limit pursuit of patrons to only one side of the political fence. She sold her novel to Chief Justice Marshall. "His keen eyes and his arched brow," she wrote, "seem to be the only parts of his venerable form that have escaped the ravages of time." Marshall was seventy-two years old. A reluctant customer was dyspeptic Associate Justice Joseph Story who, in a letter to his wife, said that "the famous Mrs. Royall . . . had compelled the Chief Justice and myself to buy to avoid a castigation." Now, what could the justice have been afraid of? [2]

The reputation of the author as a flatterer of subscribers and reviler of those who turned her down was spreading. "She is more sinned against than sinning," insisted a Rhode Island editor. "Mrs. Royall is a woman of talents. . . . We have seen nothing in her conduct to which the most fastidious stickler could take exception. It is true, she is exceedingly garrulous, and sometimes impudent; but both those faults should be ascribed to dotage." [3]

The author herself commented on the conduct of people whom she interviewed. "Since the appearance of my *Sketches,* I have observed that the moment I make my appearance in any town or village, one part of the community avoids me as they would a pestilence, while another part advances to meet me with demonstrations of anything but fear." [4]

Critics were unanimous in declaring *The Tennessean* a poor novel.

"We would wish to be as courteous as possible to our fair countrywoman," said the Boston *Lyceum,* "[but] the best meed of praise we can bestow upon *The Tennessean* is to say that it consists of 372 closely printed duodecimo pages, very vilely printed, at New Haven."

Mrs. A. S. Colvin, publisher of the (Washington) *Weekly Messenger* and foremost woman editor in the country, expressed the hope that many "readers will be pleased with the new production of a *native* novelist." Mrs. Colvin, however, had her doubts. "Mrs. R. has sinned against the canons of novel writing, in suffering her heroine to betray an inclination for so romantic and shocking a beverage as wine." On her part, the native novelist was impressed by the good looks of Mrs. Colvin, "a widow, about thirty years of age, tall and exquisitely formed." She wore her hair, "a

deep glossy black neatly rolled up, with a comb, without a cap."
Mrs. R. wore a cap with a drooping frill which framed her face.
The cap completely covered her head and that is probably why
no one has told us the color of her hair.[5]

At the final session of Congress, Anne Royall sat late into the
evening in the house gallery awaiting favorable (she hoped!) action
on a bill to "provide for officers of the Revolutionary War and
their survivors." For two months the lawmakers had quibbled,
orated and rewritten. The Senate had passed the bill, but the lower
house adjourned without taking a vote. "The Representatives in
getting drunk on the last night of the session my bill was lost,"
Anne complained to a Mobile, Alabama, correspondent.[6]

2

So Anne Royall, fifty-eight years old, resumed the road in April,
taking off for Richmond. "Mrs. R. is a traveling bookstore," said
Major Noah. She paused in Alexandria to give Mr. Clagett copies
of her two published volumes. The innkeeper was still "one of the
finest looking men in the District." Though *The Sketches* had been
less than complimentary to the town, she "met with a handsome
patronage and much good feeling."

Anne bought a ticket and boarded the steamboat to Potomac
Creek. How different was the reception on her second visit to
Fredericksburg! "Joe Young met me with a smile. I was introduced to his family, the best room in the house was at my service.
I must hear his daughter play the piano." But J. T. Sinley, director
of the stage line who earlier had refused her a ride to Richmond,
sent a note saying he was "utterly disgusted" with her book. "You
have had the impertinence to call me a brute."

In the Virginia capital, a beaming Mr. Bohannon escorted the
writer to the room she had previously occupied, by courtesy of
the editor of the *Richmond Enquirer*. "In this chamber," wrote
Anne, "I suffered more agony from the brutal usage of the world,
than I did before or since. How different were my feelings now!
Beloved and admired by the public, blessed with friends, dreaded

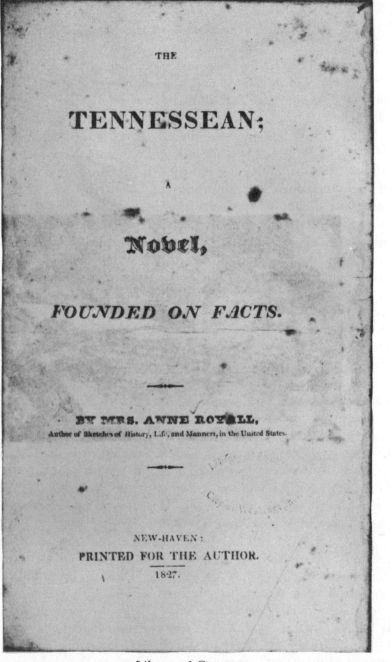

THE

TENNESSEAN;

A

Novel,

FOUNDED ON FACTS.

BY MRS. ANNE ROYALL,

Author of Sketches of History, Life, and Manners, in the United States.

NEW-HAVEN:
PRINTED FOR THE AUTHOR.
1827.

by foes, above want, I contemplated the chamber with 'a bliss supreme.' " [7]

Far from beloved, as each packet of reviews attested. Though *The Tennessean* contained nothing controversial, it whipped up more of a storm than *The Sketches*. Mr. Packard of Springfield, Massachusetts, readily picked up his abusive pen. He called Anne a "silly old hag," and suggested the place for her was "some asylum, or work house." He got a prompt reply from a New Hampshire editor. "We beg leave to inform Mr. Packard that there are different opinions . . . respecting the character of Mrs. Royall. Some of the editorial fraternity profess to regard with sincere respect that energy of mind, which has enabled her to overcome so many obstacles in her literary career." The editor of a Connecticut newspaper was "convinced" that Mrs. Royall "is either an idiot or maniac; and in either case, she ought to be placed under the care of a keeper." The (Newport) *Rhode Island Republican* wished the author "success and prosperity." The Boston *Statesman* "blushed to see the public journals of New England all joining in a tirade against an unprotected woman. Surely this is not liberty—it is the *licentiousness* of the Press!" [8]

And so it went; a repetition of the reception given *The Sketches*, but with more newspapers spoiling for a fight. *The Tennessean* was lost sight of in the controversy; Anne Royall again was under review. The strategy of the haters was not subtle. Something must be done to silence the woman. Call her names; make her look like an idiot. If she received so much attention with a poor novel what might not happen if she wrote a good book? The title *The Black Book* was ill-boding and already Mrs. Royall had announced a second volume of *The Black Book*.

William Morgan had boosted the cause of the Antis with publication of *Illustrations of Masonry*. Not long afterwards, Morgan disappeared from jail where he had been locked up for nonpayment of a small debt. Kidnapped, accused anti-Masons; bribed to disappear, countered Masons. Late in 1827 a body was washed ashore at a Lake Ontario town. Mrs. Timothy Munro identified it as that of her husband; Mrs. Morgan said she was not sure. "It is a good enough Morgan until after election," Thurlow Weed, an up-and-coming anti-Mason publisher, is reported to have said. The presidential election was a year away but already bias and slander clogged the air. Publisher Weed was as cleverly venomous as any anti-Jackson, anti-Mason editor.[9]

In Richmond Morgan's *Illustrations* "was selling as fast as clerks could hand it out." Anne Royall stepped into a bookstore where extra salesmen had been hired. The manager told her that he had disposed of only a few copies of her books.

"If you write such a book as Morgan's," he advised, "you might expect to sell better."

For once, the loquacious Mrs. Royall was struck dumb. Back at Mr. Bohannon's inn, she relieved her feelings by writing a couple of thousand words about this "Juggernaut" which captured "the minds of the weak and ignorant. I believe the Morgan book is a vile speculation to make money, and further designed as a political engine. It is a match for the missionary scheme to make money, and, like it, aims for power."

The "missionary scheme" was a derogatory label that Anne Royall had pinned on the revival movement.

Under the name of *foreign* missions, *home* missions, *Bible* societies, *children's* societies, *rag-bag* societies, and *Sunday School* societies, the missionaries have laid the whole country under tribute. This is done under the *pretense* of spreading the gospel. The gospel has nothing to do with it. The true gospel of Christ could not be bought and sold for a price.[10]

Perhaps a fattened treasury gave the Protestant churches the courage to try to move into national politics. The joint churches petitioned Congress for legislation to forbid the transportation of the mails on the Sabbath; to forbid all types of transportation, in fact. As we have seen in a previous chapter, individual churches, such as the one presided over by the Reverend Ezra Stiles Ely, had been able to interfere, to some extent, with the movement of mails in and out of Philadelphia on Sundays, by bearing down on members of the congregation who were linked, in one way or another, with postal contracts. The Third Presbyterian Church even went an annoying step farther. On the Sabbath a chain was stretched across the street in front to prevent traffic from passing.

The churches had chosen a poor way to make their bid for political participation. In and out of churchdom, discontinuance of the Sunday mails was protested and the Senate, after some brilliant oratory, voted down the proposed legislation. Anne Royall filled pages of her new travel book with warnings to readers that this single defeat would not drown evangelical ambitions. The churches would push from some other direction, until they had the power they desired. She became a woman possessed of a mission—writing, preaching, scolding, arguing, ferreting out motives behind each new churchly endeavor. Her country—the country she loved— must be saved from evangelical claptrap.[11]

3

Revival was in full swing in Virginia and Richmond appeared most hospitable to "the delusion of the missionary scheme." Anne Royall never did get along with Richmond or Virginia. Richmond "swarmed with the most ignorant rabble of any city I have seen. The Negroes insolent beyond description, particularly the female Negroes. A friend told me it was owing to the preference shown to them by white gentlemen. If this is true, it evinces, to say the least, a black taste in the gentlemen of Richmond."

The bright spot of her visit was an interview with Thomas Ritchie, editor of the *Enquirer*. She took the long walk afoot to the "splendid house on Shocko Hill," after failing to hire a carriage. "I asked for a porter to go for a coach, and he ran to the store returning with a bottle of porter." Mr. Ritchie, "a tall, spare man," greeted her warmly. "His oval face was rather pale, his eye bright blue and intelligent." They discussed "Yankees," as Mrs. Royall termed New Englanders, and Mr. Ritchie, afflicted by the southern aristocrat's stock view of the materialistic easterner, professed that he had developed an admiration for Yankees, after reading *The Sketches*."[12]

From Richmond, Anne Royall went south to Petersburg, agog to see City Point where William Royall had spent his boyhood.

Alas! The Royall family "had greatly degenerated." All that was left of the once lively harbor was "a tavern, the collector's house and a house where the widow Epps, descendant of the former owner, lives. Even the shelldrakes had disappeared."

"This species of duck is almost extinct," informed the tavernkeeper. Well, William Royall had certainly done his part in killing off the birds.[13]

Norfolk, Old Point Comfort, and Baltimore wound up the travels in behalf of *Black Book*, I. In the last city, Anne Royall had a set-to with the president of the Biddle bank—a "rough, uncouth clown!" The banker was generally unpopular. Several Baltimore friends "begged me to aid in ousting him." In Philadelphia she went to see Nicholas Biddle, whom she claimed as friend. He had bought both her books.

"Mrs. Royall," said Mr. Biddle, "we don't care for the shape of a man's face, or his manners. All we are concerned with is whether he has property enough to indemnify us, should any default occur in the bank."

Not long afterwards, the Baltimore banker obligingly ousted himself by dying. When Mrs. Royall next visited the Quaker City, Nicholas Biddle pointed an accusing finger at her and said: "I will have you tried for your life for killing my president." But Anne thought Biddle looked "well pleased." He should have been. The replacement was William Patterson, a popular member of one of the first families, whose fortune had withstood the rapacious demands of his son-in-law Jerome Bonaparte.[14]

From the urbane banter of Nicholas Biddle, Anne moved into the "radiant presence" of Catherine Potter Stith, celebrated for the attention Lord Byron had once paid her. They had met in Leghorn, Italy, at a reception honoring the frigate *Constitution* on a farewell tour of scenes in the War with Tripoli.

"When I return to Philadelphia," said Mrs. Stith with the assurance of an acknowledged beauty, "my friends will ask for some token that I have spoken to Lord Byron."

The poet took the rose from his lapel and gave it to the lady. The rose never left the reception. Byron admirers plucked out the petals for souvenirs.

The next day Byron sent Mrs. Stith an autographed copy of his poems with a note: "I take the liberty of requesting your acceptance of a memorial less frail than that which you did me the honor of requesting yesterday." The Philadelphian brought the letter safely home where she proudly showed it to Mrs. Royall.

"She is certainly the most enviable and enchanting of her sex," commented Anne. "She is tall and elegant and her face one of unrivaled beauty. She is now a widow about twenty-four years of age." [15]

4

Anne Royall had not left Philadelphia when the Reverend Ezra Stiles Ely celebrated July 4, 1827, by preaching a long sermon disclosing the master plan to create a church party. Around the nation, churchmen and laymen sputtered in dismay as they read the extraordinary words uttered by the Philadelphian.

I propose, fellow citizens [declaimed the clergyman], a new sort of Union, or if you please, a Christian party in politics, which I am exceedingly desirous all good men in our country should join; not by subscribing to a constitution and the formation of a new society. . . but by adopting religious principles in civil matters. . . . .

All who profess to be Christians of any denomination ought to agree that they will support no man as a candidate for any office, who is not professedly friendly to Christianity. . . . Let us all be Christian politicians. Let us choose men who dare to acknowledge the Lord Jesus Christ for their Lord in their public documents.[16]

Coming from Doctor Ely, the proposal of a Christian Party in politics bore the stamp of high authority. There was no branch of the soul-saving activities of the united churches over which the energetic cleric had not assumed leadership. His eloquence had persuaded the churches to unite as an interdenominational force for their own glory. He was the spearhead of revival. Having served his apprenticeship as a missionary in New York, he had created the military-like brigades and battalions beating the bushes for converts, backsliders, and contributions. He was the principal editor of literature issued by the Sunday School Union which, after three years, reported circulation of "a grand total of 3,741,341 publications." Doctor Ely had also taken on the task of rewriting text books "which in their [the Union board's] conscience believe to be false or inconsistent with the purity of divine truth." After composing the weekly sermon which he delivered to his congregation, the reverend still had energy to write a major part of the religious essays which the American Tract Society distributed to hotels, stages, and other public locations.[17]

Anne Royall had her say about the Ely proposal.

The missionaries have thrown off the mask. They are preaching to the people to elect none but godly men to represent them in the State Assembly and Legislature. They think to get these godly men into the Federal government; get two-thirds of the states to alter the Constitution and then come out with their national religion. One of two things is inevitable. Either the country must put down these men, or they will put down the country. Their object and their interest is to plunge mankind into ignorance, to make him a bigot, a fanatic, a hypocrite, a heathen, to hate every sect but his own, to shut his eyes against the truth, harden his heart against the distress of his fellowman and purchase heaven with money. This is the business of those *pious* young men who scour the country, range regularly through every street, enter every house, beg every individual for money. "You will go to Hell if you do not give money to spread the gospel." This is downright blasphemy against God as if He could be thwarted for want of money.[18]

A friend read what Anne Royall had written. "What you say," she commented, "is very true, but it is a dangerous thing to meddle with."

"My pen cannot be better employed," retorted Mrs. Royall.

She began to plan a trip which would take her into enemy territory. She would battle not only the churches, but the anti-Masons who also seemed wickedly involved in suppressing individual freedom. Again she would travel in upstate New York, grown more dangerously intolerant since her previous visit. She would invade Vermont, too, where the despised lodges had had to close down.

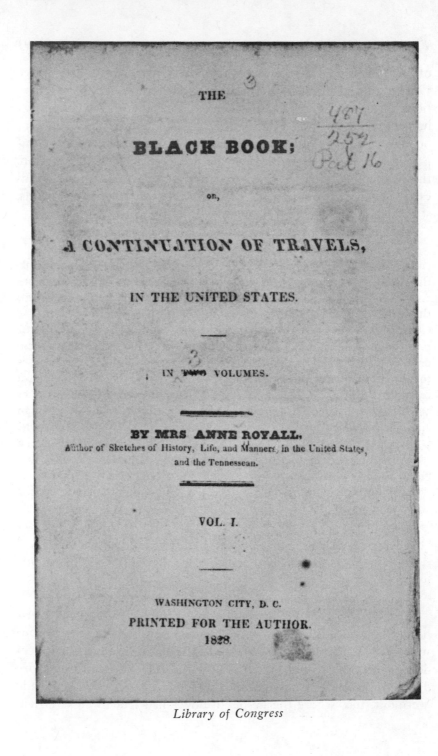

THE

BLACK BOOK;

or,

A CONTINUATION OF TRAVELS,

IN THE UNITED STATES.

IN ~~TWO~~ VOLUMES.

BY MRS ANNE ROYALL,
Author of Sketches of History, Life, and Manners, in the United States,
and the Tennessean.

VOL. I.

WASHINGTON CITY, D. C.
PRINTED FOR THE AUTHOR.
1828.

She got off to a good start in a preliminary skirmish on the Delaware River as she steamed toward Trenton. Parcels of tracts filled the decks and public rooms of the New York boat. With only a short time to work, Anne Royall began dumping them overboard. Passengers joined her; they were having fun. But the supply of tracts everywhere was so endless it was impossible to get ahead of it. "Allow me, Messrs. Editors," a correspondent wrote a religious newspaper, "to recommend to Christians who travel in steamboats, to supply themselves with tracts before they go aboard. They will find them eagerly read by passengers, and the dull and listless hours often passed on board will be occupied by useful and instructive reading."

Though she did not throw any passengers with their supply of instructive reading overboard, a voyage thereafter with Anne Royall was neither dull nor listless, especially when she stumbled onto a new way of annoying missionaries, "blue-skins," or whatever she chose to call them. Changing to the Raritan River steamboat, she "took a seat by a jolly little old lady" who was absorbed in reading a pamphlet. Anne read over her shoulder. The pamphlet was the report of the last gathering of the Presbyterian Assembly and contained a reprint of Doctor Ely's Fourth of July speech.

Suddenly Mrs. Royall stood up and shouted: "Treason!" The piercing shriek immobilized passengers, as if they were posing in a *tableau vivant*. Treason became Mrs. Royall's rallying cry; it was an attention-getter. It *was* treason, she explained, to suggest the revival of a church and state party in the U.S.A.[19]

5

In New York Anne and Major Noah had a good laugh over her dismantling passage from Philadelphia. According to the major, she concluded her story saying: "I only wish that John Knox and Ignatius Loyola lived in our day—I would pickle them for posterity."

Many changes had taken place in the nine months since she last saw the city. "The most striking was that of its increase—the crowded streets, bustle, noise, and a constant tramp, tramp, tramp on the sidewalks." Another change was the lusty new crop of religious newspapers. The most powerful was the *Christian Advocate* which already claimed 15,000 subscribers, more than the *London Times* counted in 1828.[20]

Anne Royall visited none of them, but, feeling strong in fame and finances, she again tackled Theodore Dwight, editor of the *New York Daily Advertiser*. She needed the editor behind her on the new tour. To gain his support she was willing to bite into humble pie.

"I've come to pay my respects and hope you are well," Anne said, demurely dropping a courtesy. ("If an earthquake had happened, Mr. Dwight could not have been more surprised.")

The editor was speechless. The audacity of the woman! When he found his voice, he spoke "in a tone resembling the hoarse croak of a raven": "I want none of your respects."

Clearly, time would never narrow the gulf.

Mrs. Royall did succeed, however, in her peace mission to William Leete Stone, editor of the *New York Commercial Advertiser*. Stone appeared to be grateful to her for not joining the chorus of newspapermen currently making him the butt of jokes about the Georgetown editor who had gone bankrupt and in his "editorial will," bequeathed to Anne Royall "his duelling pistols, to shoot Colonel Stone." Even so the truce with Colonel Stone did not last long. Some time later Anne wrote: "I never received the pistols, nor were they necessary. I shot Stone dead with my pen."

Major Noah was a gadfly. After proclaiming that "Mrs. Royall has extended towards Col. Stone, the Royall clemency," he urged her to try to make peace with Charles King. "Friend Charles has treated you with great contempt, not having noticed any of your literary works."

The editor of the *New York American* had also been contemptuous of Major Noah and his brand of journalism. The son of Rufus King had married into the Gracie and Low families, securing for himself an entrée, if he did not already have it, into New York's select Knickerbocker society. Doors swung wide for King where the major could not peep through keyholes. The *American* paid no attention to the stream of editorial sarcasm that flowed from the office of the *New York Enquirer;* not even when Noah began calling him Charles the Pink (the pink of perfection in manners and dress).

So Anne visited the office of Friend Charles and reported back to Major Noah who unselfishly shared her words with his readers. "Mr. King never deigned to look at me, much less ask me to sit down, or pay me the least mark of civility. In justice to him, however, I must add, he neither kicked me down stairs nor broke my head, but allowed me to depart in safety."

Because of King, Anne Royall was turned away at the door of Philip Hone, whom she wished to interview and sketch in pen portrait. A butler probably—"a saucy man"—told her "to walk off and never come to this house again." He explained it was on account of her call on "Charles King, the other day." [21]

6

Announcement of the lengthy tour Anne Royall proposed to make through New England in quest of material for *Black Book* II—and perhaps a third volume—reaped a harvest of rumors, the most malicious of which, Anne believed, originated in the Ely camp. "It was said that I was upon an electioneering expedition." If she had a favorite in the 1828 presidential race, she did not say. Adams and Jackson had each shown her friendship. "I admire both candidates," she wrote. "When either have been slandered I have vindicated them. After various fruitless attempts by the parties to win me to their side, to the exclusion of the other, the general request was 'well, Mrs. R., at least, you will do us no harm.'" Oh, yes, she would, if either candidate warranted criticism. [22]

Another rumor had it that the Masons were financing the New England trip to recoup losses in membership and prestige. The evidence is against this benison. Anne was heart and soul *for* Masonry. There was no need to buy her support at a time when bare treasuries reflected the full-blown unpopularity of the fraternity. As on all her trips, in whatever town she arrived, she expected Masons to help her with subscriptions. Some would help; others would not, as she knew from experience. Probably fewer would subscribe now because to admit Masonic membership often was not easy to do. In the end, she knew that she must rely on her own ingenuity to bring success to her venture.

Before she took off, friends expressed apprehension for her safety, especially after she told them she would enter the State of Vermont. In the complicated pattern of anti-Masonry, Vermont was a special case. Bordering on New York, the state had early joined the agitation blowing in from Lake Ontario. "Vermont was well fitted for such a movement . . . [particularly after] some of the witnesses wanted in the Morgan abduction trials had escaped to Vermont. Again the soil was favorable because the people were entirely small farmers of the religious New England type, and it was in this sort of community that anti-Masonry found its most fruitful soil." When Vermont's Anti-Masonic Party was organized, "the convention was composed mostly of ministers," who left no doubt as to their convictions in declaring that "adherence to Masonry is a disqualification for any responsible office in the State or nation." Even after the Anti movement began to peter out elsewhere, Vermont continued to pick up membership.[23]

The opposition was naturally uneasy about Mrs. Royall's new junket. She was unpredictable. The tract-dumping and the outspoken public denunciations of the churches had received bountiful publicity. She was a threat, especially if people listened to her. The church party took a new tack. According to Mrs. Royall, the Protestants "had the impudence to attempt to draw me to their side. One of their females (no less than one of their pillars) accosted me:

" 'Don't you think, Mrs. R., you would make more by writing about religion?' "

Mrs. R. chopped the pillar down short: "But I *am* writing about religion." [24]

CHAPTER XI

"A VIRAGO ERRANT IN
ENCHANTED ARMOR"

1

When the *Lady van Rensselaer* had tied up at the West Point landing Anne Royall climbed the hill in the blistering sun of August. She hunted up the "military professors" whose acquaintance she had made on an earlier visit, but they "fled like a parcel of poltroons." The superintendent, Colonel Sylvanus Thayer, previously most amiable, "hid himself." Anne smelled a "blue-skin" rat after she observed copies of the *New York Observer* strewn about and piles of tracts everywhere within reach. After everyone fled, she spent the afternoon destroying the religious literature. In the evening she looked up a "lady-friend" who, in a scared whisper, told her that "parade music was laid aside, as offensive to God's people, and the cadets were on their knees praying, the Bible on one side of them and the sword on the other." Anne used up the night writing to Congressional friends to demand an investigation. "The most flourishing and best conducted seminary is changed into a missionary school," she told them. The investigation of abuses at the Academy was a long time coming, but eventually got under way, thanks to the persistence of Representative James J. Roosevelt of New York. (He was the grandfather of Theodore.) [1]

West Point at the time of Anne Royall's first visit in 1825. Lithograph by W. J. Bennett, published by Parker & Clover, New York City. *New York Public Library*

Next day Mrs. Royall continued by barge to Albany where she changed to one of E. Young's red coaches, destined for New Lebanon. There she found "a truly Christian sect." Though the heat had intensified, she climbed a mile uphill to reach the Shaker colony. "It is hardly credible in a person of my age." With Miss Betsey, an elder, as guide, the sightseer panted through the colony.

The family houses are precisely the same, all well furnished with plain furniture, which is kept in the neatest order. The women spin, sew, knit and weave. Shakers manufacture all their clothes, bedding and shoes. The men have workshops of all their trades. Nothing can exceed the beauty and neatness of their farms and gardens from both of which they derive great profit in seeds. Their produce and manufactures have preference in all markets. All must work. They require no other incitement but their conscience.

The hot weather almost succeeded in accomplishing what her opposition had been unable to do. "I was never nearer giving up." [2]

In stagecoaches taking her to New England Anne, however, showed not the least sign of wilting. She tongue-lashed all missionaries who traveled with her, and anyone else who seemed to be a devoted churchman. She was as vicious, rough, rude and ill-mouthed as any newspaper had said. But she amused the passengers. With good listeners, the performance was at its best. One victim was Judge John Hooker, Springfield probate court and bank president. Never before had Anne laid eyes on Judge Hooker. She learned his title and business as he bade farewell to a group of friends seeing him off.

"What, more missionaries!" she exclaimed as the judge took a seat opposite her. "Keep away from me if you do not wish the top of the stage to blow off."

She laughed "at his long face," and decided he was "one of those old witch-hangers."

"How long since you hung a witch?" Silence from the judge. So she attacked the bank president: "An old, tried man of prudent years. Young men cannot be trusted with money bags." The passengers snickered.

Next question: "If you ordered my arrest, what death would you adjudge me?"

Judge Hooker took no more. "If I was to hang you," he said, "I could get enough to join me."

Between bouts, the authoress remarked the scenery—"unspeakably handsome"—except, "You are hardly ever out of sight of white steeples; so sure as you see a steeple, you find a grogshop. How the eyes of the passengers sparkle when they are drawing near one of those steeples!" [3]

2

In Boston Anne took a room in a boarding house on Brattle Street —"the noisiest street in the United States"—and then went to call on Jared Sparks. The heat wave had not broken and "Mr. S. in dishabille reposed on a sofa." He had just finished arranging General Washington's papers for publication.

It is hardly possible to conceive their bulk. One whole wall, fitted with shelves, was filled from top to bottom. The greatest part consisted of large books, into which many of his letters were copied in the general's handwriting. I looked into a number of letters and diaries. Throughout, the most minute exactness was observed. In the diaries, it was surprising, as well as gratifying, to see on every page so much in alms. The general kept an account of every cent or shilling expended from his youth up. [4]

Spruce in a new pongee dress, Mrs. Royall again made the pilgrimage to the house in Quincy where John Adams had died in the year past. President John Quincy Adams, his wife and a flock of Adams relatives were gathered at the old homestead for a reunion. The President, Anne thought, "looked quite pale and thin," but received her with "ease and simplicity with which he welcomes alike the lowest citizen and distinguished stranger." The stranger, not distinguished, was an Italian count who, with Anne, was invited to stay for tea. "In the North it is not the custom to hand tea around as it is in the South," explained the knowledgeable traveler, and so the company grouped about the dining-room table.

"Instead of tea, the President took a glass of water and a piece of bread, upon which he made his supper." The talk was of the last days of the second President of the U.S.A. A family member recalled a story John Adams was fond of telling:

"When I was a boy, I had to study Latin grammar, but it was dull and I hated it. I told my father I did not like Latin, and asked for some other employment. 'Well, John,' said the elder Adams, 'you may try ditching. My meadow yonder needs a ditch.'"

This seemed like a welcome change, and to the meadow went the youthful Adams. "Ditching" was back-breaking labor. At midday John was ready to resume his studies, but too proud to admit a change of mind. He dug one more day, but by nightfall "toil conquered my pride." To the end of his life John Adams believed that "ditching" had played an important part in building his character.

Anne Royall had never been an admirer of "those shoals of foreigners, who swarm our country and do not like us." She did not like the Italian guest and perhaps made no effort to conceal her disdain. He had never before drunk tea.

The President told him how to manage it, and the count very cautiously commenced the attack. He ventured to pour some into a saucer, but sat and looked at it a long time before he drank about one-half and refused to take any more. During this time, the President never even turned his head that way, or moved a muscle of his face, but continued to eat his crust and water. Mrs. Adams meanwhile smiled and pressed the count to eat. She has the most bewitching smile and in every respect is the most fascinating and accomplished of her sex.

That night, the impassive John Quincy Adams wrote in *The Diary* his impressions of the two teatime visitors:

Mrs. Royall . . . continues to make herself noxious to many persons, tolerated by some and feared by others, by her deportment and her books; treating all with a familiarity which often passes for impudence, insulting those who treat her with incivility, and then lampooning them in her books. Stripped of all her sex's delicacy, but unable to forfeit its privilege of gentle treatment from the other, she goes about like a virago errant in enchanted armor, and redeems herself from the cravings of indigence by the notoriety of her eccentricities and the forced currency they give to her publications. . . .

The Count dal Verme introduced himself as the son of a man of the same name, an Italian, who traveled in this country in 1783. . . . I received and treated this Count with civility, but there was something peculiar in his self-introduction and his documents that I could not resist distrust of his authenticity.[5]

Anne Royall was at least authentic. She might not have agreed with Adams's pen portrait, but no public servant ever showed her more consideration than the sixth President of the U.S.A. Twenty-one years later when Representative Adams of Massachusetts dropped dead on the House floor, he was still trying to persuade the government to pension the octogenarian widow of William Royall.

3

While Mrs. Royall tarried among sights and sounds of her favorite American city, the Med. Fac., a Harvard undergraduate club whose raison d'être was to burlesque the currently famous, bestowed on the authoress, in language clowning the awards of proper institutions, the honorary degrees of "M.D. for 1825, and M.U.D. for the year 1827." In fifteen years of existence the Med. Fac. had given degrees and diplomas to Andrew Jackson, Van Buren, Christophe and Alexander I of Russia. The Czar took his award seriously and sent the Med. Fac. a fine surgical library. Anne Royall's citation was for her "enunctae naris" and the "terrorem maximum Typographorum perambulavit" employed in marketing her words. Honored at the same time was "Johannes Randolph . . . Senator eccentricissimus, qui per diem lagaenas cerevisiae Congressional perpotat."[6]

Mrs. Royall, however, was not without a host of serious admirers among the Harvard student body. The young men were as much wrought up over anti-Masonry and the political goals of the

Protestant churches as were their elders. She received a letter from Cambridge, signed "Many Students," congratulating her on her "labors in the cause of truth and science." The students "heard with pleasure" that Mrs. Royall planned to continue the "war against the vile and unprincipled system of anti-Masonry." [7]

From Boston Anne traveled northward into a stronghold of anti-Masonry. At Salem, her old champion Warwick Palfrey, junior, greeted her warmly and wrote about her "victories over aggressors," in the *Essex Register*. The opposition newspaper called her a "nuisance." [8]

There was little novelty about her receptions which, with slight variations were repeated in most New England coastal towns. Newburyport offered a variation when a crowd followed Mrs. Royall into a bookstore. "Since I have become an authoress, I attract crowds, mostly rabble!" Anne waited "till a goodly number had forced themselves in. They were the most ignorant, dirty-faced gawks in New England. The children squeezed their hands between the gentlemen's knees and strained their necks to look up in my face. Amongst those in the store was a great rough heron—a man over six feet in height, about middle age, plainly clad."

Anne began to speak: "You are the people who send missionaries to convert the heathen. Look at yourselves—ten times ruder than the heathen. Why don't you convert yourselves?"

The "heron" flew out of the store, accompanied by most of the rabble.

"That is Bartlett who gave $30,000 to the Andover Seminary," said a friend.

Anne caught up with William Bartlett and invited him to buy a book.

"He took his watch out of his pocket and looking at the sun, said, 'You will please to excuse me now madam; it is banking hours, but I will be glad to see you at my house in the afternoon—after three o'clock.' "

Mrs. Royall arrived on the dot. Meanwhile she had collected more information on the heron. A self-made man, Bartlett proudly preserved a lapstone which he was wont to point to as the "foundation stone of his great fortune." When the banker did not show up for his appointment, Anne hunted him down at his countinghouse. He was "sitting at ease, unengaged. I came to the point and offered him one of my books.

" 'Why Mrs. R.,' said he, 'these things require consideration.'

"I told him that I had no time to wait."

Her "time was proportioned. To do equal justice to all, one day could not encroach upon the time of another. Mr. Bartlett did not intend to buy in any case." [9]

Next day she was in Exeter. Though "it rained torrents, pouring down so powerfully as to bend my shattered umbrella," Anne dutifully sloshed through the streets, determined that Exeter should have its portion of time. Before dawn the following morning she was on her way to Portsmouth, New Hampshire.

Here again she was greeted by the tale in print that she was on an "electioneering campaign" in behalf of General Jackson. Wrote the pro-Adams editor: "We well know she disclaims any partiality to Gen. Jackson, and with the characteristic duplicity of her associates, cloaks her political deformity under the specious garb of disinterested patriotism; but her temper and disposition . . . betray her false colors, and disclose the real banner under which she is fighting."

So intent was the editor on getting in his political licks that he missed a far better story unfolding in front of his office building. Ordinarily Unitarians welcomed Mrs. Royall. For some reason the Unitarian parson at Portsmouth, the Reverend Mr. Parker, ran away from her after they almost collided on the street. Or as Anne put it, "He appeared not to court my company." Hurrying to overtake him, she "could not but remark the nimbleness with which he moved. Though I walked very fast, he had a great advantage over me in the length of his legs. Noways disheartened, I was gaining fast. He ran outright. I imitated him, but being seized with a fit of laughter, I had to give up the chase."

During the Portsmouth sojourn, a party of Penobscot Indians camped on the opposite side of the Piscataqua River. Anne walked across the bridge, curious to compare them with redmen she had seen elsewhere. Many townspeople had preceded her and were already "amusing themselves by setting up cents for the Indians to shoot at with the bow." She thought the Penobscots "stouter than the southern Indians, but greatly inferior in intellect." Her opinion was influenced by a conversation with "the doctor," who spoke English. The doctor was on his way south, on advice given by "some gentlemen," to collect capital "to build himself a house, and live like a white man." His advisors had told him "to go to populous towns." His destination was populous Boston.

"Why not take these hands you have, cut down trees, and build a house for yourself?" asked Mrs. Royall. "Where I come from the Indians do so, and they have good snug houses."

"No, no," said the doctor. "Indians no build house; white man build house."

"Can you cut with an axe?" persisted the interviewer.

The doctor shook his head. "Not to build house." [10]

In the Portland stage, Anne Royall enjoyed the company of Benjamin Silliman, professor of chemistry and natural history at Yale University. Silliman was bound for commencement at Bowdoin College and so Mrs. Royall decided, then and there, she too would attend the exercises. In the afternoon the stage picked up a Bowdoin student—"a jovial, merry, stout man, who was drunk." Fortunately, the young man slept. Once he awakened to ask "if any of the passengers had a razor. The professor needs a shave." Anne laughed at herself. Though she had spent nearly two days in the company of Professor Silliman, "I never noticed his beard."

After resting the night in Portland, they traveled next day by steamboat to Brunswick. On board was "a Miss Gardiner, a daughter of Parson [John Sylvester John] Gardiner, of Boston. She was on a visit to Gardiner, Maine, accompanied by her Uncle Gardiner, of Gardiner, whose father gave his name to the town. Miss G. was very affable, but her uncle was proud, stiff and distant."

The Bowdoin commencement began at nine o'clock in the morning. Anne sat through some ten discussions, conferences, orations and debates. A sampling of subjects: conference on the characters of Fielding, Cervantes, and Scott; on benefits derived from the study of the vegetable, mineral and animal kingdoms; political, religious and intellectual progress of the sixteenth century; danger to American liberty, arising from ambition, corruption of morals, forms of government, and extent of territory; mental efforts affected by language, civil institutions, and religious benefits; the propriety or the impropriety of the banishment of Napoleon. She enjoyed most an argument delivered by a candidate for Master of Arts who "spoke eloquently against sending Missionaries amongst the Indians."

The exercises crawled to completion at three o'clock. Anne was exhausted "from the heat and the crowd," and time was running out. She had moments only for calls on several members of the Dunlap family. "It would seem that all Dunlaps since the flood have resided in Brunswick. There is the Hon. Robert Pinckney Dunlap, next Maj. Gen. Richard Dunlap, and David Dunlap." They were sons of Captain John Dunlap, son of a preacher who had emigrated from Ireland to the District of Maine. John had lived his youth in such poverty that he resolved to work hard and get rich. He made a fortune in the fur trade and was probably the richest man in Maine when he died.[11]

4

When Anne Royall traveled up the Maine coast in 1827, the state had been a member of the Federal Union only seven years. Success stories such as Captain Dunlap's were the wonder tales of almost every town. Anne liked the people, probably because Maine still was so much like the frontier. There were hateful people, to be sure, but so far her tour had not produced the quantity of intolerance anticipated. Massachusetts, some; New Hampshire, less; but nowhere had she ever received a more cordial welcome than Maine gave her.

The old trunk had been quickly emptied of books. No more shipments were expected until she returned to Portland. Still, she went ahead with her schedule—up the Kennebec River some twenty-five miles to Waterville; back to the rocky coast and into the Penobscot, beyond Bangor and to Old Town. Bad weather stalled her two weeks in Hallowell on the Kennebec, where she enjoyed herself immensely. The editor of the *Hallowell Gazette*,

Henry Knox Baker, printed excerpts from newspapers from Boston to Portland, praising her current tour.

Together she and Baker concocted an absurd story explaining the "mysterious disappearance" of Henry Clay from the Washington scene in the midst of the political campaign. Adams's aspiring Secretary of State, harassed by the "corrupt bargain" charge, had gone "to the West from fear of Mrs. Royall!" The *Gazette* was for Adams, as was the rival *American Advocate*, which also eulogized Anne Royall. "This far-famed female quixote," wrote Editor Calvin Spaulding, "is remarkably active, voluble, blithe, and gay, and has an eye of peculiar brilliance. . . . The ambition of petty accomplishments, and mere personal attractions, find no place with her. She inculcates and values nothing but the dignity of knowledge and the irresistable power of independence."

After such adulation, no wonder the *American Advocate* scooped the *Gazette* by publishing a letter Anne wrote Major Noah from Hallowell.

At this fearful distance from you and my other friends, I haste to apprize you I am in the bosom of my favourites, the Yankees. I threatened these saucy Yankees with my black book, and they received the threat with the best natured smiles. I am everywhere hailed with true Yankee benevolence. For this remark, however, I must except the Missionaries, who do not seem to extend to me the right hand of christian love and fellowship. Pray give my love to my friends, and my forgiveness to my enemies.

Mr. Spaulding printed the letter, but Editor Baker went further. With his reprint he tried to find an "angle," speculating in a fashion Major Noah himself might have done. Like most younger newspapermen of the day, Baker greatly admired the New Yorker's journalistic style. The lady's attitude towards the great editor seemed quite "saucy and intimate." Could the letter indicate a romance between Anne and Noah? After guiding his readers out on a limb for a column, the Hallowell editor abandoned them. No, it could not be romance. He decided Mrs. Royall is a woman who lives for the world and future times. Major Noah is a determined old bachelor, "fat, fair and forty." A month later the determination of the forty-three-year-old bachelor collapsed. He married a seven-teen-year-old Jewish girl who was as devoted as he was to alleviating the lot of poor Jewish immigrants pouring through the Port of New York.[12]

"The pride of Hallowell" was Doctor Benjamin Vaughan, an Englishman "who inherited most of the land where Hallowell stands." Anne called at the Vaughan house and was agreeably surprised when the venerable doctor himself "opened the door and showed me into the parlour." Upon her arrival in town, she had remarked the number of fine cows which roamed the streets. Many of the cows—Vaughan cows and kin—were descended from a bull taken from an English vessel captured off the coast during the War of 1812. Doctor Vaughan's fortune was not as large as it once was because he had laid out large sums to import seeds, plants, implements, and so on, for the benefit of the state's agriculture. Quite a man this Doctor Vaughan, who had been a "pupil of the great Dr. Priestley." [13]

As was her custom in towns visited, Anne Royall went to church on Sunday. In Hallowell, in the company of the innkeeper and his wife, "Mr. and Mrs. Brown," she attended the Baptist Church and was most pleased with the preacher. "He spoke well—not a word about Missionaries or spreading the gospel. He spread it more effectively by letting it alone, and preaching up charity to the poor." Mr. Brown appears to have taken the sermon to heart. When Mrs. Royall was ready to leave Hallowell, he gave her a bill, charging her two dollars for two weeks.

In Waterville, where Anne spent the next Sunday and attended a Universalist church, the landlord, "J. Dow," refused to give her a bill. "I should be far from thinking it proper to charge a person who is rendering a benefit to the country," he explained. Belfast outdid Waterville. "When I was just going to set off on my journey those immeasurably kind people flocked around and, upon shaking hands, every man left a dollar!" And she had not one copy of a book to leave in return.[14]

Returning to Portland she picked up a new supply of books and ran over the city. "Let our citizens keep in mind," warned a newspaper editor, "that her ladyship has a black book. . . . For the benefit of our most distant readers, Mrs. R. is a little, short, snug-built, sharp-eyed lady, who looks just as if she were ready to give you place on her black list." [15]

Nevertheless "patronage was great in Portland," though the snug-built lady found getting around the town most unpleasant because the streets were unpaved. "The slightest breeze raises the dust." She took time to see the governor, younger brother of Levi Lincoln, currently in his third term as Governor of Massachusetts. Here was a dynasty. The father of both popular executives had also been a governor of Massachusetts.

"Governor Enoch Lincoln of Maine is most plain in his dress," said Mrs. Royall. "Not a gentleman in the State but who has more style in his house and appearance. I found him in a plain parlour, scarcely with what might be called furniture. He is good-natured, simple, affable." [16]

Mrs. Royall rode out of Maine on November 3, in a snowstorm. It had been a wonderfully successful tour, exceeding all others in book sales; and people had taken her to their hearts.

5

Four days later the shivering traveler arrived in Concord, New Hampshire. "I greatly suffered from wind and snow, and would certainly have frozen, had it not been for the kindness of a friend [in Dover], who furnished me with a warm coat." As she had done earlier in heat and rain, she was out early next morning, plodding through drifts taller than she was. She called on Governor Benjamin Pierce, "about seventy years of age, a tall noble figure. He served the whole of the Revolutionary War. Governor Pierce is a farmer. He was dressed quite plain and wore a cocked hat."

Isaac Hill, editor of the *New Hampshire Patriot* and political godfather of Pierce, saw to it that the homespun governor kept his cocked hat on. New Hampshire had been solid Federalist territory when Hill began working to bring it under the influence of the Democrats, as the Jackson party now called itself. The lame, gaunt editor lay great store by an agrarian party which he was promoting in support of Old Hickory's election. (Jackson carried New

Hampshire in 1828.) Anne Royall thought Hill worked too hard. "Hill's face is thin, furrowed and grave." After wandering among the snowdrifts, Anne herself was grave. She had picked up some frightening tales of the extreme religious fervor rampant in the Green Mountain State. Momentarily her "ardor" to contend against Vermont blueskins had "somewhat cooled." An acquaintance pleaded with her not to go into the state. Anne, however, decided it was her "duty" to rescue Vermonters from the missionaries.

"You will be up against a snag," warned her friend. Thus, in subsequent adventures, Mrs. Royall called Vermont "The Land of Snags." [17]

Halfway across the state she hit her first snag. At Waterbury, the landlord asked her, please, not to stop at his tavern; he "had been warned against her." She stopped and moved on next day. On the night of December 16, snow still falling, Anne reached the outskirts of Burlington. The stage broke down and the driver guided her afoot to the tavern of Captain Henry Thomas on Court House Square. Next morning ex-Governor Cornelius P. Van Ness, brother of Washington's General Van Ness, brought a group of Masons to call. Fearful of the effects of an unfavorable description in the *Black Book*, the visitors had come to talk of their town's good points. There were blueskins, they admitted, but Burlington was also the home of many enlightened persons; even of a Unitarian Church.

From the window of her room Anne looked across the street to a general store. One of her callers said that inside was a "very good specimen of blueskins." As soon as she had visited the two newspaper editors—"one was an Adams, the other a Jackson man"—she tramped through the snow to the blueskin's lair.

The house had high steps before the door, from which the snow had been removed. Upon going in, I found a gloomy looking man, about fifty years of age, wearing a wig of sandy color. His face looked as though it had lain out on a frosty night.

"Are you Mr. Hecock?" I asked.

"Yes," he replied.

I informed him who I was, and that I had called on him for his patronage.

"Yes," he said, "I'll patronize you. I have heard of you."

"And now you see me."

"Yes, I see you ought to be put in the workhouse."

"And pray, sir, what have I done to consign me to the workhouse?"

I was about to open a paper [the subscription list] to convince the gentleman that I was not a fit subject for the workhouse. Hecock walked deliberately to the door, and opening it, walked back, took hold of me with a hand on each shoulder, and pushed me [through the door] with such force that he sent me to the foot of the steps, into the street. The height of the steps must have been not less than ten feet, and had it not been for the snow I must, inevitably, have been dashed to atoms.

Anne Royall lay helpless. Mr. Hecock let her lie. Passers-by delivered her on a sled to the tavern. A doctor was called and then a second doctor, and a third who was a surgeon. The diagnosis was that Mrs. Royall had suffered "a contusion, a dislocated ankle, a fracture of the larger bone of the leg, a smaller bone broken above the ankle, knee badly sprained and the flesh much bruised."

The pain gave her sleepless nights, but during the day she scribbled away on the third volume of the *Black Book*, in which Samuel Hecock ("base coward!") received his share of attention. Serving as her attorney, ex-Governor Van Ness threatened the storekeeper with a damage suit. Samuel Hickok—Anne misspelled his name—was not a poor man. He had made substantial contributions to the University of Vermont.

"The Hero of Lake Champlain," as Anne named Hickock, was quick to see that moneywise he was a most vulnerable defendant, if Mrs. Royall should take him to court. He tried to squirm out of the situation saying that a dog had pushed Anne down the steps. His attorney "settled the business." What the payment was we do not know. Mr. Hickock did not realize how much he got for his money. He had inflicted a permanent injury on Anne Royall. For the rest of her days, though the fighting front appeared bold as ever, she lived in fear of religion-crazed blueskins.[18]

6

The publicity value of her sufferings in the Land of Snags was not allowed to languish. In Burlington, neither the Jackson nor the

Adams editor printed a line about the broken leg. As far as I know, no Vermont newspaper mentioned the incident. Anchored to a splint, Mrs. Royall scribbled letters through the day, broadcasting to the outside world the nature of her wounds and how she acquired them. Friendly newspapers were indignant over the brutal handling of "our venerable friend." Unfriendly journals were not worked up. "From the manner in which it was hinted the accident occurred, we infer that the literary virago has at last received what she long merited—'a brief ejectment.' " [19]

She was a wretched invalid. Often, when the doctor came, he found she had removed splint and bandages. Anne was impatient to be on her way. The first two volumes of the *Black Book* were waiting in Washington to go to press. The author should be *there*. After five weeks, Mrs. Royall "stole away" from Burlington one morning at two o'clock. Scared of being waylaid by enemies, she kept her departure a secret. Averaging about ten miles a day, she traveled the length of Vermont stretched out on the back seats of stagecoaches, bundled in buffalo robes. Every jolt was a stab of pain. She worried constantly about a setback to her mending bones. Each night when she arrived at a tavern, a doctor was summoned to examine her leg and wrap it tightly with fresh bandages. Thus she journeyed to Fishkill, New York, where she was carried aboard the steamboat *Rising Sun*. In New York City she transferred to a coach of the Citizens Line "which runs to Philadelphia in opposition to the Union Line. Both lines advertise a fare of $2.00, but these proprietors, up to cheating and fraud in all seasons, always take care that the two dollar line is full. So I paid five dollars." Nothing new under the sun!

After a winter of heavy snows, New Jersey roads were in bad shape. "Scarcely a trip was made without oversetting." Mrs. Royall's coach keeled over in the night near New Brunswick. She was lifted out, her leg apparently none the worse, and laid on the roadside to wait while the driver went for help. At midnight she was carried into a New Brunswick inn "not without my share of New Jersey mud." At two o'clock in the morning the journey was resumed; breakfast was eaten in Trenton. On February 12, seven weeks after the Burlington mishap, the cripple arrived in Washington.[20]

Sally Stack was waiting. All her orphans had good jobs and Sally was alone. Her husband had quit his Navy Yard clerkship and sailed for Mexico to seek his fortune. Regularly he sent money home. Sally's little daughter, just beginning to toddle, had suddenly died of croup. So Sally was ready to bury her sorrow and loneliness in the care of Anne Royall. She had told Daniel Carroll that the broken and bruised author was returning and that good gentleman had provided a house—"gratis"—in Carroll Row, on the east side of First Street, between East Capitol and A Street. Their new home was known as the Bank House, having once sheltered the Bank of Washington.

Sitting up in bed Mrs. Royall prepared her two books for the printer and wrote the third volume. Doctor Edward Cutbush, surgeon to the Navy, attended her daily. Somebody with influence must have got him for her—"gratis." Dr. Cutbush found her a difficult patient. From her bedroom window, she had a view of Capitol Hill. She pestered the doctor to let her hire a carriage and be carried through the halls of Congress on a litter. She wanted to know what was going on there and to see for herself what progress the churches had made burrowing into government. Let them beware! "I'll drill an army of women and shoot every Presbyterian I can find!" The surgeon was not amused; he was afraid that one day Mrs. Royall would do just that.[21]

Anne was to blame for her slow recovery which delayed publication of the first volume of the *Black Book*. It did not appear until late May.

"She has drawn a hideous portrait of many," said a Baltimore newspaper. "These, we think, will not sit again for a second likeness."

It remained for Major Noah to point out to future portrait-sitters the lessons to be had from *Black Book* I. "Mrs. Royall's rude sketches convince us of one fact, that there is a great portion of pride and haughtiness among men of our country, whom fame and public employment have designated as prominent citizens. Civility is so cheap a coin . . . that he is a fool who rejects it."

The reviews showed so much interest in the pen portraits that Anne Royall resolved to include more of them in succeeding publications.

"Why don't you wait until we are dead?" asked a gentleman.

"I might die myself meantime," replied the author.[22]

7

Not long after *Black Book* I came out, Anne Royall was carried onto the Senate floor (only male visitors sat in the gallery, ladies and foreign representatives being seated along one side of the chamber) to hear the final round of the debate on the "abominable" tariff bill. Her entry stopped the oratory as senators hastened to shake her hand. The proud author "was much gratified to see my *Black Book* on several desks."

The debate, which had agitated the nation for almost four months—"being the event from which a serious division dates between the North and South," wrote Senator Benton of Missouri—had momentarily taken a diverting turn. A vintner living near the Capital claimed he had grown grapes and fermented wine the equal of any shipped from France. He asked Congress to protect his product with a high tariff on imported wines. Senator John Branch of North Carolina argued for protection. Senator John H. Eaton, a competent judge of vintages, depicted in such graphic terms the ravages inflicted on the digestion by domestic brew that he "set the Senate to laughing and Mr. Branch was defeated."

Anne Royall dug her hand into her reticule and pulled out pad and pencil, but she complained to her neighbor that the restlessness of senators interfered with portrait-writing. She could not write an accurate description unless she looked into the eyes of her subject. Senator Robbins of Rhode Island annoyed her most. He "was continually skipping over to chat with the ladies. He is a *wee* man, something like myself. The ladies call him 'their sweet little robin.'"

For the first time Anne saw Judge Hugh Lawson White, Senator Eaton's Tennessee colleague who had stood up in debate to Daniel Webster of Massachusetts, spokesman for tariff protection which his manufacturing constituents demanded. Never was Judge White diverting in debate; only logical and a guardian of the south's economy. When he was twenty years old he had won national acclaim by dispatching a Cherokee chief who tried to block the western progress of the frontier. Thereafter White's political rise was rapid, a statement which does injustice to the integrity of the Tennessean. He was, of course, a member of the Jackson coterie though no servile vassal of the hero. Later they fell out over Martin Van Buren whom the justice looked upon as inferior presidential material.

Anne Royall described Senator White as a "modern Socrates. Of good height, he seems to be nothing but skin and bones. He rises from his seat, when about to address the chair, and with eyes resting on the floor, and his body bent forward, he commences, speaking at first low, but by degrees his voice assumes a bolder tone and his body becomes erect."

That day began for Anne a long and advantageous friendship with another slayer of an Indian chief. Colonel Richard M. Johnson, senator from Kentucky, was well along in his career before he killed the Shawnee leader Tecumseh. For many years Johnson was a neighbor and during this time Anne Royall said she "never knew want." One Christmas Colonel Johnson sent her a "handsomely engraved portrait" of himself. Anne coyly commented that "we should have preferred the original." Anyway she enjoyed hearing the handsome Kentucky colonel's declamations in the Senate. "His words flow like a torrent, marked with boldness and energy peculiarly his own. He is of middle age, common height, face round, arched brow, manly countenance, and complexion pale. His hair is a light auburn." The senator also showed boldness by paying no heed to unwritten rules of moral conduct that constituents expected from their representatives. Johnson, as far as we know, is the only political careerist to reach the vice-presidency of the United States, while living "open and above board with a mulatto mistress, by whom he had two children." He was so popular in Kentucky, where he won the fight to banish imprisonment for debt, that "his conduct was not held against him." [23]

After two hours Mrs. Royall was carried out of the Senate "in great pain." She "doctored up" for a couple of days and returned to the Capitol to be juggled up the "dark, narrow stairs" to the Strangers Gallery of the lower house. The noisy "too dark hall" was a medley of sartorial creations, ranging from the stylish ingenuity of eastern tailors to the handiwork of wilderness seamstresses. Representative Davy Crockett, who masqueraded as a "coonskin Congressman" back home in Tennessee, startled Anne Royall with his formal attire. But his greeting did not match his modish turnout. "He is a true specimen of the Tennessee character —warm-hearted, brave and generous." The representative paid for a book, though protesting "he was not a great scholar, since he only learned to spell as far as baker. He is one of the best-tempered men in the world, full of fun and spirits, and by his wit and sprightliness is the life and soul of friends and foes." At the moment everyone was chuckling over Davy's encounter with a foe. To promote their candidate, the Adams party had begun a new publication called *We The People*. Among the first Jacksonians attacked was Crockett. Stowing a Bowie knife in his belt, the angry Tennessean went to call on the editor. From the uplands of his more than six feet, Davy gazed down on a puny little man. How could he fight such an undersized opponent? His wrath changed to laughter. "He told the editor 'he had a great mind to grease and swallow him.' "

No greeting came from Representative William S. Archer of Amelia County, Virginia, the cousin who had sided with the Roanes in the contest of Major Royall's will. With restrained pen, Anne noted the presence of her in-law. "He is reckoned a man of talents. His language is good, but his style prolix and he loses his subject in a multiplicity of words."

George McDuffie of South Carolina, who "deals forked lightning and thunderbolts upon his adversaries," was a disappointment. "When he is silent you would scarcely know him to be the same man." And McDuffie, whose vehement speeches usually crowded the gallery, that day was silent. "I expected to have seen one of the most shining gentlemen in the world, and so perhaps I did, but the gold is in his mind, and not in his exterior, which is by no means striking."

Mrs. Royall waited at the bottom of the stairs for the congressmen to recess.

I was highly displeased to find Miss F. at her old stand, and the grog tables sitting as thick as ever. As the representatives came severally up to speak to me, I pointed out those nuisances and threatened them with a fair tornado. Since then Miss F.'s temple is torn down and she and the grog-sellers, cake sellers and fruit women and other women are banished the place." [24]

8

As soon as she was able, Anne Royall hobbled along Pennsylvania Avenue, selling and trading. She needed money; the Bank House needed furniture. From Mr. Wilson, a "fashioner of chairs," she bought "3 second hand chairs at 50 cents." Anne rested on one of her purchases before advancing on the store of Mr. Ratsbone, merchant tailor. "He had a few fancy articles, which I cared nothing about, but for the sake of getting acquainted, I struck up a trade for the *Black Book*." At the third stop she exchanged for "a cambric handkerchief, the first time I had been able in some years to treat myself to such a luxury." With Raphael Jones she bartered for a pair of silk stockings. "I am unfortunate in finery. The stockings were stolen from me a few minutes afterwards."

Not everyone was willing to trade. The man who had exhibited a painting of Niagara Falls in the Capitol rotunda and was now showing it on the avenue refused to admit Mrs. Royall free. "You can see it by paying 25 cents," he said curtly. Anne did not see it. She ran into Mrs. Carlisle, "one of the warmest friends I had," but Mrs. Carlisle's greeting was cool. She scolded Mrs. Royall for being "too severe on the missionaries." Others she met also condemned her attacks on the Protestant churches: "My old friend Mrs. Cruikshanks, once a fine woman, but in the missionary ranks"; Darius Claggett, proprietor of a dry goods store, who nodded agreement when a customer suggested Mrs. Royall was a "drunkard"; Pishey Thompson, the English bookseller—"I saw him through the window, and kissed my hand to him. He did not return my greeting. Surprising!"

This was a long-standing feud which began when Pishey Thompson refused to stock Mrs. Royall's books. "They will not sell in my store," he said, although he had already disposed of five copies. With an Englishman involved, Anne went off on her usual tangent. She surmised that Thompson deliberately plotted to discourage the rise of native writers, while boosting the books of his countrymen. "The daring Tory advertises whole columns of Hinglish books." Anne warned him: "I assure you Mr. Pishey, I will be a thorn in your side." She kept her promise, beginning with a pen portrait. Thompson, in shape,

resembled a stuffed Paddy of middling age, with red face, cheeks puffed out as if holding wind in his mouth, two little round, winking eyes, and an arrogant countenance. But his manners! If you can imagine haughtiness, pride, malignity, scorn and contempt combined in both look and action—his sleek coat and black silk vest, his pretty ruffle, partly displayed, you may form some idea of this monarch of booksellers.

Mrs. Royall blamed "Viceroy" Thompson for the sudden cooling of Joseph Gales's friendship. The editor of the *Intelligencer* published no notice of her new volumes. Anne sent Gales five dollars to pay for an advertisement. He returned the money without a word. When an announcement was still not forthcoming, the author could do no better than accuse Gales & Seaton of being under the thumb of Thompson. "We have four editors in the city, three of them are English. We have three booksellers and two of them are English. We have English and Scotchmen in our departments and at the head of our public works. Is there no talent to be found in Americans?" [25]

Continuing the tour of Pennsylvania Avenue, Anne rested at "Doctor Todd's—he needs no puffing, everyone knows Todd the druggist man." She bought matches.

"Are these matches good?" she asked.

"I expect they are," said the druggist man. "But if they should not light quick enough, Mrs. Royall, just look at them and they will be sure to take fire."

Anne limped across the street to Gadsby's Hotel—"an elegant and most splendid establishment—the largest I have ever seen except

BROWN'S INDIAN QUEEN HOTEL, WASHINGTON CITY

Lithograph published by Endicott & Swett, 1843. *Library of Congress*

the Exchange in Boston." As always "Mr. G. was very polite," but she was more fond of Jesse Brown of the Indian Queen, a hospitable Marylander who welcomed his guests at the curb. "The main stay of the Indian Queen," said Mrs. Royall, "is Mrs. Brown. She is to be seen everywhere, late and early, and not a particle of the culinary department is performed that does not pass under her eye." The charge for room and board at the Indian Queen, with brandy, rum, gin and whiskey free with meals, was one dollar and seventy-five cents per day, or ten dollars the week; less by the month.

These were the "two mammoth hotels of the city," patronized for the most part by politicians and out-of-towners. For wining and dining and the inauguration balls, Society went to Carusi's. No fashionable party was fashionable if Carusi were not the caterer. Anne Royall was hardly a prospective client, but she listened with interest while Louis Carusi talked nostalgically of his native land. He remembered the vastness of St. Peter's. "When standing at the entrance to the church men at the opposite end looked no larger than infants." Carusi's outsize assembly rooms were not the equal of St. Peter's in size, but Mrs. Royall was impressed by the spacious- ness that the Italian provided for entertaining in the six-story build- ing at the corner of Eleventh and C Streets. "The upper room, where the inaugural balls are held, is adorned with handsome paint- ings; the lower room, where the parties take supper, is adorned with handsome columns. There are smaller rooms for refreshment." Anne endorsed Carusi, "a very intelligent foreigner."

Though her leg stood up well under the test of the Avenue outing, Mrs. Royall hired a carriage next day to make the rounds of "the Departments. The whole of these departments wants over- hauling." Entering the State Department, she jumped on her good friend Colonel Graham, commissioner of the general land office, "for letting the books lie on the floor, covered with dust." The commissioner protested the fault was not his. "I must blame Con- gress; such is the Spirit of Retrenchment." [26]

The debates on retrenchment had been as "inflammatory and dis- graceful" as those touched off by the tariff. In the election year, accusations had been hurled against candidates without regard for truth. President Adams was accused of extravagant spending. Much was made of a billiard table installed in the White House when most households were still feeling the pinch of hard times. To present the Administration in a better light, Adams representatives in Congress began snipping away at budgets. Anne thought little enough of the cuts made in the State Department. "These books have value. They should be secured."

The news "flew around like a whirlwind" that Anne Royall was rampaging through the offices and "there was a terrible scampering." One faithful clerk stuck to his desk in the Treasury Department, but at sight of Mrs. Royall his courage failed. He ran into a private office and locked the door. Anne banged on the door. "How dare you shut the door against one of the sovereign people!" she shouted. The clerk did not open up.

In the Navy Department, another clerk refused to announce the sovereign lady to the Board of Navy Commissioners. Mrs. Royall pushed past him and opened the door on a conference between two commissioners. Commodore Lewis Warrington remained seated, put his hand before his face, and refused to speak. The other commodore, "a stout man, but much older," retreated through a side door—"all those doors ought to be nailed up." Who was he? No less than Commodore John Rodgers, ranking naval officer in the War of 1812. Anne hastened after him. A diplomat interrupted the chase, offering to buy a book for the commodore.

"I will not have his money, nor shall he have my book," said the author. She glanced at Commodore Warrington as she swept out of the conference room. "He looked cannon balls at me!"

The War Department produced "none but gentlemen," including Colonel David Brearley, agent in charge of removing the Creek Indians from Alabama to new settlements. "The Creeks have become so attached to him they will follow him anywhere," declared Mrs. Royall. "He has done more toward civilizing the Indians than all the missionaries on the globe. The missionaries hate him because he will not let them delude the Indians. The colonel is a noble looking man, about middle age, very much sunburnt." [27]

So the summer passed, Anne Royall writing, interviewing, prowling streets and offices where she made new friends and enemies. The gossipy, rambling *Black Book* I sold well and almost everyone wanted to meet the author, or, at least, see what she looked like. Capital Society still kept aloof, though visiting English writers who swarmed the country about this time were wined and dined. Thomas Swann, the district attorney, was a cordial exception.

"Why, I expected to have found a woman of coarse vulgar manners!" he exclaimed when Mrs. Royall called at his office.

A train of the curious gathered round. "O, buy her book and she will speak well of you," one of them advised the attorney.

Swann did not buy a book, but he invited Anne Royall to his house. She was too busy to accept.

Samuel Harrison Smith, head of the branch of the Bank of the United States and one of the truly in-people, did not invite her to his house and so Anne had no opportunity to meet his famous wife. Still, without their patronage, she spoke well of the Smiths, praising the latest novel of Margaret Bayard Smith. "*What is Gentility* is an excellent and interesting work taken from life." All of which proved, Anne pointed out, that "it was untrue that if you buy my book I will speak well of you."

She could not speak well of the District, which showed slight improvement in the years she had known it. "Very few houses have been built. Capitol Square does not look well. The trees are not thrifty from want of water and poverty of the soil. I have often suggested the propriety of manuring and flooding."

The majority of the Capital's inhabitants also suffered from poverty.

There is not a spot on the globe containing the same number of people that is oppressed with more indigence and human distress and more cursed with dissipation than Washington City. And yet no one seeks the cause, much less to remove it. The cause has grown up with the city. The great number of mechanics employed in building, instead of laying up their earnings, consume it in drink. For want of means their children are growing up in ignorance and contracting all manner of vicious habits. Mother and children obtain a few cents from charity and many of the mothers, merely for want of work have, like the men, become confirmed drunkards.

Another cause of distress is the number of free colored people allured to the city to get money in an easy way. These almost outnumber the white population. They take the work and of course the bread out of the mouths of white widow and orphan. They will meet the members of Congress on the road and engage their washing. They are talking of liberating the slaves in the District of Columbia. They had better liberate the white people. But it appears that the Negroes are very popular, as many of them hold lucrative places under the government, and I must say they are more sober, saving and industrious than the white people. The godly people have raked and scraped every cent from the poor, instead of relieving them. If there is a place of punishment hereafter, every one of these blackcoats will be found in it—if it will hold them. The missionaries now issue two newspapers in the capital. They have also built a large splendid church in the heart of the city. Well, they have enough money to build a church on every square of the Capital. Hail Columbia, happy land! [28]

CHAPTER XII

"BLUE-SKINS, MAY ALL THEIR THROATS BE CUT"

1

The building of a costly canal system had brought the Commonwealth of Pennsylvania to the brink of civil war. Many taxpayers failed to foresee that the waterway, connecting Pittsburgh with Philadelphia and thence with European ports, would benefit them financially, and so grumbled disturbingly over mounting taxes. Lancaster County was a case in point. The prosperous county was content with the well-established trade route along the Susquehanna River to the Port of Baltimore. Why chip in to excavate another channel? When the governor budgeted nearly four million dollars more for internal improvements, including completion of the canal, Lancaster threatened revolt against the state government.

Discord was just what the U.S.A.'s newest political organization thrived on. The Anti-Masonic Party moved in, pouring out sympathy for the oppressed taxpayers, and within a year Lancaster County became the center of the party's operations in Pennsylvania. Two successful newspapers were launched and the profits used to finance additional publications. Between editions presses were not idle. "Morganic books, almanacs and ridiculous Masonic bugaboo pictures were peddled and distributed without number wherever the people were supposed to be sufficiently credulous to be imposed upon." [1]

Religious wrangles among the various Protestant sects (German and Scotch-Irish) of the large state also contributed to the rapid success of the Anti-Masonic Party in Pennsylvania. The churches quarreled among themselves over interpretation of tenets, but presented a solid front against "oaths and secret societies." In this made-to-order situation, anti-Masons had no more to do than toss a little fuel on the fire, now and again, to keep dissension simmering. [2]

The popularity of *Black Book*, I, had thickened Anne Royall's mail. "Go on, Mrs. Royall," letters urged. "You are doing good, but you have much more to do." Pennsylvania correspondents, anxious over illiberal developments within the state, informed her of the rising tide of anti-Masonry. They pleaded with Mrs. Royall to come, as she had gone to New England, and see that "justice is done." The indomitable tourist needed little urging. Long confinement—still lame and suffering pain—made her restless to be on the move. Ultimately she convinced herself she should make the Pennsylvania tour "merely for amusement." That notion, of course, turned out to be an "absurd conclusion." [3]

The second volume of *The Black Book* appeared in the middle of September. On the nineteenth, loaded with books, and more to follow, Anne Royall began the familiar journey to Philadelphia. In Baltimore she learned that Miss Elizabeth Chase, breathing fire, had waited two days at Mr. Coale's bookstore to "whip" her. Miss Chase was the sister of the late Supreme Court Justice Samuel Chase, a signer of the Declaration of Independence, and daughter of the Reverend Thomas Chase, well remembered as the first rector of St. Paul's Church. On a previous visit, hearing that Miss Betsey had published some books of verse, Anne had sought her out and given her a conspicuous place in the first volume of *The Black Book*. Her aim was solely to aid the impoverished author whom she found living in a "wretched apartment, gloomy and almost destitute of furniture." Miss Chase showed Anne her books and lied about the vast number of copies sold. She was preparing a manuscript of her father's for publication and talked about it in a grand manner. Her visitor was not fooled. The "intolerable pride" of a southerner who had known better days was not a new experience to the traveler. "Wishing sincerely to do her benefit," Mrs. Royall volunteered to distribute a prospectus of the new work during her travels. She even offered to buy a subscription. Miss Chase haughtily informed her that she already has as subscribers "a great many of the *first* people." Anne thought the statement untrue and so persisted in trying to assist Betsey Chase. Unfortunately she wrote realistically of the appearance of the apartment and its unattractive occupant, "a masculine woman." The characterization enraged the poet. The clerks at the bookstore told Anne they expected Miss Betsey "at any moment. This intelligence was rather alarming. Because of my lameness I could not have outrun her. I called for a hack and rode off as fast as horses could take me." She hid aboard the Philadelphia boat and did not emerge from her cabin until the paddle wheels were turning.

The publisher of *Niles' Weekly Register*, Hezekiah Niles, and his wife, were passengers on the steamboat up the Delaware River. The *Register* had paid no attention to Mrs. Royall's literary output and Mr. and Mrs. Niles ignored their traveling companion. Anne did not ignore Mrs. Niles in her next book:

A great fat, round faced, ignorant tory-looking woman, whose tongue ran like a clapper. She is a great missionary, and had a basket and reticule stuffed with tracts; and kept handing them out. I was tormented by her eternal clack. Mrs. Register N. was dressed in fine costly clothes—her fat sides wrapped in rich satin and superfine cloth cloak. Weep Columbia! As late as this day, September 30th, I was without a cloak!

In Philadelphia, Anne's first call was on the bookseller Mr. Griggs. "He had been very successful in sales of the 1st vol. of *The Black Book*, but the 2nd vol. is not going well." Why? "Mr. G. said it was because there is nothing in it about Philadelphia. They shall not have that to say about my new book."

Next call was on John Hare Powel of the Pennsylvania legislature, "who has immortalized his name in his opposition to clerical tyranny." Earlier in the year, the American Sunday School Union had placed before the legislature a bill asking permission to incorporate. The debate had been bitter and Senator Powel was credited with bringing about defeat of the measure which he described as one more step in "a systematic effort [by Doctor Ely] to boldly assume the despotism of a dictator . . . [and] make all men and all doctrines subservient to an established orthodox creed." The legislator demolished arguments favoring incorporation with quotes from the Reverend Doctor Ely's famous Fourth of July speech of the previous year. He quoted also from the Union's annual reports, penned by Doctor Ely, which further made plain the plan to establish an ecclesiastical domination of the United States. "The experience of the civilized world demonstrates that the character of the man is built upon the principles instilled in the mind of the child," the preacher had written. "In ten years, or certainly in twenty, the political power of our country would be in the hands of men whose characters have been under the influence of Sunday Schools." The prospect frightened the lawmaker. "The Presbyterians alone could bring half a million electors into the field." [4]

Mrs. Royall was not disappointed in the appearance of Senator Powel. "He is tall and stout and under middle age, though gray; his face fair and oval with a keen dark eye. Nothing like flattery or bombast in his language or manner."

As was her habit, Anne Royall visited the "good Samaritans" of her first entry into the City of Brotherly Love. The Horse and Groom in Strawberry Alley, where she "had suffered much," had a new landlord, but she took a room there "because the house is dear to me." At the corner the tobacconist Mr. Dick was still in business. Again Mrs. Dick was exceedingly helpful. "She took upon herself to have my winter clothes made, which relieved me from a great deal of trouble." Further afield on Walnut Street, near the state prison, was the "humble shop" of J. L. Baker, broker and artist. Anne had nearly fainted from hunger and pain in front of the shop. Mr. Baker had given her "every assistance in his power and from that day to this I never fail to call and acknowledge my obligation to this worthy man."

Out of pure deviltry she banged again on the door of "my dear friend and patron" Robert Walsh. "Pa is engaged," one of his children parroted as before. Through the half opened door Anne caught a glimpse of the editor's "long narrow back, covered with a threadbare rusty black coat." Walsh had never been a good samaritan to her and so she felt no compassion. "May he never have better until he learns to respect the genius of his country."

At the moment the most notorious editor in Philadelphia was John Binns, publisher of the *Democratic Press*, previously a devoted supporter of the Jackson party, but violently opposed to Old Hickory in the 1828 campaign. Working to defeat Jackson, Binns had published the famous "coffin handbill," a lurid broadside depicting the coffins of six militiamen who by Jackson's order had been executed for insubordination in the War of 1812. For good measure, Binns added two more coffins to the handbill. In the "most scurrilous campaign of vilification the country had known," the coffin handbill walked away with honors until the caustic pen of Isaac Hill of the *New Hampshire Patriot* pricked the balloon. "Pshaw! Why don't you tell the whole truth? On the 8th of January, 1815, he [Jackson] murdered in the coldest kind of cold blood 1,500 soldiers for merely trying to get into New Orleans in search of Booty and Beauty." Indignant Democrats followed up by wrecking the Binns home. Subscribers vanished overnight. Mrs. Royall had become acquainted with Binns on her first trip to Philadelphia. This time, when she went to see him on the eve of the election, he was near to bankruptcy. The editor begged her to help him. Apparently he believed current gossip that Anne had influence with the Jackson party.

"Oh, Mrs. Royall, you must put in a good word for me," pleaded Binns.

"You thief!" retorted Anne unsympathetically. "What can I say in your defense?"

All she wanted to know from Binns was why he had published the handbill in the first place. The editor gave her no answer. He lost his newspaper not long afterwards and wound up a once brilliant career as an alderman, available for oratory at a negotiable fee.[5]

Anne Royall visited most of the Philadelphia editors.

"How shall I proceed with this Pennsylvania tour?" she asked Joseph R. Chandler, editor of the *United States Gazette*, who had "sheltered my widowed head from bitter storm."

"You know better than anyone can tell you," replied Chandler.

The editor knew many things himself better than most of his contemporaries. In four years he had returned the floundering *Gazette* to prosperity. He gave his readers ample local reports and printed letters from European capitals which he wrote—a well-kept secret—from material picked up at the wharfs where Atlantic packets put in. But he had live correspondents in the principal ports of the U.S.A. and their reports were not only interesting to most readers, but especially helpful to Philadelphia's shipping trade. The partner and business manager George H. Hart worked toward a list of twelve hundred subscribers. Then, he estimated, "all will be right." All had been right with the *Gazette* for some time.

For the sake of a long-standing admiration of his talents, Anne Royall looked up William Duane, once the Democrats' most powerful editor. Duane's newspaper had lost its advantage with the removal of the National Capital from Philadelphia. A heavy contributor to his downfall also was the enmity of the Federalists who, in revenge for Duane's crippling attacks, got him charged with sedition. President Jefferson saw to it that the charge was dismissed, but the damage to the editor's reputation was permanent. Presently William Duane held a minor political appointment with the Pennsylvania supreme court.

Mrs. Royall came upon him . . . walking to and fro before his little office.

He looked disconsolate and thoughtful and was doubtless walking the pavement to warm himself, as the morning was cold. We stepped into the office, and sat down and consoled with each other in our reverses of fortune; he, in a dirty little police office, pocketing fipenny bits, and I trudging through the towns, travelling in hard going stages, and sometimes pocketing a dollar and sometimes an affront. We comforted ourselves that the world is unworthy of us.[6]

2

Mrs. Royall left Philadelphia at six o'clock in the morning of
October 14, the date chosen by some Pennsylvania towns to ballot
for the President. This was a very special election. Since the
muddled outcome of the 1824 election, manhood suffrage had not
only been extended, but, for the first time, voters cast their ballots
directly for electors. Only two of the twenty-four states—Delaware
and South Carolina—clung to the old mode of plucking presidential
electors from their legislatures. Like New York, Pennsylvania was
regarded as a "crucial state" and the Jackson organization had gone
all out with decorative trappings to catch the eye of the electorate.

The stage clattered through frosted towns expectantly awake and
festive with tall Jackson hickory poles from which flapped the
national flag slightly above the gay banners appealing in large
letters for "Jackson and Liberty." The stage driver resolutely prepared himself for the responsibilities of the occasion. "He stopped
at every grog house and tavern, and for taverns and tavern signs
Pennsylvania exceeds all other states—sometimes lions grinning at
you, sometimes eagles that seem ready to pick out your eyes, bears
and turks. Sometimes the driver would drop off to sleep, drop the
reins and lose command of the horses altogether." Anne was not
reassured when he told her in fifteen years he "never had any bad
luck but once." She did not ask him about the once, but was sure
this trip would add a twice to his record. Still and all, he was a good
fellow. "He seems to know every person on the road, nor did he
fail to call at many houses. Yet, we arrived in Easton precisely on
time, at sunset."

She put up at "Chippy" White's hotel, drank tea and went to
bed, without listening to one of the anecdotes for which the host
was famous. Anne was about her business bright and early next
morning. After several calls, she made her way to the terminus of
the Lehigh Canal, a marvel of the period. The canal connected
Easton with the anthracite mines at Mauch Chunk, after a thirty-
six-mile climb through fifty locks. In eight years of the canal's existence, shipments of coal to Philadelphia had risen from three hun-

dred tons annually to more than 77,000. Philadelphia manufactures had increased accordingly.

Mountains of coal framed the waterway's terminus where "long, flat, shallow boats" were being loaded for the downriver trip. Of course! These were the Durham boats, those heroic craft of the Revolution which had converged on Trenton on a dismal December day in 1776 to help George Washington and his defeated army make good their icy retreats from Long Island and White Plains. In peacetime, design unchanged—"shaped like a very long Indian canoe, with wide board extending the whole length of the boat on each side, where the men walked propelling the boat"—the Durham boats carried farm products to the Quaker City market. But now the prosperous anthracite mines kept them far more occupied. They floated effortlessly with the tide downstream, but the return was toil with the long poles.

In the afternoon, Mrs. Royall rode the switchback railroad which brought coal down the mountainside to Mauch Chunk. It was not precisely a railroad. Mules pulled the empty cars, or wagons, up to the mines and gravity brought them back down to the loading chutes. The ride up was "delightful, steady, swift, and not a jolt." Anne happened to ride down in an empty car. "Away we flew— birds, cats, dogs and cows flying for their lives before us." (With the passing of time the railroad appears to have found its true destiny. "When the 'Switchback' was abandoned as a coal carrier in 1870, it was turned into a scenic railway.")

Mrs. Royall said that "many hands are employed in loosening the coal and loading the wagons. They receive from 80 to 90 cents per day. Some of the workmen are Irish, some German, and some Yankees; they work, drink whiskey, fight, receive their money in the fall, go home, spend the winter, and return in the spring."

The sightseeing round about Easton had been adventurous and informative. But "Chippy" White, the noted humorist, was a disappointment. "He charged me the highest bill I ever paid in the United States—$3.62-½ for two days." [7]

Mrs. Royall moved on to Reading. Her stay there was remembered by an appreciative chronicler of the town. "Without her recital, many historical details would be entirely lost. For instance, there is no one living who can testify either by observation or tradition as to the celebrated wooden figures on the old Penn bridge." The bridge, wrote Anne, "is one of the finest in the United States. It unites beauty and strength, is handsomely carved, and cost $30,000. The figures are designed to represent commerce and agriculture—a female reclining upon a wagon laden with yellow wheat, just reaped; the wagon is drawn by oxen, and the wheat is hanging down upon the heads of the oxen." She did not know the name of the woodcarver—"someone from Philadelphia"—but she thought she detected "the hand of a master. This is the first carving I ever had the patience to look at." She had made a good beginning. Besides his accomplishments as woodcarver and sculptor, William Rush was the nation's most famous creator of figureheads which adorned the prows of American and foreign ships.[8]

Mrs. Royall arrived on schedule in Lancaster the day before the town voted in "the Presidential." A holiday atmosphere prevailed. "As I drove into the principal street, I was no little amused at a large body of men singing Jackson's march, and dragging a great hickory tree large enough for the mast of a 74-gun frigate. I waved and was cheered down the street to the tavern." The tavern was filled. Anne sent a note to Congressman James Buchanan, leader of the Jackson forces, who came quickly to settle her at the White Swan Tavern where she had a bedroom, "an elegant parlor, and always a good fire." She could not have done without the parlor. "It was seldom empty during my visit, and the society equal to any met with."

Such was the reception in Pennsylvania's hotbed of anti-Masonry where nothing short of bloodshed was anticipated when the aroused citizenry went to the polls. The Anti-Masonic Party had put no candidate in the field, but their campaign had been rabidly anti-Jackson. The proprietor of the White Swan, Edward Parker, was a Jackson man. He and his wife "surfeited" Anne with attention. Mrs. Parker bought material and made her a new dress. Before her trunk was unpacked, Mr. Parker had her out at the stable, exhibiting his thoroughbred John Stanley, recently judged best in the Chester County horse show. The following year, matched against Hickory, John Stanley won first prize of a thousand dollars.

From the stable, Mrs. Royall walked to her bookseller, Mrs. Dickson, a widow who continued to edit her husband's newspaper, the *Lancaster Intelligencer.* "I hope she will meet with liberal patronage," wrote the visitor. On her part Mrs. Dickson urged subscribers to rally round Mrs. Royall. "We hope she will not be without support from every gallant who admires her spirit." Hugh Maxwell, editor of the *Lancaster Journal,* also gave Anne a boost, but the anti-Masonic press did not notice her.

Next morning Mrs. Royall took a seat before her bedroom window to watch the balloting at the courthouse across the street.

. . . the Sheriff made proclamation that the polls were open. The few round the court-house did not go into the court-house to vote; none but the judges go in and the door is kept shut. The voters walked up to a window, slow and solemn, and slipped the ticket through a slit. Then they walked off, no crowding, no taking aside, no whispering.

Everything was as still as a funeral till the election was over, which was about sundown. Then the city rang with acclamation and huzzas for Jackson. [The general had won hands down.] The band struck up, and a large party walked through the streets preceded by music. I saw several large lights of a deep red approaching. The sight startled me—moving, firey machines, revolving on a pole, high in the air! They were transparencies! the first I ever saw. They came under my window and the bright light within the four sides made script and figures easy to distinguish. The figure always was General Jackson, arrayed in a rich suit—his sword, epaulets, &c., shone like the sun. One side depicted the general riding in a cloud of glory. They paraded through the streets long into the night.

The transparencies, Anne Royall learned, had been executed by fifteen-year-old Julius A. Keffer. Since the election had not resulted in carnage, Anne returned to her stock and trade. She interviewed Julius. The young artist said he had sketched all the figures and lettering. Each side of the largest transparency—"with a large pyramid on top representing Pennsylvania"—measured three feet six inches.

On the afternoon of the fifth day, Mrs. Royall held court in her parlor at the White Swan and bade goodbye to a flock of new-found friends. She was flanked by an alderman and Congressman Buchanan, and felt greatly honored. At the time public appearances of the congressman were rare. He was still mourning, as he mourned all his life, the death of his fiancée.[9]

Mrs. Royall rolled away from Lancaster in the chilly night, on her way to Harrisburg. Her stay in the Pennsylvania capital was brief; she would stop again on her return from across the state. She came solely for an interview arranged with Governor John Andrew Shulze of whom she had heard "a thousand remarks, such as he is a great awkward Dutchman, bigotted priest-Federalist, Jew, Gentile, did not know a spit box from a tea-pot; and again, a good-natured fool, a tory, a whig, a gentleman, a clown." Much of the criticism was heard in Lancaster, still angered over expenditures for the canal the county did not want. "Oh, well," observed Mrs. Royall, "tongues like wheels were made to run."

In search of truth, Anne knocked on the door of "a very plain common brick house overlooking the Susquehanna River." Governor Shulze himself opened the door and led her into the parlor. "It was just the kind of parlor I like, and at my favorite point, on the north of the building." The governor only laughed as she repeated the criticism of his policies. He was not "ignorant, but a man of good mind." Mrs. Royall believed the legislature had made a mistake in not backing to the hilt Shulze's proposals for extension of public elementary education. She judged him about "fifty years of age, over six feet in height, remarkably erect, with fine features and lively black eyes." With only one year remaining of his second term, the governor was already a dead duck, because of his forays on the state treasury in behalf of internal improvements. Two years earlier, Shulze had been reelected "by the unprecedented majority of approximately 72,000 votes to about 2,000 for his opponent." If he found any consolation for the sorry ending of his public career, it was that the publicity stirred up by his projects for the betterment of the state paved the way for improvements initiated by his successors in the next decade.

Though Pennsylvania was displeased with the governor, the state capital was delighted with the visit of the "much talked of female writer who now obtains the greatest share of publick attention of any of her literary compeers." All who met her, said one newspaper, "acknowledged she was a *rara avis*. All, too, admired the great conversational powers of which she is possessed—the witty attack—the prompt repartee." [10]

3

So far everything had gone smoothly. Not one anti-Mason or Presbyterian had bothered her. At Carlisle, less than twenty miles from hospitable Harrisburg, the storm broke.

I had been solicited for two years back [said Anne Royall], to visit Carlisle and give them a dressing, as they had become formidable to the peace, safety and liberty of all who refused to receive the mark of the beast. Some of our first men have been educated at Dickinson College, and speak of the faculty in the highest terms. But since the church and state scheme, Carlisle's college has become the rallying point of "good sound Presbyterians." I found the town and college worse than I would dare imagine.

Dickinson College locked windows and doors—front and back—against entry of the visitor. An inquisitive professor peeked at her from behind the corner of a building, but Anne never caught up with him. She was not as fleet as she had been. She knocked on the door of the president's house and was informed the president had gone to the college.

"Has he breakfasted?" asked Anne.

No, he had not breakfasted. The determined caller returned half an hour later. The president was "in," but refused to receive Mrs. Royall.

A call on the Reverend George Duffield of the First Presbyterian Church would have been as fruitless. Before her arrival in Carlisle, the Reverend Mr. Duffield told his flock that Mrs. Royall "was doing more mischief than any other person in the United States." The congregation accepted his verdict. "Not one of the ladies," and few of their consorts, visited Anne. "Many of the Presbyterians said they would consider themselves disgraced to have me speak well of them." "Pious females" were especially zealous in

their efforts to discomfit the mischievous guest. Accompanied by
Doctor W. B. Powell, one of the town's "liberal and decent men,"
Mrs. Royall drove in a chaise along the main street. As she rode
past a group of women, one of them observed in a loud voice that
the doctor could "be after no good when he gallanted a harlot."

The remark furnished the theme for a lengthy letter to Mr.
Wightman, editor of the *Carlisle Gazette*, in which Mrs. Royall,
after telling of the incident, gave Carlisle the "dressing" solicited
from her. "But what does this and sundry things communicated to
me in Carlisle prove?" concluded the letter.

The vilest hypocracy! Do they learn this out of the Bible? This
outrage upon the rights of hospitality is disgraceful. It will not sound
well to the world because it shows the danger of those religious
tyrants. Not an editor in the place, I am told, with the exception of
yourself, has the courage to publish any liberal sentiment!—so much
so are they afraid of incurring the displeasure of the priest-ridden
gentry. But I hope my friends the editors will sound the alarm from
one end of the Union to the other to put our country on its guard
against religious tyranny. I was told in Carlisle, that many who did
not, would have visited me, but were afraid of the blue-skins!—Mark
this, ye who prize your liberty! It savors of church and state.[11]

The "Carlisle Letter," as it became known, "flew over the State
like wildfire." In Bedford Anne Royall walked into the littered
office of Charles M. McDowell, editor of the *Gazette*. He was
working frenziedly to meet his deadline, preparing to reprint the
Carlisle letter for the second time. People had borrowed the lone
office copy of the first printing "till it was worn out." McDowell
prefaced the second printing with announcement that Mrs. Royall
had arrived "in our goodly (not godly) town. . . . She is a
sprightly, active, bustling little woman—she uses no ceremony—is
plain and blunt, which we like, and afraid of nothing." Oh, but
she was. There was an inward trembling at each encounter.[12]

4

At dusk, on December 4, "one month and twenty days" from
Philadelphia, Anne Royall rolled into Pittsburgh, "having lost

everything but the clothes on my back and the reticule in my bosom." The trunk had been missing five days, but was brought in sometime after her arrival at Mr. Griffin's. Anne's room had two beds and she invited an old lady who had come with her in the coach to occupy one of them. "She was unaccustomed to travelling and seemed fearful of keeping by herself." Next day Landlord Griffin requested Mrs. Royall to move. She had "insulted the agent" of the stagecoach, accusing him of stealing a bundle of books which she had not received and never did receive. Calling on Anne about this time was Mayor M. M. Murray. She asked the mayor to find her other accommodations. E. J. Roberts, clerk of the United States Court, and clerk of the Common Council, took her into his home.

Pittsburgh further filled her with "dread." It was unlike any city she had visited, with "volumes of smoke, fires, thundering steam factories, and the fumes of furnaces," extending into the suburbs.

All the houses are colored quite black with the smoke; the interiors of the houses are still worse; carpets, chairs, walls, furniture—all black with smoke. No such thing as wearing white; the ladies mostly dress in black, with a cap or white ruff. Put on clean in the morning, ruffs are tinged black by bed-time; the ladies are continually washing their faces. The smoke is most annoying to the eyes; and everything has a very gloomy, doleful appearance.

The doleful scene worsened directly after Mrs. Royall began her sightseeing. The town's water pipes burst and mud covered the paved sidewalks. Walking was slippery and arduous, "too great for a female, particularly one of years and lame." Still, off she went, day after day, from early morning to dusk, visiting and describing glass factories, construction of steam engines, manufacture of paper, the town, the people. "I spent thirteen days in the manufacturing houses and founderies. During the whole of my visit to the factories, I never saw an instance of intoxication. Had they been expecting me, I should have thought their manners assumed." She ascribed the soberness of the workmen to the advanced development of organized labor. That year the first labor party in the world organized in Pennsylvania and issued the first labor journal.

At the Columbian Steam Engine Company, the traveler gazed in awe at the nearly completed one-hundred-horsepower engine ordered by a Philadelphia company. Once the powerful engine was ready and functioning, it would be taken apart and sent east over the mountains by wagon.

But Bakewell's is the place. Whoever wishes to see the blowing of glass done with ease and dispatch, let them visit the glass-house. One man alone makes 240 decanters per day. The furnace has been in blast five years. The establishment is entirely devoted to the manufacture of white or flint glass, and has succeeded in producing the best specimens of this article ever made in the United States. The quantity, variety, beauty and brilliancy of the endless miles of glass at Bakewell's is the greatest show I have ever seen. The factory has introduced a new fashion of stamping figures on the glass while it is warm.

Pittsburgh newspapers fought over Mrs. Royall. Fortunately the score was three to one in her favor. Three published the Carlisle letter, but the fourth denounced her in the usual fashion. For the first time she received a batch of anonymous letters, "abandoned and obscene."

"Throw them in the fire, Mrs. Royall," advised her host, Clerk Roberts.

"No sir," said Anne. "These letters will show how *godly* these Presbyterians are making their women."

Selecting the worst of the lot, she tacked it on the wall of Mayor Murray's office for all to read.[13]

Anne Royall had intended to turn back east from Pittsburgh, but, hearing that Fanny Wright was scheduled to lecture at Wheeling, she accepted the invitation of "H. Holdship, Esq." to go with him and his daughter by steamboat as far as Steubenville where Mr. Holdship owned the Clinton Paper Mill, "the greatest paper manufactory in the western country." Anne inspected the mill and then parted with her friend to visit the school conducted under the Pestalozzi method, a Swiss importation which had brought advanced educational ideas to the New World. Francis Joseph Nicholas Neef, an Alsatian who had introduced the method in Philadelphia and then, by invitation, taken it to Robert Owen's colony in New Harmony, Indiana, had opened his school in Steubenville, after failure of the Owen experiment.

Mrs. Royall spent a day observing Mr. Neef at his task as teacher.

Because of my poor comprehension I cannot do the Pestalozzi system justice in this description. The scheme supposes that man is essentially an active and social being. The effects of one man's activity must, of course, affect his fellow man. If nothing beneficial results from their coming together, then the negative effect is harmful. The scheme goes on to prove by what means we can produce happiness to ourselves and the greatest sum of good to all our fellow creatures. Nothing new is taught, but old things are taught in a new way. The teacher tries to develop what is found within the pupil. Thus the faculties of the pupil unfold, and, in the end, he finds himself qualified to be happy and to dispense happiness all around him. He is taught arithmetic, grammar, chemistry, natural and moral philosophy, astronomy, geography, ethics, &c., all without the help of a, b, c's, [the learning of which Signor Pestalozzi was convinced took more time than they were worth. Shades of Major Royall!]

Throughout the day Mrs. Royall followed Mr. Neef from one class to another. She thought him "most witty" as he explained the Pestalozzian reclassification of verbs. "He annihilates our grammar with a dash of the pencil. 'I march,' he said, 'is a neuter verb. It denotes neither action nor passion. I love is an active verb. When a young man is whispering soft nonsense in the ear of his mistress, to be sure he is the busiest man in the world.' "

Mr. Neef conducted nature study classes in gardens that he himself had planted. "The whole kingdom of plants undergoes a thorough examination—their uses to mankind, their diseases. Thus he goes on, observing, describing, and analyzing the earth, water, stones, metals, trees, plants, birds, worms and so on."

The school day finished, Mrs. Royall took a moment to write a description of Mr. Neef. He was not handsome, but "polite, lively, gay, middle-aged, middle height, rather heavy. He was plainly dressed in gray surtout." His most outstanding feature was "profuse hair which lay in clusters over his forehead." Finally she tested him on his religious views.

"All religions consist of dogmas and morals," said Mr. Neef. "All religions oppose crimes, as they ought to do, and they try to inculcate virtue, as they ought to do." He kept hands off religion in his school. His pupils were free "to think as they please." Personally Mr. Neef was opposed to missionaries and because of his opposition "the missionaries were already great enemies of his."

"I should rejoice to see a school of this description in every county, town, and city of the Union," said Anne Royall.[14]

Mrs. Royall rode the stage south, hoping to reach Wheeling in time for Fanny Wright's lecture. She liked what she had read of the Scotswoman who jolted tradition by taking to the platform to expound her liberal views. Miss Wright "attacked religion, the influence of the church in politics, the existing system of education based on authority, and defended equal rights for women." A handsome, bosomy woman nearly six feet tall, Fanny Wright had come to the U.S.A. with Lafayette in 1824. She was in her midtwenties and their association, as she followed him about the country, might have become a scandal if the ancient hero had not been so much revered. After the Marquis returned to France, Fanny, who had inherited a fortune, remained to work for causes. She had bought a tract of land in Tennessee to initiate a scheme to emancipate Negro slaves. She purchased slaves and put them on her land, calculating that after five years they would have earned their freedom. (In 1830 she shipped the first boatload of freedmen to Haiti.) Inevitably her social views brought friendship with the Owens, father and son, who were struggling to create a better way of life for mankind at their New Harmony colony. Her connection with the Owens confirmed the public's opinion of Frances Wright: She was a socialist and a believer in free love.

Arrived at the tavern in Wheeling, Anne Royall was disappointed to learn that "Miss Wright, after lecturing several nights to crowded houses, had left town two days since."

"She is very popular," remarked Anne.

"Very popular amongst the gentlemen," interposed a female voice. "She is not respected among the ladies."

In the privacy of her room, Mrs. Royall had to admit to herself that "Miss Wright goes farther than I do." She referred, of course, to woman suffrage, a movement she never approved. It was simply a difference of opinion, and that was all right. She admired what "Miss Fanny has done to arouse working men to a sense of their rights, by encouraging general education, and abolishing monopolies, &c." [15]

Anne Royall returned to Pittsburgh on Christmas day, which she spent alone. At three o'clock the morning after, with "my heart palpitating with a species of delight," she boarded the stage for Denniston, now become a town, to visit her sister Mary whom she "had seen but twice in fifty years, and her husband never." At the Denniston farm she was greeted by William Denniston, son of John and Nancy Denniston. The elder Dennistons were both dead and so was their son John. The farmhouse she had known so well had been torn down. Nancy Denniston "had no recollection of me! I was rather hurt." Still they sat and talked nostalgically of old times and "the best room in the house was fitted up for my use."

Anne's sister lived on Mount Pisgah where the Newports had first settled in Pennsylvania. The place was still hard to get to. No one seemed to think that Anne Royall should ride a horse and she herself had doubts not having sat a horse in half a dozen years. But she was willing to try. In the morning Anne mounted the gentle Mrs. Fly and rode off with William Denniston. They followed the Loyalhanna most of the way and for the visitor it was a trip down Memory Lane. They passed the sites of the Blane place, the Parr brothers' farm and the block house at Shield's.

Mary received her sister with "a most inhospitable frown and a cold eye." Anne immediately "set her down as a missionary." And she was correct. Mary was "a mighty pious Methodist." The husband, Mr. Cowan—she never knew his first name—greeted his sister-in-law warmly. Cowan was a Mason. The Cowans had eight sons "all living, and four daughters. None of the sons lived with them, most of the children being married and gone." If they talked of Anna Malvina, Mrs. Royall makes no mention.

The younger sister was properly impressed when a boatload of men came across the river from Saltsburg to meet Mrs. Royall.

"Mary was surprised that so great a mark of respect should be paid me."

So the sisters met as strangers and strangers they remained.[16]

From the Denniston farm Anne Royall went to Lewiston to see Colonel DeWitt Clinton, junior. Lewiston was the "rendezvous of all the canal people" and Clinton was chief engineer of the project. They talked sadly of his father, dead less than a year. The son had "the same eyes, chin, forehead of the father. He was very pale, doubtless from intense application to his duties."

Lewiston proudly sent Mrs. Royall off in a stagecoach especially outfitted for her comfort. "The coach had been neatly painted, stuffed and lined anew, the stage-lanterns were shining, the horses the best in the line, and the driver no way behind." On the outskirts of Harrisburg, the stage tried to pass beneath a temporary bridge that canal workers had stretched overhead across the road. "The top of the stage was torn off and a shower of wooden fragments fell over me. Our escape was miraculous in that the wood did not pierce our skulls." So that was the end of the beautiful coach decked out to honor the crusading Anne Royall. At dawn, in a snowstorm, "a very genteel man" took Anne in a sleigh across the Susquehanna to the state capital.

The hazards of arrival in Harrisburg were soon forgotten in an enthusiastic welcome. Next day was Sunday and Mrs. Royall was invited to attend church. General Ogle, a veteran of the Revolution and sire of a progressive Pennsylvania political dynasty, escorted her to the Episcopal Church. We have a short eye-witness account in the letter of "a gentleman" sent to the Charleston editor who was never a friend to Mrs. Royall:

She is a woman probably seventy years of age [!] with very sharp eyes, and a great deal of vivacity, possessing the highest veneration for the masculine fraternity, and a most cordial detestation of priests, missions, bible societies, tract societies and christianity in general. . . . On leaving the Church, a splendid barouche drawn by a pair of cream colored horses, attended by six out-riders, was in waiting. . . . It so happened, whether from the prevalence of an epidemic at Harrisburg, or for some other causes . . . the General, the Lady, all their attendants wore spectacles, those of the outriders, green ones. This spectacle, or rather spectacles, must have been novel to the citizens of Harrisburg, as a large concourse of spectators assembled at every point from which a view of it was likely to be obtained. On the day following she was escorted to the capitol in the same style.

The Senate and the House honored Anne Royall with a banquet. The members who had voted for chartering the Sunday School Union were pointed out. Anne had intended to chide them in her Pennsylvania book, but then decided the legislators "do not deserve a place." The only one to receive a "place" was the "Hon. Logan who is keen for uniting *Church and State;* he openly avows it, and is a warm friend of Dr. Ely's. May both their HEADS be severed before we see the day." She stood up and gave a toast: "*Blue-skins—may all their throats be cut!*" [17]

CHAPTER XIII

"LIKE RAVENS AROUND CARRION"

1

Triumphant, Mrs. Royall came home to Washington feeling better than at any time since the Vermont "ejectment." She settled to work on the third volume of *The Black Book*, paying slight heed to a cold parlor where a cleaning woman had neglected to lay a fire. Six weeks later *Black Book*, III, as peppery as promised, was on sale and the first volume of *Mrs. Royall's Pennsylvania or Travels Continued in the United States* was being made ready for the printer.

On March 4, 1829, Anne Royall put down her overworked pen to attend the inauguration of Andrew Jackson. The coming of the new order was pregnant with anticipation, for rich and poor. In the days before the inaugural she had watched the common man and his family trooping into the Capital, in wagons and afoot. The District had never before seen the motley likes of the droves of arrivals. Through cold nights they slept in wagons or in the public parks, confident that the hero they had elected to the Presidency would tear down the wall of privilege which had shut them away from a golden life. In the warmth of their comfortable beds, the privileged few slept fitfully, afraid of what the uncouth hordes had in store for them. "My fear is stronger than my hope," wrote Senator Daniel Webster to worried manufacturers in Boston.[1]

"To grace the occasion," Anne Royall spent two dollars for a new dress. At an early hour she went to the Senate Chamber to witness the swearing in of new members. The foreign ministers, "covered with gold lace," glittered undemocratically. "The Danish Minister must have had several pounds weight of gold upon him. General Jackson was the plainest dressed man in the Chamber, in a suit of black, and with a cane. After taking off his hat he bowed respectfully. He was thin and pale and his hair, which was black when I first saw him, was now almost white, and his countenance was melancholy." Melancholy he was, though inwardly on fire. Sitting about him in the Chamber were men of desperate political ambitions whom he blamed for the cruel death of his beloved Rachel. On Christmas day, ten weeks earlier, he had buried his slandered wife in the garden of The Hermitage and then taken off by carriage for Washington, with no heart for the work ahead.

Inauguration Day was "mild and serene," by comparison with what went on behind the scenes.

The officials at Washington, who were friends of Mr. Adams, had agreed not to participate in the inaugural ceremonies, and the only uniformed company of light infantry commanded by Colonel Seaton, of the *National Intelligencer*, had declined to offer its services as an escort. [The day before, the Adams family had quit the White House to visit friends in a suburb, thus avoiding any show of hospitality to the new President.] A number of Revolutionary officers, however, had hastily organized themselves, and walked with General Jackson from Gadsby's Hotel to the Capitol.[2]

A few minutes before noon Mrs. Royall moved toward the east portico of the Capitol "to select an eligible place," where she could view the first outdoor inaugural. By "hard squeezing," she achieved the entrance and was

. . . wedged up. Not only every seat, but every inch of platform was crowded with men, women and children. These had forced the guards, and taken possession. I saw nothing of the President but the top of his head; nor did I hear one word of his address; much less did I hear him taking the oath. The firing of the cannon, and the shouting of the multitude proclaimed the new President. The earth was literally covered with people, who maintained neither order nor regularity. If ever I am caught in such another crowd, it will be an accident.

She did not give up. "I ran upstairs to look out some upper windows, and here I found a colored man in a violent passion. He had been locked up.

" 'I was always for Jackson,' said the prisoner, 'but if this is his way, I wish Adams was President again.' "

Mrs. Royall returned to the Senate Chamber where the session had resumed. She gazed about, noting improvements made during her absence in Pennsylvania. "The old gallery has been torn down, and replaced by another, more beautiful, and infinitely more convenient." Unfortunately the beautiful gallery "was crowded with a vast number of gaudy-dressed women," who overflowed onto the floor and "intruded upon the members. It is evident these women only come to show their finery."

Sitting beside Mrs. Levi Woodbury, wife of the senator from Maine, Anne greeted old and new members, who congratulated her on the Pennsylvania tour. Senator Augustus S. Foot, of Connecticut, "a handsome, middle-sized Yankee and anti-Federalist, rolled his black eyes" coyly and said:

"There's no escaping you." Hoping to make the senator curious enough to buy a book, Anne told him she "had him down in *The Black Book*."

"Ah!" said Senator Foot, "I have been down many times."

The ladies tittered and remarked how "clever and amusing the senator is."

No less ingratiating was John Tyler of Virginia, "a fine-looking man." The senator introduced his wife and daughter, "a little sylph," who remained to ask innumerable questions about note-taking. Until publication of the next opus, the senator from Virginia seems to have been apprehensive as to what Mrs. Royall might write about the Tylers. One can almost hear him sighing with relief when he wrote his wife: "Mrs. Royall's book is here at last. . . . She speaks highly of all of us." [3]

Reluctantly Mrs. Royall abandoned the Senate to do her duty by the House of Representatives where she always had "labored under great disadvantage, from distance and want of light." This time she was not so distant that she could not see copies of *Black Book*, III, which had been placed on congressmen's desks, as a reminder they were for sale, had disappeared. Alas! The books had not been sold but "pilfered by the rabble." Only one representative "sent me a quarter of an eagle in gold [about $2.50]."

The first House interview was with the "affable and genteel" James K. Polk of Tennessee. "He is of middling height, with fair good face, high smooth forehead, and light gray eyes."

Anne gave her relative-by-marriage a breezy nod. John Randolph of Roanoke did not nod back. Even so, the lady could not refrain from admiring his "black, piercing eyes."

The thrill of the day was an introduction to Governor William Clark, superintendent of Indian affairs, up from St. Louis headquarters to witness the resurrection of democracy. The surviving partner of the Lewis and Clark expedition could still boast "a pretty fine figure" in his sixtieth year.

In company with a "mob, black and white, of all sorts," the weary author trudged to the White House to attend the inaugural reception. A crowd already jammed the East Room, "neatly though plainly furnished, not a particle of alabaster." A fortunate omission this was, in view of the havoc wrought that day by the celebrants. "They clambered upon the satin furniture with their muddy boots. . . . Only after disgraceful scenes in the parlors, in which even women got bloody noses, was the situation relieved by the device of setting tubs of punch on the lawn to lure the new 'democracy' out of the house."

President Jackson kept his composure, even displaying, said Anne, "great courtesy," as he submitted to interviews "with both high and low, rich and poor." Another observer declared that he behaved like the "servant in the presence of the Sovereign, the People."

Among the People, Anne Royall was "astonished to encounter that insidious advocate of Church and State," the Reverend Ezra Stiles Ely. It was out of character that Old Hickory, "hostile to the Hartford Convention, should countenance" the Presbyterian, members of whose family had participated in the secret Federalist gathering to talk up peace at any price in the War of 1812.[4]

Ever suspicious of the clergy's rise to power, Mrs. Royall began to look about her for an explanation of Doctor Ely's presence. Jackson's political opponents, those who had not spurned the reception, concocted a story to muddle her and poke fun at the new executive. Doctor Ely was slated, they told her, to be the new Secretary of the Treasury. Anne was not misled. She stumbled upon part of the Ely design (the rest would come out shortly and nearly shatter the new administration). The Reverend Doctor Ely had come close to the throne through friendship with the religious Emily Donelson who, upon the death of Aunt Rachel Jackson, had consented to serve as the President's hostess. Emily's cousin and husband, Andrew Jackson Donelson, was his foster father's private secretary. Unabashed by the high station of young Emily, Anne Royall asked her why she had invited to the reception a clergy-man so opposed to "the firm republican principles of General Jackson."

"Doctor Ely is a very fine man," said Mrs. Donelson, and walked off. Anne walked off, mumbling: "She is a very ignorant woman." [5]

2

In the days immediately following the inaugural, Mrs. Royall reported that adherents of Doctor Ely were "thickening in the city, particularly around the person of the President." Still, she expressed "great confidence in the integrity of Old Hickory."

Her confidence appeared justified when, in May, 1829, Jackson removed George Watterston from his post as librarian of Congress. Anne crowed.

Home from Pennsylvania, she had been shocked to come across books and pamphlets of the Sunday School Union scattered over reading tables of the Library. "How dare Mr. W. suffer the books of Dr. Ely to be put there! Does Congress want to be instructed by these books?" Anne had protested against the stock of Ely books and Mr. Watterston ordered her from the Library room. "He was very insolent," though his discourtesy pricked her sensitive nature less than the conclusion that "there appears no longer any doubt of Mr. Watterston having gone over to the black coats." She did not hesitate to spy on the librarian. "He entertains shoals of these missionaries. Pass his house when you will, you will find it enveloped in a flock of black coats, like ravens around carrion." She canvassed the House, recommending a congressional investigation, but decided little could be expected in this quarter. There were "traitors in the service of Doctor Ely in the House." [6]

How correct was her surmise as to the bond between Watterston and some House members, Anne Royall was never able to pin down during her lifetime. Proof of one of the librarian's extracurricular entanglements is presented here for the first time, as far as I know. It was found in a letter sent by Watterston to Representative Edward Everett of Massachusetts in January, 1829, shortly before Jackson moved into the White House. Everett, a former Unitarian minister, was chairman of the House committee for the Library of Congress. Wrote Watterston: "I have delivered to Mr. Coyle the Sunday School books and as many bibles and testaments as he wanted agreeably to the order of the Committee." John Coyle was an elder of the First Presbyterian church, presently employed as clerk in the office of the First Auditor. Remember him. He will play a most unchristian role in this history of Anne Royall.

What Mrs. Royall suspected George Watterston guilty of had nothing to do with the dismissal of the librarian from the government office he had occupied for fourteen years. Political gossip had it that Watterston was fired because he had supported Henry Clay in the 1828 campaign for the presidency. Not only did Jackson believe Clay had entered into a "corrupt bargain" in the 1824 election, delivering his block of supporters to the Adams party in exchange for appointment to the office of Secretary of State, but Jackson also blamed Clay for circulation of slanders against Rachel Jackson with which the Kentuckian had hoped to disgrace Jackson and so win in the 1828 campaign. With the passing of time, the "corrupt bargain" might have dimmed in importance, but Old Hickory could never forgive attacks on the good name of his wife.

The Kentuckian was no less bitter toward the man who had

frustrated him in attainment of the highest office in the land. Until
he resigned from the Senate in 1842—even until 1848 when his
party once again declined to nominate him for the Presidency—
Clay strove to "weld together all the elements of protest against
Jackson." In the Senate, to which he was returned in 1831, Kentucky's "favorite son" unremittingly "attacked Jackson and harassed him," all to no avail. Tennessee's "favorite son" remained
the people's choice.

From his Kentucky plantation, Henry Clay wrote to console
the jobless Mr. Watterston:

Your removal from the office of Librarian . . . was a step in keeping with the despotism that now rules Washington. . . . I rejoice . . .
to perceive that you possess a soul which is not to be subdued by the
exertion of tyranny. . . . I hope both you and I shall live to see the
Nation rid of its present misrule, and the Jacksons and the Greens and
the Eatons and the host of kindred spirits driven back to their original
stations and insignificance."

After two weeks, the ex-librarian, his soul subdued by the needs
of a livelihood, went to work as an editorial writer for the *National
Journal* (anti-Jackson). His first contribution was an unsigned
editorial assailing his discharge. It was "a gross outrage on the rights
of Congress." Duff Green's *United States Telegraph* (pro-Jackson)
replied: "The astonishment was that an individual altogether unfit
for the situation should have been so long tolerated. . . . The Library . . . owing to the carelessness and incapacity of the Librarian, was in a state of great derangement." The *National Journal*
defended its new staff member and the *Telegraph* had a reply for
that. The tit-for-tat argument might have gone further, if Anne
Royall had not suddenly become the hottest news in Washington.[7]

3

Mrs. Royall had been quick to note that many changes had taken
place in the neighborhood of the Bank House during her absence
in Pennsylvania. "Capitol Hill is a den of blackcoats." The first

Sunday morning she was awakened by "stones rapping against my windows. Looking out, I saw several little boys and girls around the [Columbia] Engine House. They seemed trigged up neat and clean, but continued to fling stones."

"What are you doing?" Anne shouted.

Permission, it developed, had been given to hold Sunday School and church services in the Engine House. The trigged up children smashed a couple of Royall windows and Anne retreated to await the arrival of parents. She met them on the sidewalk. Her complaints were coldly received. She was face to face with readers who disapproved what she wrote about the Protestant churches. Still, these churchgoers adopted what they must have believed was a Christian attitude in dealing with a misguided woman. That Sunday night and for many nights thereafter, groups of them gathered beneath the broken windows to pray for Mrs. Royall's salvation. They carried "loads of tracts to my door, crying out 'who wants to go to heaven? Here is your passport.'" Anne wanted only to go to sleep and rest for the labors of the morrow. The monotonous intoning was "torment," but, we can be sure, she did not accept it without protest. The Anderson kitchen vocabulary was resurrected and poured forth full strength on her would-be redeemers. John Coyle, senior, the "commander-in-chief" who led the nocturnal vigil, later testified that Mrs. Royall called him a "d——d old bald headed son of a b——h." Not once, but three times!

"He is the only person in the world who ever heard me swear," commented Anne.

Redemption got out of hand. "Holy mobs of boys (black and white)" joined the Engine House evangelists, not to pray, but "to shower the house with stones, yell and blow horns." Holy Wiley, as Anne named Coyle, had to abandon his night work which was getting nowhere and meet with aides to discuss what should be done about the "stubborn spirit" of Mrs. Royall. It was this meeting, according to Anne who appears to have received a full report from a friendly spy, that decided she had to be "removed." "This woman is beyond grace," one member said. Holy Wiley presented his views. "If we let her alone, gentlemen, to write more *Black Books,* she will *Black Book* us out of being. A civil presentation is our only hope. Some slight crime that will put her in the work-house. Our business is to find the evidence; for instance, drunken-ness." While the "gospel spreaders engaged in prayer and suppli-cation to heaven to aid them," inquiry went on all over the U.S.A., but Holy Wiley had set them on the wrong track. No one had ever seen the widow of Major William Royall take an alcoholic drink. So the council reconvened with attorneys. They decided to present charges to the Grand Jury.[8]

On June 1, after hearing the testimony of the four Coyles—father, son, daughter, son-in-law; of John Watterston, John O. Dunn, House sergeant-at-arms; and Lewis M. Machen, Senate office clerk, the Grand Jury indicted Anne Royall on three counts. Number one charged her with "being an evil-disposed person, a common slanderer and disturber of the peace and happiness of her quiet and honest neighbors." The second count accused her as a "common scold." The third reiterated the second, Mrs. Royall having continued her "annoyances" while the grand jury investiga-tion was in progress.

As with criticism that ensued after publication of each travel book, the press lined up pro and con, politically and religiously. Though delighted with the assurance that Anne would be "sup-pressed as a nuisance," a Boston editor fretted lest banishment from the District of Columbia might work a hardship on the New England city. "We feel a terror at the very idea of her coming this way." As to be expected, Major Noah's *Morning Courier and New York Enquirer*, the new name of the major's merged journals, stood gallantly with Anne. "She has fallen into the pit and we hope may be dealt with in a lenient way, corresponding with her age and infirmities."

But Major Noah could not let well enough alone. After a few days, with impish cleverness, he spun a tale about the marshal delegated to serve the bench warrant. Although a veteran of the Battle of Bladensburg, the marshal was "quaking in his boots." He said he preferred an encounter with a "rhinoceros rather than come within the pale of Mrs. R.'s tongue." But the servant of the law got around his dilemma. "The marshal . . . has so contrived matters," continued Major Noah, "as to afford her [Anne] a hint

of her intended arrest, and she has taken advantage . . . and de-
camped." Mrs. R. herself rebuked the major for the slur on her
want of courage. "Be it known," apologized the editor, "Anne
Royall continues to reside on Capitol Hill, receiving the daily
homage of her friends, and dispensing terror and dismay among her
enemies."

Noah blamed his misinformation on "our Washington correspondent"—at the time James Gordon Bennett, a staunch defender
who sat beside Mrs. Royall during the subsequent trial in the circuit court, advising and consoling. Bennett viewed the action as
nothing less than an attack on the freedom of the press.

William Leete Stone's *New York Commercial Advertiser* lavishly
complimented the Grand Jury. "It required no ordinary share of
. . . courage, in any three and twenty men to make so daring an
attack upon the rights of this belligerent woman." Later the *Advertiser* printed a lengthy letter from a phrenologist who signed
himself "Phren and Logos." He said he had "seen, conversed with
and observed the Phrenological indications in Mrs. Royall." His
conclusion: "Gentlemen, she is beyond a doubt PARTIALLY
insane."

Mrs. Royall took up so much space in the public press that even
the complacent *Niles' Register* unbent. "This female having obtained considerable notoriety in the United States, as a traveling
merchant*ess*, for the sale of her own 'home-made books'—some may
be interested in learning that she was presented to the court of the
U. S. sitting in Washington, as a 'common scold.' "

"An *uncommon scold*," corrected a South Carolina editor.

The *New York Observer*, a religious journal of rare dignity,
for the first time admitted the name of Mrs. Royall to its columns.
Despite the indictment, reported the *Observer*, the culprit was "as
free of limb and tongue, and came into court . . . for the purpose of obtaining a list of the Grand Jury. . . . She menaces them
with a fearful visitation of her displeasure, and her menaces seldom
evaporate in thin air."

A Bedford, Pennsylvania, newspaper gave a different version of
Mrs. Royall's appearance in court. She "made her *debut* like a ver-
nal morning, bright with sunny smiles." [9]

4

Her debut took place at the preliminary hearing before the United
States circuit court of the District of Columbia, which occupied a
room in the nearly new City Hall situated in Judiciary Square.
Chief Justice William Cranch, a Jefferson appointee who was on
his way toward establishing a record of fifty-four years service with
the circuit court, threw out the first and third counts of the indictment and ordered trial on the second count which charged Anne
Royall with being "a common scold."

Reluctantly Thomas Swann, the prosecuting attorney, accepted
the curtailed indictment, but Richard Coxe, an outstanding member
of the bar who had volunteered to defend Mrs. Royall, moved
for a new trial on the ground that the code provided no punishment to fit the misdemeanor charged against his client. "By the
common law," contended Mr. Coxe, "the only punishment of a
common scold is ducking—a mode of punishment which is obsolete
in England, and was never inflicted in Maryland, under whose
common law the prosecution was commenced."

After deliberation, Justice Cranch ruled that "although punishment by ducking may have become obsolete, yet the offense still
remains a common nuisance, and, as such, is punishable by fine and
imprisonment." [10]

Trial of Mrs. Royall was postponed for a few days while court
concluded another case. Meanwhile, press and public, ignoring the
words of Justice Cranch, went wild over the prospect of a public
ducking.

"She is destined to immortalize the Tiber,—alias Goose Creek,"
informed a Boston newspaper. "Perhaps from two to four hours
will be thought long enough for her to remain under water."

"We recommend to the marshal to postpone the execution of the
probable sentence, until winter," wrote the *New York Commercial
Advertiser.* "A dozen such lavations during the dog-days would
only be so many refreshing luxuries."

Niles' Register, usually so concise within the limited space of its undersized pages, confounded readers with a lengthy history of the obsolete law which Justice Cranch said would not be resurrected.

The term *scold* is of uncertain signification—the offense is not well defined. . . . Jacobs' Dictionary . . . says "a woman indicted for being a common scold, if convicted, *shall* be sentenced to be *placed* on a certain engine of correction called the *trebucket, tumbrel, tumborella, castigatory*, or *cucking-stool*, which in Saxon signifies *scholding stool;* though now it is frequently corrupted into *ducking-stool;* because the *residue* of the judgment is, that when she is placed therein, she shall be plunged in the water for her punishment."

Snatching a moment for courtroom oratory the prosecuting attorney ignored Justice Cranch's ruling to "express his desire that Mrs. Royall should enjoy the benefit of a cold bath with as much privacy as possible." A newspaper reporter wrote that Anne looked up from her notebook and "smiled very graciously" at Mr. Swann.

The Navy Yard likewise paid no heed to the justice's words. On Navy Yard Hill was constructed a ducking-stool, which brought out crowds to inspect the engine of punishment which would never administer Anne Royall's chastening. One may wonder that a branch of the federal government should employ time and money in this fashion, but if there is an explanation we do not know it. Commodore Isaac Hull was no friend of Mrs. Royall. Recently, making the rounds of Washington, she had called at the Yard and sent her name into the commodore. Hull instructed a servant to say he was ill. It was the old snub.

"Is there any hope of his death?" Mrs. Royall asked, walking away from the grinning messenger.[11]

The correspondent of the *Morning Courier and New York Enquirer* observed that "two topics alone appear, for the last four or five weeks, to have engrossed . . . the attention of the good people of this district." The first topic was the trial of Mrs. Royall and the second the insufferable heat of the humid Washington summer. Despite the humidity, the courtroom was filled the day the trial began. An excess of attorneys came to listen to the unusual proceedings, as well as wives of high government officers and of lesser

"City of Washington from beyond the Navy Yard." Lithograph, 1834. *New York Public Library*

employees, and those "gaudy-dressed" ladies already complained of. The ladies did not usually show themselves in court, but word had gone out that *this* was a spectacle not to be missed.

Anne Royall sat next to her attorney "pen in hand, taking notes . . . scorning the public gaze with surprising intrepidity." There was an effusive welcome for Francis Scott Key who was shortly to succeed "Granny" Swann as United States attorney for the District. Magnanimously Anne overlooked the crop of hymns and remembered him solely as the author of the *Star-Spangled Banner*. Never especially fond of children, it pleased her to have a handsome boy, Master Richard Wallach, hanging "over my chair the whole time, with the affection of a son." Handsome Richard was destined to become a newspaperman and later a popular Washington mayor. Another old friend, Clerk of the Court William Brent, danced attendance.

As the trial proceeded newspapers commented on the number of inner-circle Administration members gathered round the common scold. "She's a good Jackson *man*," declared one writer. To be so classified that overheated summer of 1829, Jackson's first in the White House, was of dubious value. The new President's popularity had tumbled as he began to turn out government officers and employees, devitalized by long service in a soft snap, and to replace them with younger men from his party. The jobless were resentful and vocal, as were their slews of deprived relatives.

But, as Anne Royall gazed about and compared her witnesses, several most distinguished, with the mediocre lot dredged up by the plaintiffs, she felt confident the verdict would be in her favor. She had wanted to summon President Jackson as a character witness, but "he was very properly excused." In his stead he sent Secretary of War John H. Eaton. Pressed for time, the tall, auburn-haired secretary was permitted to give his evidence out of turn. He said no more than that Mrs. Royall had always conducted herself like a lady when she came to his office seeking interviews.[12]

The prosecution produced ten witnesses, three of them members of the Coyle family: Coyle, senior; Coyle, junior; and son-in-law J. C. Whitwell, listed in the same order in the annals of the First Presbyterian Church as the first ruling elders. Lined up with the

Coyles were ex-librarian Watterston, a sprinkling of minor government employees and a boardinghouse keeper, neighbors of the
Coyles and of Mrs. Royall. They testified to "outrages . . . most
abominable and violent" which the defendant had committed. "She
had not ceased to pour out on every one of them torrents of the
most coarse, vulgar, and obscene language, until they could not
appear even at the windows of their house." Other witnesses testified to the abuse of sisters and mothers. A circumstance which
influenced a Pennsylvania newspaper to observe that "had she confined her attacks to men alone, the prosecution would never have
been undertaken." [13]

The Coyle witnesses were grim and dull, hardly worth sweating
it out for. The flagging scene came to life with the first character
witness for the accused. He was H. Tims, Senate doorkeeper, nick-
named "Little Tims" by the solons he served. The correspondent
of Mr. Stone's newspaper wrote as good account as any reporter of
Little Tims's appearance on the stand and so we quote him.

"Coxe began by asking him [Tims] if he knew Mrs. R. to be a
common scold? . . .

"Pray sir," asked Tims. "what is the proper and legal definition of
a common scold? When can a scold be said to be common?; for as
to being a scold, you know all women are that." . . . Changing the
shape of his question, [Mr. Coxe] said, "Well, then, Mr. T. did you
ever know of Mrs. Royall's slandering anybody?" Tims promptly
answered, "Yes, sir—she has slandered *me*." This was rather a stumper
—coming, too, from her own [Mrs. Royall's] witness. "You, Mr. Tims?
how so?" "Why, sir, she has said, and printed it too, in her book, that
I am very clever—and to that I make no objections; in fact, I believe,
on the whole, it is true. . . . But she adds—and a very *exemplary* man.
Now that's a slander."
This was too much. The court roared: bench, bar, and jury. . . .
Tims himself was the only person left unmoved. He looked round
grave as an owl. Just opposite him stood Mr. Waterston [sic], the ex-
librarian, laughing immoderately. Tims catching sight of him, again
opened his oracular jaws. "Yes, sir, and I know of her slandering another person besides me." "Indeed! who is that?" "Why there is Mr.
Waterston, she says in the same book that he and Joe Gales are the

handsomest men in Washington; now I leave it to all the world if *that* is not a slander." The effect of this you may imagine. In vain the constable roared out "silence!" The court room shook to its foundations; and it was sometime before the trial could proceed.

Little Tims was the star performer. Witnesses who followed him were high-class, but their lines were run-of-the-mill. Among them were Mrs. William Greer, wife of a newspaper publisher and printer of several of Mrs. Royall's travel books; the faithful Sally Stack; and John Underwood who, as inheritor of the C Street Spring, gave the District its first water system. All pronounced Mrs. Royall of excellent character. Listening to them, Anne was certain that she would soon walk out of Justice Cranch's courtroom a free woman. But, before her exit, Anne Royall had something to say to the jury.

Solemnly she rose from her seat and

advancing her wrinkled visage [Mr. Stone's correspondent again] she proceeded to obtest and objure them, as they loved liberty and their country, not to sacrifice both in her person. They stood not only for the present age, but were the guardians of posterity. This prosecution was but one branch of the general conspiracy of the blue and black-hearted Presbyterians, the priests and missionaries, against the freedom of speech and of the press. If they were to succeed . . . nothing would be safe—bigotry and all the horrors of the inquisition would overwhelm the land; nothing would be left of all for which her husband and other worthies of the revolution had shed their blood.[14]

Messrs. Coxe and Swann agreed to submit the case to the jury without argument. Unmoved by Mrs. Royall's plea, the jury took only a few minutes to return a verdict of guilty. Justice Cranch imposed a fine of ten dollars and ordered Anne Royall to post a bond of one hundred dollars to guarantee that she would keep the peace for a year. Ten dollars! She did not have it! As for a hundred dollar bond—how long since she had seen a hundred dollars! Anne asked permission to leave the court and hunt up friends who would pay her fine. Before permission was given word of her conviction had been carried to Secretary Eaton who with Major William B.

Lewis and Doctor William Jones, the postmaster, all members of Old Hickory's inner circle, dispatched the ten dollars to the court. Their money was not needed. Two newspaper reporters, employees of Gales & Seaton's *National Intelligencer* "stood up for the honor of the press and the gallantry of the profession," paid Mrs. Royall's fine and went security for her good conduct. One was Thomas Donohoo and I know nothing more of him than his name. The second was Thomas Dowling with whom Mrs. Royall had become acquainted a year earlier when she described him as a "genius." No genius, really, though Dowling did very well for himself, having begun life, "a friendless, homeless orphan."

Naturally Anne Royall was disappointed in the outcome of the trial. She had so much wanted to vanquish the Coyles and their ilk. But perhaps the Coyles were not altogether winners. The trial had given her a forum and much publicity. She had been able to get across her warning message nationally—to all the U.S.A. It was possible that her defeat would make a shambles of the church and state party.[15]

CHAPTER XIV

GARDEN SPOT OF THE SOUTH

1

The trial increased demands for Mrs. Royall's books. After five years of traveling and writing, she had seven volumes available. The best was the first—*Sketches etc.*—and the worst her novel *The Tennessean*. In the works, and probably best of all, was *Letters from Alabama*.

Flushing buyers for her wares was, as we have seen, a very personal pursuit. After a short rest from the court ordeal, the sixty-year-old author, laden with a trunkful of books, headed for New York to cash in on her new-found fame. As a "good Jackson man," she traveled free in stages and on the steamboat lines of John E. Reeside, whose political fealty had been rewarded with a government contract to carry mail between New York and Ohio. Ben Perley Poore facetiously gave Reeside the title of "Land Admiral," but Mrs. Royall put him in the army with the rank of colonel. She described Colonel Reeside as "of towering height, with neat, erect, slender figure." Poore smartens up his admiral with "red hair and side whiskers," who dismissed as unimportant the current transportation revolution. "He used to ridicule the locomotives . . . and offer to bet a thousand dollars that no man could build a machine that would drag a stage from Washington to Baltimore quicker than his favourite team of iron-grays."

Stopping in Baltimore, Mrs. Royall went to look at the few miles of Baltimore and Ohio track which nonagenarian Charles Carroll, last surviving signer of the Declaration of Independence, had inaugurated a year earlier. Anne seconded the opinion of Colonel Reeside. "I think the undertaking one of the wildest schemes for men in their senses; to think of carrying it over the Allegheny at this point, it will take all the iron in this country and Europe." [1]

Next stop was Philadelphia where the author was pleased to find "my books were all gone." She "ran over the city in a trice" and steamed off to New York for hasty calls on booksellers and editors. She "was surprised by the death-like stillness" of Broadway. The citizenry blamed the funereal aspect on tariff legislation sponsored by the Jackson party to win votes in the Middle States and the South. Anne was unsympathetic with the whining metropolitan merchants. "New York has had her good things; let those good things go around." On a following visit to the city, she remarked that storekeepers were even more "distressed and gloomy." With seventy-five cents which a Pearl Street dealer paid her for a book, she started a subscription fund to relieve the down-hearted business-men. [2]

After twenty-four hours Colonel Reeside's guest began the return trip south. She slept the night in Philadelphia and made a dawn start down the Delaware River to explore the new water route to Baltimore. "The day was tempestuous and the boat crowded. The ladies' cabin being too small, we sat with the gentlemen." No great hardship that; Anne joined a group of Jackson's staunchest supporters in his battle to place Peggy Eaton on equal social footing with other Cabinet wives: Major William B. Lewis, a Tennessee crony of the President, Postmaster-General William T. Barry, and Doctor William Jones, postmaster at Washington City. They were escorting Mrs. Eaton—"what an elegant figure!"—back to the Capital.

Poor Peggy Eaton! her days were numbered. Even while she sailed down the Delaware, Doctor Ely was at the White House demanding that the President remove the Secretary of War from the Cabinet because his wife was "unchaste." He had come to the inauguration bubbling over with gossip of an abortion which Mrs. Eaton had submitted to before she married the Secretary. Face to face with Andrew Jackson, Ely had lost courage and so went home to Philadelphia to put his accusations in a letter. Old Hickory, loyal to his friend John H. Eaton, refused to believe the Presbyterian minister, but all the king's horses could not have held back the climax in 1831 when Jackson's Cabinet broke up, because the wives still refused to receive Mrs. Eaton.

Time ran off merrily for Anne Royall in the distinguished company aboard the river steamboat. A widower, Auditor Lewis announced that he had placed his daughter in school in Philadelphia. Anne bridled. "I do not approve. In Philadelphia, there is neither refinement, taste, nor science; nothing but tracts and Sunday School Union." The auditor did not argue but continued to keep the party in an uproar with an assortment of tricks and jokes. At the entrance to the newly opened Chesapeake and Delaware Canal, passengers debarked and splashed through the rain to board "an elegant barge drawn by six horses." The steamboat captain held an umbrella over Mrs. Royall as he led her to the canal craft. She fared better than the shapely wife of the Secretary of War. "I happened to turn around when lo! Mr. Lewis, full of mischief, was conducting Mrs. Eaton with the umbrella carefully held over *his* head."

The barge "was much more pleasant than the steamboat, having large windows. The canal is wide and must have cost a vast sum. In order to prevent the clay from washing down into the cut, the sides have been thatched with straw." [3]

2

From Baltimore Anne Royall sailed down the Chesapeake to Norfolk in the *Pocahontas*, "the most splendid boat on the Atlantic waters." She was on her way to Richmond to attend the Virginia Constitutional Convention. At Norfolk she changed to a James River steamboat and from City Point rode the stage to the Virginia capital.

The convention, already in session a month, had been called at the insistence of transmontane Virginia which demanded equal representation with Tidewater in state and local governments. "There never was a greater assembly of men," wrote an enthusiastic historian. The roster was indeed impressive: Madison, Monroe, Marshall, Tazewell, Randolph, Mason, Tyler, Giles, Barbour, Ritchie, Mercer, Cabell—to pick a few names at random. A wall of gawkers shut Anne Royall off at the entrance to the capitol. John Randolph, shriveled and sickly in appearance, stood beside her, likewise frustrated by the throng.

"Sergeant," the congressman called out, "I would thank you to put me in the convention."

The sergeant maneuvered an opening and Anne, clinging like lichen to a rock, followed the delegate inside. After squeezing into a gallery seat, she was annoyed that her view of the dais was blotted out by a "line of big bonnets," the so-called "convention-bonnets, made of white silk, with feathers stuck in them of one yard in length." Mrs. Royall had not traveled hundreds of miles to be thwarted by "silly women who thought to captivate with umbrella bonnets." In a loud voice that carried beyond adjacency, she said:

"I am astonished the sergeant-at-arms would suffer those mantua-makers and milliners to intrude upon the convention."

Next day not one convention-bonnet was seen in the auditorium.

For the first time Anne Royall saw James Madison. "He is a small, aged man. He was dressed in plain Quaker coloured coat, and his hair is powdered." The ex-President, in his seventy-ninth year, earlier had called the delegates to order and, in a quavering voice scarcely audible, had nominated James Monroe to preside. Mrs. Royall worked her way closer the center of oratory. "Several of the members bowed to me, and amongst them Mr. Monroe. I think he is the most diffident man in the world."

The western delegates made Anne Royall "feel proud," especially Philip Doddridge from Brooke County, an isolated finger of Virginia land squeezed between the Ohio River and the Pennsylvania border. (Brooke County threw in with West Virginia when the new state was carved from the Old Dominion.) In debate Congressman Doddridge outshone the famous Randolph at the convention, though the man of Roanoke was the performer the crowds had come to see. "It is difficult to explain," wrote a contemporary, "the influence which he [Randolph] exerted. . . . He was feared alike by East and West. . . . The arrows from his quiver, if not dipped in poison, were pointed and barbed, rarely missed the mark, and as

seldom failed to make a rankling wound . . . What made his attack more vexatious, every sarcasm took effect amid the plaudits of
his audiences." Plaudits were won by Doddridge's runner-up Chapman Johnson, presently residing in Richmond, though representing
his constituency beyond the Blue Ridge, when he bested Randolph
in debate. Glancing down at the wasted form of the congressman,
Johnson said nastily: "Sir, it needs no ghost to tell me *that*." [4]

Johnson, in common with all the westerners, argued for a census
upon which to base a proportionate representation in the Virginia
assembly. Westerners were wont to compare their lot with that of
the earlier colonists. "Taxation without representation." Randolph,
a member of the Old Guard, fought to prevent changes in the constitution. Proportionate representation, recognizing voting privilege without benefit of property ownership, would have weakened
the supremacy of the low country's landholding gentry.

Hearing that several favorite slaves from Peter's Mountain had
fallen into the hands of Mr. Johnson, Anne called at his house to
inquire after them. Chapman Johnson, it will be recalled, had been
the Roane's attorney. She did not get inside the door. Mrs. Johnson
barred the way, saying she was "ve-ee saw-ee," but the household
was busily engaged. "I wonder at Mr. Chapman's choice of a wife,"
mused the rejected visitor, "but suppose she was ve-ee rich." Could
be; she was a daughter of the flush Nicholson clan.

Learning that the Madisons had taken rooms about a mile and a
quarter from Richmond's center, Anne Royall tried to hire a
carriage for the hot, dusty trip. The hackman said "he must have
$1 for hitching, and $2 an hour." The price was outrageous and
so Mrs. Royall "took it afoot." Losing her way, she walked perhaps
three miles before she found the house. But the effort was worth
the greeting Dolly Madison gave her.

I expected to have seen a little old dried up woman; instead a young
active, elegant woman stood before me—the self-same lady of whom
I had heard more anecdotes than any family in Europe and America.
No wonder she was the idol of Washington. Chiefly she captivates by
her artless though warm affability. She and affectation are farther apart
than the poles. She is a tall straight woman, muscular, but not fat,
and as active as a girl. Her face is large, full and oval, rather dark than

fair; her eyes dark, large, and expressive. She is not handsome, nor does she ever appear to have been so. She was dressed in a plain, black silk dress, and wore a silk checked turban. Her curls were black and glossy.

The former first lady busied herself making the visitor comfortable. "She would run out—bring a glass of water, wipe the mud off my shoes and tie them. She pressed me with much earnestness to await dinner." Anne did not wait. With proper directions she walked back to town thinking about the gracious Dolly Madison. "She appears young enough to be Mr. Madison's daughter." [5]

The convention was crowded and the air stale and oppressive. Anne spent less and less time listening to the toiling debaters. Tidewater, "as perfect an aristocracy as ever existed," was winning. She wandered through Richmond, selling her books and collecting snubs. The capital was still the preserve of her in-laws who had never let up with blackening her character. She approached a group of Lowland delegates and all scattered except one. Mr. John Mason Young of Southampton, why didn't you run? "Madam, I should have ran, but I am lame!" He had sprained his ankle. Westerners, however, gave her generous patronage, all except Colonel Andrew Beirne who would not speak to her. In *Black Book*, I, she had reported that around Monroe and Sweet Springs, "he used to be called the greasy peddler."

One day, as Mrs. Royall sat writing at a table in the public room, a portrait painter made a "miniature likeness" of her. The artist was Harvey Mitchell who, even as a boy growing up in Lynchburg, "manifested a talent for drawing, painting and taking likenesses." He painted portraits of the townspeople, quite a few of which are still in the hands of descendants, and then went to South Carolina. Of Mrs. Royall's miniature, there seems to be no trace; nor has any likeness of her ever been found. [6]

3

The convention had a long way to go and so had Anne Royall. Hurriedly she retraced the route to Washington. Aboard the

Pocahontas, she met a little old lady from Charles City who told her that James Roane had died. "Old Roane drank himself to death and his estate went to the dogs," said her informant. Anne had no time to dwell upon the past. Her future lay, in part, with the mail contractors assembled in Washington to negotiate new agreements with the Federal Government. She was getting ready for a tour of the South which would probably require three volumes. The stage owners readily agreed to her proposition that "they frank me through their lines." Mrs. Royall had been an asset to them during the fight to continue Sunday mail service. She might be useful again, for the church opposition was still hammering away at Congress for legislation. The Philadelphia legislature meanwhile had handed Doctor Ely a setback, passing an act "forbidding chains to be drawn across the streets on Sunday in Philadelphia and throughout the state."

Before starting the southern trip, Mrs. Royall sat in the Senate chamber during several sessions listening to the lengthy Webster-Hayne debate. Too close to the event to take in its gravity, she decided to leave it "to Mr. W. to be the conciliator of those conflicting interests which are now convulsing the Union." As for the "muleish Congress," indifferent to revision of the Pension Law—"I leave them to their wine and sins." She said goodbye to Washington January 30, 1830.[7]

The tour began uncomfortably—cold and damp inside the coach and snow falling outside. Rumors of her itinerary had preceded her and unfriendly crowds awaited her at most stage stops. "The Presbyterians have the whole of Virginia under their thumbs," Anne decided. With the memory of Vermont ever present, she was uneasy in the predominantly Protestant territory, and therefore a less aggressive tourist than formerly. In towns where she spent the night or a few days, friends greeted her and their presence was reassuring. People and the snowstorm retarded her progress. To keep to schedule she arrived in Warrenton on a horse, "riding rather unpleasantly behind a young man." Court was sitting and the county seat overflowing with visitors. Major Mark Russell, a high Mason and well-to-do farmer, took charge of selling her books, determined to send the widow of Major Royall on her way with her pockets filled. Each night after supper he climbed the stairs to Anne's parlor to take his "toddy," bringing with him a considerable company of Masons. The flow of toddies brought out the poetic side of the visitors. One visitor recited:

> Hail Virginia old and crazy
> The people poor and lazy.

Another extolled the fame of the state for

> Lowering mountains and broken lights,
> Methodist-meetings, and fist-fights.

Sheriff James lifted his glass:

> Democrats abroad, aristocrats at home,
> Virginians everywhere drink whiskey and chew tobacco.

At the end of each recitation, coins were pitched on the table. After an evening of toddies and doggerel, Major Russell scraped up the cash and dumped it into Anne Royall's lap. She remained four days in Warrenton.

In Winchester Anne accompanied her landlord and his wife on Sunday to the Lutheran Church. "The discourse was not the best I ever heard. Moreover, three little girls stood before me and stared the whole time, with their fingers in their mouths." She admired the "handsome, fine featured, graceful ladies of Winchester," and was pleased to note that the "education of females is liberally encouraged there."

On a bitter cold morning Mrs. Royall departed in Mr. Becket's stage. "Mr. Becket is an elderly man, and has carried the mail on this route since the Post Office was established. Hot or cold, he generally travels with the mail himself and has honest careful drivers. Being told that the contractors franked me on the routes, the dear old man said he could be as generous." She defrosted and rested in Staunton and paid for a seat in the stage to Charlottesville. The agent accepted her money, but in a few minutes came to her room to return it.

"There are fourteen or fifteen officers of the U.S. Army, just arrived from the West," he said, "and they say you cannot go on."

"Take my baggage downstairs this instant," Anne ordered. "I would not give up my seat to the President of the United States."

She kept her seat and in the stage delivered "a speech to these men of war, to teach them the difference between defending our rights and invading them." The day-long ride was not pleasant for the military. She badgered General Henry Atkinson, in command at Jefferson Barracks, near St. Louis, and so irritated him that finally one of the officers threatened to stop the stage and put her out. She *dared* him to try.[8]

The snowfall was heavier when she reached Charlottesville, and she hired a carriage to take her around the university town. Bundled in rugs, her identity should have remained hidden, but a crowd of students spied her out. From time to time, they rushed the vehicle, "yelling hideously to frighten the horses, but the driver managed to hold them in check." In the evening the "ruffians" stormed her tavern suite. The landlord rounded up some "genteel citizens" who forced the students to leave. Next morning a rowdy group began to gather early in front of the tavern, and by evening the crowd was "formidable." The apprehensive innkeeper led his frightened guest down a private staircase to his quarters. The mob, however, discovered her retreat, "forced the guard and the door, and rushed in." Meantime the genteel citizens arrived and once again drove off the hecklers. During the long night, they stood outside, stomping and shouting, and every once in a while one of them managed to shove an obscene note under the door. "Thus it has happened to the celebrated University of Vagabonds."

To the regret of the landlord, his guest did not depart next day, but, escorted by two army officers (not of the Atkinson party), went up the mountainside to visit Monticello.

It was a severe undertaking, colder than the previous day and the snow falling in a shower. I never flinched! I had all the Southern States to visit and were I to stop for every snow, I should never accomplish my plan.

In the garret we found Mrs. Jefferson's spinnet partly broken. It was the first I ever saw. It stood amidst heaps of coffee urns, chinaware, glasses, globes, chairs and bedsteads. My hands were so numb I was unable to write. From this cause, my sketch of Monticello is imperfect.[9]

Before sunup the following day Mrs. Royall took the stage south for Farmville, not far from Hampden Sydney College "where they manufacture blue-skins, by wholesale and retail." Though Charlottesville had "unnerved" her, it was her duty to show herself unafraid in Farmville. She unnerved Farmville. Rumor of her arrival circulated rapidly. Anne sat at her tavern window

. . . witnessing with amusement the terror of the town. Stores and shops were soon emptied. All business ceased. Some took shelter in one or two shops and the postoffice, while others were running through the streets and hiding behind houses. The bravest strode across the common and arrived before my window, taking care, however, not to approach me. Why did they not trust in their God, the hypocrites! If they are afraid of one heathen, how are they going to convert the whole nation?

Still, she met some "fine, noble-looking gentlemen" in the flourishing village which "by right, was the property of my husband's heirs, but from want of attention slipped into the hands of Hon. John Randolph." [10]

Leaving Farmville she rode two miles through "farms, lands, plantations, or what might constitute a Principality, or Dukedom of the Honorable John Randolph. His plantation lies on both sides of the Appomattox River. He has his gates and bars all through his lands—the driver had to get down and open every gate and bar."

When the stage stopped to water the horses, passengers were rewarded with a glimpse of the lord of the vast domain. He was mounted on a "large pampered white horse, very sleek and rather restive, a great contrast to his master. Mr. R. rode up to the stage door, and touched his hat, and no person can do this with more grace than Mr. Randolph." To Anne's surprise Mr. R. greeted her by name. She returned his greeting and inquired after his health.

"My health is very bad indeed, madam. Your servant, madam."

Whereupon the white horse bore Mr. Randolph away at a gallop.[11]

Despite unfriendly demonstrations, Mrs. Royall did very well marketing her books in Virginia. Content with her prosperity she crossed into North Carolina two days from Farmville. She did not sightsee much of the state, but what she saw pleased her. From her reception, she assumed the Presbyterians were less powerful than in Virginia. In Raleigh she was overawed by the handsome new State Capitol. So much did she admire Raleigh that she was pained to report the "strange infatuation of the females of the town for the unbounded use of snuff. They do not snuff it up the nose, but take it into the mouth; they call it dipping."

The criticism was not published until some months afterwards, in the first volume of *The Southern Tour*. Meanwhile, all was sweetness and light in the North Carolina capital.

On Friday last, our city was visited by Mrs. Royall [reported a local newspaper]. Her fame had long since reached us; and her arrival threw our tranquil metropolis in commotion. Many visited her, while others seemed desirous of avoiding her. . . . All who saw her affirm that they had never seen her like before; and all who came within range of her colloquial power, were fully convinced that she wields a weapon equally as powerful as her pen.[12]

Our heroine rolled away to Wilmington to venture on her first ocean voyage. She promoted a passage in the sloop *Providence*, bound for Charleston with a load of lumber. Before the freighter sailed out of Cape Fear River Anne was "pretty tolerable sick." Mindful of her duty to readers, she lay uncomfortably atop a stack of lumber taking notes of the shore "lined with evergreen and cypress swamps, but very few settlements. The cypress stood as thick as canebrakes, with their accompaniment of leafless knee-knees." The sloop went aground at the mouth of the river. Captain Bray carried Mrs. Royall below and waited for the next tide.

4

Without meeting "anything but a few gulls and porpoises," the *Providence* anchored four days later in Charleston Harbor, amid

the Sunday clanging of church bells. "Cold chills ran over me!"
Captain Bray escorted Mrs. Royall to a boardinghouse on King
Street.

Of all parts of the United States, I had promised myself most pleasure in Charleston. I had often met with the citizens of this once pol-
ished city years back, at the watering places. They seemed to belong
to another species. Their looks, their manners, their dress and their
conversation were distinguished by super-elegance. They had all that
simplicity of dress and charm of manner of the Boston people; but
there was an easy dignity, or higher order of nameless graces about
them, peculiar to the South. Alas! the only reputable people I found
in Charleston, were Jews and a few Yankees.

No one called during the first few days and no books were sold.
In alarm Mrs. Royall stopped by the office of the *Charleston
Mercury* to advertise her presence. The editor Henry Laurens
Pickney refused to receive her. He was sick. "All these mean people
are sure to take sick when I arrive." So it was that Charleston ac-
quired "The Pink," of matching editorial hue with his "Pinkship"
Charles King of the *New York American*.

Angered by the rebuff, Mrs. Royall rushed into the office of the
Southern Patriot where she "opened the floodgates" upon the editor
Jacob N. Cardozo. A "charming Israelite" Mr. Cardozo soon composed the ruffled feathers. He noticed Anne's books in the *Patriot*
and wrote of the "pleasure" he had from her call.

Mrs. Royall is certainly an exception to her sex in all particulars.
The ordinate influence of the clergy and the Ladies, in American
society, were the burthens of her complaints, and she rated us, in our
editorial capacity, in good set terms, for our submission to such influences. She would accept of no apology in justification for yielding
to the soft sway of the Ladies and discredited our chivalry utterly.

But Mr. Cardozo proved she was mistaken about him. He sent his
friends to King Street and Mrs. Royall's evening "levees" became
popular. Especially attentive were the two Joseph brothers and their
wives.

Their kindness knew no bounds. They took me to their houses, they fed me, and clothed me, they took me in their elegant barouche on a tour through the city and suburbs. I write this of the Josephs, particularly as they are Jews. The Christians, who never offered me a drink of water, despise this honorable sect, and talk of converting them! And the Mrs. Josephs—the wives! I never saw a Jewess before— I was delighted. They are both young, beautiful women, with sparkling black eyes, and the most hospitable ladies in Charleston.

Anne "picked up" acquaintance with Doctor John E. Holbrook, a Yankee from Massachusetts who was founder of the South Carolina Medical College. Doctor Holbrook was thirty-six years old and a "gentleman of superior endowments. He has few rivals in surgery or medicine. His whole soul breathes love to mankind." What probably brought on the exuberant description was discovery that Doctor Holbrook, "like the strong oak, which defies the storm, is proof against the overwhelming destruction of Presbyterianism and tracts." But Anne reported erroneously when she praised him as a surgeon. The physician was not even a contender in the field. Says the *Dictionary of American Biography:* "His tenderness of heart and distaste for seeing suffering led him to refuse all cases of childbirth and surgical cases involving serious operations." The literary attainments were, in the main, papers dealing with studies in herpetology and ichthyology, twin passions pursued outside the walls of the medical college.

Before sunrise one morning Anne Royall visited the market which she praised as "more interesting" than any seen in the North. "It not only puts the seasons forward about one-fourth of the year, but also presents us with the fruits of the West Indies." She ate her first banana—"perhaps four inches long and crooked like a long-necked squash; it has a sweet, insipid taste." The market "was a very pleasant place to walk," because not crowded. White ladies did not "attend"; they sent their Negro slaves. "Ladies appear to walk very little in Charleston. They ride out in their own carriages, generally in the evening." The market was as "neat as a lady's parlor," thanks to the buzzards, "gentle as doves," who "removed the filth." The buzzards gave her a retaliatory line to hit back at the city for its indifference. "They say the buzzards go regularly to church." [13]

In a mood mixed with bitterness and raillery, Mrs. Royall wrote "My dearest Friends" of the *Morning Courier and New York Enquirer*. Mergers of Major Noah's journals had brought together a group of Anne Royall's favorite newspapermen. They were young men who reported in the Noah style and had always shown interest in whatever Mrs. Royall undertook. They saw the major's point; her activities were news. At this time, "My dearest Friends," were James G. Brooks, James Watson Webb (co-owner), James Gordon Bennett and, best of all, Major Noah. After complaining of the "degradation and contumely" suffered at the hands of "barbarians and blue skins," Anne Royall settled down to amuse her "friends," and so assure publication of her communication.

What is the reason you make no mention of my triumphal march through the South? From the days of my predecessor, Queen Elizabeth, no woman has enjoyed such fame—such *eclat* as I have. I say this with all becoming Modesty, for every one who knows me is aware how sensitive I am on this point. [Momentarily Charleston was her most sensitive point.] "South Carolina is eternally kicking up rows. There was I, Anne Royall, in Charleston, hunted into a grocery store by some madcaps, and not only that, cheated out of my passage money to Camden. I have been told that South Carolina intends to put herself upon her sovereignty. [In the Webster-Hayne debate, the South Carolina senator had leaned heavily on argument favoring sovereignty of the states.] She had better put herself into an honest bib and tucker, and behave like an honest woman who never yet twice married. I hate all those who marry second husbands. It is a monstrous departure from the purity of our first love.

We can throw no light on the grocery store incident, but Anne herself wrote of the disaster that marked her departure from the Garden Spot of the South. At the stage office, her pocketbook was stolen and also her subscription list, with the names of all the subscribers laboriously obtained in Virginia and North Carolina. She hurriedly wrote a note to Mr. Cardozo, asking him to advertise the theft. Neither list nor pocketbook was ever returned.[14]

How different was Camden, a detour of a hundred miles, but worth it. "I shall never forget the thrill of pleasure I felt when the gentleman who helped me out of the stage said, 'I am Daniels!'" Constans Freeman Daniels, editor of the *Camden Journal,* was an old friend, though they had never met. He had defended the common scold throughout her trial and never once poked fun at her erratic deportment or at what she wrote. Two years after their meeting in Camden, Daniels was called to New York to become an associate editor of the *Courier and Enquirer,* and thus became one more "dearest Friend" in Mrs. Royall's favorite group of newspapermen.

Mayor Thomas Salmond sent two councilmen to conduct her on a trip around the city. "I wished to view those places where the sons of freedom had fought and bled, in which my husband bore his part." To read about the Battle of Camden, even today, brings a lump to the throat. The Americans held on, held on, though there was little hope of winning. The idealistic German Baron De Kalb fell at Camden, together with nearly one thousand of his troops, a large battle loss for those bygone days of lesser population and feebler engines of war. In the end, the surviving Revolutionary soldiers had to flee. Captain Royall, as we know, retreated in disorder to North Carolina, along the way fighting a couple of delaying actions.

Mr. Daniels rounded up congenial companions and patrons. Some of the loss suffered in Charleston was recouped. With financial worries dispelled and a new subscription list healthily underway, Anne Royall could enjoy herself. Ever long on gratitude, one of the first calls made was upon William Nixon, father of Henry G. Nixon, who had paid her stage fare out of Saratoga Springs on the initial trip to the spa in 1826. The son, only twenty-nine years old and "a darling of the community," had been killed in a duel a year earlier. As in Charleston, she encountered an impressive colony of Portuguese Jews, descendants of late seventeenth century immigrants. "The gentlemen are among the most upright, honorable men, in Camden. All are Masons."

The Camden sojourn was fruitful beyond expectations.

This is very happifying to us [wrote Daniels]. "Mrs. Royall is, without flattery, the most extraordinary woman we ever saw. . . . A certain people . . . in the interior of Africa, distinguished a portion of their Chronology . . . as "the year in which the white man passed." The annals of Camden will hereafter show . . . 1830 as the year particularly glorified by the transit of Mrs. Anne Royall.

The day came, all too quickly, when the visitor had to say goodbye to the felicitous town which had restored her morale and refilled her purse. "Farewell, dear Mrs. Royall," wrote Constans Freeman Daniels. "She is indeed the *dearest* of women. . . . She considers Camden the garden spot of her travels, while our citizens look upon her as the *Queen of Flowers*."

The stage creaked south with the Queen of Flowers bathed in tears. "My bill was paid by the City Council." [15]

5

After the cold and snow of Virginia, Mrs. Royall rode in "oppressive heat" to Augusta, Georgia. The exertions of the tour began to tell. She complained: "At every town, I have to go through the same labor. People gather round me, I have to converse, and often take my meals at the same time. The only rest I have is in the stage." She complained, too, if no people gathered round. At one road stop, she breakfasted at sunrise, and was taken aback when the stage manager said "he had never heard of me!"

"I travel free," Anne informed him. The manager was unmoved. "He liked money."

In Augusta a Catholic priest bought her dinner and from him she learned that "Augusta has its share of tract gentry. Most of the women belong to Dr. Ely."

For the duration of her stay the town belonged to Anne Royall. "Nothing was talked of, or heard of, or thought of, but Mrs. Royall. On Thursday she received company, and every body—that is any body—not to mention some whom she has set down as nobody—paid their respects to her in person . . . and her rooms were a squeeze." Anne "was truly gratified to find Masonry prospering. The miscreant blueskins kept out of my way." [16]

In cool comfort aboard the *William Gaston*, Anne Royall chugged out of Augusta down the Savannah River bound for the city at the mouth. The steamboat was squeezed between two flat-boats piled high with five thousand bales of cotton. "We looked like floating mountains." She took her meals with Captain Bowman and a young man passenger. In addition to Mrs. Royall the captain had three freeloaders stowed away on one of the flatboats—a family of Irish immigrants to whom he sent bountiful trays of food. "They sat on the stern of one cotton boat, the man tending the child, while his wife washed their thin rags in the cold river water, leaning over the side of the boat." Anne scrambled over cotton bales to talk to them. Some months earlier the little family had left Ireland to join the husband's older brother who had prospered in the New World. The brother received his kinfolk coldly and put the younger man to work in his fields. His wife helped out in the kitchen. They got no wages. The newcomer decided to look for work in Savannah. The successful brother permitted him to depart —without a penny. "I maintained you all winter and that's enough," he said. Thus, as hitchhikers, the family had wandered into the hospitable orbit of Captain Bowman. Anne made a contribution, and, as she watched the husband later walk ashore at Savannah with step "firm and independent," she had no doubt that he would get along.

The river was the scene of continuous entertainment. "Vast rafts of timber floated down. Georgia was on one side, South Carolina on the other." The "natural growth" along the shore—cypress, holly, sycamore—was an unfamiliar sight to the voyager.

The second day we began to look for alligators. I had never seen one. As we gained upon the south, they became quite numerous, some quite near us lying on logs as still as though they were dead. The largest might be 8 to 9 feet long. The captains of the steamboats generally carry a gun, powder, and shot, and the passengers amuse themselves by shooting alligators. Our young gentleman went into action. He must have killed from 60 to 70. They are a most frightful and disgusting animal. They are formed like the lizard, only magnify the lizard many times. Were it not that such numbers of them are shot, they would overrun the country. They often go on shore and destroy young pigs.[17]

In Savannah, Captain Bowman deposited Mrs. Royall at New-comb's Tavern. Her first caller was the mayor, Colonel William T. Williams, who had received a note, introducing her, from Robert Berrien, Attorney General of the United States. The mayor's side-line was a bookstore. Mrs. Royall saw to it that he was well stocked with her volumes.

Business out of the way, Anne took "the happiest walk I have enjoyed in many years." This was so, although the "streets are one sea of sand" and walking was difficult. The people of Savannah, she noted, had developed an unusual gait—a "wading step, slow, regular and long, head thrown back, the better to breathe, I suspect, and they rise and fall at every step."

Quiet, clean, smooth river travel had turned Mrs. Royall into an avid sailor who had no further bouts with *mal de mer*. She wangled a passage by steamboat to eliminate part of the dusty overland trip to Macon. At the last moment, the captain informed her that his paying passengers "objected" to her company. "I suspected the truth. There were missionaries aboard." [18]

So off she galumped over the hot dusty road in an uncomfortable coach. In Columbus her first caller was the handsome editor of the *Columbus Inquirer*. In a few years Mirabeau Buonaparte Lamar would leave Georgia to make history in Texas, at the battle of San Jacinto and as president of the new republic. Lamar was thirty-three years old, in the "bloom of manhood," said Mrs. Royall, "a very smart, intelligent man, with finely formed figure, fair manly face, soft black eye, and a countenance indicative of deepness of thought." Recent successes gave him an air of cocky confidence. As secretary to Governor George M. Troup, he had played a promi-nent role in the campaign to expel the last of the Cherokee and Creek tribes from their Georgia lands. Leaving Columbus, Mrs. Royall rode through one hundred miles of the Creek Nation, al-ready abandoned by the affronted Indians, though the treaty would not become effective for another year. "The whole country is a waste," wrote Anne.[19]

In nostalgic mood she crossed into Alabama. "From the day I left Alabama till I returned, I have seen no state or country to equal it—land rich, fields large, rivers deep and smooth, lofty bluffs, majestic trees, dark green forests." In Montgomery she was amused by a nephew of Henry Ward Beecher. Uncle Henry forwarded a continuous stream of tracts. "There are a great many goats in Montgomery, and Mr. Beecher [nephew] stuck tracts on their horns, and sent them forth to spread the gospel."

Mrs. Royall obtained free passage in the steamboat *Herald*— "fastest boat on the Alabama River—she goes downstream at 25 miles an hour." Captain Young was a "noble, fine fellow, and a Mason," and she told him she would "immortalize his boat."

"You're too late," said the captain. "It has already been done by Bazle [sic] Hall."

The aristocratic English traveler and his wife had been passengers on the *Herald* two years earlier. "He was reserved and sulky all the way," said Captain Young, "and Mrs. Hall was busy writing all the while." For the convenience of shippers, river boats signaled arrival at a landing by firing a small cannon. Captain Hall requested Young "to stop the firing, he disliked the noise."

No one would expect an Irishman holding the upper hand over an Englishman to fly in the face of his good fortune. Young's answer was to fire the cannon off *twice* at landings. "Captain Hall was a proud, distant, haughty man," he told Mrs. Royall. According to the editor (English) of Mrs. Hall's *Letters*, "Both Captain and Mrs. Hall disapproved on principle of everything that America presented of equality and fraternity and were completely out of their bearings in a society unmapped by class distinctions." [20]

The Halls had arrived in the U.S.A. with more than one hundred letters of introduction and, wherever they went, were given the drawing-room treatment. Harriet Martineau, who traveled a few years after Anne Royall, brought only fifty letters. Her two travel books about America were probably the most objective to come out of a period when droves of English were crossing the Atlantic to pen their views on the republican experiment. Anne Royall preferred Mrs. Trollope's *Domestic Manners*. She was not angered by the Englishwoman's criticisms of Americans. She had known these Americans whose domestic manners Mrs. Trollope found fault with. Like herself, Mrs. Trollope had no letters, only bitter experiences after living for several years with money troubles

in the U.S.A. Anne Royall believed Mrs. Trollope had succeeded
in reaching into the basic daily life of Americans and reporting on
aspects of our society which lady observers in the throes of lioniza-
tion had no opportunity to plumb. As a biographer wrote: "The
majority of the people Mrs. Trollope came in contact with never
entertained her or put themselves out for her. She was just an
ordinary, unconsidered person, adjusting herself painfully to the
framework of an uncouth pioneer society." The description fits
Anne Royall, except that she had had no adjustments to make in a
pioneer society.

Mrs. Royall was impatient to reach Mobile and a bookshop and
read what Captain Hall had said about the river trip. What he wrote
was no immortalization of Captain Young and his steamboat. "He
merely remarked that the *Herald* was a fine boat, but badly managed." His wife echoed the complaint: "Clumsily managed."

Immortalization was therefore still within the province of Anne
Royall. "My poor talents are inadequate to do justice to the worthy
Captain Young. He is sober and attentive, allows no liquor to his
hands, and keeps the best of servants. His garb and manner are
plain, but under these is concealed the best heart that ever beat in
the breast of a high-minded independent Irishman." [21]

6

The "rendezvous of renegades, outlaws, pirates and obnoxious
characters," Mobile was an uncomfortable city for a frail female.
They thundered on the door of Anne Royall's tavern room and
"raced through the passage in front of it." She cut short her visit
and one dawn started across country on the journey which was to
deliver her to New Orleans. By sundown the stage had reached
Pasacougla, Mississippi, where passengers piled onto the steamboat
Mount Vernon! Yes, the very same in which Anne had set out
from Alexandria for Richmond. Captain Queen greeted her and
she went to look for Emma, the chambermaid, who had been so
kind to her. Emma had not come south with the crew. "But my
eye rested with pleasure upon the little stove, round which Emma
and I sat, she the only human being, at that time who seemed to

have the least friendship or feeling towards me." The *Mount Vernon*, Mrs. Royall perceived, carried a load of tracts. She threw them overboard. "Captain Queen is highly censurable for uniting with a gang of religious pirates."

By night the *Mount Vernon* crossed Lake Borgne, passed through the Rigolets and emerged into Lake Ponchartrain. Early morning the steamboat picked a slow passage through narrow, winding Bayou Jean, docking at midday the first of May two miles from New Orleans. "I am 1189 miles from Washington City, having travelled rather more than double the distance in all my windings," calculated Anne Royall. She hired a carriage and was driven to Chartres Street and the boardinghouse of Madame Herries, a long-time fugitive from the French Revolution. The room was pleasant, with high ceiling and faced in the direction of the river whence came a breeze, if any. Anne felt called upon to immortalize Madame Herries because another traveler, the Duke of Saxe-Weimar, "mentioned her house unfavorably in his book of travels. Her house is the best in the city." The price, Anne thought, was high—three dollars a day with meals—but that was no concern of hers. Her bill (for two weeks) was paid by Mayor Dennis Prieur and John H. Holland, Grand Master of the Masonic fraternity in Louisiana. Mayor Prieur called promptly to inquire whether Mrs. Royall was satisfied with her accommodations. He explained his "duties were so oppressive," that he had assigned Mr. Holland to look after her. His only free time, he said, was on Sundays. Then he would be happy to attend Mrs. Royall wherever she wished to go.[22]

Like many a tourist, before and since, Mrs. Royall breakfasted early the following morning (a Sunday which the mayor had already promised elsewhere) at the French market, "astonishingly crowded with vegetables and flowers. Everything is sold and principally bought by female negroes. These old negro women gabble French so fast that it appears to be nonsense."

For the first time Anne saw Negro convicts at work outside prison walls. "They have a chain round one ankle. It reaches up to the waist, around which it is fastened. These convicts are kept at work on the streets, levee, and about the prison, and do not seem

at all impeded by the weight of the chain. Those I saw this morning were carrying water on their heads to the prison."

Anne went to mass in the St. Louis Cathedral.

It was certainly the most solemn scene I ever witnessed. The
Cathedral was crowded with well-dressed people, amongst whom were
many blacks. I never saw such devotion before. Every soul of them
was deeply engaged, with their eyes shut, and seemed to be totally
disengaged from earth. They were all upon their knees. This is the
Cathedral where thanks were returned for the delivery of New Orleans,
and where General Jackson was crowned in honor of the victory."

From the Cathedral, she walked toward the Mississippi River,
amused at the sight from the below-sea-level city of vessels which
appeared to be "borne aloft." Sunday was not a busy day and
May was not a busy month, but the visitor speculated on how it
was possible to make room for more people or more goods.

Vessels lined the shore for miles, the levee strewed with goods, bales
of cotton and boxes, the streets choked with people, drays, carts and
porters and the owners of the freight flying from vessel to cartmen,
without taking time to eat or drink. It appeared as if the whole world
was in New Orleans and the Sabbath is not kept holy. All the stores
are open, as busy on Sunday as any day in the week. The only people
who keep Sunday here are the lottery men. Their doors are shut.

These observations were remembered in the evening when Anne
Royall sat on the balcony outside her room.

The four corners of the world seemed to have met in New Orleans.
They were chanting vespers in the Cathedral; playing billiards in a
second floor room of a long building in front of me; singing and acting
in the French Theater next door, praying in the negro Methodist
Church nearby; playing cards in the tavern; all in peaceful harmony
on Sunday. Dr. Ely ought to come here and convert the heathen.

Monday morning and to business. Blue Monday it was when Mrs.
Royall learned that the bookseller Benjamin Levy—introduced to

her several years previously in Washington by Senator Edward Livingston—had lost, through neglect, the 104 volumes shipped him. The books had arrived by boat from New York, damp with sea water. Levy had not troubled to open the two boxes, but dumped them into an open shed where frequent rains doomed the entire contents. Anne was furious. She was sure that Levy was working with the blueskins to keep her books from readers, and so offered words of caution:

"Booksellers have more bearing on our liberty than we are aware of. The blueskins attempted first to bribe me and then to murder me. Well may they bribe booksellers."

Checking accounts, Anne found that Benjamin Levy had "charged me $9.87 commission on $35.50, and had the use of the money for two years." That, she admitted, was not quite as bad as the Portland, Maine, bookseller who had owed her $200 for two years and on settling up, paid her no interest. "But he repented afterwards and cut his throat. I forgave him. If Levy will do the same I will forgive him too." [23]

Benjamin Levy, Anne estimated, had cost her at least one hundred dollars. Fortunately, she was traveling with a fair supply of books and could fill the shelves of the two bookstores Mr. Holland recommended to represent her. Generous patronage by the Masons helped to offset the Levy loss. Anne herself, walking the highways and byways of the hot, humid city, pushed the sales of her wares, although everyone told her she had arrived too late and the town was "empty." The previous year New Orleans had suffered a disastrous yellow fever epidemic and the exodus of residents to healthier climates had begun unusually early in the spring of 1830. Mrs. Royall thought the stories of the plague "exaggerated," but she was careful. Nighttimes she slept under three mosquito bars and daytimes she raced around town, probably faster than any stegomyia could keep up with her.

Anne called at the seminary recently opened in Conti Street by Mr. Pichon to provide schooling for the "quarteroons." (She misspelled the Spanish word and crossed it phonetically with the English quadroon.) Apparently, until Mr. Pichon came along, these lovely creatures who, from the cradle were taught to please their white patrons, were excluded from institutions stressing education in the three R's.

Mr. Pichon has attained a most astonishing degree of improvement [said Mrs. Royall]. Never did I witness such ardour and application. I was amazed at the eyes-downcast-modesty of the little girls. They averaged about twelve years of age. They were reading and writing and many of them were perfect in geography and grammar. The beauty of the quarteroons is celebrated to distant lands, but whoever wishes to see beauty ought to see these children, so pretty, with the loveliest features, the sweetest black sparkling eyes, and black glossy hair; their complexion though dark, blooming as a rose.

Anne had already studied the grown-up quarteroons:

They are not so handsome as I had expected. They are naturally well-shaped, and many have fine features. They dress equal to those who are called white ladies, except white ladies wear bonnets, and the quarteroons throw a rich veil over their heads which is decorated with a wreath of flowers, turbans, etc. This distinction is strictly adhered to. Some of the quarteroons are immensely rich. They have their slaves, and are usually attended by one in the streets. They have separate balls and do not mix with the white ladies who are seldom seen in the streets.

The diversity of skin colors, from "snowy white to sooty," kept Mrs. Royall frowning. It was worse than what she had seen in Alexandria. The Negro mixture with Spanish, French and Germans, made the populace more polygenetic than any seen elsewhere.

Here you see a little squat, yellow foreigner from the West Indies—from South America—who can say from whither—covered with the finest laces, yards of it, and glittering with jewels. And again, a tall, elegant figure from France—England—Netherlands or Poland. Sometimes a face of inexpressible beauty, and again one of horror; sometimes a face of lily whiteness, and next one of saffron, and so on to coal black.[24]

On the outskirts of the city Mrs. Royall came onto the Poydras Female Orphan Asylum, sitting on a rise of land which provided the "best view of New Orleans and the suburbs. You see miles checkered with fig groves, young orange groves, and squares of smooth softened green, studded with brilliant flowers; the river lined with sloops, steamboats and squareboats; all this with the magnolia and live-oak exhibiting a prospect of unrivalled splendor."

Inside the "large, lofty elegant building" were sixty lucky inmates. In the dining room hung a painting of the founder Julian de Lalande Poydras, who was so destitute when he arrived in New Orleans in 1768 that he might have been a candidate for admittance to an orphan's home. Monsieur Poydras was a hustler, however, and very soon outfitted himself with a pack and went off into the wilderness of the Lower Mississippi Valley looking for customers. Think of it—forty years before Thomas Jefferson made the Purchase! Before long he opened a trading post and after that came plantations and other prosperous ventures. Poydras had died a very rich man about six years before Mrs. Royall visited the Crescent City. A bachelor, he left his fortune to the orphan asylum, the Charity Hospital, to colleges and other public institutions. In Pointe Coupee parish where he had his plantation, he had set up a fund to provide dowries for poor girls.

Anne was pleased to learn that the Poydras orphans were taught English and French alternate weeks. No one, however, had learned English well enough to converse with her.[25]

In either language, New Orleans, booming center of the Mississippi Valley trade, was then the most expensive city Mrs. Royall had visited.

Every man, woman and child, who can use his hands and head, is at once a mint within himself. A woman here gets five dollars for making a plain calico dress! From eight to twelve for a full dress. What would she get in New York or Philadelphia? Fifty cents at most for the first, and from one dollar and fifty cents to two dollars for the latter, and out of work two-thirds of the time while she would pay double for provisions, fire-wood and house rent. When a mantua maker came to make me a plain calico dress for five dollars, I sent her off. But five dollars is as easy to get here as five cents in any part of the Atlantic country. In Washington City a poor woman gets 12-½ cents for making a cotton shirt, and not more than two jobs a week. I gave a dollar for a yard of lace, and another dollar for quilling it on my cap! [26]

As the guest of James H. Caldwell, actor-manager of the St. Charles Theater, Anne Royall frequently attended performances, sitting in the fashionable pit, where the seats "are boxed up like the pews in a church." She met an old acquaintance who had acted in her New York benefit—"lovely and celebrated" Caroline Placide who had since wed William Rufus Blake, star of the benefit play. He was not with the company in New Orleans. Anne saw Miss Placide perform in *Imogine*, the *Soldier's Daughter*, and *Alonzo the Brave*. The last play had to do with skeletons rising up from their tombs in The Escorial, a scene which Mrs. Royall praised as "inimitably fine." The visitor did not attend the French Theatre, "no doubt of the first distinction in the United States." She had enough trouble with the language on her daily rounds.[27]

7

Finally the Sunday arrived when Mayor Prieur was free to accompany Mrs. Royall to the site of the Battle of New Orleans. He brought along two more gentlemen and the party "pranced" off behind a "sprightly match of horses," following the road atop the river levee. For most of the four miles Anne was "in despair for words to portray the beauty, the colorful flowers, the groves and gardens, the boxwood trimmed into innumerable shapes."

The party climbed over a fence and at last the "good Jackson man" was thrilled to stand on the battleground where the ragtag American troops—"Dirty Shirts," the enemy called them because of their homespun clothing—had, in a few hours, licked the elite British legions—veterans of Waterloo, of victories over Napoleon in Spain, of the burning of Washington, and crack regiments summoned from round the globe to win back the colonies. Twenty-five years later and

. . . not a vestige is left of those great contending armies but the ditches. I saw the spot from where Gen. Jackson directed the defense, and the swamp where stood the brave Gen. Coffee with his invincibles, and walked over the bones of the British, over which the plough now runs and cane is growing. The mayor also pointed out where Pakenham fell and where the greatest slaughter took place. What a waste of human life! That rational men should think it an honor to come so far from home to be shot down is making a bad use of reason, to say the least.

"They did not come all the way here to be killed," corrected the mayor. "They came to kill." [28]

CHAPTER XV

RIVER RABBLE AND TRACTS

1

Captain Rian, the "best river commander," piloted the *Atlantic* upstream against the stubborn Mississippi current. Anne Royall was his guest, on her way to St. Louis. She had quickly elicited information that the steamboat was 170 feet long, accommodated four hundred passengers, and had cost $30,000 to build.

. . . an extravagant price [she decided]. "Contending against the gigantic current soon shakes a river boat to pieces. The islands, without end, are hazardous to navigation. In the course of the day we met a monstrous flood bringing down great trees. The *Atlantic* received severe shocks from these trees as they struck us, and captain and crew had their hands full for about twenty-four hours.

The Bible Belt settlements behind the levee were as unfriendly to Mrs. Royall as the Father of Waters was to the *Atlantic*. The church people knew all about her and showed no disposition to be enlightened about the plot for a church and state party. They were prayer-meeting people, and they could hoot, holler, and hiss. In her book, Mrs. Royall did not describe them as blue-skins, but said their ramshackle towns were the haunts besides of "outlaws and vicious characters." She had not been up to doing battle with any of them. It had been a long, hard trip and fatigue and fear took hold. She had a valid claim on both. At Vicksburg, the crowd was so hostile that Anne vowed not to put foot on shore until St. Louis.

The *Atlantic* passed Memphis during the night and tied up at midday at New Madrid just beyond the Missouri line. From the deck Mrs. Royall could make out "traces" of the earthquake of which New Madrid had been the center twenty years earlier. In an attempt to disguise the disaster, the proud town had built up sunken areas to a level with bluffs which had not been flattened. But no one was fooled. "People are afraid to build there," Anne reported. The shocks had persisted for nearly a year, rumbling through thirty thousand square miles and altering the course of the Mississippi River. Few persons were killed and damage was slight. New Madrid then was frontier and sparsely populated. Even so, the earthquake is still said to have been the greatest known in the history of the United States.

At the mouth of the muddy Ohio, Captain Rian brought Mrs. Royall a glass of water to compare with the Mississippi water drunk throughout the voyage. "The captain filters the water of the Mississippi through a porous stone and keeps it in great stone jars as large as barrels. There is as much difference between the Ohio and the Mississippi water, as between a fountain and a duck-puddle." [1]

Twelve hundred miles from New Orleans and four weeks later, the *Atlantic* came abreast of Jackson Barracks on a Saturday afternoon. Officers and men frolicked in the river and sunned on the bank—stark naked! They did not retreat, and so Anne primly retired to her cabin and turned her guns on the vast "fortifications of so much style and cost. What enemy would come here? Not the Indians in the heart of the country. Why were these fortifications not built at New Orleans, where a foreign enemy might one day invade us?"

Mrs. Royall had looked forward to a cordial reception in St. Louis because of acquaintance with General William Clark, superintendent of Indian Affairs. The general gave her a whacking snub before she stepped off the *Atlantic*. Clark was known as a considerable host, keeping open house for Indians who came in their canoes bringing their problems from far up the tributaries, and for merchants and traders from the vast western reaches of plains and mountains which he and Meriwether Lewis had opened to settlement more than a quarter of a century earlier. The general did not call on Mrs. Royall, a courtesy she was accustomed to; he did not invite her to visit the agency, and he did not answer her note advising him of her arrival and requesting aid in locating accommodations. At this period St. Louis was a wild, rough, over-crowded frontier town and a tavern room was not easy to find. Besides, it was no place for a lone female.

Anne Royall vowed she would not honor St. Louis with her presence. Captain Rian invited her to stay aboard the *Atlantic* as long as the boat remained at dock. But the problem was to get her elsewhere. Rian made the rounds of the steamboats, but no pilot wished to deprive him of his notorious passenger. Hearing of a captain who might sell her a ticket, Anne broke her vow and went ashore.

"I must go to the mouth of the Ohio," she told the captain. "I will give you double the price."

"I will not take you for any price," retorted the riverman.

Naturally the unsuccessful ticket buyer blamed her dilemma on Presbyterians and tract societies. "It is very plain that the Presbyterians are in possession of the Indian agency and the army. Remote from the great mass of people, their plot could ripen, before the people are aware of it." [2]

A St. Louis newspaper took its cue from General Clark. "From the reception, or rather non-reception, Mrs. R. met with here, we may expect from her a royal edict for expulsion of Missouri from the Union."

Mrs. Royall left the *Atlantic* for the second time to confront the editor who printed the item. The newspaper belonged to Senator Thomas Hart Benton, with whom she had always been on friendly terms. But she never spoke her piece; maybe she remembered the Davy Crockett story. Keemly, the editor, looked such a "poor wretch," that she had not the heart to add to his miseries.

Her heart, however, was firmly set on a confrontation with General Clark. She was certain the general would continue to avoid her. Before spying him out, Anne obtained a plan of the interior of the agency in order to locate precisely the general's headquarters. "I found the house very large; part of it was filled with trifles to allure the poor Indians out of their annuities—another part of the house, under the appearance of hospitality to the Indians, the more readily to fleece them, is allotted to those unsuspecting visitors. This was a large room on the first floor, and was then full of Indians. I pushed on briskly through them, and found Clark in a remote room, cooped up like an old rooster."

"I am sick, madam," protested the cornered general. "I cannot see company today."

Clark *was* sick, Anne agreed. "He is only the shadow of a man, scarcely sane, reduced to a skeleton, feeble, superannuated, and fit for no business in the world." Once again her piece went unspoken. In a moment, agency guards had tracked her down.

"Come, madam, pack off," ordered one. Without protest she complied.[3]

On Sunday a host of the curious came to the dock for a glimpse of the strange creature who had the whole town talking. Daring ones ventured aboard the *Atlantic* for a closer view. Anne was cordial and did her entertaining best to offset unworthy reports. She was working hard to get a room. The excursions into town had changed her mind: It was her duty to stay. But none of the Sunday sightseers was charmed into offering accommodations.

Next morning an unexpected invitation was delivered. "Mr. and Mrs. Shepherd's respects to Mrs. R. and would be happy to see her at their house, which is at her service as long as she may think proper to remain in St. L."

The Shepherds owned and taught a school in a "large, brick building." There was plenty of room for a visitor. Anne found the couple "very amiable." Once on land, however, her uneasiness returned. Whenever she walked out, she was sure she was being followed. The Shepherds, too, were alarmed by her state of mind. With her hosts Anne Royall began to plot escape from St. Louis. In case the flight should fail, she wrote Secretary of War Eaton where she was going and asked him to call out the troops if she should not show up at her destination. On a dark night, by backstairs and back streets, she was taken to the ferry which operated back and forth across the Mississippi. Apprehensively she crossed

to the Illinois landing and then rode the stage to Belleville. Governor Ninian Edwards, whom she had known as a senator in Washington, waited to receive her. The governor guided Anne to a
tavern which received her with "kindness and respect." Suspicions
once more dissipated, she "forgot St. Louis as though it were a
bad dream." [4]

2

In a couple of days, nerves calmer, Mrs. Royall rolled off in the
direction of Nashville, Tennessee. The trip made her proud of the
U.S.A.

The whole distance comprehends one of the richest and most
delightful regions on earth—natural meadows, succulent grasses, the
finest navigable rivers, tall timber. There are doubtless more bees in
Illinois than in the whole United States. The great number of flowers
on the prairie attracts them. What a retreat this state is for the poor
man! [But already the best land was in the hands of speculators.]
A curse must pursue those speculators who keep up the price of land,
and so keep our suffering poor a dead weight in our Atlantic Country.
Congress is blind to the interests of the poor. That such a fine country
should have been so slow in settling, can be ascribed to the high price
of land. As slavery is prohibited, the poorer sort should come here.

After four days Mrs. Royall continued southeast to Shawnee-
town, covering a little over two hundred miles, or half the distance
to Nashville. During the final hour of the journey, the stagecoach
bogged down in mud. Anne was the only passenger. The driver
unloaded her trunk and the mailbags and the lady took the reins,
whipping up the horses while the poor fellow pushed and strained
to release the vehicle. It was almost the first of July and the heat,
which set a record that year, was near to unbearable without exer-
cising any additional strain.[5]

Next evening Anne Royall boarded an Ohio River steamboat
which took her to the mouth of the Cumberland River and thence
to Nashville. As the much touted friend of President Jackson, she
expected an enthusiastic turnout of "brave Tennesseans" to wel-

come her. No one met the boat. The two newspapers did not announce her arrival. One editor told her he would write about her visit after she left town, an arrangement which would hardly promote immediate book sales. Anne handed the editor of the *Nashville Republican and State Gazette* a dollar and "requested him to say Mrs. Royall is in Nashville." The editor refused the money, explaining, "We are not in the habit of flattering people to their faces."

Anne related the incident in a letter to the publisher of the *Murfreesboro Courier*. "Considering the politeness of these editors heretofore, I can think no other than that they are bought up by the U.S. Bank." [6]

Momentarily, she had let up on the Presbyterians for an old whipping boy, the Second Bank of the United States, a subject to which the Jackson Administration was giving more and more attention. She went into "raptures," however, over one Presbyterian in Nashville—Doctor Philip Lindsley, president of the University of Nashville. Anne had refused to visit the university because of its religious affiliation, but Doctor Lindsley came looking for her. "A clap of thunder would not have surprised me more! He was most captivating, young and liberal and quite qualified to preside over the education of youth."

Doctor Lindsley introduced her to the university's star lecturer, Doctor Bertrand Troost, head of the departments of geology and mineralogy, and chemistry and natural philosophy. Anne Royall examined his collection of thirty thousand minerals. She was "much astonished to hear that no ladies attended the lectures on chemistry, or, indeed, scarcely any of the citizens of Nashville. I should esteem it a great treat to attend the lectures of Doctor Troost, one of the most learned men in the world. He had written many of the books I saw in his library."

Doctor Troost and the university came cheap enough. "The cost per session (6 months) for tuition, including library and servants hire, is $25 only; board $1.75 per week." [7]

After a week, Anne Royall took the stage for Louisville, shaking her head sadly over the desolation in "once flourishing Nashville." If anyone wanted to see first hand the "horrors of banks and the tyranny of priestcraft let them visit the Tennessee city. Independence crushed, the citizens stripped of their all, not only in Nashville, but the state is swallowed up by monied monsters." She herself once again was fleeing in panic. Her seat on the stage was booked in the name of a friend, "lest another attempt be made on my life." After three days she arrived in Louisville, dusty and worn out by the heat. No one turned out to meet her. The rumors had flown ahead. One tavern refused to take her in; a second accepted her but, when the landlord learned her name, he put her out.

"You can't stop here!" he shouted, shoving her trunk onto the sidewalk. "Go about your business!"

Mrs. Royall left her luggage with a cabinetmaker across the street and went hunting for friends. They took her to a hospitable inn and again her fright subsided. S. Penn, junior, a descendant of William Penn and publisher of the *Daily Advertiser*, gave her reams of publicity; the mayor called, as did judges and officials. Most of the callers were Masons and Jackson men. Her bookseller W. W. Worsley "was doing good business."

Escorted wherever she went, Mrs. Royall did a thorough job of sightseeing in Louisville. She visited the pavilion built in a treetop where "large parties of pleasure assembled in the heat." The roots of the tree were in the bed of the Ohio River and the pavilion in the branches on a level with the bluff. She saw numbers of "tract people" about, but they did not bother her.[8]

3

Quite relaxed, Mrs. Royall moved up the Ohio in the steamboat *Telegraph* to visit her mother and her half-brother James Butler who, after many ups and downs, had settled in Connersville, Indiana. As she stepped ashore at Lawrenceburg, she was hailed by Thomas Dowling, one of the Washington newspapermen who had paid her fine after her conviction as a common scold. Since her departure from the Capital, Dowling had come west to edit a newspaper.

No stage ran the sixty or more miles to Connersville. Everyone advised Mrs. Royall to be patient; soon someone would be going to Brookville, more than half the distance, and would give her a ride. From there she could arrange further transportation. Sure enough, in a couple of days, she was sharing a carriage to Brookville, the route so close to the state line that sometimes they were "in Ohio and sometimes in Indiana." Brookville gave her a warm reception. "The Indianians, though not wealthy, are very kind and hospitable. All united to hire a man and a little wagon to send me to Connersville."

And so, six months after leaving Washington in a snowstorm, Anne Royall arrived in "blazing" July sun at the Indiana farm of Colonel James Butler whom she had not seen in fifteen years. ("Colonel" may have been the outcome of service in the War of 1812; more likely, it indicated current service in the militia.) Mary Butler no longer lived with her son. The last time James heard of his mother she was residing in Edinburg with the Cowan family, offspring of the marriage of Anne's sister Mary. Edinburg was less than a hundred miles west.

The Butlers begged Mrs. Royall to stay with them. Though ready to collapse with fatigue, Anne was doubtful that her brother's household was a place to rest. James now had "ten, or perhaps twelve children." She was persuaded to settle away from the Butler house in a "rustic, rusty cabin" which one of James's tall sons patched and hammered into a "pleasant bower." Her brother, she regretted to observe, had no ambition. "He is diffident and his spirits depressed. He lives on rented land which his lusty sons cultivate. He had a most luxuriant crop growing. They live plentiful and his wife clothes him and the family with the labor of her own hand, and that of a daughter nearly grown."

For eleven days Anne Royall relaxed and wrote in her bower, and then one night her brother's "unmannerly" sheep staged an invasion. "They scattered papers and ate some of my notes. They must have been missionaries—wolves in sheep's clothing!" [9]

Next day she moved into a hotel and quickly became popular in the town. One admirer was Samuel W. Parker, editor of the *Political Clarion*. Parker, a native of Kentucky, was a Clay man and felt certain that the visitor would eventually see the light and abandon the Jackson camp. He found her "fair minded" on the subject of politics. Of the handful of newspaper reports of the *Southern Tour* that I have had the good fortune to collect, I think Mr. Parker—age twenty, said Mrs. Royall—"wrote just about the best." There's no embroidery in his style; just what he observed, no bias, no attempt to be clever at the author's expense, no unnecessary adulation. The first account runs nearly a column. A sampling:

> She devotes . . . all the time she can . . . to the writing out of her tour. Though the undisguised independence of this lady has rendered her obnoxious to a few of the powerful classes of the country, yet her literary talent . . . and the deserved celebrity of many of her literary productions, will elicit the attention of the public wherever she may go. We never spent an hour more agreeably than in her company. She is very communicative—all life and interest. Her minute observance of all the public evolutions of several of the recently passed years—the extensive range of her travels and intelligence . . . and the fervid rigor of her imagination—together with a never flagging vivacity of countenance and conversation, conspire in giving her, and her writings, a peculiarity of zest and texture.
>
> . . . She declares that all of our public officers . . . care for nothing in reality but themselves; and relative to their extravagance, she advises the application of the caustic without a tittle of abatement. The prolific characteristic of the "Great West" has stricken Mrs. Royall even with the extravagance of astonishment! She deems that Indiana and our chivalrous sister on the other side of the "beautiful river" are showered with the multiplicity of their "pigs and children" in the same manner that the ancient Jewish wanderers were with heavenly manna!!
>
> In some of the departments of writing, we consider Mrs. Royall as having few equals. . . . We have just been dipping into her *Letters from Alabama*, a work which has issued from the press during her present tour. . . . [There are] some sketches of fascinating interest. . . . We predict, with confidence, a favourable reception for this book. . . .[10]

The visit to Connersville was the beginning—by correspondence —of a friendship with the Clay editor. Over the years he kept Anne Royall informed of developments and happenings in the Middle

States and she shared his letters with readers of the newspaper she later published. It was as good as having a correspondent in a distant land, a land neglected by eastern journals whose focus remained on the Old World.

Newton Claypool, "probably the wealthiest man in Connersville," sent his carriage for Mrs. Royall and she had a delightful visit with him and his wife, "the first white child born on Scioto River, Ohio." She had been born Mary Kerns in Ross County and Anne described her as "plain, kind, charitable and good natured. She was acquainted with my mother. Mr. C. is a young, active business man who lays his hand to everything." He had kept a store in Ross County, then moved to Indiana where he opened a trading post. "He rented a sawmill nights where he sawed lumber for the hotel that he himself ran up. It was Connersville's first hotel. As a sideline he raised hogs and drove them himself to the Cincinnati market." When Anne met Claypool he had just become a member of the state senate.

At her hotel there was a string of callers—judges, lawyers, doctors, the sheriff, and two merchants in partnership—Lewis and Clark. "Success to them!"

A Presbyterian missionary, arriving ahead of Mrs. Royall, had boasted of "having converted more women than any other man in the same time." Anne thought the boast might be true: "He is a handsome man." But she told the citizens of Connersville to watch their money and spend it in the town.

It is a new and flourishing town, most of the buildings elegantly built of brick. The handsome courthouse cost six thousand dollars, which is a lot for this country. The whole place looks fresh, as though it had sprung up in one night. The streets are wide, crossing at right angles. There are but seven hundred inhabitants. The land is rich and all around the country is beautiful.[11]

After a few days of hotel life, Mrs. Royall continued west in search of Mary Butler. Mr. Claypool sent her in his carriage as far as Rushville, seventeen miles distant. Rushville had succumbed to the blue-skins and so Anne left the town as quickly as she could hire a "shocking carriage without cover or seat" to take her twenty-five miles to Shelbyville. All the way she sat on her trunk, holding a borrowed umbrella over her head. She was welcomed by Captain John Walker, whose father had come to hunt with Daniel Boone, stayed, and so became the first white settler in Indiana. Captain Walker owned extensive lands, lived in a beautiful house, and operated a flour mill. "He builds large boats and ships flour (via the Big Blue River) from his door." She departed Shelbyville in the Walker carriage, accompanied by a son and a daughter, for Edinburg, where she hoped to find her mother.

But Mrs. Butler had moved on, which was just as well because an epidemic had sent the frightened populace scampering. "The few that were there were all down with the fever." Anne Royall learned that her mother's latest transplant had taken her clear across the state to the Illinois border and a new town called Springfield, in Vermillion County. The Walker children hurriedly faced about and went home. Anne Royall prepared to proceed west.

Had I known this when I crossed into Illinois from St. Louis, I could have saved some hundreds of miles. But I had the pleasure, and no small one, of seeing the country. From the time I left Ohio until I reached Springfield, I crossed White Water River, Flat Rock River, Blue River, White River, Eel Creek, Mill Creek, White Lick, Racoon Creek, Sugar Creek and the Wabash, all considerable streams, and besides a number of smaller ones. As to soil and water, Illinois and Indiana are worth the whole United States. Not an inch of ground that I have seen in either state but is rich and can be cultivated. Unfortunately Indiana is thinly settled.

She waited almost two days for the stage to take her from afflicted Edinburg. Next stop of importance was Indianapolis. "It is finely situated on the White River and has a number of good buildings, but it is settled by a low rabble. It is the most blackguard town in the western country." Presbyterians, of course. The Methodists, a few years before, had fought and lost the battle for spiritual possession of the Indiana capital. The victory was won with money. "The Presbyterians have tract depositories, a press, and several societies in the place, and people hired at sixty dollars per month to carry tracts through the state." Mrs. Royall was soon "embroiled. In my room the table was loaded with tracts." She threw them out. In retaliation "one of the tract girls stole my traveling map and tore it up." Anne was outnumbered and again frightened. There was no transportation in the direction she wished to go.

She sent for Noah Noble, brother of Senator James Noble, one of Indiana's first representatives elected to Congress, and asked his "protection." He was "sick." The senator's son-in-law, however, "behaved very gentlemanly," taking Anne under his wing and paying for a carriage to carry her part way. In Danville, probably alerted by Indianapolis, the tract society serenaded her "with obscene songs. The windows being up, they threw in dirty water, and rioted till late in the night." Still, she was able to say Danville "is one of the healthiest and handsomest spots in the state." After Edinburg, she concluded that Indiana was "not as healthy" as Illinois. The fault lay with the "heavy timber" which covered the state. "The air cannot circulate." [12]

She fought the tract society doggedly all along her route and the society fought back. When she parted with the carriage hired in Indianapolis, she faced no further obstacles in hiring transportation, although no stages rattled over the unmapped, rutted road she followed. Sometimes Anne advanced in wagons, often on horseback, but she never traveled alone.

And thus, after three days, she arrived in Springfield. "The settlement is only a few months old, but has reached a fair size. It is on the Vermillion River, two miles above where it empties into the Wabash and in sight of Eugene, an older and faster-growing town strongly opposed to Springfield. It is laughable to see how each is trying to outdo the other in putting up houses. (Eugene won and the hated rival vanished.) Springfield takes its name from a remarkable spring which gushes out of a bluff of solid rock forty feet high. The steamboats come so near the bluff in high water, that goods can be laid directly on them."

Mary Butler was in her seventy-eighth year and Anne thought the sudden appearance of her eldest daughter, whom she had not seen in five years, might be too much of a shock for the elderly woman. Accordingly, she hunted up the Cowans who kept a mercantile store. Patrick Cowan, a nephew, went to look for his grandmother. Like old times, Mary Butler was at the house of a neighbor helping to tend a sick child. By degrees Patrick broke the news. Mrs. Butler took it calmly and hurried home to change to her best dress. Anne found her seated and waiting.

The dear soul sprung with the rapidity of lightning and caught me in her arms. The first words I could distinguish were "Well, never, never did I expect to see you again!" Her voice is so low and inarticulate that I had trouble understanding her. For years she has suffered from a shaking palsy. It is worse and has affected her voice, though not her mind. The family, accustomed to her speech, had to interpret most of what she said. The palsy I attribute to the immoderate use of strong coffee.

My mother is a low, light woman, and once the handsomest of her day. She is now considerably bent, her features grown longer, and she is much burned by the climate. But her eye (and such an eye!) was as brilliant as ever. She can still outride any female on horseback. She devotes much of her time to the afflicted. They say her knowledge of medicine is such that she is often consulted ahead of the physician. After experiencing every vicissitude of fortune she has the pleasure of seeing her family respectable and flourishing and finds a most comfortable asylum in its bosom.

This was Mary Butler's epitaph from the pen of her famous daughter. There is no further reference to her in Anne Royall's subsequent writings; not even mention of her death, which could not have been too long in coming.[13]

4

Two days were all Anne Royall could spare for Springfield. Back across Indiana she racketed and wrangled, hurrying to Cincinnati, where she wished to report on the banking situation. "I had a most lamentable account of the oppression of the U. S. bank in Cincinnati." Most of the news coming out of Washington City these days had to do with the agitation over the renewal of the charter of the Second Bank of the United States. Though the charter would not expire until 1836, Nicholas Biddle, the bank's president, had decided to press for earlier renewal, before opposition to his institution got worse. President Jackson in his first annual message had served notice that he disapproved of the currency policy of the bank. That was enough for the people. If their hero did not embrace the bank, then they would not. The decision was not just; there were faults on both sides. The main trouble was that our young nation was a novice at banking. People, of course, were not necessarily in need of the President's viewpoint to make up their minds. Many of them were already unemployed and had lost their homes to the "monster."

The U.S.A. stood on the threshold of one of the worst panics in its history. Officially the beginning year is put down as 1837, but discomfort was felt much earlier. As with all our panics it was the old story of boom and bust; too rapid expansion, reckless speculation, reckless spending, no planning for crop failures, inflation, and a poor banking policy. The effects of the panic were to fall heaviest on the South and the West. In Tennessee, the President's state, Mrs. Royall had already briefly written of the "gloomy picture" created by the "monied monsters." Booming Cincinnati had suffered even more.

E. Flint, son of Timothy Flint, and Judge William Burke, the postmaster, met Mrs. Royall on arrival in Cincinnati and took her to a tavern where rooms had been engaged. When the landlord learned her name, he would not let her stay. Anne was delighted. The inn was on the bank of the river and the clientele appeared to be "ruffians and thieves," types such as she had seen along the Mississippi River. Settled in a boardinghouse more to her liking, the visitor went to call on her old friend the Reverend Timothy Flint of whom Frances Trollope wrote: "He was the only American I ever listened to." Said Anne Royall: "I never longed to see, not even my mother, more than I did Mr. Flint." She was distressed to hear that Flint had had to quit publication of the *Western Monthly Review* for want of support. "Cincinnati is unworthy of him!" she declared indignantly. Born in Massachusetts, the Reverend Mr. Flint had come to the Queen City of the West as a missionary. "In his daily life he was frankly outspoken and critical, often to his own hurt, and some of the many troubles he met with in his honest preaching to the frontier heathen, resulted from his plain speaking." It led to his break with the missionary society which had sent him west. At heart, the reverend was as much of a gadabout as Mrs. Royall. They had met half a dozen years earlier when both were on the road gathering material for books. Flint had discovered the Mississippi Valley as a source for his researches, and probably his most important work was the four volumes published in 1826 under the title *Recollections of the Last Ten Years, Passed in Occasional Residences and Journeying in the Valley of the Mississippi.* More or less an extension of his Valley wanderings, the *Western Monthly Review* had concentrated on little known history of the section.

He is far superior to Walsh [said Anne Royall]. As a man of strong mind, deep conception, classical elegance, and inventive powers, he is second to no American writer. His teeming mind dresses his lively ideas with a magic sweetness which never fails to charm; nor are we less pleased with his sprightly wit and descriptive powers. Had he written tracts, which his soul disdains, he would have been supported.

And with all these endowments, Flint was a tall, handsome man. "His face is round and thin, with delicate features, much sun-burnt. His eye is black, rather small, but of such riveting keenness it startles the beholder."

Mrs. Royall was enchanted by all the Flints. "I have now traveled through every state in the Union and have not met with a family more pleasant and more interesting." Besides E. Flint, the son, there was a daughter. Mrs. Flint, the patient Abigail from Massachusetts, was "very fair and blue-eyed." Micah, the eldest son who had already won a reputation as a poet, was absent in Alexandria, Louisiana. Like his father, Micah was fond of roaming the country and writing about it.[14]

Despite the crumbling economy, Cincinnati was also interesting and the scenery most beautiful, except—"There are 23 churches and 50 societies for spreading the gospel in Cincinnati." Mrs. Trollope, who departed the Queen City previous to the arrival of Mrs. Royall, wrote vehemently of the churches' dominance over the women.

There are no public gardens . . . and were it not for public worship . . . all the ladies in Cincinnati would be in danger of becoming perfect recluses. The influence which the ministers of all the innumerable religious sects . . . have on the females . . . approached very nearly what we read of in Spain. . . . I heard of Presbyterians of all varieties; of Baptists of I know not how many divisions; and Methodists of more denominations than I can remember; whose innumerable shades of varying belief it would require much time to explain and more to comprehend. . . . Every evening that is not spent in churches and meeting houses, is devoted to . . . prayer meetings. . . . It is thus the ladies of Cincinnati amuse themselves; to attend the theatre is forbidden; to play cards is unlawful; but they work hard in their families, and must have some relaxation.

Anne Royall concentrated on the bank and Presbyterians. Her views were not objective. "The Presbyterians here, as at Nashville, are at the head of the U.S. Bank, and have left the citizens nothing. The city displays a most melancholy picture of poverty, vice, tyranny, slavery and distress."

A later writer has confirmed report of the bank's despotism, though without blaming the Presbyterians: "A large part of the city, its hotels, iron founderies, unimproved real estate, warehouses . . . passed in title to the Bank of the United States. . . . The West was prostrate at the feet of what it had come to call 'the Monster.'" Perhaps part of the explanation of Mrs. Royall's indictment lay in the fact that the Presbyterian Church, at that period, had the biggest bank roll, and therefore the closest banking ties.[15]

The tavern where Anne Royall stayed had been taken over by the bank. The cook, a white woman and mother of several children, worked barefoot because she could not afford shoes. Anne gave her fifty cents and told her to ask the other boarders for more.

The poor thing burst into tears, called me an angel, and said if I had not given her the money the constable would have taken her that night. "This is just what I owe the tract society. So sure as I haven't the money to pay, the constable is sent for me. He took me away once."

"But why do you subscribe?"

"You are obliged to subscribe, if you work for a living, or nobody would hire you. All the servants and waiters about the tavern have to subscribe $5 a year!" Several of them were standing by and said it was true.

Even so Anne praised the tavern as one of the most delightful met with in her travels. There were several foreigners, looking about for opportunities in the New World, but apparently of superior lineage, education, and a charming sense of humor. She especially liked the widow of that archconspirator General James Wilkinson, and her daughter Elizabeth. Wilkinson had gone off on another grandiose scheme and died in Mexico, leaving his family in "low circumstances." Anne hoped they would find friends to help them. "Miss Elizabeth is beautiful and charmed us with her skill on the harp. Her mother is a French lady from New Orleans."

So the longest tour was about to end on a happy note, when up sprang a bothersome blueskin, a "gentleman of the cloth," with a letter to a newspaper, inviting Mrs. Royall to a "public discussion" of her views "in relation to Bible, to Tract, and to Missionary Societies." Anne published her acceptance of the challenge the day after the preacher's communication appeared. Not only that, she told him in advance what her views were:

I view all those schemes as vile speculations to amass money and power and the Sunday Mail plainly proves your object is to unite church and state. I am opposed to those schemes because the money is taken from the poor and ignorant, as no man of sense would pay for the gospel which is to be had without price. I will be happy to see you at my rooms or in public.

Her correspondent, who had signed a "fictitious name, neither replied nor showed his face." [16]

5

In October, after a period of rest, Mrs. Royall began the return trip to Washington. In November she was detained in Pittsburgh for a couple of weeks by a shabby incident which could have cost her life. The Capital first learned of her narrow escape from a few paragraphs in the Jackson newspaper.

A clerk in a bookstore in Pittsburgh was fined . . . for an assault and battery on Mrs. Royall. . . . The *Pittsburgh Statesman* says—"It appeared that the assault and battery was committed with a cowskin—that several strokes were inflicted which left marks on her person, and drew blood from her face."

The same authority says, that Mr. G. W. Holdship testified on the part of the defendant, in substance, "that Mrs. Royall had advised defendant's employers, if they desired decent people to come about their establishment, to employ, etc." She spoke something about the tail of a monkey, but owing to the low voice in which the witness gave testimony. . . . [the correspondent] did not distinctly understand the expression. The defendant then got a cowskin, followed the complainant downstairs, and inflicted the assault and battery. Such was the provocation for an assault upon an aged and infirm woman.

"Why is the name of the defendant suppressed?" asked the Washington editor.

The defendant was Charles Plumb, clerk in the bookstore of G. W. Holdship, brother of the paper manufacturer with whom Anne Royall had voyaged to Steubenville, Ohio, a couple of years earlier. Plumb pleaded guilty, but his attorney argued that "the penalty ought to be merely a nominal fine, owing to the bad character of the prosecutrix, and in particular, because of her abuse of the Antimasons. He said that no individual, who happened to be Antimason, could escape the foul defamation of her tongue and pen."

The prosecutor insisted that "no provocation could, in the slightest degree, extenuate the offence by a *man* who struck a woman [and] . . . the Court should not stop short with the infliction of a fine." His assistant made the point that "personal security was a right more sacred than any other. What would become of it, if nominal fines only were imposed for its violation? Whatever the irritability of the plaintiff's temper, or the scurrility of her tongue or pen, she . . . was entitled to protection from violence and outrage." Furthermore, she had the right to "question the correctness of antimasonry, without being cowhided for it." [17]

Plumb was fined twenty dollars and costs, apportioned as follows: "Atty Genl. $3.00; county, $4.00; sheriff. $1.37; Ald. Murray, $3.41; state $7.13." (It does not add up and I cannot explain the Ald.'s cut.)

Mrs. Royall wrote Major Noah the trial was "a farce." Plumb should have served time in jail. All that saved her from death was a new bonnet which she had bought the day before the "outrage." Heavy padding broke the force of the blows on her head. She believed the clerk had been inspired by her opposition to the Bank of the United States, rather than denunciation of Antimasonry.

Holdship was my firm friend until he found I was opposed to the Bank. He manufactures paper for the Bank. He has all the presses indebted to him for paper . . . [and] ships vast quantities to the Western and Southern States. If the Bank, which I suspect for this foul deal, would do such a thing now, what will it do if rechartered? Therefore, ye who value liberty, crush the monster before it be too late.[18]

CHAPTER XVI

"THE WELFARE AND
HAPPINESS OF OUR COUNTRY"

1

What a pile of manuscript Anne Royall had ready for the printer! Her custom, when traveling, was to sort her notes and write down events of each day before she retired. Later she rearranged and edited. All this had been done during the month she tarried at the pleasant boardinghouse in Cincinnati. The three volumes of the *Southern Tour* were the last of the travel books. They were, in fact, the last books Anne Royall wrote. Her sixty-one years were not up to riding in stage coaches or running after subscribers. The cowhiding in Pittsburgh had added to her distrust of Doctor Ely's followers. Still, she was not ready for the shelf.

"Home to Washington, by 6th Dec. last," she wrote her brother in March, 1831. "Opened from 30 to 40 letters pr. day—received company, and replied to correspondents. I have been ever since shipping books to South and West." [1]

In May, a bundle of books delivered to the Lafayette Hotel, Fayetteville, North Carolina, burned up along with most of the town. "Dreadful Literary Calamity," headlined *Niles' Register.* "We have heard nothing like it since the destruction of the Alexandrian Library." Anne Royall estimated her loss at $190, a lot of money for her. Moreover, the stopover in Fayetteville had been profitless. After paying stage fare ($2.50) and tavern bill, she sold only one subscription and the blueskins gave her a scary time. Her judgment of the town: "Fayetteville is the poorest hole I ever was in." [2]

In the face of all the problems perplexing the nation, the aging crusader was not encouraged to take it easy. In the spring the Eaton affair broke up Jackson's cabinet. It also shattered the White House ambitions of Vice-President John C. Calhoun and boosted the political fortunes of Martin Van Buren, who stuck with Old Hickory and tried to maneuver the wife of Secretary of War Eaton into the Cabinet wives' social circle. Anne Royall was a good friend to most of the secretaries and others involved. She was a great admirer of Calhoun. "Few men understand the science of government better than Mr. Calhoun." If only Mrs. Calhoun had consented to receive Mrs. Eaton! It is told that the bemused, white-haired old gentleman from the scrubby Waxhaws called on the unyielding Floride Calhoun of Charleston. Wordlessly she heard out his plea for peace and then coolly summoned the butler to show the President of the United States to the door. Unsullied Floride retreated from the Capital, leaving the Vice-President to finish out his term of office without a wife to comfort him as disappointments accumulated.

Throughout the year President Jackson battled against renewal of the charter of the Second Bank of the United States. Mrs. Royall stood with him, firm in the conviction that her country should be free of the growing economic power of the "monster." Nicholas Biddle played a deep game and his craftiness worried Anne, lest the Administration should be hoodwinked.

In September, in preparation for the presidential election in 1832, the Anti-Masonic party organized nationally. It was the first third party in the history of the U.S.A. The nominating convention, assembled in Baltimore, chose William Wirt as candidate. Anne had lost her respect for John Quincy Adams's attorney general when she interviewed him that first summer in Washington. She was not unhappy that he was the nominee. "His prospects are not bright!" A more popular candidate might have transformed the anti-Masonic sentiment into real danger. [3]

Perhaps it was the threat of the third party which returned Anne Royall to the political battleground. Early in November, she and Sally Stack went to New England. Along the route—Baltimore, Philadelphia and New York—they visited newspaper editors and collected funds to start a weekly newspaper. Mrs. Royall was surprised to learn later that support had come in abundance from the states of "North Carolina, Georgia, Alabama, and Ohio." As usual friendly editors were encouraging and enemies scoffed. Missing from the ranks of former stalwart supporters was Major Noah. A contribution from him was unacceptable. Noah and his partner J. Watson Webb had borrowed nearly $50,000 from the obliging Biddle bank. "The *Courier and Enquirer* was in some financial difficulty," explained James Gordon Bennett, who quit the newspaper after the debt became known, "and Mr. Noah, when he saw the breeches pocket of Mr. Biddle open, entered it immediately." Shortly a Congressional investigation revealed that the major had joined a numerous and select company of editorial "borrowers": Duff Green, the Jackson editor who would go over to Clay in the 1832 presidential contest ($20,000); Gales and Seaton ($44,695), Robert Walsh ($11,541), Thomas Ritchie ($10,900) and Jesper Harding of the *Pennsylvania Inquirer* ($36,916).

Mrs. Royall was terribly upset over what Noah had done. "Shame! shame!" she admonished. "The major was an able general, endowed with talents worthy of a better cause than the one he has chosen. [He was] an old and admired friend, but we love our country best." A lesson should be drawn from Noah's perfidy: "The people have a most lamentable evidence of the dangerous engine of oppression and corruption that the Bank is." [4]

In Boston Anne and Sally took time out from fund raising to visit a display of monsters. "The Great and Unprecedented Attraction" frightened "Secretary Sally nearly to death." She ran into a corner and refused to look at the "beautifully preserved body of a New Zealand tribal chief." Massachusetts shipping families had a special curiosity about the aborigine. He had been "one of the perpetrators of the massacre of the ship's company of the *Argus*, in 1816, when all were murdered except five of the crew."

Secretary Sally showed a stiffer backbone several weeks later when she called at the White House for a subscription to Mrs. Royall's new enterprise. Jim the porter [Jimmy O'Neal] had been instructed to take one subscription, but he wrote "none" on Sally's list. The secretary told him the word began with an *o*. Suspicious of what he was ignorant, Jim demanded that Mrs. Stack repeat the vowels of the alphabet. Without hesitation Sally ran through them and left the executive mansion with *one* subscription.

Meanwhile Anne Royall dashed about picking up a discarded Ramage press and wheedling Duff Green into giving her type discarded by the *Telegraph*. She hired a tramp printer (probably a discard too) and, as was an editorial custom of the day, acquired two orphans as printer's devils. While serving their apprenticeship, they received their keep. A neighborhood "carrier boy" named the newspaper *Paul Pry*.[5]

2

On December 3, 1831, the first issue of the four-page *Paul Pry* was run off in the Royall kitchen at the Bank House around the corner from Capitol Hill. The newspaper made it clear that Mrs. Royall was embarked on a personal adventure in journalism. Up to then, Washington newspapers—and elsewhere—published little local news. "Scissors editors" clipped and reprinted items that originated with their colleagues, or might even be a clipping of a clipping. The press of the District abundantly displayed the propaganda of the political party of the ambitious politico who footed the bills. Sometimes the newspapers went so far as to announce the coming of a distinguished visitor, but he was never molested by interviewers. *Latest Intelligence from Europe* had to do with the arrival of ships at Atlantic ports and, judging by the space allotted *Intelligence*, was the information most eagerly awaited by subscribers. The few columns of advertising were frequently more newsy than the editor's contributions.

Paul Pry was gossipy, with considerable personal propaganda of an anomalous female who had so much to say that there was little necessity to paste up what other editors wrote. "No party," an-

PAUL PRY.

EDUCATION—"The main pillar which sustains the Temple of Liberty."—JOHNSON.

VOL IV   WASHINGTON CITY, D. C. DEC. 20, 1834.   N 2

PAUL PRY,

PUBLISHED EVERY SATURDAY, BY
MRS. ANNE ROYALL.

TERMS.

Two dollars and fifty cents per annum, paid in advance. One dollar and fifty cents for six months, including the Session of Congress.

Subscribers may discontinue their papers when they think proper, by giving notice to the publisher. All letters must be post-paid.

Mrs. Royall has removed her residence and Printing Office, a short distance west of the Capitol, at the corner of East Capitol and 2nd Streets, near the Hill Market.

Advertisements received at this Office, as usual.

HOLT'S HOTEL.

THE above establishment having been in successful operation for eighteen months, is now in complete operation for the accommodation of Ladies and Gentlemen visiting the city, either on business or for pleasure.

HOURS FOR MEALS.

Breakfast from 7 to 9 | Tea from 7 to 9
Dinner,   do. 12 to 4 | Supper, do. 9 to 12
Doors never closed.

New-York, July 12, 1834.   STEPHEN HOLT.

NOTICE
TO EASTERN TRAVELLERS

THE proprietors respectfully inform the public that they have established a new line of mail coaches, between Washington city and Philadelphia, by way of York, Lancaster, &c.

THOS. COOKENDORFER.
Washington city, March 12, 1834.

EDUCATION.

I inform the public that I intend to commence the instruction of youth on Monday, the 1st of December next, in the school house on 9th, between E and F streets, at present occupied by Dr. F. Smith.

JOHN McLEOD.

P. S.—If Parents and Teachers would understand each other, teach their duty, and perform it, the children would do theirs, and we should have few complaints concerning improvement or conduct.

T. P. PENDLETON,

HAS this day received a fresh supply Clothes, Cassimeres, (Cassimere of a entire new style,) and Vestings, which he pledges to make up to order in the best and most fashionable style, at S. Ditty's old stand, one door west of Brown's Hotel.
Nov. 12, 1834.

MARBLE YARD.

J. P. PEPPER, Pennsylvania Avenue, near the National Hotel.

Continues to manufacture Marble Mantles, Monuments.

TOMBS, HEADSTONES, &c.

Marble work in general furnished to order. Also keeps constantly on hand, a full supply of

SOAP STONE.

Suitable for coal grates, backs, jams, hearths, &c.

FIRE BRICK.

Fire brick, and fire slabs, an entire new pattern, with bevel tops, and fire cement, an excellent article to setting grates. December 6.

THE PIEDMONT LINE.

Leaves Washington every day for Warrenton, except Monday, at half past 6 a. m. For points south of Warrenton, it leaves Washington on Sundays, Tuesdays, and Thursdays.

Washington December 6, 1834. THE PROPRIETOR.

A. MARMION,
GENERAL AGENT,

Corner of 13th and E Streets, Washington City.

Keeps constantly on hand, and will sell at the lowest prices, every variety of Stationary, such as Paper, Quills, Ink, Pens, Pencils, Inkstands, Sealing-wax, Wafers, Wafer-seals, Band-Boxes, &c.
Dec. 6

MRS. E. W. STROTHER,

Having removed her large and commodious house (on 18th street, near the Pennsylvania Avenue, and in the immediate vicinity of the Globe office,) would be glad to accommodate, on liberal terms, members of congress, clerks, and other gentlemen. Two washes and carriage houses on the premises.
December 6, 1834.

MICHAEL McDERMOT,
Coach and Harness Manufacturer,

Corner of 4 1-2 and C Streets.

Tenders his respects to his customers in Washington city, and to the public generally, and informs them that he still carries on the Coach and Harness making business, in all its variety, at the above stand, where he will be ready at all times to execute orders confided to him, in the neatest manner and at the shortest notice. All work warranted—repairing done as usual at short notice.

Silver and Brass Plating

He has also employed a first rate Painter, and will do all kinds of plating. Dec. 6.

EXCHANGE HOTEL.

The subscriber begs leave to inform the public that he has taken his home, on Penn. Avenue, opposite the Globe office, formerly occupied by Mr. Faunt.

B. S. MOYELL.

CITIZENS HOTEL.

BY MR. M'KEON.

Near the corner of 9th St. and Pa. Avenue.
February 3, 1834.

BOARDING.

The subscriber respectfully informs the members of Congress and strangers visiting the city, that he is prepared to accommodate, in handsome style, those who may favor him with their patronage.

R. H. CLEMENTS.

December 6.

BOOT AND SHOE
MANUFACTORY.

WM. I. WHEATLEY, respectfully informs his friends, and the public generally, that he carries on the above business in all its various branch, and will be found at all times on New Jersey Avenue, near the Capitol, three doors above James Young's Esq.

BOOTS and SHOES repaired at the shortest notice and in the neatest manner.

Washington City, Dec. 1834.

Our friends will have the goodness to forward the needful to us, through their Members at Washington.

YOUTH AND AGE.

BY SOUTHEY.

With cheerful step the traveller
Pursues his early way,
When first the dimly dawning east
Reveals the rising day.

He bounds along the craggy road,
He hastens up the height,
And all he sees and all he hears
Administers delight.

And if the mist, retiring slow,
Roll round its wavy white,
He thinks the morning vapors hide
Some beauty from his sight.

But when behind the western clouds,
Departs the fading day,
How wearily the traveller
Pursues his evening way!

Sorely along the craggy road
His painful footsteps creep,
And slow, with many a feeble pause,
He labors up the steep.

And if the mists of light close round
They fill his soul with fear,
He dreads some unseen precipice,
Some hidden danger near.

So cheerfully youth going begin,
Life's pleasant morning stage;
Alas! the evening traveller feels
The fears of weary age.

From the Commercial Herald.

WAIL OF THE WARRIORS.

On the low grounds of the Rivanna, about two miles above its principal fork, there is, or rather there was, an Indian mound:—"A party of Indians passing about thirty years ago, through the woods directly to it, without any instructions or enquiry, and having staid about it some time, with expressions which were construed to be those of sorrow, they returned to the high road which they had left about half a dozen miles, to pursue their visit, and pursued their journey."—*Jefferson.*

Still grows the grass upon the grave
The stream runs fast to view,
And still the piney forests wave,
On yonder hills of blue.

The valleys and the hills are yet
Robed in their summer bloom,
And blazing suns still rise and set
Upon our father's tomb.

But oh, how silent here where erst
The wail of sorrow rose,
Or whoops of warlike triumph burst,
To greet them in repose.

Fathers! who still in dreamless sleep,
Lie free and happy here,
Or o'er Elysiums grassy steep
Still chase the bounding deer,

Rest, rest; or if our sorrow break
The quietof your cell,
Forget that this your children take
Their last, their last farewell.

Sleep on, sleep on—the sage and brave,
A glad and glorious band;
To wake would be to find your grave

Within the stranger's land.

The days of glory you have seen,
The deed that ye have done;
The battle-frays in forests green,
That ye have lost and won;
These be your dreams, your days of fame
Alas, that they are o'er;
Nor heed if never tongues shall name
Your proud achievements more,
Ye are happier in your home and grave,
Than we who wail you thus;
While our old vales and mountains have
No home, no grave for us.

R. M. B.

Dreadful Tragedy.

The Philadelphia Inquirer of Friday last says, "A great sensation was produced in Southwark last evening, in consequence of the death of two individuals under circumstances of the most melancholy character."—*Jeffersonian.*

[They must have been hopefully converted—been to a four days meeting likely.—How many strange things those office-holders papers have, to attract the attention of the people till they pick their pockets.]

SERMON FOR BACHELORS.

The Hartford Mirror contains a lay sermon, for the special benefit of the Bachelor's Club, founded on the following text:

"And they called Rebecca and said unto her, wilt thou go with this man, and she said I will go."—Genesis, 25, v. 23.

"Jacob kissed Rachael."

"Jacob kissed Rachael,
And lifted up his voice and wept."

How pathetic! The fact is, time and the fashions make strange inroads upon poor human nature. Here was Jacob scouring the country to look for a wife, and on the fine sunny day, in the valley of Padaram, he saw her at a distance, drawing water from a well, being barefooted, and without ceremony ran towards her, and in the language of the good book, he "kissed her, and lifted up his voice and wept." We have no account that Rachael boxed his ears for his rudeness, as in these days of simplicity and innocence would have been done, particularly in "Good Society."

A Dutchman, not one hundred miles from Middleburg, having suddenly lost an infant son, of whom he was very fond, thus vented his inconsolable grief over the corpse of his child. I dont see wot did make him be, he was so fatter as pottar, would'st had him lie for ten shillings.

A witness being called to give his testimony in Court, in the State of New York, respecting the loss of a shirt, gave the following:—Mother said that Ruth said that Nell said, that Poll told her, that she saw a man that was a boy run through the streets with a streaked flannel shirt, all checker checker; and our gals wont lie, for mother has whipped them a hundred times for lying nounced the introductory editorial, outlining the course Mrs. Royall proposed to pursue.

The welfare and happiness of our country are our politics. We shall expose all and every species of political evil, and religious fraud, without fear or affection. We shall patronize merit of whatsoever country, sect, or politics. We shall advocate the liberty of the press, the liberty of speech, and the liberty of conscience.

The initial exposé of political evil called for the dismissal of M. St. Clair Clark, clerk of the House of Representatives, who "has but too plainly indicated his unfitness by his trucking to the monopolizing schemes of those employed under him—particularly the Burch family." Seven members of this "pampered" clan were on the payroll, not including Captain Benjamin Burch, doorkeeper of the House for close to thirty years. An anecdote circulated on Capitol Hill told of the patriarch's surprise when called upon to "assist a distant connexion to obtain an office. He expressed astonishment that he had a relation who was not already provided for."

Besides the Burches, Mrs. Royall listed various "faithless employees," unworthy to serve the government. A sergeant-at-arms who had succeeded his father in office had been charged with "using the public wagon and horses together with a driver, to take him to the theater." He had not denied the charge and he had not been removed. Another doorkeeper, "a habitual gamester" who held his job through the influence of "the iniquitous Bank" and against whom frequent charges of "mal-conduct" had been made, was still at his post. The secretary of the Senate, Walter Lowrie—"The most superficial observer can see that his talents are far from adequate to his station."

Lastly there was Mountjoy Bailey, the Senate doorkeeper. "He is accused of dispensing the favors which his station places in his hands with the sole view to his private emolument. He is known to have employed Negroes to transact official duties, while he pocketed a portion of their wages."

The last paragraph was addressed to members of Congress:

"Look at the disgusting picture we have drawn and ask yourselves if it is not time to apply the besom of reform."

Anti-Masons were attacked as they were in nearly every issue thereafter. Mrs. Royall told of an interview with "one of those poor ignoramuses."

We asked him "if he knew any harm of Masons."

"No," he replied, "but they ought to be put down."

"Why?"

"Because they have secrets."

I asked him "if he intended to kill every Mason, or what did he mean by putting them down?"

"Why we will keep every one from joining them, and then they will die, and Masonry will be destroyed."

Congratulations [to Mr. Wirt, the nominee of the Anti-Masonic Party]. Were we in his place, we would much rather have both legs shot off in the defence of our country, than to stand with the Anties and attract the contempt of every true patriot.[6]

There were cheers and brickbats for *Paul Pry* depending, as usual, on the political and religious sentiments of the critics. "No paper, perhaps, has ever had so many enemies," Mrs. Royall observed not without pride. "Let her be patronized!" urged Constans Freeman Daniels. "The Old Hag!" shrieked the Connecticut journal of which John Greenleaf Whittier was editor. "*Paul Pry* contains all the scum, billingsgate and political filth extant," declared another Connecticut editor. From New Bern, North Carolina: "My dear Lady: Your paper is the most ridiculous thing I ever herd [sic] in my life. It has almost made me thro up." In Indiana, Thomas Dowling, editor and publisher of the *Greensburg Political Observer*, advised readers that *Paul Pry* "is edited in that fearlessness of spirit for which the lady is remarkable."[7]

Paul Pry was only a few months old when Anne Royall commented, at length, on Mrs. Trollope's book. The Englishwoman must have been delighted to read one favorable review from an American. The uncouth sights that had disgusted Mrs. Trollope—men spitting and missing filthy spittoons and hogs wallowing in the muddy streets—were so familiar to Anne Royall's eyes that she had long since ceased to notice them. Fearlessly, the editor of *Paul Pry* reprinted a chapter from *Domestic Manners of the Americans*, in which the Englishwoman, after describing the hysterical carryings-on at a Methodist camp meeting, ended on an innuendo: "Before our departure we learnt that a very satisfactory collection had been made by the preachers for Bibles, tracts, and *all other religious purposes*." No wonder Mrs. Royall declared the book a "most able exposition of clerical tyranny over our women."

Championship of Mrs. Trollope evoked the suggestion from the *Baltimore Chronicle* that a purse be made up to send "Mrs. Royall to England to describe the 'Domestic Manners of John Bull.'" Anne replied snootily that she was not for hire. "We will take care of the Mr. Bulls on this side of the water." [8]

For the most part, subscribers to *Paul Pry* encouraged the editor. "Cut up the nullifiers—give it to them Mrs. Pry." Some of her mail tickled Anne. "Brother editors living at a distance addressed her as Miss Royall or Dear Sir." In Alabama she had a newspaper name-sake—*Mrs. Ann Royall, jr*. She was pleased to note a second name-sake—the *Ann Royal*, a canal boat operating out of Hollidaysburg, Pennsylvania. "We beg leave to remind the gallant captain to give us another L. Our name is Welsh."

Anne Royall was not so gentle when it came to correcting some of her own errors. "Speaking of Attorney General B. F. Butler, we were made to call him 'a detestable reptile.' It ought to have read 'detestable hypocrite.'" [9]

3

"Who is Mrs. Ann Royall?" asked a pamphlet-letter addressed to President Andrew Jackson in 1831 by an upper-class Philadelphia lady. "This Joan of Arc still abides by her first sentiments and . . . continues a member of your party."

The Philadelphian was in error. After little more than a year the sentiments of our Joan of Arc had changed. The voices of the bells told her that Jackson was not doing enough for betterment of the nation. *Paul Pry* found much to criticize in the December, 1831, message.

The President, among other things, congratulates the people upon the happiness and prosperity of our country; speaks of the march of science, and says a great many fine things—we cannot for the soul of us see these fine things. We have just been through the U.S., and with the exception of Louisiana and Georgia, we saw nothing but fraud, violence and oppression—distress of all sorts, vice the most abandoned. The President, we fancy, does not pry into these things as we do, though he need not go out of Washington to find ignorance, vice and distress.

And the Second Bank of the United States? The message barely mentioned it.

The absence of diatribe deceived Mrs. Royall as well as Nicholas Biddle, who, in company with Henry Clay, eager presidential candidate of the National Republican Party, was lulled into believing that Jackson had been too uncertain of his ground to bring up renewal of the charter. In February, 1832, four years before expiration of the bank's charter, bills for a new charter were introduced into the Senate and the House by direction of Banker Biddle. Thomas Hart Benton, Jackson's Senate floor leader, was glumly sure the legislation would pass, but continued to assail with his customary flow of political diatribe. Clay was overjoyed that he should have so pregnant an issue to campaign for, and money back of him too. This was the first election in which the political parties adopted platforms. The businesslike steward of the bank moved on Washington with "an advance guard of crack lobbyists." On June 11, the Senate voted 28 to 20 for renewal and on July 3 the House echoed with a favorable vote of 107 to 85. "When Biddle made a smiling appearance on the floor after the passage, members crowded round to shake his hand. A riotous party in his lodgings celebrated the victory late into the night."

Paul Pry warned the bank's friends that their jubilation was premature. Though sharply critical of the Executive, Anne Royall recognized the character of the man. "They infer that the President for the sake of securing his election will sign the act of recharter. They know little of General Jackson." In a couple of weeks they knew. Jackson vetoed the bank bill and returned it to the Senate with a memorable message which dwelt on the government's obligation to protect the American people against monopoly by the few.

Anne Royall went to the Senate to hear the veto message read and the debate to override. Clay and Benton were the protagonists. She stared long at Benton, whom she had never met, though the probank faction "had accused us of plotting the downfall of the bank together." She had never admired Benton's ". . . manner. On the bank veto, his words rolled in torrents, mingled with thunder and lightning, transfixing listeners. It was a succession of electric shocks." *Paul Pry* noted that a Louisiana newspaperman, translating Benton's speech into French, said he "could compare it to nothing but 'writing with a red hot iron upon naked flesh.' "

Anne had more admiration for Henry Clay, "a beautiful and fluent speaker." During most of Benton's searing philippic, Clay sat beside the editor of *Paul Pry*. Oh, what would Gallant Harry not do to get into the White House! As the Kentuckian rose to begin rebuttal, he asked Mrs. Royall if he might "notice our presence on the floor." She was "honored" and Clay opened his speech remarking that the "Senator from Missouri has adverted to the fact of crowded galleries. . . . The member ought not to be dissatisfied today from the presence of those who are around him; for among them is a lady of great literary eminence." ("Alluding to a noted female of the name of Royal," explained the reporter for the predecessor of the *Congressional Record*.) [10]

When the veto was not overridden, the lady of literary eminence said it was too bad that "Clay is always on the wrong side." Too bad also for Nicholas Biddle of whom she was fond. "It is Mr. Biddle's misfortune that he has become entangled with the Bank." These kind words set afloat a rumor that Mrs. Royall had gone over to the "Bank party." "Another Editor Bought Up" headlined the *Pittsburgh Manufacturer*. Anne retorted sharply: "The United States Bank never had money enough to buy us up." Her value as a publisher was better appreciated by the (Montgomery, Alabama) *Journal* which commented: "Mrs. Royall has a rare knack of castigating an enemy. If they think she has no power to hurt them, they deceive themselves, for she cuts deep as any of the Washington editors."

She had "castigated" Representative George McDuffie of South Carolina for lining up on the side of the bank. One morning they sat with several southern legislators in the Capitol restaurant, sipping coffee.

"I gave it to you pretty well, sir, I think," said Anne.

"I think you did, madam," agreed Mr. McDuffie.

Anne looked the congressman square in the eye and told him he could have been House leader, "had it not been for his audacious impudence in advocating the bank." [11]

She had neither advice nor sympathy for Major Noah who, with humor and cajolery, tried to win her back. Now and again, he published an engaging editorial intended to close the gap.

> Our friend—our favorite—our protegé—Mrs. Royall . . . has discarded us [he wailed one morning]. We always looked up to her as the source of our opinions—the individual that gave us the cue—the bugleman of the liberalists—the trumpeter of the anti-hypocrites. . . . In comparison with Mrs. Anne Royall, we said that Robert Walsh, jr., was a school-boy; Edward Everett, Domino Sampson; and Daniel Webster, a mere country lawyer. . . . We blew off the anti-masons for breaking her leg; we praised the Doctor who mended it.

And so on.

Paul Pry reprinted Noah's lament, commenting that it was

> . . . one of those fiddle-faddle articles, with which Major Noah is wont to amuse his readers. He says "we forget what he has done for us." No, never. We owe him a large debt of gratitude and will acknowledge it to our latest hour. But we put no private friendship—no individual obligations in competition with the liberty of our country.[12]

4

What a year of crises 1832 was for Andrew Jackson! He came out of the bank crisis riding high, only to face nullification. All the while a cholera epidemic, a repetition of the decimating epidemic of the previous year in Washington, was taking a nonpartisan toll of rich and poor, Jackson men and Clay men, Masons and anti-Masons, Presbyterians, Unitarians, etc.

Paul Pry hopped on "Josey" because of his editorial policy during the first epidemic.

Last year, when the hearses had scarcely enough time to carry the dead to their grave, he was silent lest the report might injure the bank-men, who own property in the city. That the location of Washington is unhealthy cannot be denied. The principal part of the city [Pennsylvania Avenue], being built in a marsh, which a common shower overflows, and from want of sewers and proper attention, it is overspread with standing puddles which are choked with filth. The whole flat land between the settled part of the city and the Potomac, much of which is marsh, is also overspread with stagnant pools. There are besides great, oblong, deep holes, from which the earth has been scooped out years past, intended for a canal, but has been the receptacle for dead cats, dogs, puppies, and we grieve to add, infants. Scientific men ought to be engaged to put in sewers and drain the marsh.

Belatedly engineers returned to work on the canal, laying down sewers and paving Pennsylvania Avenue. The laborers were principally Irish and German immigrants, who lived in slums, or ghettos, as we now call them. Many workmen were soon laid low by cholera. Even so, the task of making the Capital more sanitary proceeded apace and there was no return of cholera in epidemic proportions after 1832.[13]

As early as February, 1832, Mrs. Royall was complaining about the "shameful high price of FLANNEL—fifty to seventy-five cents for narrow stuff through which you may dart straws. Thus human lives have been sacrificed to the cupidity of a moneyed aristocracy who care not who sinks, provided they swim."

Hers was the universal complaint against tariffs through the ages. The legislation of 1828 and 1832 was highly protective of the New England woolen manufacturers, too high to please the South's cotton growers, and not protective enough of new industries coming to the fore in the Middle States. The tariff had been used to gain advantages for Jackson in the 1828 election. No use fighting for

New England votes; they would go to Adams in any case. Jackson, it was assumed, had the southern vote in his pocket. And so the wooing of the Middle States with promises which, if kept, would be at the sacrifice of other sections. The consumer was loser, in the end.

Unfortunately, at this time, a more dangerous sentiment was boxed in with the tariff's sectionalism. Even before he became Jackson's Vice-President, Calhoun "had begun to lead South Carolina on the road to nullification, which was to end in secession a generation later." Slavery was not an issue earlier. After the Eaton scandal, the Vice-President perceived that the tariff controversy provided him with a platform for a political comeback and he started elaborating on his belief in the superior rights of the state over the sovereignty of the Union.

Aware of the general dissatisfaction with the tariff, the President at the beginning of 1832 asked Congress to moderate the legislation. The new regulations still hit the agricultural states harder than the northern factory states. A South Carolina convention adopted an ordinance nullifying the tariff acts of 1828 and 1832. The legislature approved, declaring the state would secede from the Union, if the Federal government sent military might to enforce the law.

Thus, on the eve of the presidential election, after fighting off recharter of the Second Bank of the United States, Jackson was confronted with a nullification crisis, which threatened to spread from South Carolina through all the southern states, the solid core of his political support. For the sake of holding onto votes, the candidate for reelection did not hesitate. A year previously he had lifted his glass to make his famous toast: "Our Federal Union—it must be preserved." In a proclamation to the people of South Carolina, he described nullification as an "impractical absurdity. . . . To say that any State may at pleasure secede from the Union is to say that the United States is not a nation."

With no Gallup poll to deliver a hurried sampling of reaction nationally, Jackson did not know how the voters felt about the proclamation, when they trooped to the polls in December. After five months, he did not know whether they approved his veto of the Bank Bill. If he read the newspapers on the latter subject, he should have felt utterly defeated. "Two-thirds of the press . . . supported the Bank." The loans to editors gave Mr. Biddle the right to turn the screw.

Capital newspapers backed Jackson on his nullification stand, none more enthusiastically than *Paul Pry:*

> We say PRESERVE THE UNION; and if the Constitution does not bear equally on all, call a Convention of the States and amend it. The bill now before the House promises relief to every reasonable man. While we advocate equal rights, we shrink from the idea of treason and the civil war of the nullifier, as much as we do from the manufacturing monopolist who from a selfish desire of individual wealth would see the United States sunk ten thousand fathoms under water, provided he could heap up money.

Jackson won overwhelmingly. Martin Van Buren succeeded Calhoun as Vice-President. The charming, volatile Clay, having linked his fortunes with the bank, anti-Masonry, and the Church party—"always on the wrong side"—ran a poor second, with forty-nine electoral votes to Jackson's 219. William Wirt carried Vermont only. South Carolina contemptuously threw away her votes on a candidate who was not in the running. Still, the proud southern state was made a degree happier by the new tariff bill. Andrew Jackson began his second term once again a national hero.[14]

5

For all the ensuing worry, Anne Royall certainly made a mistake when, for the second time, she attempted to invade the theater. *Paul Pry* was only a few months old and funds were running low. The approaching panic was the neon sign of the times. Distress notices began to appear nearly every week in the columns of the newspaper: "May we ask our friends to forward the needful. Can they suppose we can print and live on air?" It was a losing proposition. The needful was insufficient to pay the bills. And so Anne dashed off a "comedy": *The Cabinet or Large Parties in Washington.*

In March, 1832, *Paul Pry* announced *"The Cabinet* will soon be ready for the stage." The first performance, however, did not take place until a year later and we have only inklings as to the confusion behind the scenes. First, the author quarreled with the manager of the Louisiana Avenue Theater—Joseph Jefferson, father of the famous Joseph who was a four-year-old toddler at the time. A partial explanation was published by "card" in the pro-Administration *Globe:* "Mrs. Royall is sorry to inform the citizens of Washington City, that Mr. Jefferson, of the Theatre, refuses to bring her play *The Cabinet* &c on the stage; and she has good reason to believe his refusal is governed by political motives, through the influence of the Editors of the *Intelligencer*." (Mrs. Porter wrote that the play was not given because "ecclesiastical and anti-Masonic influences were brought to bear on the owner of the building.")

The notice dropped opportunely into the laps of the anti-Administration editors Gales & Seaton. The *Intelligencer* reprinted Mrs. Royall's notice, with comment.

We congratulate the Public, but more particularly the Administration, upon the able coadjuvancy which has been secured to the Official Editor in acquiring the assistance of Mrs. Royall in preparing the *Globe* paragraphs against the *Intelligencer*. . . . We suggest the expediency of an union of the journals whose talents thus combined . . . with title of *The Globe and Paul Pry*.

Anne Royall paid for publication of a second "card" in the *Globe*, apologizing for having "been the innocent cause of an unmanly attack by the *Intelligencer*."

The playwright, after moving mountains, staged the play on her own. She "engaged" Masonic Hall for one night—the night of March 5, 1833—and with roles played by "a company of young gentlemen, who have kindly volunteered their services," scenery and benches borrowed from a school, "we amused our friends." It was the day after President Jackson took his second oath of office and so cold that the ceremonies had been moved inside the same Masonic Hall. Mrs. Royall reported that though "the house was thin, we made our expenses and something over." Magnanimously she expressed her sympathy for the misfortune of Mr. Jefferson who had advertised the appearance that evening of the Kembles. "Because of the most stormy evening of the winter," the popular father and daughter team, on tour from England, had failed to arrive in the Capital in time for the scheduled performance.

The following week *The Cabinet* played "to a good house, though the evening was again unfavorable." Once more, Producer Royall triumphed over competition. On the same night, Mr. Jefferson had billed Edwin Forrest, a rising young star from the Park Theater in New York.

In February, 1836, a performance of *The Cabinet* was advertised for the benefit of J. A. Gibson, member of the original cast. By then, the title had been changed to *The Kitchen Cabinet, or Life in Washington*, from which we may assume the recent difficulties of President Jackson were the inspiration. With the exception of the addition of two new parts, the original characters were the same. We list them, inasmuch as no copy of Mrs. Royall's comedy appears to have survived:

> Williams
> Jedediah Ploughshare (a Yankee)
> Mons. Furnish (a Frenchman)
> Peter Paperkite (a Virginian)
> Dennis (an Irishman)
> Hal
> Jim
> First Gentleman
> Parson Sneak
> Mrs. Foolscap
> Mrs. Legible
> Mrs. Furnish
> Miss Mariah Davis

The benefit did not take place and *Paul Pry* published an apology "to the citizens of Washington," saying the manager closed the theater.

Three years later, in March, 1839, Mrs. Royall permitted herself one more involvement with the drama. The Thespian Benevolent

Society of Washington customarily staged an annual production for the aid of a selected charity. This year the play was announced "for the benefit of Mrs. Royall." Financially Anne was living in the darkest depths of her career. During this period *Paul Pry* published many "thank-yous" for donations of wood, food and clothing. Members of Congress, who were frequently among contributors acknowledged, unfortunately did not muster sufficient votes to pass the pension bill which Mrs. Royall was always counting on to relieve her. Instead of passing the Widows Bill, "they passed the champagne." So the Thespians came to her aid. They rehearsed a play entitled *William Tell*.

In fifteen years of charitable playacting, the membership, though winning plaudits for zeal to do good, had won none for "ability in the histrionic art." Well-wishers bought tickets "liberally." Mayor Peter Force "remitted the theater license," and the commandant of the marine garrison agreed "to furnish the music when lo! word arrived that the proprietor of the Theatre refused to let the company have it!" Mr. Carusi, the caterer, came forward with the offer of his "saloon," but that rendezvous of fashion was booked until the hot summer months. "Take care of your tickets until September," Mrs. Royall advised purchasers. The benefit was never again announced. Anne managed to make out in the lean months ahead, but it could not have been easy.[15]

6

President Jackson made out rather well during his second term in office and that, too, was surely not easy. Interpreting his victory as a mandate from the people to continue his battle against the Second Bank of the United States, in the Fall of 1833 the President delivered the *coup de grâce* by removing the government's deposits and parceling them out among state banks—"pet banks," sneered the opposition. Though the attorney general gave it as his opinion that Jackson was treading on firm legal ground, Old Hickory had to fire two treasury secretaries before he got one who agreed.

Paul Pry again applauded the bank policy of the President while continuing to lambaste him for not clearing the deadwood out of government offices. Mrs. Royall wrote numerous editorials pointing out that officeholders, in order to perpetuate their trifling jobs, were building up a hierarchy that should permanently keep the Democratic forces in the saddle. Anne was particularly critical of the Post Office Department, and here she had plenty of company. Postmaster General William T. Barry was a good ordinary appointee, a politician who ran his department like a Tammany ward heeler. Jackson had rewarded him with the federal office because of faithful service. Barry doled out post office jobs on the same basis. Contracts for carrying the mail went to favorites, though it was said they paid high for the privilege. A Senate investigating committee was looking into the charge that the postmaster was less than a fastidious bookkeeper. (The findings were never made public.)

Paul Pry's attacks on the postal system were based, for the most part, on firsthand experience suffered during the editor's travels, and visits to government departments. She objected to free franking tracts by postmasters in cahoots with blue-skins; nondelivery of her letters and newspapers by postoffices which she had criticized (for two years none of her communications had reached friends in Montgomery and Mobile, Alabama); postmasters who could not read; nonobedience to regulations, such as opening mail bags in the presence of anyone who was not a postal employee. Of course, Anne Royall plugged for newspapers to be sent free through the mails. Payment of postage on them, she argued, represented a "tax upon the diffusion of political information."

The persistent denunciation of Postmaster Barry produced an unexpected result. "A man named Ferguson," a postal clerk, "came armed with a pistol" to the office of *Paul Pry* "and threatened a young man who was at work there." The man named Ferguson was got rid of before harm was done, but Mrs. Royall's receptions at the general post office grew more and more hostile because of her criticism. "In the General Post Office they have a bull dog, one Douglass, to seize people who enter the department," she complained. "I would thank Judge Barry, if he is compelled to keep bull dogs, to have them chained." [16]

In time the clamor forced Barry to resign. His successor was

Amos Kendall, an able politician and public servant who had written many of Jackson's best speeches and papers. Anne Royall did not like Amos Kendall and Kendall did not like Mrs. Royall. In his *Autobiography*, Kendall devotes a couple of pages to telling about his first and last meeting with Mrs. Royall. He bought one of her books. "Thus cheaply I purchased my way into the good graces of Anne Royal." How wrong he was! He fell from grace over the gift of some wood. One day Sally Stack went to his office to tell him "that Mrs. Royall was sick and suffering for the necessities of life; that although she had a little food on hand she had no means of cooking it, being entirely out of wood." Kendall sent a load of wood. A few days afterwards Mrs. Royall, presumably having recovered after eating a cooked meal, stormed into the postmaster's office.

"Well, Mr. Kendall, you sent me a load of wood," she said in an unfriendly manner. "It was very mean of you."

"Mean?"

"Yes, mean—you ought to have sent me a cord of wood!"

"Thus far I had in relation to Mrs. Royal been influenced more by thoughtless amusement than any other motive," explained Mr. Kendall in the *Autobiography*. "But now I discontinued taking her paper and took no notice of her abuse, which, indeed, I never heard of except through the thankless kindness of officious friends." He missed some good reading. *Paul Pry* praised him for firing worthless postal employees. If Kendall "is aiming for the Presidency," said Mrs. Royall, "we should prefer him ten thousand times to Mr. Van Buren." [17]

Andrew Jackson wanted Martin Van Buren and, long before Old Hickory's second term ran out, the hierarchy of government clerks had begun massing behind the Vice-President. *Paul Pry* was frothing over the political situation:

We are just as great a personal friend to Mr. Van Buren as ever. But whether we are his friend or foe is not the question. The question is whether we will submit to receive a President forced upon us by a treacherous combination of office holders who, under the name of

"Jackson Democrats," have been entrenching themselves and their families in the Government for the last twenty years.

Succeeding weeks produced more editorial outbursts.

It is apparent to all that something is fundamentally wrong, either in our institutions, or in the administration of them. Corruptions, frauds, impositions of the clergy, and the treachery of political aspirants have become the base instruments of contending parties, whose antagonism against each other would lead us to suppose they would sacrifice half the United States, provided they could reign over the other.

Anne Royall's disappointment over what Andrew Jackson had failed to accomplish was painful to bear. "While Jackson was a plain republican and acted for the good of his country, he deserved the esteem and confidence of the people." Presently he "was governed by sycophants" and "did not act for the general welfare." He was, in fact, the "royal prisoner of Major Donelson [Emily's husband] and Mr. Blair [editor of the *Globe*]." [18]

For a minority a flicker of hope flashed across the national sky when the Workingmen's Party agitated for political and social reforms. "Workingmen are very strong, they are numerous, let them be united," advised *Paul Pry*. "Let them cast an eye over the country and mark those massive buildings rising up in every part of the land: colleges, churches, &c., &c., all in the hands of our deadliest foes, the church and statesmen." Alas! The Workingmen's Party failed to unite and so expired from multiple disjointure.

Next began the development of trade unions, based solidly in intercraft associations, and *Paul Pry* gave them a hearty welcome. "These unions will form an era in the history of the world. We find them attracting great attention throughout our own country, and in Europe and look upon the trades unions to burst the chain of ignorance and set us free from the monster money craft."

Mrs. Royall hailed "the arrival of a weekly newspaper called *The Female Advocate and Factory Girl's Friend*," which was issued "in Lowell and Boston, alternatively." The textile publication declared it would not take part "in the disputed topics of religion and politics," but would "expose abuses and impositions practiced on laboring women, and promote equal justice between the employed and employer."

For all her enthusiasm for trade unions, Anne did not put her stamp of approval on a strike called by the typographers against Duff Green's *Telegraph*. "They turned out and left some hundreds of dollars worth of paper wet down. A few printers of the city, induced by benevolence alone to save Green's paper, helped to work it off." The publisher refused to rehire the strikers and took on a whole team of new hands, paying them slightly higher wages. The strikers attacked their successors in street fights and even in their homes. Pistol shots rang out wildly and the police did their duty. *Paul Pry* disapproved of the strike. "Those midnight ruffians call this 'defending their rights.' We hope the court may make an example of them, and learn them what it is to invade the rights of others."

But this isolated incident hardly does justice to the early struggles of the trade unions to organize the crafts. After the tragedy of the typographers' strike, Anne Royall settled down to thinking how the labor problem must be settled. Her analysis was ahead of the times.

It is futile to expect that these United States can remain free and happy, if one portion of the citizens is allowed to hold the rest in subjection. One thing is certain: Oppression on one side will beget resistance on the other, and the strongest party, which is beyond doubt the working class, will become tyrants and usurpers in their turn. Therefore the present tyrannical acts to subdue the workingmen and reduce them to slavery, will have no other effect than to engender strife and discontent, which must end in the destruction of one party or the other."

The editorial appeared as the Panic of 1837 closed in on the nation. It swept by the boards a decade of laborious years devoted to building up the trade unions. But the memories were not laid to rest.[19]

7

We have already remarked that Anne Royall did a heroic job, scrimping along during the Panic—before and long afterwards. An empty pocketbook could not eliminate this durable product of the frontier in the struggle for survival. As the Panic gathered momentum, she lost her "rooms" in the Bank House where the kindhearted Daniel Carroll had waived the rent for six years. The Bank House had been sold. Sally Stack went looking for a new home and found it, but unfortunately those Christian complainants in the common scold trial, Messrs. Coyle and son-in-law Whitville, persuaded the owner not to rent to Mrs. Royall. She had continued to annoy them with sharp words, oral and written, and they wanted her out of the neighborhood, far away from the Engine House where church services had not ceased to be held. At the moment, Anne Royall was laid low with a fever—"for the first time since our residence in the city"—but Sally, on the hunt again, located two small rooms "east of the Capitol, in B Street, between 1st and 2nd Streets." Sally was short $2.50 for the first month's rent which the owner demanded in advance. She canvassed the Hill, collected the rent money and the editor of *Paul Pry* was carried into the cramped lodgings on a litter.

Throughout the hard times Mrs. Royall published weekly appeals which, if read serially, give a grim picture of the struggle to keep afloat.

"Our friends of Boston will have the kindness to forward to Mrs. Royall their subscription. She is in want of money."

"The sudden and unparalleled rise of provision [prices] is such that many persons must perish of starvation. For our part it is fortunate we can live very well on bread, but poor Sally! coffee she says she must and will have."

Urgent pleas were made to members of Congress to leave a present for Sally before departing after adjournment.

The members must recollect that the winter was severe, yet Sally waited upon them with the paper regularly through storm and sunshine. After devoting nearly the whole of every day in the year, except Sunday in aiding us, she hastens home to her three orphans, often wet and weary, to provide wood and food, with but a few minutes of daylight, and but a few cents in her pocket, and too often not that.

Anne herself was desperate. "If our patrons intend to assist us— now is the time. Send some, if you cannot send all."

"With the most heartfelt gratitude we acknowledge the deep obligations we are under to the citizens of WASHINGTON, particularly to the MASONS and other MECHANICS, engaged on the new Treasury building." [20]

When banks suspended specie payments, Mrs. Royall gladly shared her store of experience on how to get along without cash.

Those who have no money, if known to be punctual, can buy on credit at Parker's on the Avenue. Mr. John Lynch is also very generous. He will credit till Congress meets. His grocery is on Capitol Hill, opposite the Market. Messrs. Stetinius, Dry Goods Merchants, near Brown's, on the Avenue, will credit till times are better. These gentlemen all deserve great credit for their prompt humanity in times like these.

A year later: "We are almost famished of want, and was never nearer giving up the p-e-n." Which was a weakening of an earlier resolution: "Everything shall stop before our paper."

"We sent Sally to Philadelphia to collect our subscriptions. It cost her $14 the trip, and she brought home $20, out of which she owed $5 borrowed."

Dead beats were indignantly exposed and pursued. "A Mr. F. Scott left Sparta, Geo., and is said to have settled down in Lumpkin County, Geo. We will be thankful to any person who will inform us how to come at this Mr. F. Scott, who left Sparta without paying for his papers." [21]

Mrs. Royall got down to bedrock with an accounting of her finances. How unbelievably little she needed! "The Post Office having suppressed my whole southern and southwestern subscription, has cut off one-half of my publishing expense, reducing it from $30 to $15 per week. I have also reduced my rent from $9 to

$6 per month, by giving up my kitchen." The editor figured her weekly publishing expenses—in the depression year of 1838—at "$16.50 per week, or $858 per annum. I have about 200 *good* subscribers, which amounts to $500. This, with transients, will doubtless meet expenses."

The "transients" were nonsubscribers and visitors to the Capital. Like a hungry hawk, Sally swooped down on them. If she was alert enough and had a little luck, she could wipe out the deficit with sales of single copies of *Paul Pry*. But often the deficit accumulated and the editor resorted to her old standbys. "Mrs. Royall has the pleasure to return her cordial thanks to the gentlemen attached to Congress, messengers and guards; also to gentlemen of the Treasury Department, and sundry others of their kind, for their liberal donations. This act of generosity in her hour of need will ever endear them to her heart."

Another generous act touched her deeply. She had gone to the office of former mayor William A. Bradley who turned down the request that he subscribe for her newspaper.

"Well, sir, just contribute a trifle to help me along," she begged, but Mr. Bradley did not contribute. Mr. Gales—"Josey" of the *Intelligencer*—whom she insulted nearly every week, overheard Bradley's refusal and followed Anne out of the office. He gave her five dollars.

"Take this, Mrs. Royall, it is all I have," he said.

The gift did not silence attacks on "Josey."

The ladies, too, gave "generous and timely assistance. May heaven reward them and bless them as they deserve," Mrs. Royall having been reduced to her last loaf and last stick of wood.

She looked around and turned up a new field of revenue.

The Marine Corps, having learned with regret the poverty and suffering of Mrs. Anne Royall, whose husband was a soldier in that glorious war that made us a nation, do respectfully think every good, charitable and patriotic citizen, ought to contribute their mite for the relief of his aged widow and aid in soothing the pillow of her declining years. She, like her husband, has always been true to the cause of liberty. For her relief we therefore contribute the small sums affixed to our names.[22]

The eulogy should have touched the unrelenting heart of Congress which, year after year, received the petition of Mrs. Royall for an amendment to the law which would give her a pension as the widow of a Revolutionary soldier. But Congress was untouched, although the petition was eloquently presented annually by Congressman John Quincy Adams of the Plymouth District, Massachusetts. There remained the old limitation as to the year the veteran had taken a bride. The law *was* amended, but Anne's wedding date was still one year short of qualifying. So, through these poorest of her poor years, Anne waited out each session of Congress, hopefully looking to Uncle Sam to drop down her chimney and fill a threadbare stocking. The anticipated pension was at least good for a little credit with grocers.

8

In one bad year of the Panic, Congress did come through with an unexpected blessing, awarding the Widow Royall twelve hundred dollars, which represented half-pay due Major Royall for five years' war service. The Royall in-laws promptly took two-thirds of the payment. After the long economy drought, Anne threw caution to the winds and broke out in a spending spree. She paid a few debts, "treated Sally with a new cloak and ourself with a new cap and cape," closed down the newspaper for a month, and caught "the cars" to Baltimore, taking along as guests Secretary Sally and the foreman Mr. Terry, "a handsome and accomplished young gentleman," though "rather bashful." Mr. Terry's boss could not have boosted his *amour propre* when she published his description: "The down had just begun to sprout on his chin, when he engaged with us; but by care and combing, he has now a very respectable crop of whiskers." [23]

In Baltimore the travelers boarded the steamboat for Philadelphia. Mrs. Royall walked into a familiar scene. "Someone had scattered tracts over the deck, and threw them in the window of the ladies cabin. Seeing no one pick them up, we did, and threw them overboard."

The softly-bearded Mr. Terry parted company with the ladies

in the Quaker City. Mrs. Royall called on old friends, beginning
with Governor George Wolf down from Harrisburg for a few
days and a guest of Mrs. Yohe's North American Hotel on Chestnut Street. The governor, a Jackson man, though pro-Biddle, was
basking in congratulations over the triumph of his battle in the
cause of education. The Pennsylvania Legislature had, at last, passed
the free school act, for which Wolf had pleaded during two terms
in office. The governor received Mrs. Royall ahead of a line of
party members and ordered coffee and cakes served her and his
other caller, the Right Reverend Henry Conwell, bishop of Philadelphia.

"Ah!" exclaimed the Catholic divine. "I like you. You are independent!"

She visited newspaper offices, looked into the post office—it was
well run—and investigated the progress of the school to which
Stephen Girard had bequeathed a fortune. A French emigrant,
Girard had died in 1831. In his will he had adequately remembered
relatives, employees, hospitals, and other charities, but left the bulk
of his estate in trust to the City of Philadelphia to establish a college
where poor white orphan boys should receive an education. *Paul
Pry* had hailed Girard as a "great benefactor," only to find itself
once more in a row with the churches. In his twelve-thousand-word
will Girard had specified that "no ecclesiastic, missionary, or minister of any sect shall ever have hold or exercise any station or duty
whatever in the college." Religious publications were quick to jump
on the legator. Obviously he "was opposed to the Christian creed."
Paul Pry was as quick to defend the Philadelphian searing, among
others, the Georgetown editor who said that "Stephen Girard was
now in hell." That pious writer "belonged to the most wicked and
dangerous class of men in the U.S.A."

Another specification of the will should have discouraged disgruntled heirs: "No man shall be a gentleman on *my* money." At
the end of a long court battle, the will proved unbreakable, but
meanwhile Mrs. Royall's current investigation turned up a snarl
of "city authorities," quarreling over the administration of the trust.
"They indicate a wish to expend the funds on the building. What

wicked creatures!" Not until twenty-seven years after the benefactor's death did Girard College open its doors to students.

After a pleasant family evening with Colonel Reeside—they met
his "enchanting son" named for Andrew Jackson—Anne and Sally
rode out to Bristol atop a wagon piled with mail to entrain for the
twenty-eight-mile run north to Morrisville, end of the rail line,
where a stagecoach took over. Though enveloped in darkness, "the
two women were unafraid." Colonel Reeside accompanied them to
New York singing "some excellent Scotch songs," through the
night. Contrary to his former misgivings about railroads versus fine
horses, the colonel had surrendered to progress and invested in the
People's Line. In the beginning Reeside had advertised that, having
in mind his "first care" was the community, the company "was resolved not to use steam carriages, and thus not to place it in the
power of an agent to sport with the lives of passengers at forty
miles an hour." But the colonel, reading the handwriting on the
wall, had again changed his mind. He retired the horses.[24]

In New York Mrs. Royall was the guest of the Holt Hotel, a
square of granite stretching the length of Fulton Street, between
Pearl and Water. Holt's was the talk of the town, if only for the
"four or five hundred persons victualed per day." When Anne first
ran onto Stephen Holt and his wife, they were owners of a popular
little hole-in-the-wall restaurant where they toiled long hours to
recoup losses from a fire which had destroyed their former public
house on Water Street. Serving "shilling plates (thirteen cents) of
the best Fulton Market beef and poultry and potatoes," they had
earned their way back into big-time hotel business. The new cara-
vansary also featured shilling plates and customers crowded in to
enjoy the tasty, low-priced luncheon. Though she did not pay,
Anne Royall thought the cost of a room—one dollar and a half per
day—was "exhorbitant."

Mrs. Holt took the visitor on a tour of the hotel and to the roof
"from which the whole city, the bay, the shipping, the islands, and
the State of New Jersey are all seen." As housekeeper Mrs. Holt
had at her disposal the most modern equipment. "The whole is so
regulated that very few hands are necessary; much of the labor is

performed by steam, even to the grinding of pepper!" And Stephen
Holt had taken forehanded measures against a second burning-out.
"The great cisterns and hose and the facility of giving the alarm in
any part of the building, exceed belief. The wooden furniture &c.
cost fifty thousand dollars. The bedding and table linen are the
work of Mrs. Holt's own hands. A most extraordinary woman!"
Mrs. Holt also had made a patchwork quilt for each bed.

Thanks to Benjamin H. Day, a tramp printer and born newspaperman of Mayflower ancestry, who published a sensational
"penny paper" called *The Sun*, we have a description of the cap
and cape to which Mrs. Royall "treated" herself. "The Joan of
Ark (sic) of the corps editorial, Mrs. Ann Royall, Esquire," according to Day, walked into his New York office one Sunday
morning at nine o'clock. She had a "handsome round face, small
blue eyes, a middling nose, and dimpled chin. Her outer person consisted of a plain snuff-colored frock, a green mantle, fastened at
the neck with a neat silk cord and tassel—a snow-white cap with a
fantastically-crimped border, and a figured lilac fashionable hat." [25]

As was her custom in New York, Anne Royall called on "those
amiable men," the Messrs. Harper. "Their honesty and public spirit
have been crowned with success. The American people are indebted
to them for the diffusion of useful and amusing books." This time
the usually peaceful Harper office was in a turmoil. Philadelphia
booksellers had boycotted a biography of Andrew Jackson by William Cobbett. The book was highly complimentary to the President, but not to Nicholas Biddle and his bank—"the accursed
scourge of paper money." Cobbett was a brilliant Englishman, a
political essayist who spoke his mind with sharp words and was
frequently in hot water.

Anne Royall expressed sympathy for the Harper brothers; and
for the author, too. He had the right to express his opinion.

She was back in Washington in time for the opening of Congress, and very much amused when she received two votes for
chaplain of the House of Representatives. "We have advised Congress to do their own praying." [26]

CHAPTER XVII

LET NO MAN SLEEP AT
HIS POST

1

Andrew Jackson's candidate to succeed him attracted more politi-
cal nicknames than any Chief Executive in our history. A few:
The Magician, the Red Fox, the Weasel, Sweet Little Fellow,
Political Grimalkin, Little Squirt (wirt-wirt!), Flying Dutchman,
Mistletoe Politician. Though fighting Martin Van Buren's candidacy with "pen dipped in bile," Anne Royall's belittling contributions were mild and unamusing—sometimes Vanny, sometimes
Matty. She insisted that she held nothing personally against Martin
Van Buren, except that he was the nominee of a "Third Party—
the Office Holders." Still the editor of the *Boston Commercial
Gazette* chided her for pursuing "Mr. Van Buren with great feroc-
ity—a constant fire." Anne denied this was so. "We do not keep
up 'a constant fire'; Mr. Van Buren is rather small game." [1]

She was not so briefly squelching with a young man who came
to see her on a stormy January morning in 1836. He was twenty-
five-year-old Phineas Taylor Barnum, editor of the (Bethel, Conn.)
Herald of Freedom. Anne Royall had begun a correspondence with
Barnum when he was serving a sixty-day jail sentence for libeling
a church deacon. They greeted each other like old friends, but
unfortunately got onto the subject of politics.

Signor Vivalla, "who performed certain remarkable feats of balancing," under the management of P. T. Barnum. Anne Royall and Sally
Stack attended a performance in Washington. This is one of the few
illustrations published in her newspapers. Reproduced from *Paul Pry*,
January 30, 1836.

"By the way, Barnum, whom do you support for President and Vice-President?" Anne asked.

When Barnum replied that he would vote for Martin Van Buren and Colonel Richard M. Johnson, Mrs. Royall exploded into a "tempestuous passion." "I have seen some fearful things in my day," the promoter wrote in his autobiography, "but never have I witnessed such another terrible tempest of fury as burst from Mrs. Anne Royall."

It took time, but Barnum was relieved to observe when Mrs. Royall ran out of steam. With the last gasp she apologized for her outburst.

"Now, I want to have a real good talk with you," she said.

They went into the printing-office-kitchen where a man and a boy worked at the press. There were no chairs in the dark room and Anne invited her caller to sit on the dirty floor and help wrap newspapers for mailing. He saw Sally Stack, "a tall woman of about thirty, somewhat ragged and considerably dirty." Barnum folded papers for an hour, but later confessed that, although Anne "was the most garrulous woman I ever saw, I passed a very amusing and pleasant time with her."

The budding impresario had come to Washington with his second venture in showmanship, Signor Antonio Vivalla, an Italian deft in feats of balancing, stilt-walking and plate-spinning. Barnum had found him in Albany, New York, fancied up his name and hired him for a year "to exhibit anywhere in the United States at twelve dollars a week and expenses." The signor was a great success in New York and Boston, attracting as much as $150 net per week for his manager. But, in the Capital, a blizzard ruined attendance. Even the weekly twelve dollars were difficult to pick up. Anne agreed to give Signor Vivalla a "puff" in *Paul Pry* and she and Sally received complimentary tickets to the show. Barnum tried to sign up Mrs. Royall for a tour of the "Atlantic Cities" to lecture on the government. Anne turned the offer down. "I am sure the speculation would have been a very profitable one," wrote the showman. "I could not engage her at any price," Barnum said with more verity than intended. He had not the price. From the office of *Paul Pry* he hunted up a pawnbroker who lent him thirty-five dollars on his watch and chain, thus providing the stake for the exhibition of Signor Vivalla's talents in Philadelphia.[2]

The house at the corner of East Capitol and Second Street, near the Hill Market, increasingly became an attraction for an assortment of visitors. New members of Congress paid courtesy calls at the beginning of the sessions. Sightseers walked by to stare and titter. The common scold often came out to greet them with a sermon on whatever current wrong was bothering her. Ahead of Barnum had arrived Virgil A. Stewart, the man responsible for the capture of the land pirate John A. Murrell and his band. Stewart asked Mrs. Royall to contradict the published report of his death. "We can do this with propriety," wrote Anne, "for we had him by the hand."

She held on while Stewart told her about the trapping of Murrell. With a gang numbering one thousand, the "last and most dangerous of the land pirates" had operated out of Tennessee and into the South and Southwest. The son of a prostitute, Murrell had beautiful manners, talked softly and killed without conscience. Horse-stealing and highway robbery were petty side rackets compared with Murrell's slave trade. He was the first gangster syndicalist, tying in his desperados with other bands who terrorized the Mississippi Valley. Stewart ran into him when he was looking for two missing slaves. Murrell liked him and Stewart, under an assumed name, joined the outlaws. He won the bandit's confidence and learned that he was organizing a slave revolt, a dangerous business in the hot-headed time of nullification. Before the rebellion erupted, Stewart took his man. Murrell and henchmen were sentenced to ten years in a Tennessee penitentiary.

Stewart told Mrs. Royall that he was being called a coward in Yalobusha County, Mississippi, where he had lived for a time after Murrell was put behind bars. People were saying that he left the state "clandestinely" to live in Tennessee because he was afraid of an encounter with the land pirate. Stewart showed Mrs. Royall an affidavit which he asked her to publish. The affidavit was the statement of a Yalobusha storekeeper who declared that Stewart "had called at my store . . . and informed me that he contemplated leaving the county on the day following; he also declared the same facts openly in the presence of all in the house." *Paul Pry* printed the affidavit and Mrs. Royall appended a note, assuring Stewart's friends "that he is the same fearless and intrepid" hero who had captured Murrell.

At every opportunity the intrepid crusader kept her own private war going, though not with the same vigor of the beginning days. Noting that a religious paper published in Columbia, South Carolina, "asked why the people of Tennessee suffer the infamous man [Murrell] to live," Mrs. Royall set the editor straight with a lesson in jurisprudence. "It is because the people of Tennessee have a reverence for the laws and the demands of justice." [3]

2

Anne Royall was as broke as Barnum when she rejected his offer, though she turned "summersets," as she wrote the word, to keep her newspaper going. She decided to dump the bankrupt *Paul Pry* and start afresh. She moved into another house, a block away "at the corner of North B and 3d streets." This was her ultimate home in Washington and from the few descriptive details appears to have been more attractive than the couple of rooms—sometimes with, sometimes without kitchen—where, for half a dozen years she had bedded down with printing press and mounds of exchange newspapers. A white picket fence enclosed the "white cottage" and before the door was a well of cool water, which neighbors and callers alike enjoyed. Even the restless Anne Royall took pleasure sitting in the shade of a tree beside the well with a pet cat.[4]

As with the launching of *Paul Pry,* Mrs. Royall made a hasty trip east to collect funds and advice. In New York she made a beeline to the damp cellar at 20 Wall Street where James Gordon Bennett published the *New York Herald.* Only a year old, the *Herald* was wonderfully prosperous. Like Benjamin H. Day, Bennett sold his four-page daily for a penny while developing the appetite of readers for lively news. "Local news [was] comprehensive, piquant, and bold. . . . Editorials were brief, pungent, independent and lighted up by a vein of Mephistophelian mockery." He had begun with $500 capital, no debt to Nicholas Biddle, and

James Gordon Bennett. *The Bettmann Archive*

no political obligations. Until he got over the hump, Bennett was editor, staff and janitor. He worked sixteen hours a day, but still had time for frivolity—in his newspapers. Boldly he laughed "at the churches, politicians, and pompous public characters." His readers laughed with him. He exposed "financial rogues" and to this category he consigned his former boss James Watson Webb, needling him to such a degree that Webb twice assaulted him on the street. If Bennett did not come off best with fists, his amusing account of the scuffle in the pages of the *Herald* won the day for him.

"I stripped him of his integuments," Bennett wrote and the whole town picked up the little-used word which invited indelicate jests.

"Ha! ha! ha! So you did, so you did," chuckled Anne Royall after Bennett, no shrinking violet, had given her a blow-by-blow description of his victory. "You rogue! And so you've quit politics?"

"Absolutely. I despise politics and politicians."

"You are perfectly right," agreed the Washington editor, with a sigh, "but I must do something for my country—I must put down corruption."

Bennett could have told her that mockery paid off better than dull crusading, but no doubt realized Mrs. Royall's limitations. He was not above mocking a trusting little old lady, so long as his readers were amused.

"I want good lodgings," said Anne. New York's great fire in December, 1835, had cut down the supply of accommodations.

Bennett knew just the place. "The Astor House."

The hotel had recently opened and the bar already become a mecca for men about town. Mrs. Royall, unfamiliar with the haunts of New York society, asked: "Where's the Astor House?"

"Go from my office across the Park, and the first house on Broadway that looks like a Penitentiary or State Prison, is the Astor House."

Anne hustled off in search of the Astor House. "Her reception there . . . was funny," reported Bennett. The hotel disdained her patronage which she offered in exchange for a "puff." Perhaps she mentioned Bennett's name which made her even less welcome.

She soon found out he had used her, in his devilish way, to annoy the manager—a Mr. Boyden whom John Jacob Astor had imported from the Tremont House in Boston. Bennett, who boasted he needed no friends, but could stand on his own, if worthy, had promptly sailed into the Bostonian's management. "Boyden must get more table linen, and not send the napkins wet from the washtub to the table." Less than a week later he made a second attack: "The management of the Astor House is getting to be a serious blot upon the character of New York. Every week some serious affray or riot takes place at the establishment. Boyden is unfit for his post. It requires a gentleman." When a new manager replaced Boyden, his first administrative act was to bar Bennett from the Astor.

The knowledge that Bennett had tricked her did not alter Anne's esteem for the editor. He had had a hand in editing *The Sketches* and he had sat by her side giving encouragement during the common scold trial. As long as she lived Bennett had at least one friend. *Paul Pry* echoed the criticism of Boyden: "He is not fit to run a dog kennel." For Bennett, there was only admiration: "He is a beacon set upon a hill, and keeps a good lookout for the movement of those wily Church and State men. He is one of the few in New York who dares warn the people of their danger from religious intolerance and power." [5]

Mrs. Royall returned to Washington with ninety-nine subscribers to her new weekly, fifty-one dollars in cash, and promises of more subscription payments. *Paul Pry* announced its own demise with a backward look at accomplishments.

Always in the van of the editorial corps and attacking the enemies of its country in their strongholds, *Paul Pry* was the first to sound the alarm that traitors were in the camp. *Paul Pry* was first to proclaim the abandonment of reform by Gen. Jackson. It was the first to discover and the first to challenge the Post Office loans and the Post Office frauds. It was the first to challenge the Indian land frauds of the great land companies. *Paul Pry* was the first to put a stop to the enormous swindling of a knot of "God's people," as they impiously call themselves. That is, "good, sound Presbyterian yankees." The Editress has only to say that, if the people will do their duty to themselves as faithfully as she had done by them, all will yet be well! Let no man sleep at his post. Remember, the office holders are desperate, wakeful and vigilant.[6]

The last issue of *Paul Pry* appeared on November 19, 1836, and two weeks later, on December 2, *The Huntress* made its debut.

The name is not inappropriate as we have often followed the chase in our young days [wrote Anne Royall]. My stand will be precisely where it always has been—on the side of the PEOPLE. If I have any particular leaning in politics, it is in favor of States Rights, in opposition to the encroachments of the General Government. Against the untiring strides of the Church and State Party to dissolve our Republic and establish a religious despotism upon its ruin we shall maintain an unflinching and uncompromising hostility. The only difference between *The Huntress* and *Paul Pry* will be the introduction of amusing tales, dialogues, and essays upon general subjects.

3

There was one noticeable difference. Mrs. Royall's attitude toward President Van Buren softened. She attended his inaugural and was "pleased" with the inaugural address.

His style and language are more correct and courteous by far than that used by General Jackson. One was always pained by the great number of I's in Gen. Jackson's written speeches. Mr. Van Buren speaks of himself in the 3rd person. "The President thinks this, or does that," sounds better than—I did this, and I did that—and I and I, to the end of the chapter.

For a while she called him the "Gee-Gaw" President, a bit of ridicule which should be set down as the characteristic reaction of frontier upbringing to the fashionable New Yorker. Despite Van Buren's style of speaking, she suspected that somewhere a flaw lurked within his well-groomed frame. A few months after the inaugural Mrs. Royall called at the White House, hoping perhaps to put her finger on the weak spot.

We were disappointed! [she confessed]. A very genteel porter led
the way upstairs. Upon reaching the President's parlor door, he
announced us for the first time. We were immediately admitted, and
found Mr. Van Buren well. After chatting a few minutes and exchang-
ing reciprocal good wishes for each other's health and happiness, we
took leave, much pleased with our visit.

The lovely spring afternoon was ideal for acceding to Sally
Stack's often expressed wish that she visit the Congressional Cemetery and view the spot where Sally's parents had been laid to rest.
For company Anne picked up Mrs. Deneale who lived near the
"burying ground." Mrs. Deneale was the "daughter of one of the
original proprietors of the District." She lived "in very primitive
style on the family patrimony, and received us with a smile and a
brow as smooth as her own *Ana Costa*, which glides by her door."
The strollers admired the cemetery, "beyond doubt the handsomest in the United States; shade trees neatly trimmed and thriving;
wide and neatly gravelled walks; the whole had the appearance of
a village."

Sally's family was buried in unmarked graves, which the keeper
located from records. Their anonymity was out of keeping with
other tombs of "great size and handsome workmanship." Anne
stood before the recently completed granite vault of an old friend,
John Gadsby, whose popular hotel on Pennsylvania Avenue continued to flourish under his son's management. Gadsby's resting
place was as commodious as one of his suites and "very beautiful."

From the cemetery Anne walked alone to the Navy Yard where
she had a flare-up with a Captain Smoot. When the captain recognized the common scold, "he started to run. We gave him chase;
and finding we were gaining on him, he jumped into a skiff. We
were near to losing him. From the favor of a small cable, his vessel
entangled in a rope and we were there.

" 'Surrender, you coward,' we said.

" 'I'm in a hurry,' the Captain said and rowed off." [7]

Captain Smoot should have studied a page from the p.r. book
of The Little Magician. Anne Royall responded as readily to kind
treatment as she did to the plight of an abused underdog. At the
moment, she was fighting to obtain justice for Richard H. White,

in jail four years charged with setting fire to the treasury building. Mrs. Royall did not believe White guilty. "We said last year that from the conduct of the secretary [Louis McLane], clerks and messengers, that the fire was no accident. It now turns out that copies of the Post Office contracts were burned up. There was a fireproof room in the department. Why were not all valuable papers kept in it?"

At the end of White's third trial, when the jury failed to convict and the prisoner was returned to his cell, *The Huntress*, bold as ever, insisted "there is some mystery in the rigid and cruel persecutions this man undergoes from the government." Mrs. Royall charged that the treasury "had been laid to ashes to conceal frauds."

White was freed after an inconclusive fourth trial, thanks to the statute of limitations. He went to the *Huntress* office to thank Mrs. Royall for her support. "He is a young, fine looking man," said Anne. "He has suffered unspeakable oppression. His property is all gone and his wife—one of the best of women—worn out by toil and suffering."

Mrs. Royall's belief in White's innocence must have had sound basis. In 1841 President Tyler gave him a full pardon.[8]

After the drab tale of White's misfortunes, it was a pleasure to report the wholesome activities of her neighbors and long-time friends, Mr. and Mrs. James Maher. Mr. Maher was the public gardener. Under his care the Capitol, and especially the Hill, showed "visible improvements." The public squares and the "President's house" were colorful with "new shrubbery and a variety of flowers, all among the best specimens." Mrs. Maher was a true helpmeet. She ran a boardinghouse and, through their lean years, did not forget Mrs. Royall and Sally with samplings of her savory platters. It was hardly a surprise therefore when Anne stopped by the Mahers one morning and the lady of the house proudly handed her a letter to read:

We the undersigned chiefs and interpreters of the Sac, Fox, Sioux, and Ioways, of the Missouri River, do hereby tender our grateful thanks to our most kind hostess, Mrs. James Maher, for her most kind treatment to us during our stay in Washington.

A-sa-so
Su-e-ah-sah
A-sha-tu
Ma-ka-ush-ka
A-ka-ake
So-ca-pee
Pa-co-ma
Interpreters: Jas. Mattel, Zephine Rencourt.

The Indians left Washington far more satisfied with Mrs. Maher than with the treaty they had signed ceding their land in Iowa Territory to the United States at ten cents per acre. There was no help for it. Land-hungry emigrants pushed the redmen aside like the wild growth they cleared from the land.

Despite the frightening experiences of her childhood on the Pennsylvania frontier, Anne Royall displayed a sympathy for and understanding of the Indians that Americans who lived in security far from the bloody scenes usually lacked. Benjamin H. Day, of the *New York Sun*, reported a discussion he had with her about the removal of the Indians. He wrote that he was impressed with her exposition of the redman's point of view. Said Mr. Day at the close of the interview: "Then you understand the Indian character?" "Yes, sir," replied Anne, "and the white man's character, too."

The Sac treaty ended what is known in the history books as Black Hawk's War, a most sad war. Anne Royall thought little enough of the military conquerors.

It took four generals, and with "*squadrons*" [a new name for land troops] of we do not know how many men, to whip Black Hawk and his handful of undisciplined, starved, bark eating Indians. What a valorous army we have! A captain's company, were they worth their salt, ought to have drove Black Hawk out of the country five months since. I think it best hereafter to send our young men to Black Hawk to learn military tactics.

Some while later when a final treaty was negotiated with the Creeks and the Cherokees—a negotiation with the latter tribe terminated with a decision by the United States Supreme Court ruling the Cherokees had to go because they were a "foreign" nation within the State of Georgia—*Paul Pry* reported, through a correspondent, on a few iniquities perpetrated by Americans during the removal to western reservations. "We have been told the moment the Indians receive their annuity a host of speculating merchants and tract people fly amongst them and snap it up in a trice. The people of the United States pretend to sympathize with the Poles, and deplore the barbarity with which they have been treated. Look at home! There never was such barbarity as that practised toward the Indians."

Those foreigners—the Cherokees—were living in Georgia when DeSoto marched through in 1540. They sold out to the U.S.A. Their 7,000,000 acres brought them $5,000,000. But not all Cherokees were content with the sale. Along with dissident Creeks and northern Florida Seminoles, they holed up in a swamp between St. Augustine and the St. John's River. The army had a problem dislodging them. Anne Royall seized on a newspaper dispatch to puncture the reported heroism of the expedition's commander:

"Genl Clinch," read the item, "behaved like a gallant officer."

"Ma conscience!" commented Mrs. Royall. "He must have wounded someone's tom cat!" [9]

4

Though the government of President Van Buren gave the public better grammar, the lively news that underscored the Jackson administration was missing. The columns of *The Huntress* reflected the more tranquil political atmosphere, as well as the advancing age and ever present financial worries of the editor. She wrote more and more about neighbors and personal incidents encountered on strolls about the Capital rather than problems which had once stirred her wrath. The walks were not solely for news-gathering. Anne Royall was again reduced to panhandling. One such excursion yielded an open break with General John P. Van Ness whose wealthy wife had been for many years a steadfast alleviator of Mrs. Royall's destitution. A coolness had developed during the fight over the recharter of the Second Bank of the United States. The general, president of the Bank of Metropolis, was pro-Biddle. So angry was he with President Jackson that he joined the new Locofoco party, a radical offshoot of the Democrats and an odd transfer for a conservative banker. One morning Anne showed up at the Bank of Metropolis and was probably inviting an old friend, Jesse Brown the hotelkeeper, to "assist" her, when General Van Ness broke into the conversation.

"Madam, you must not come here. Go out!"

Anne Royall had no choice but to go out. She went away thinking that the general was not so angry with her as he was "in a violent pet at the downfall of the locofocos." On the eve of the party's death rattle, she had written about the "feast" given by members. "It took five cart loads of champagne to satisfy their locofoco stomachs. The pity is they did not choke on the first bottle."

As she wandered about the city, Mrs. Royall pushed a new source of income: advertising. She wrote the chatty advertisements, which were often unintentionally informative on customs of the day. One such was the announcement of J. F. Callan who kept a drugstore at the corner of E Street and 7th. He advertised that he had "just received COLD CREAM, FLORIDA WATER, BEARS' OIL (scented with Persion Otto [sic] of Rose), HONEY WATER (a wash for the hair, or for imparting a mild fragrance to linen), OTTAR [sic] OIL SPIRIT OF ROSES, ROSE WATER, and AMBOYNA LOTION (for preserving teeth and gums, and purifying the breath)." Obviously Anne Royall was no user of cosmetics.

A more practical announcement was that of a new grocery. "Mr. James Given has the honor to inform the Public that he has just opened a grocery store in that noted building on Penn Avenue, near the Railroad Depot, formally [sic] occupied by Mr. Dunnas a furniture store. Ye all know *Jemmy Given.* Some call him *cheap* Jemmy, some *handsome* Jemmy. Call and see him—all our pets are good."

Anne Royall reached such straits that she threatened to remove herself and *The Huntress* to the Mississippi Valley. Some people no doubt prayed for her early departure, but she really had no intention of forsaking the District. Over the years, though she complained and scolded, she had grown to love the place. During the summer of 1839, she enjoyed it as never before. "Never did Washington afford a more pleasing treat to the lovers of taste than at present. Besides the fine band at the Capitol three times a week, the beautiful walks, bordered with a profusion of flowers of the most surprising beauty and variety, afford a treat to the pedestrian." [10]

5

The presidential campaign of 1840 was a rollicking songfest. The Whig candidate was General William Henry Harrison who, several decades past, had defeated Tecumseh near Tippecanoe River in Indiana Territory. Thurlow Weed, the upstate New York editor-politician who guided the Whigs' choice, settled on Harrison because "he had no important political enemies [and] enjoyed a reputation as a hero." Weed, one may recall, was the anti-Mason who had tried to defeat Andrew Jackson's candidacy in 1828 with a corpse of William Morgan. Harrison's running mate was John Tyler of Virginia, a states' rights man who had broken with Old Hickory during the nullification crisis. Martin Van Buren was renominated by the Democrats.

Weed built General Harrison up as a homespun hero who preferred a log cabin and a jug of hard cider to the elegant furnishings and French wines such as President Van Buren served at the White House. Actually Harrison had been born into a Tidewater family, far more distinguished than the farmer forebears of Van Buren. But the general kept his mouth shut, as he did on most subjects. He had to. Aware of the candidate's limitations, Weed set up a committee to attend him and censor his utterances and correspondence.

The Whigs offered no platform, no issues, nothing controversial. Besides their Weed-loomed hero they relied on an out-of-focus portrait of the urbane New York candidate. Historians generally agree that Van Buren merited reelection. He was unreasonably blamed for the Panic of 1837 and that calamity alone had enough victims with votes to defeat him. Not a figure to excite popular enthusiasm, he could not counteract the warbled fervor of the first campaign song in our history.

> The iron-armed soldier, the true-hearted soldier,
> The gallant old soldier of Tippecanoe.

The composer was George Pope Morris, of *Woodman, Spare That Tree* fame, though verses were sung to the tune of Samuel Woodworth's *Old Oaken Bucket,* a title which might have described the Whigs' Presidential candidate. To the opposition, the unsung Democratic candidate was merely "Little Van, a used up man."

Anne Royall, fearful of one-party rule by leftover officeholders from the Jackson regime and whom Van Buren, in her opinion, had not cleared out, came out for Harrison. "General Harrison has served his country in the field with honor to himself and the applause of all good men. He never had a father-in-law, two or three nephews, a brother-in-law and some two or three cousins packed upon the people at large salaries." But she held her enthusiasm in check. "It is impossible to tell what the future may bring forth. We had the same opinion of General Jackson. The result proved otherwise." [11]

In her more than a dozen years' residence in Washington, Anne Royall had acquired cynicism, though she was always hopeful that some paragon would arrive on the scene inspired by love of country rather than by personal ambition. There were no statesmen such as animated the early days of the Republic. "Too much politics, too much President making," lamented Anne. "Consider the present Congress. With important legislation pending, the "people-loving members adjourned to see Fanny Elssler dance." On the November night when the election results became known and "a perfect jubilee" broke out in the Capital, Anne Royall was so little interested that she retired early. She refused to get up when "the young Harrison men waited on her for the purpose of presenting a Harrison banner." "A petticoat," guessed an anti-Whig newspaper which had offered statesmanlike opposition by calling the general "Granny Harrison." Anne woke next morning and, with a flash of humor wrote: "Should our pension claim before Congress fail of success, we petition for the LOG CABIN."

She did not attend the inaugural ceremonies. The day was cold and snow was falling. A couple of weeks later, when the weather improved, she "waited upon the President at the White House," to congratulate him. She was annoyed by the "host of office seekers, who thronged the portico and public rooms." Harrison presently came out of his office to shake hands with all. Mrs. Royall thought he "looked well, happy, honored and triumphant, though a little fatigued." In less than two weeks the old soldier who had stood bareheaded in the freezing weather to take his oath was dead of pneumonia. His final words: "These applications—will they never cease?" [12]

6

The new Congress pleased Mrs. Royall. "There were never so many young men in any previous Congress. This has doubtless a good effect, as they have done more business in one month, than was formerly done in six. Old members had too much caucussing and self-aggrandizement for the general welfare of the country."

Time was moving ahead—rapidly. A new generation had caught up with the old reporter. Colonel William Jack, son of the heroic Captain Jack of Anne Newport's Hanna's Town days, was among the new representatives. "He hails from noble stock." Henry Van Rensselaer, youngest son of "the great and good Patroon, of Albany, N.Y. seems to possess all the amiable qualities of his noble sire." Alexander H. H. Stuart, of Staunton, "whose father and grandfather were once our neighbors, has won much esteem for the short time he has been in Congress." The replacement for Colonel Beirne was George W. Summers. "When we left Virginia Mr. Summers was a boy."

Mrs. Royall was impressed by the energetic young Tammanyite Fernando Wood—"a promising young man, gentle, modest and winning, very tall, rather wan, but no member retains his natural

color long in this place." She met also an energetic Roosevelt—
James, junior, of New York (Theodore's grandfather). "With
papers in hand and people tugging at him, he could not stand still
a moment." Another new member from New York was Hamilton
Fish, "tall, stout, and of showy appearance." [13]

Samuel F. B. Morse, whom she had met eighteen years earlier,
was presently demonstrating his invention in a small room at the
Capitol. Congress had reluctantly voted $30,000 to stretch an ex-
perimental telegraph line between Washington and Baltimore over
which the famous message, "What hath God wrought," had been
successfully transmitted. Mrs. Royall wormed her way through a
crowd to the table where an operator

. . . was intently striking a brass key with his finger. We requested
the gentleman at the key to say Anne Royall was present. He had just
finished the last stroke when a small wheel on his right began to turn
slowly, and the gentleman reached over and tore off a narrow slip
of paper under the wheel and handed us the reply from Baltimore:
"Mr. Rogers respects to Mrs. Royall." A wonderful triumph of the
human mind!

She made her way to the far end of the table where the inventor
stood with folded arms watching the operator. He had aged considerably since she first met him at his father's house in New Haven.
"He was then in the bloom of manhood. He is now thin, gray
and careworn. We think very highly of this amiable man and our
opinion is that his country is unworthy of him." She referred to
the fact that Morse had been unable to persuade the government
to buy his invention for $100,000. Eventually it fell into private
hands.[14]

For a couple of weeks Anne had to quit her meanderings to
pamper a sore eye. "Our friends say the pain in the eye is occasioned by looking at such a number of handsome gentlemen."
Well again and on a tour of "the departments," she met the handsomest of them all—John Howard Payne. Though fifty years old,
the author of *Home Sweet Home* was "young looking. His eye is
the point of attraction—large, of a dark, liquid blue of uncommon
luster, and sparkles with a joyous vivacity. His conversation em-

bodies much in a few words, while his voice has a peculiar sweetness and harmony, not common to Americans." The actor-playwright had followed a steady downhill progress in the eighteen years since he incorporated his nostalgic song in a light opera first produced in London. But his fortunes had improved since he threw in with the Whigs. Anne Royall met Payne in the State Department directly after President Tyler had appointed him consul at Tunis.[15]

About this time began a delightful editorial "romance," reminiscent of the days when Major Noah published love letters to Anne Royall in his newspaper. The new admirer was L. R. Streeter, editor-owner of the (Richmond, Virginia) *Daily Star and Transcript.*

"We have no less an honor," wrote Streeter, "than a proposed exchange from our sweet friend Mrs. Ann Royall, who chucks us under the chin with the title of 'Leander of Richmond.' . . . Well, dearest Madam, we salute you most profoundly. . . ."

Some months later when Streeter closed a squib with a loving "squeeze" of Anne's hand, *The Huntress* editor hurriedly protested: "Pray do not talk of squeezing our hand. It had a squeeze five weeks ago in the press which will serve for six months to come." Mrs. Royall told her readers that the *Star* "in wit, humour, good sense and anecdote is not to be surpassed." Streeter, more rooted in the U.S.A. than Noah, made it so. He invented two characters—Ephraim and Simon—to clown his homely imagery:

Ephraim: I'm so rejoiced the Florida War is settled. [Second Seminole War to remove resisting Indians west of the Mississippi.]
Simon: So I think. And so is Grandmother Squibbs' rheumatism settled—in her left leg. The thing is to unsettle it.

Anne Royall tried to fall in step with the Virginian's comedy, utilizing Jeff, her printer's devil, but Jeff was no match for the newsprint fantasies of Streeter. One Christmas he planned a trip to Washington, but illness kept him at home. He and Anne never met. After five years *The Star* was sold.[16]

There were no coy exchanges with Horace Greeley, though Anne Royall had only praise for *The New York Tribune.* She "heard" the editor was an "accomplished gentleman—a fine Belles Lettres scholar, with strong reasoning powers, mild in temper, and suasive in manners." Greeley's aloof dignity seemed to affect her writing when she mentioned *The Tribune*, though it never cowed James Gordon Bennett, who referred to the editor as "a galvanized squash."

Anne Royall ran across Greeley one day as he was looking over his mail at the Congress Post Office. Though it was winter the New Yorker wore his customary white coat. Anne walked around him, studying the profile and the light blue eyes, "soft and innocent as a babe," which had won him the nickname Baby Face. She introduced herself and Greeley shook hands limply. "His manners are distant," reported *The Huntress*. "He has whitish hair, a red beard, and a soft sweet voice." [17]

For a time the *Baltimore Sun* was a favorite, although newspapers were not exchanged. "We take the *Sun* and pay for it, because we get the news generally 24 hours sooner than in our city papers," explained Editor Royall. The *Sun* fell from grace after publishing a paragraph of "falsehood and low insolence." "She [Mrs. Royall] is the strangest *female* (query?)," proclaimed the Baltimore journal. "She attacks everybody and nobody, and when neither everybody and nobody will notice her slang, she attacks herself. A *Royall* idea!" Anne canceled her subscription.

A Vermont newspaper complimented Mrs. Royall and five other "female" newspaper editors for their journalistic labors. Anne was displeased to be linked with "female" editors who were campaigning either for abolition or for woman suffrage, or both. She did not approve of slavery, but she did not like the quality of those who ranted against it. She was dead set against woman suffrage. Her preference was for a "womanly" woman. She joined masculine editors in ridiculing the costume worn by Amelia Jenks Bloomer, editor of the *Water Lily* and one of the five lady editors cited. "We think bloomers indelicate, unbecoming and highly inconvenient," said Mrs. Royall. "Do our sisters intend to part with their last and best treasure—modesty; that grace of symmetry in motion, the sweet rounding waist, the unspeakable charm of a swelling bosom. 'It is food for health,' say the doctors, 'no more wasp waists, no more lacing.' But why is there no medium between corsets and immodesty?" [18]

Of them all, though, Anne decided the "best newspaper in the United States" was the (New Orleans) *Picayune*. "We find news in the *Picayune* found in no other paper. It gives the best and truest reports of Congress and we often read items of things passing in this city, for the first time in the *Pic*. In religion and politics, the editors are liberal and independent." The *Picayune* was blessed with one of the outstanding editors of the day; blessed with two, in fact. George Wilkins Kendall, the equal of Bennett in smelling out news and irritating people, had established the newspaper in 1837 in partnership with Francis Lumsden. Lumsden, the balance wheel, tended to business while Kendall buckled on his armor and dashed off with the Santa Fe Expedition which Mirabeau Buona-parte Lamar, Mrs. Royall's old Georgia acquaintance and now the first president of the Texas Republic, dispatched west to claim more dominion from Mexico. The expedition had been hurriedly planned and poorly equipped. Kendall and his companions-in-arms wound up in a lepers' prison in Mexico.

To the New Orleans editor probably belongs the honor of being the U.S.A.'s first war correspondent. He had sent back to the *Picayune* exciting accounts of the progress of the march. Anne Royall was one reader who could hardly wait for the succeeding installment. When the reports broke off suddenly, she was "in mourning for the loss of them." Several years afterward she would be able to pick up the thread when Kendall, returned to his native soil, wrote a two-volume history of the expedition. The publishers were Messrs. Harper of New York who, from time to time, sent Mrs. Royall a book to review. They did not send her the Kendall volumes, but instead she received *The Tourist*. With no show of enthusiasm, *The Huntress* acknowledged *The Tourist* as "an interesting little book intended for colonists." [19]

7

The conquest of Texas by American colonists, aggravated by the Mexican government's broken promises, appeared to New Englanders a predatory act. The West, to whom strife over land acquisitions was daily fare, considered the deed necessary. Anne Royall had never ceased to be of the frontier. First sight of Sam Houston had evoked a gushing description of the tall, personable Tennessee congressman. A second encounter drew a deep frown of disapproval. This was in the spring of 1832 when Houston, arrayed in beads, feathers, buckskin, and long hair, had accompanied a delegation of protesting Cherokee Indians to the Capital. In addition to battling for the redman's cause, Houston got into a street fight on his own. With a cane whittled from the branch of a hickory tree at The Hermitage, he thrashed Congressman William Stansbery of Ohio for what he considered a derogatory remark uttered on the floor of the House. Stansbery's colleagues ordered Houston to stand trial before the House. The trial was an absurd performance, with flag-waving speeches and hysterical women throwing bouquets at the feet of the handsome pseudo-Indian who swaggered and hammed like the worst actor. Houston's punishment was an indifferent reprimand by the Speaker of the House. *Paul Pry* criticized the "shameful waste of the people's money" on the farcical trial.

Then, in February, 1836, Houston, with haircut and wearing the uniform of commander-in-chief of the Texas army, made a hasty trip to Washington for consultations, and incidentally to recruit volunteers for the ultimate showdown.

Gen. Houston comes [reported *Paul Pry*], with the sole intention of representing to our citizens the destitute condition of the soldiery as well as the inhabitants of eastern Texas. He will return in a few days to that country and would be the willing and faithful instrument in forwarding bequests of money or provisions which the friends of Texas might be disposed to make.

Mrs. Royall published a call for "Volunteers and Troops for the aid of Texas." General Houston "recommended them to come by sea and land at Matagorda," the quickest route. "By the first of March, the campaign will be open."

The timing was almost accurate. The Alamo garrison was slaughtered on March 6. By then Houston was back in Texas, pulling his angered troops together through a series of retreats, until he had the pursuing Mexican army wedged into favorable battle terrain at the junction of the San Jacinto River with Buffalo Bayou. The victory was a month old when *Paul Pry* flashed the news:

"We have barely room to congratulate every man who has Anglo-Saxon blood in his veins, on the redemption of our brethren in Texas from Spanish power. The whole country resounds with joy at the capture of Santa Anna. His capture will crown Governor Houston with more laurels."

Two days later Anne Royall devoted most of her newspaper to an interview with General Memucan Hunt, minister to Washington from the Texas Republic. "The republic is filling up fast," said General Hunt. He predicted that "ere long it would have one of the most dense populations in North America." "Emigrants" were warned that "provisions have become very scarce," and advised to bring all supplies possible. Besides Texas prices were sky high:

Axes	$4.00
Butter	1.00 per pound
Eggs	1.00 per dozen
Meal	None
Oats	9.00 for 3½ bushel sack
Rice	.20 per pound
Vinegar	1.00 per gallon
Whiskey	2.00 per gallon

We are gratified [wrote Mrs. Royall], that the young Republic has the friendship and good wishes of a large majority of the southern and southwestern States, and no less so that she is upon the alert against criminals and outlaws, who flee from the States to Texas. A number of new counties and towns are now being organized. All kinds of mechanical labor are very high in Texas. The Texans are forming treaties and cultivating a friendly intercourse with neighboring Indians. With these advantages, added to her fine climate and rich soil, whether Texas be admitted into the Union or not, she bids fair to be a great and independent republic.

The possibility of admission had set in motion intrigues, at home and abroad. Texans themselves worked energetically for annexation; England schemed to keep Texas an independent republic. The South favored annexation. With a preponderance of southern settlers, the new state would be an ally against abolition. The North was against annexation of another slave state. Mexico puttered about with reconquest. Capitol Hill solons were mostly noncommittal, waiting for a sign from heaven to direct their decision.

Anne committed herself without cue from on high.

We have many friends in Texas, and were we to follow our own feelings exclusively, we should be in favor of annexation. But if it would endanger the liberty and happiness of the United States, farewell to friends and all. It is our opinion that many of those who are so pressing upon the subject, care very little either for their own country, or the exclusive welfare of Texas, but are governed by other motives, such as prejudices, self interest, &c.

Four days before he left office, President Tyler signed the annexation resolution. The Republic of Texas had only to vote acceptance. General Houston returned to Washington in 1846 as United States Senator from the new state. Anne Royall interviewed him.

"We found him less changed by the vicissitudes of time, than any one would expect. He once, and still is, one of the most elegant figures of the human family. His eye is not so bright as formerly and his hair is turning gray." Houston had had a rocky time with Texas. One day he would be hailed as hero; next day, he had no friend west of the Sabine River. With Anne Royall, Houston "laughed heartily" as he reviewed his "persecutions." His "countrymen" had made him out "the greatest rascal in Texas." When he had ordered the retreat from the Alamo, he was "accused of selling Texas to the Mexicans and joining in a conspiracy with Santa Anna." That accusation appeared to irk him most, particularly since his order was ignored and brave men died in a hopeless defense.[20]

Simultaneously with Texas' annexation, the Oregon question had the United States in a dither. By treaty this distant kingdom of fantastic proportions was jointly administered by the United States and Great Britain. Western emigration had suddenly taken a spurt at the beginning of the Forties and eager pioneers were unhappy with the dual government. In his first annual message to Congress in December, 1845, President James K. Polk demanded an end to shared authority and definite demarcation of boundaries. An expansionist, Polk had set his sights on more Oregon country than the U.S.A. was entitled to.

Anne Royall was not an expansionist. Like many another American, including Senator Daniel Webster, she considered the faraway western region "worthless." The Oregon pioneers were mainly missionaries. Anne was glad to see them go, though she felt sorry for the Indians. Characteristically, land companies had begun grabbing early. The *Huntress* published a stream of editorials, condemning both groups and assailing members of Congress for luring more settlers (not missionaries) with

. . . false inducements when they have a knowledge of the sterility of the distant Territory. Those who are in favor of settling Oregon are little concerned for the good of the country. [A raid on] the Treasury and speculation are at the bottom of the agitation. $100,000 are already voted to fit out a Standing Army. Most of those who have to pay this money will never perhaps be benefitted in dollars. The Standing Army to protect the emigrants, as in the Florida War, must be supplied from New York and Boston. The first can furnish war implements and champagne; the latter, silk gloves, hosiery and vests. Ohio and Kentucky can furnish provisions and wagons. Fortunes can be made in wagons alone. All this, as in the Florida War, will secure a strong party of votes.

What troubled Anne Royall most was that expansionists might push the U.S.A. into a war with England which still entertained thoughts of recovering her lost colonies.

The Oregon dispute was, as we know, concluded peacefully by treaty. The U.S.A. did not receive all that President Polk had staked out, but the new boundary took in more land than the earlier covenant specified. The awkward rule by two nations ended. Now came the task of organizing a territorial government. Here, as in Texas, North and South fought each other over slavery. The abolitionists wanted slavery forbidden in the Territory. States righters contended the Federal government did not have the authority to tell settlers what property they might bring with them over the Rockies.

On a steaming Saturday night in August, 1848, Anne Royall went to the Senate gallery—"for the first time in two years"—to listen to the climax of the debate on whether or not to restrict slavery in Oregon. "The crowd was immense; Mr. Webster was to speak." A nonexpansionist, the Massachusetts Whig had been woefully distressed by the annexations of the Forties—Texas, Oregon, California, New Mexico—and had "no disposition to make a speech." "I have nothing to say," he wrote a friend. "I have steadily resisted all annexation and acquisition, but there are those who would have territory, or pretended that they must take it. I feel much inclined to leave it to them to say what they will do with it, now that they have got it."

Anne Royall was shocked by the senator's physical appearance. He had aged greatly since she last saw him. He was thinner and looked worn and tired. "He spoke slow and feeble-like, his former fine voice and fervor seemed to droop, doubtless owing to his recent calamity." (The senator had lost a daughter, and then followed the death of a son, stricken with typhoid while on duty with the army in Mexico.)

But Mr. Webster's old strength flared when he rose to speak on Oregon Territory. His abhorrence of slavery was stronger than the earlier inclination not to intervene. That August evening the enfeebled senator from Massachusetts triumphed over States Righter Calhoun and settled the future course of slavery in Oregon. No slavery.[21]

CHAPTER XVIII

THE WHOLE COUNTRY SEEMS
TO BE OUT OF JOINT

1

By the middle 1840's a smidgin of economic security had settled over the roof of *The Huntress*. Nothing to splurge on; rent still six dollars a month, in advance, and always hard to scrape up. Anne Royall would appear to have accomplished the impossible. Riding out the Panic, she had lined up a small army of regular contributors who provided her and the loyal Sally with a meager living and made up the weekly publishing deficit. Thriftily the women put by savings during the winter to tide them over lean summer months when Congress went home. One time they had accumulated forty-five dollars which Sally sewed "fast to the pocket" of Anne's dress. A Negro washerwoman, "an old penitentiary bird," stole the money. "Poor Sally! We pitied her, she grieved so sorely about it." Sally was a dedicated dun. If donors fell behind on pledges, she did not scruple to hunt them down and extract contributions. It helped collections that the attitude of the Capital had changed toward Mrs. Royall in recent years. Her exploits were remembered, elaborated on, and repeated with gusto. She had passed into folklore.

Political independence was a financial handicap to *The Huntress*. Poor as she was, Anne Royall clung to her ideals. By endorsing no party she kept her field wide open to criticize. "The most unamiable trait in Mrs. Royall is that she dips her pen in the bitter ink of politics," complained the New Orleans *Picayune*. "Not so," Anne snapped back. "Our object is to expose, strip the mask off hypocrisy —defend the innocent, detect treachery, and hold the traitor up to public view. We are neither whig nor democrat when we think the parties do wrong. We look after the great enemy of our country— despotism!" [1]

On foot Anne made weekly rounds of the government offices, public buildings, hotels, and any other place which might yield a news item. She dragged herself up to Fourteenth Street to report on the big hotel Henry A. Willard was superimposing on the skeleton of the old City Hotel. "Those who were acquainted with the previous establishment would not recognize a single feature of the new edifice."

Observing a light in the Adams "mansion" on F Street, she assumed the Massachusetts representative had not left the Capital for Quincy whither he was reported to have gone to recover from his "feebleness." "It is the long sessions of Congress that are oppressive, not only to Mr. A., but to *all* the members." Mr. A. received Anne, "with his usual soft smile of welcome," in the same parlor remembered for the gift of a shawl by Mrs. Adams, "twenty-one years since." But the parlor was different and "did not yield us the pleasure we had anticipated. Mr. Adams explained that he had had a part of it cut off for another parlor." Despite rumors of illness, Anne found the ex-President "looking well and as cheerful as we ever saw him." [2]

Along Pennsylvania Avenue were a string of daguerreotype galleries. Mrs. Royall, as curious as any sightseer, wandered into Plumbes "next door above to Mr. Brown's hotel to investigate the new photography." Mr. Plumbe took her picture, after telling her to straighten her "cap border." (We have not located the daguerreotype.)

Though the crusading fire burned less brightly, *The Huntress* had not fallen into a rut. Editorials were fewer and shorter, but more space was given local news, all written by Mrs. Royall. She clipped more than formerly, publishing poetry, some very bad jokes, and recent novels in serial form. An Englishman, Dickens was a favorite. Unprotected by international copyright, he cost her nothing. More and more advertising filled the columns. Sally was a good saleswoman, and agreeable to payment in trade.

One afternoon Robert Owen drove up in a carriage accompanied by a beautiful Polish lady. She was Mrs. William E. Rose, born Ernestine Louise Siismondi Potowski, well-known in London and on the Continent for her labors in behalf of the poor and for women's rights. With her English husband she lived in New York and at the moment was on a lecture tour which would take her as far west as Michigan. Anne was charmed by the "beautiful creature," but not by all her causes. She welcomed Mrs. Rose and Robert Owen to "our frail old shell of a frame-house which lets in the wind, the rain and the snow, but takes good care not to let them out." Owen was an enthusiastic talker, though he seems not to have talked about the breakdown of the New Harmony, Indiana, colony. Instead, he reviewed his earlier success with some two thousand children whom he had found working in cotton mills bought in Scotland. Under him, the mills prospered without child labor and Owen built schools and besides gave the youngsters a good diet. Unfortunately, the formula did not succeed in Indiana. The colonists were not children, but adults, too many of them crackpots and individualists. Owen had returned to England to continue his earlier good works.

"Mr. O. is seventy-five years of age, but does not look so old," said the *Huntress* whose editor was seventy-four and no doubt looked it. "He is a stout man, at least six feet in height, with a good figure and proud athletic limbs. His forehead is remarkably high, deep, wide and retreating. His eyes are pale blue, calm and inspiring. He comes nearest to what we may fancy to have been the appearance of a Roman senator."

Owen was on a visit to his son Robert Dale Owen who had remained in the U.S.A., and, after a tempestuous national campaign in the company of Fanny Wright in behalf of liberal causes, settled in Indiana and presently represented the state in Congress. Representative Owen was engaged in a struggle for legislation to begin construction of the Smithsonian Institution. The funds were in hand, bequeathed by an Englishman who had died in 1829, but

Congress quibbled over the mechanics of setting up the foundation. Matters moved faster after Robert Dale Owen introduced a bill in 1845. Mrs. Royall attended the laying of the cornerstone on May 1, 1847. Judge William Cranch also attended and the common scold was "happy to meet this gentleman who has been very ill." [3]

On the score of health, the two veterans had much to confide. In the autumn of 1845, after getting through an exceedingly hot summer, Anne Royall suffered a severe bilious attack, with typhus following. "Say what you will, Washington is a sickly place," she commented. After these illnesses, she habitually remained indoors during the summer months. Still, as the years passed, the number of attacks mounted. Another summer, when cholera again threatened the District with an epidemic, she went to a deal of trouble to "discourage a visit" from the killing disease. "We owe an apology to our patrons for the shortcomings of last week's *Huntress*. We were white-washing and cleaning up." [4]

While Mrs. Royall was recuperating from typhus, she received word that Colonel James Butler had died in Logansport, Indiana. After his sister's visit in 1830, James had moved to Cass County, bought a farm, and, as a Harrison Whig, represented the county for two years in the legislature. An obituary in the local newspaper described James as "esteemed . . . kind and unassuming, intelligent, of the most incorruptible integrity." A newspaper feature writer, passing through Logansport some thirty years later, dug up James's political "sobriquet." Because his "legs extended so far below his pants he was known . . . [as] 'Short Breeches.' "

The *Huntress* did not record the passing of Mary Butler who was old enough to have gone to her reward before her son pulled up stakes for Logansport. We know that at least one descendant, in the grandmother's tradition, advanced westward with the frontier. For a time Anne corresponded with Samuel Butler, whom she addressed as "Dear Nephew." (Probably a great-nephew.) Samuel then lived in Sugar Creek, Cedar County, Iowa, a transient settlement which has passed into limbo. In a letter to Samuel, Anne invited him to "come and see me this Fall. I have something for you to do and you can finish your education here." Samuel did not come, but sent a poem which he wrote.

> O where are they, the glorious great?
> Who once our nation's glory were
> Who nobly filled the chair of State,
> And ruled with pride their country dear.

And many more verses, all reflecting Auntie Anne's nostalgic thoughts on American leaders of bygone days.[5]

A caller who poured balm on an ancient wound was Thomas P. Lewis, grandson of the proprietor of the Sweet Springs. "We were in raptures!" Mr. Lewis held a government job in Washington. After five generations of ownership, the Lewises had lately sold the Springs to Oliver and Christopher Beirne, "in association with Allen T. Caperton and John Echols, connected by marriage with the Beirnes." Descendants of the old peddler did not let him down. When Andrew Beirne passed on in 1845, his estate was valued at one million dollars. His son Oliver built the family fortune into six million dollars.

Sixteen-year-old William Darby, junior, whose father had been the only subscriber in Philadelphia to the *Sketches*, was another welcome caller. One evening Mrs. Royall entertained two visitors who were currently guests at the White House—James Hull, nephew of Commodore Isaac Hull who commanded the *Constitution* during the War of 1812, and "Master Lawrence, nephew of President Fillmore. They are the most promising young men we have seen in years."

Another young man in the uniform of the Navy was a timely visitor, enabling Mrs. Royall to pass on useful information to the congressional committee investigating whipping in the Navy. Since late in the Thirties *The Huntress* had published editorials protesting the "barbarous conduct" of flogging seamen. The New Orleans *Picayune* had backed Anne up. "We are not among those who would say that our soldiers and marines should not be punished, but we say punish them in some other way than that of whipping them upon their backs, and with that cruel instrument cat o'nine tails." Anne was already objecting to an even more cruel instrument—"the Colt, a rope with a knot on the end of it." Acquaintance with the young Navy man who called dated from an earlier period.

He was the son of "a poor widow who died and left nine children entirely destitute. We flew around and collected a trifle, but lost sight of them and supposed they had scattered about among their relations."

"Are you going to remain in the Navy?" Anne asked.

"No, madam, no money would tempt me to return."

"Why so?"

"I will show you, if you will have the goodness to excuse me."

He removed his blouse and showed his back, cut up into great ridges by a Colt. Not long afterwards, as a result of the congressional investigation, the whipping of seamen in the United States Navy was prohibited.

On a December morning in 1847 Mrs. Royall answered a knock at the front door. She was "saluted politely by a tall genteel looking man, with a cane in his hand. From a slight lameness, it struck us he must be Colonel Jefferson Davis," of Mississippi, lately returned from the War with Mexico. The pen portrait was all too brief: "About six feet in height, with erect commanding figure, face fair and thin. His soft blue eyes were as serene as the 'stilly night'; his manners extremely winning." Thus Jefferson Davis on the Royall threshold; on the threshold too, of an ill-starred career.[6]

2

Suddenly, in July, 1848, Congress performed a miracle, voting a change in the pension law which gave the widow of Major Royall an allowance of $480 a year, or $40 a month. Sally wanted to take a trip to Niagara Falls, a bonus promised her during years of waiting. But they did not go; probably too old for the long excursion. Calling to congratulate Anne Royall came Major J. M. Scantland, also a hero of the War with Mexico. "He was in seven Pitched Battles! A ball entered his right eye, and came out behind his left ear." Congress was in a generous mood. The major was not kept waiting until he was almost eighty years old. He was unanimously voted a pension of thirty dollars a month for life.

The pension award started the rumor that Mrs. Royall "is one of the richest women in the country." Some contributors dropped away. With needs less urgent, waning energy was not used to bring

them back into the fold. Anne and Sally had income enough to
exist and publish in a small way, and with years of training, both
knew how to get along with very little.

Looking over the record, the federal government appears to have
played a miserly role in taking care of Revolutionary widows. In
the peak year of 1838, there were 11,191 such widows on the pension roll. Ten years later, when Mrs. Royall qualified, she was one
of 2,774 surviving widows. An appropriation of little more than
one hundred thousand dollars took care of them. For years employees had plundered the bureau. President Jackson had inherited
the scandal and promptly took steps to end it. He "had a list of
pensioners printed, showing what each one was entitled to receive.
This disclosed the fact that some of the agents had been continuing
to draw the pensions of deceased soldiers years after their death,
besides retaining portions of the pensions of others." [7]

The Pension Act of 1848 inappropriately was not the handiwork
of Representative John Quincy Adams, of Massachusetts, who, for
nearly a decade, had sponsored the petition of Mrs. Royall at the
beginning of each session of Congress. "Most valued friend," she
addressed him. "I should be happy if convenient to you, sir, to let
the petition be the first offered this morning." On the theory, no
doubt, first come, first served. For several years Mr. Adams had
been in poor health. On a February morning in 1848, after answering the roll call, he toppled from his seat in the House and shortly
was dead of a stroke.

The *Huntress* mourned him with heavily leaded columns and
eulogy. The *Huntress* also published a poem "written for Miss C. I.
Edwards of Quincy, Massachusetts," by the ex-President, the day
before his death.

> In days of yore, the poet's pen
>   From wing of bird was plundered,
> Perhaps of goose, but, now and then,
>   From Jove's own Eagle sundered.
> But, now, metallic pens disclose
>   Alone the poet's numbers;
> In iron inspiration glows,
>   Or with the minstrel slumbers.

> Fair Damsel, could my pen impart,
>   In prose of lofty rhyme,
> The pure emotions of my heart,
>   To speed the slight of time,
> What metal from the womb of earth
>   Could worth intrinsic bear
> To stamp with corresponding worth
> The blessings thou shouldst share?

Sometime before the death of Mr. Adams, Mrs. Royall, on a visit to the House, penned a sketch of the Massachusetts Representative, which was one of her best.

Mr. Adams is readily distinguished by his quiet and venerable appearance, presenting a marked and prominent contrast to that of every other representative. Since the hot weather, he wears a snow white roundabout [a short jacket] which sits easy and becoming upon him. The rest of his dress is in corresponding plainness. His hair has become whiter, his face thinner, and his nose more pointed than formerly, but no wrinkles are visible. There is an innocence and composure in the countenance of Mr. Adams. He is the picture of peace and tranquility. His left arm is carelessly thrown over the back of his chair, while he gently beats his fingers against the side of it, apparently in deep thought, unmoved by the continual uproar of the House. His face is never contorted by the various passions common to most of the members.[8]

3

Anne Royall "wrapped up warm and bent our way to the Capitol" to witness the inauguration of President Zachary Taylor, the first inaugural she had gone to since the stampede at the swearing in of Andrew Jackson. Taylor led the procession to the Capitol, but, with her usual luck in a dense crowd, she "only saw part of his head and face."

For the old resident, everything had grown "dense" in the District—so many more people, so much more government, more buildings, more congressmen from more states, the city spreading. Mrs. Royall complained of the labor involved in keeping track of what went on in the Capital. She ventured out to observe the new President because she admired "his patriotism and good sense." During the Mexican War, *The Huntress* did not hesitate to print what others whispered. General Taylor was "the man who ought to have been in Gen. Scott's place" as head of the troops below the Rio Grande. Taylor had not campaigned for the Presidency, but worked on his Louisiana plantation, chewed tobacco, wore old clothes, and told the Whigs that if they wanted him for President, they had to elect him. He carried approximately half the States— seven in the north and eight in the south. A split in the Democratic party in New York, which gave birth to the Free Soil Party (antislavery), won the election for Taylor.

Mrs. Royall applauded the inaugural address, but the opposition, as an opposition must, found fault. "There is no doubt whatever that the distinguished general is the sole author of the message," wrote Isaac Hill, editor of the *New Hampshire Patriot* and once Andrew Jackson's ghost writer. "It is neither mule nor jackass, but a sort of hybrid." *The Huntress* chided the editor who had long been her good friend. "Once Hill was a clever man, but has of late become a poor loathsome, emaciated, heartless apology for a man."

Like most Americans, Mrs. Royall was cheered by that part of Taylor's speech wherein he promised to devote his greatest effort to conciliation of sectional differences. He faced a mammoth problem. Slavery was fast ripping the Union apart. Each new acquisition of territory deepened the antagonism between North and South. Though a southerner and slave owner, Taylor believed the new annexations should be admitted without commitment on slavery. It was a matter to be settled, in time, by those living within the new territories. And he was against secession.

Anne Royall's heart was as torn as any patriot's over talk of secession. She had learned from William Royall that slavery was a ruinous economy for Virginia. "The slaves instead of being a benefit have proved a serious injury to the planters," she had written when she saw the tobacco fields for the first time. The Royalls had kept few slaves at the Sweet Springs. Systematically they freed them, but freeing them had always been a problem. With his profound belief in the importance of education, Major Royall prepared his slaves for freedom.

With tongue in cheek *The Huntress* offered a simple remedy for the slavery dispute. There was "an ox which had gained the first prize" at a cattle show in England. The "purveyor of Queen Victoria" bought the ox and was instructed to offer "through the French Embassy to present his Majesty Louis Phillippe with a sirloin, a rump, and an aitch bone for his festival on New Year's Day. The offer was accepted and both their majesties of Great Britain and France had their royal tables supplied with meat off the same animal." Apparently the beef ended a quarrel which had threatened the peace of the two nations. "Now why doesn't Massachusetts and South Carolina follow their example?" recommended *The Huntress*.

No sirloin steaks were exchanged. Early in 1850 the U.S.A. approached one more crisis when Henry Clay introduced his series of compromise resolutions which postponed the Civil War for a decade. Mrs. Royall was on hand in March when the Great Debate on the resolutions opened in the Senate. She heard Webster begin what was probably his most famous speech: "I wish to speak today, not as a Massachusetts man, nor as a Northern man, but as an American." *The Huntress* described the argument as a

. . . triumph of Reason, Virtue and Patriotism, unrivalled in grandeur of style, and the most undaunted independence running through the whole of it. He is a bold, demonstrative speaker. He separates truth from falsehood and detects sophistry quickly. He is not a flowery speaker, but has such an eye when he grows warm that it transfixes the beholders while the stillness of death reigns in the Senate chamber.[9]

She heard Clay too—"his heart is patriotic"—and the reading of Calhoun's argument (he sat in the Senate, too ill to speak), but could not have agreed with him. He was not even mentioned in *The Huntress* three weeks later when he died. And, in these days, hardly a week passed that *The Huntress* was not mournfully leaded for the passing of someone Anne Royall had known.

4

The District's spreading density introduced into the White House a new regulation which annoyed Mrs. Royall. Now the President could be visited only by appointment. Gone were the times when she might drop in and chat, if she happened to be in the neighborhood. No chance now of a repetition of that little episode for which Old Hickory was kindly remembered. This was when President Jackson, catching sight of a skinny partridge in her market basket, invited her to have midday dinner with him. What a wonderful meal it was after the lean rations she and Sally lived on! "I came in just as the old lady escaped with her partridge," recalled Francis P. Blair, editor of the *Congressional Globe*. "The President told me the story, saying he made it a rule . . . that nobody should ever go out of his house hungry."

The last President to receive Mrs. Royall without appointment had been Benjamin Harrison. When she called on his successor, the porter was most apologetic—"Mrs. R., I am much grieved that you should leave the House with a single wish ungratified"—but he did not admit her. She was given an appointment with President Polk a few weeks after his inauguration, but found the Mansion "filled with visitors of all ages and dimensions. He is tormented by applicants for office." Anne was not an applicant and so did not bother to wait her turn. But when she was invited to President Taylor's "levee" in November, 1849, she closed down *The Huntress*, spent a week getting her clothes in order and took Sally and "our help Caroline [an orphan]" to the White House. Eager to greet the hero, her little party was the first to arrive. The reception room soon filled up. Anne kept her eyes on the door through which President Taylor should pass. Promptly at noon, a "portly man entered bareheaded, and walked directly toward us with a slow dignified step and a smile on his countenance."

[Anne] sprang to meet him, taking the hand he offered. President T. salutes with warmth and ease, and if there be a man on earth without a particle of pride, he is that man. He is a genuine copy of nature,

"President's Levee of All Creation Going to the White House." Lithograph by Robert Cruikshank, published in *Play Fair Papers*, 1841. *Library of Congress*

viz. grandeur without art. From his appearance he must have been a
man of great physical strength in his day. His face, round with regular features, becomingly full and originally fair, is now weather-worn.
In his manners and dress he is plain and artless, traits which are in-
separable from all men of sense.

From the levee Mrs. Royall went to visit the stables and pay "a
small tribute of respect to Old Whitey," retired, Taylor's campaign
horse. Old Whitey looked the visitor full in the face "without
winking. He is the purest white horse we ever saw; he is over the
common height, stout and heavy in girth. It is said you may fire a
cannon off his back and he will give only a loud snort, but he will
never move." Regularly Old Whitey was turned out to graze on
the White House grounds where he always drew a crowd of
souvenir hunters who plucked hairs from his tail.

Perhaps Old Whitey, like the general, longed for the simple
peace of northern Mexico's desert where both had understood
better how to deal with the enemy than with souvenir hunters and
politicians. Taylor was unable to calm the quarrel between North
and South and his disappointment was grievous. Some six months
after Anne Royall attended his levee, President Taylor died of
cholera morbus. Death may have come as a welcome release. He
was spared confrontation with a scandal in his cabinet involving a
trusted friend. Settling a prerevolutionary claim, Secretary of War
G. W. Crawford had pocketed the interest on the seventy-three-
year-old claim.

Vice-President Millard Fillmore, the disillusioned general's successor, held his levees every Tuesday at one o'clock. Mrs. Royall
said the ceremony was different from any she had previously attended. "Only the ladies walked into the reception room, took
seats, and awaited the appointed hour. President Fillmore then came
in and, going up to each with or without an introduction, shook
hands and then it was the gentlemen's turn to be admitted." The
President needed no introduction to Mrs. Royall. Ten years earlier
she had described the New York Representative as "one of the
most splendid men in Congress—a masterpiece of nature."

Fillmore was in office only a few months when he signed the

Fugitive Slave Law which placed the pursuit of escaped slaves under federal authority and provided stiff punishment for anyone who aided the flight of a runaway. The new law brought down a "torrent of abuse" from the abolitionists and lost Fillmore the renomination in 1852. The Democratic candidate, Franklin Pierce, was elected.

"This is probably the end of the Whig party," predicted *The Huntress*. It was. After twelve lean years, surviving hopefuls of Andrew Jackson's old political party looked forward to a time of plenty.[10]

5

No one was more saddened by national developments than Anne Royall. Birth and growth of the Republic spanned her lifetime. She had proudly and lovingly watched the climb to greatness and now all, all was crumbling, for want of honorable men to hold the course. "There are loud professions of patriotism, but it would require a close search to discover the retreats of patriotism and virtue, such as we have known of old. The whole country, perhaps we should say the political country, seems to be out of joint."

The multiplication of truculent political factions kept the U.S.A. in a ferment of threatened disasters—secession, war and maybe both. *The Huntress* had lost hope: "If the peace question were settled by legal authority—Congress—and all granted that was asked for, these parties would pick a quarrel about something else."

Anne Royall returned to an old quarrel on which she had written little, since the exile of the Reverend Ezra Stiles Ely to the Missouri steppes.

There are two dangerous parties in our country: Church and State, alias Free Soilers, and the Demagogues, alias office-seekers. The Free Soil men are doing their utmost to annihilate the constitution and put an end to freedom.

The second party calls themselves Jefferson Democrats. They likewise look forward to an absolute government. Their avarice and the lawless means they pursue to gratify their lust for money is not surpassed even by the Church and State Party.[11]

The enormous acquisitions of new territory, which deepened the hostility between North and South, kept Anne Royall awake nights, "pondering upon the future." Her U.S.A. had grown beyond her comprehension. "Only think of it! from ocean to ocean, and from Canada to—we forget where. Can this vast domain be held subordinate to our government? We have our fears!"

She had no fear attacking what she better understood and, at this late date, the Pilgrims came within her line of fire. Their descendants were celebrating an anniversary of the Plymouth Rock landing. She sailed into them for the slaughter of the Pequot Indians and the torture of their own people during the witch-hunts.

The tortures these human beings endured from the hands of these fiends to make them confess their dealings with the Evil One, no language can express. These are the wicked barbarities they commemorate annually. They are getting ready for the onset against "heretics." Look at them at this moment rearing their snaky heads in our town under the name of "Free Soil." [12]

The outburst against the revered Pilgrims filled her mail with protests. Old newspaper enemies and new ones, too, wrote columns of denunciations. Anne talked back and more than likely enjoyed all the hullabaloo.

Having raked Pilgrim descendants over the coals, she was in fine fettle to assail *Uncle Tom's Cabin.* "If Mrs. Stowe had been familiar with the South, she would know that the best servants on a plantation would be the very last articles sold for money, even under the pressure of debt. And yet she forces the master to sell his faithful foreman, and the mistress her favorite houseman."

With ill-concealed joy, Anne reprinted an "ably written letter" from a "scholar," who had been a neighbor of the Beecher family in Cincinnati. "They are people of some intellectual capacity," pronounced the scholar, "but all fanatical and fond of notoriety." After reading the charges made by the Reverend Joel Parker, pastor of the Bleecker Street Presbyterian Church in New York City, Mrs. Royall declared that Mrs. Stowe was "no lady of honor. The Reverend accused the author of quoting him in the *Cabin* on the subject of slavery, from letters he had never written. He asked for a retraction, but Mrs. Stowe never complied; or did she answer his communications." The controversy waxed long and bitter. The *American Courier* of Philadelphia urged the clergyman to

. . . proceed with the libel suit he has threatened . . . Dr. Parker has now an opportunity of doing the country a great public service. . . . A verdict . . . [in favor of Parker] should stamp the character of this book, whose gross fabrications are now so widely abusing public confidence on this side of the Atlantic, and to a far greater extent on the other.

Doctor Parker did not sue. Mrs. Stowe kept mum and her brother the Reverend Henry Ward Beecher stepped into the spotlight to defend her. *The Huntress* joined the chorus which accused Beecher himself of "signing that gentleman's [Parker's] name without authorization." The letters were "forgeries," declared Mrs. Royall. Until he died the Parker forgeries haunted Beecher's public life like an unlaid ghost. He lived down other scandals, but not the Parker letters.[13]

6

During most of the year 1853 an increasing number of illnesses kept Anne Royall in bed. In summer months when she did not go out, *The Huntress* suffered from scant content and poor make-up. In 1850 she had looked at the "tremendous" marble stairs of the Capitol and climbed them for the last time. "They came near costing us our life this day from fatigue." What a sad fate to overtake those overworked "limbs!" Summer evenings when everyone was near prostration from the heat, the fireplace glowed in her bedroom. "We deem the practice indispensible in low countries or near large watercourses. Noxious dampness is invariably found near rivers."

Sally brought her some "powders" from Doctor Green—"4-½ street next door to Mrs. McDaniel." Anne published a letter in *The Huntress*—"because I fear to go out"—thanking the good doctor for the relief his doses gave her. Doctor Green's treatment was homeopathic and so *Huntress* readers were regaled with information concerning the therapy. "It *is* good for indigestion, sneer as you may." It was better, at any rate, than her previous treatment: "A mustard plaster on our breast and nearly half a pint of vervain tea."

Sally, too, was getting on in years, and sometimes she was in worse health than Anne Royall. One week when Sally was too ill to work the editor undertook to deliver the newspapers. Her problem was "to find the subscribers." Sally carried the subscription list in her head. "The first day we took it afoot, with girl and bundle, and found two subscribers, got our face peeled by the wind, gave it up and returned home. Next publishing day we took a hack and did well, for Sally was there, though weak as an infant." Anne's day was made when she learned that one subscriber was Banker William Wilson Corcoran.

The Capital abounded with tales of the rapid rise to wealth of the poor Irish immigrant. Corcoran lived near Lafayette Square in a house on H Street which he had bought from the improvident Daniel Webster, and here Anne Royall sketched her "pen portrait" of the banker. "Mr. C. is about average height, with a stout, regular build. His countenance has a mingled expression of frankness, vivacity, probity and benevolence. But it is the capacity of this gentleman for business which has made him the wonder and admiration of the country." The reporter was getting old. She completely overlooked the art gallery which the gentleman of business had already begun to assemble in an extension built onto the Webster house.[14]

As one reads the names of the many printers or foremen who came and went over the years, the wonder grows that the newspaper continued to appear as regularly as it did. For pressmen *The Huntress* was a stopover until better jobs were found or until something was in hand for another spree. It was inevitable that *The Huntress* should be used in this manner. Salaries were low, discipline nonexistent, and there was no future. "I write one inside page—for the country's good exclusively," explained the editor, "and give the printer the remainder to fill with prose or poetry as pleases him best. We allow him the liberty of speech." This was true. On the inside page Anne Royall might support one political cause, while the printer was pleading for the opposition in his space.

Some of the printers could not resist getting mixed up in the Royall battles and so remained or returned to fight the good fight. Though employed elsewhere, they helped Anne out in spare time. She had help, too, during most of the District years, from prosperous newspaper publishers.

William Greer, publisher of the *American Statesman and Mechanics and Manufacturers Advocate,* printed most of her books. Probably she was never out of debt to him. Mrs. Greer, like Mrs. Maher, was ever a good friend. She gave Anne most of the furniture inside the little white cottage. Mrs. Tims, wife of the man who had turned the common-scold trial into a farce, contributed two beds. Another good friend was Mrs. William C. Rives, whose husband was partner of Francis P. Blair in publishing the *Congressional Globe.* The Rives had a farm near Washington and Mrs. Royall was the recipient of many baskets of food and dairy products produced there. The *Globe,* as well as Joe Gales of the *Intelligencer,* passed on castoff type to *The Huntress.* As far as the record shows, Anne Royall bought new type only once during the more than twenty years of newspaper publishing. Sometimes the paper looked pretty awful—the print faint and ink smeared, and badly ruled. Another contributor was "our gallant friend Mr. Sahe of the *German Gazette,* who sent his whole force to put our press in first rate order." Captain Easby who owned a shipyard kept her supplied with "big chips, winter and summer." Wood arrived regularly from Maria Indiana Kinzie Hunter, wife of Major General David Hunter who served under Taylor in the Mexican War and was to fight beside Grant in the Civil War. Other donors sent her flour—"We never bought a barrel of flour, since our residence in the city." Anne Royall herself was no negligible contributor—reporter, editor, and giver of more than she could spare from her pension to keep alive a losing proposition which to her could not lose, if she helped the U.S.A. Moreover, those worse off than she was, found her sympathetic and generous and so came "flocking to our door." At the end she could truthfully say that "the kindliness and liberality of Washington City and Congress (all but the ungodly) have enabled me to publish. I do not work for profit. I write for the benefit of my country." [15]

Like the printers, the orphans also came and went, stole and fled. Anne Royall relied heavily on them. "We have four in all. The two little ones help about the press-roll, turn the cylinders, go to market, go on errands, help Sally to carry out the papers, and bring water. We have none who cannot earn their victuals and clothing." Well, she had one—Bill Drury, an attractive scamp, sixteen years old and already tattooed with "stars, banners, ship anchors." Bill's father put him in school, but he "played truant and ran away. He would be seen fighting, swimming" and led a gang of marauding boys of whom he was "commander-in-chief."

At length his father lost all patience and whipt him with a rope. From pity we took him conditionally and put him to printing. We dressed Bill up with two new shirts, new shoes and stockings; and a fine cap, at $1.25 and a new jacket. He worked and behaved well and while we all thought he was on the road to virtue, we were startled one morning at a visit from the police constable who enquired for "little Bill," saying he had broke open Mr. Mitchels hen house, and stole two roosters. From the time Bill had arrived we heard complaints of hen roost robbers from all our neighbors. Sometime during the night Bill packed up his all and decamped. The next we saw of him was nearly two years later on the fourth of July. He was lying in the street beastly drunk. Meanwhile, his father had bound him to a tailor and he misbehaved. Next he was bound to a saddler, but was soon on the wide world again.

Each time Bill was on the wide, wide world, Anne lost chickens. Depopulation of the henhouse ceased when ultimately Bill and tattoos joined the Navy.

The most responsible orphan was John Henry Simmes who remained with *The Huntress* fifteen years. His sister Caroline, two years younger, was also part of the household. "John being an apt scholar we kept him at school. We would stint ourselves rather than he should go without an education." While John Henry still bore the title of "devil," Anne asked jokingly "if he could help us write."

"Yes, I can," replied John H. confidently. He returned with a composition:

"HARD TIMES!!!! HARD TIMES!!!! This is the cry indoors and outdoors. Here I have to wait upon the Foreman, & another chuckle-headed boy, his helper. I have to set type—learn Grammar—and spell words for Mrs. Royall—pump water (thank my stars the pump is at the door), and then I have to wash inky aprons. I saw wood and carry water and do heaps of things besides. Mrs. Royall tells me, if I be a good boy and stick to learning, I may one day be a great lawyer, and then a member of Congress. Mrs. R. learns me herself.

In 1854 the name of John Henry Simmes with the title of printer appeared in *The Huntress* masthead beneath that of the publisher and editor. He was the only individual ever to be so honored. John Henry had earned his credit line. By this time he was writing almost all of the newspaper, even a considerable portion of the editor's inside page. A temperance man, he expressed himself often and at length in editorials on the "Evils of Rum," warning the "Young Men of Washington City against the Pernicious Habit of Drinking to Excess." He ground out a stream of sentimental poetry. An early poem, *The Orphan*, reveals the loneliness of his boyhood:

> No father—as the Vine support,
>   So we a father need,
> Whose bright example we may trace
>   And noble precepts heed.
>
> No mother—as the lamb its fold,
>   So we a mother need,
> To shield us in her fervent love,
>   Our infant mind to feed.

John Henry relieved Anne Royall of a load she was no longer able to carry. Nearly every issue of *The Huntress* reported the poor health of the editor. Added to her older complaints—dyspepsia, diarrhea, swollen limbs—her hands trembled, as Mary Butler's had in old age. She was grateful to her orphan and published a paragraph praising him. "FAST WORK. On last Friday, Mr. John H. Simmes, printer, set up three columns and pressed off twelve quires of the *Huntress* paper in five hours and twenty-two minutes." [16]

But fast work did not allay the hunger in the heart of the orphan who pined for the love of mother and father. The pangs were momentarily stilled after J.H.S. found the one and only girl, as we learn from a poem dedicated "To Mary." He had high hopes

> That thy love may prove a guiding
> Star of faith and joy to me.

He worshipped Mary's beauty in a flow of stanzas:

> Soft as the hue
> Of Heaven's own blue
>   My Lady's eyes . . .
> The Wild bee sips
>   From off her lips
> The nectar'd dew. . . .
> Her graceful neck
> Without a speck,
>   Is white as pearl. . . .

But John Henry's hopes of bliss were dashed, an advertisement in the newspaper reveals: "WANTED—An intended bride who is willing to begin housekeeping in the same style in which her parents began. Enquire of Mr. Simmes, at *The Huntress* office."

Perhaps the beautiful Mary was practical and pointed out that they could not live on the wages Mrs. Royall paid. And perhaps John Henry was loyal and grateful and said he could not leave his elderly guardian. The appeal for a wife ran through six successive issues of *The Huntress* and then love seems to have found a way:

"MARRIED—At St. Peter's Church, Capitol Hill, March 12th, 1854, by the Rev. Mr. Knight, MR. JOHN HENRY SIMMES to MISS MARY ELIZABETH HIGDON, both of Washington."

Anne Royall wrote the unhappy notice which followed the wedding announcement. "We shall issue no *Huntress* for some weeks, if ever. We are tired of newspapers. Our printer has left us and we are not able to set type." [17]

7

This was not quite the end. Little Bill Drury was not around, but the henhouse was again robbed. Anne lost her "pet hen who was setting upon the finest Shanghai eggs." The thief took the eggs, too. On June 24, 1854, *The Huntress* resumed publication in pamphlet form, with eight elfin pages. It was the "first number of the new series," for which the editor had bought "larger and more legible type, rules, etc. We are getting stronger and feel blithe and gay as ever!" Anne had celebrated her eighty-fifth birthday the week before, leaving her house for the first time in many months to attend President Franklin Pierce's levee. She had known Senator Pierce when he was a convivial lawmaker on the Hill. His wife, not so convivial and in poor health, went home to the serene New Hampshire hills. The Senator dutifully resigned and followed her to New England. However, he was the type of man who could not escape popularity no matter where he lived. Anne Royall observed obvious changes that had taken place in the time he had been away from Washington. "His countenance used to be gay and full of vivacity, but it now wears a calm and dignified composure, tinctured with melancholy. We could not refrain from dropping a tear, when we inquired after the health of his lady."

The "new" *Huntress* survived three puny issues. Anne Royall spent her all to put them on the press. In the last pamphlet she wrote she had "but thirty-one cents in the world, and for the first time since we resided in the city (thirty-one years) we are unable to pay last month's rent. Had not our landlord been one of the best of men, we should have been stript."

She was enthusiastic, however, about her new medicine—Dr. Morse's Invigorating Elixir. She eulogized the Elixir and closed the forms of *The Huntress* for the last time with a "prayer that the Union of these States may be eternal." [18]

She died on Sunday morning, October 1. Religious services, with the Masons in charge, were held next day at Grace Episcopal

THE HUNTRESS.

EDITED AND PRINTED BY ANNE ROYALL.

Vol. 1.]　　　　　NEW SERIES.　　　　　[No. 3.

WASHINGTON, D. C., JULY 24, 1854.

CONGRESS.

HOUSE OF REPRESENTATIVES.

SPEECH OF HON. JOHN J. TAYLOR,

OF NEW YORK,

On the bill to organize the Territories of Nebraska and Kansas ; delivered in the House of Representatives, May 9, 1854.

The House being in Committee of the Whole on the State of the Union—

Mr. TAYLOR, of New York, said :

"Mr. CHAIRMAN : On a subject exciting so much interest as that now before the committee, it seems almost necessary for a representative to give his reasons for his votes. Perhaps, for another cause, I ought to say a word on this subject. It has been brought to the notice of the House by my colleague, [Mr. BENNET]—unnecessarily, as I thought, though I do not complain of it—that a respectable number of my constituents differ from me in reference to this measure. It would be pleasant, certainly, if we could agree with all our constituents, and act according to the views of them all. But as this is a thing impossible, the best course, doubtless, is for each one, unless duly instructed, to follow the dictates of his own judgment and conscience, trusting they will not lead him astray."

Mr. Taylor, like all of that name—for we believe in names—is modest, mild and unassuming in his language, and by kind persuasion he would convince any one but an idiot. But the leaders of the opposite faction do not desire conviction—they know well enough the desperate game they are playing, and are only afraid their duplicity will be discovered by their own great party, which they have been training for years past, under various names. They have no feeling against slavery ; their object is to put down the action of Congress, create discord, and delay the business of that body. See the length they go in endeavoring to persuade their poor dupes that slavery has been established in Kansas and Nebraska. They keep constantly at it—ding, dong—to provoke a civil war ; and no doubt many of their ignorant proselytes believe that Congress (who has left it to the people of these Territories) has verily established and confirmed slavery therein. They are actually bullying Congress to pass an act prohibiting slavery in Nebraska—a thing they cannot constitutionally do. Was there ever seen such glaring and empty-headed knavery ? But hear Mr. Taylor : —

"At the present day, nobody denies that a State has the entire control of the institution of slavery within her limits—that she has a constitutional right to do with it what she

Last issue of *The Huntress,* printed less than three months before. Anne Royall's death. *Library of Congress*

☞ Perhaps we may never publish another paper. Life is uncertain. though we are at the present writing in perfect health.

☞ We return many thanks to our friends in Philadelphia for their kindness in sending us their papers, viz: the Post, American Courier, and Saturday Evening Mail—without any return. This is too much kindness, especially as we can get them at Shillington's for a trifle. Gentlemen, do not kill us with kindness.

CONGRESS.—We trust in heaven for three things. First—that members m.y give us the *means to pay for this paper*, perhaps three or four cents a member—a few of them are behind hand; but the fault was not theirs; it was owing to Sally's sickness. Others again have paid us from two to six dollars. Our printer is a poor man, and we have but thirty-one cents in the world, and for the first time since we have resided in the city, (thirty years,) we were unable to pay our last month's rent, only six dollars. Had not our landlord been one of the best of men, we should have been stript by this time; but we shall get that from our humble friends.

Second—That Washington may escape that dreadful scourge, the Cholera.

Our third prayer is that the Union of these States may be eternal.

☞ We have neglected to notice the amiable Mr. Dent, of Georgia, from want of time and space, but it will be repaired.

But can we ever forget t at ministering angel who sprang to our relief, at the risk of ruin to her splendid attire, to give us drink when near 'fainting. This happened at the fountain at the Capitol. Her name is Waugh, if we do not mistake. May guardian angels watch over her, and may she never know sorrow.

☞ If you want a good paper, take the "Stark County (Ohio) Democrat, published every Wednesday, by A. McGregor, at Canton.

DR. MORSE'S INVIGORATING ELIXIR OR CORDIAL.

CURE OF NERVOUS DISEASE.

No language can convey an adequate idea of the immediate and almost miraculous change which it occasions in the diseased, debilitated, and shattered nervous system. Whether broken down by excess, weak by nature, or impaired by sickness, the unstrung and relaxed organization is at once rebraced, revivified, and built up. The mental and physical symptoms of nervous disease vanish together under its influence. The stooping, trembling victim of depression and debility becomes a new man. He stands erect, he moves with a firm step; his mind, which was nervously sunk in gloom, or an almost idiotic apathy, becomes bright, buoyant, active; and he goes forth refreshed, regenerated, and conscious of new vigor, to his accustomed occupations. Nor is the effect temporary. On the contrary, the relief is permanent, for the cordial properties of the medicine reach the constitution itself, and restore it to its normal condition. Well may the preparation be called the MEDICINAL WONDER of the nineteenth century. It is, as the first scientific men in the old world have admitted, that miracle of medicine heretofore supposed to have no existence.

Its force is never expended, as is the case with opium, alcoholic preparations, and all other exitants. The effect of these is brief, and it may well be said of him who takes them ' the last state of that man is worse than the first.' But the Elixir is an exhilarant without a single drawback, safe in its operation, perpetual in its happy influence upon the nerves, the mind, and the entire system. In cases of neuralgia, headache, loss of memory, hypochondriasis, dyspepsia, general prostration, irritability, nervousness, inability to sleep, liver complaint, and all diseases incident to females, hysteria, mouomania, vague terrors, palpitation of the heart, impotency, barrenness, constipation, etc., from whatever cause arising, it is if there is any reliance to be placed on human testimony, absolutely infallible

It is the only infallible remedy yet discovered for Nervous, Head, and Mind Complaints; it is the mental physic long sought for, and never before found, the only natural agent that can administer to a mind diseased. It will increase and restore the appetite, strengthen the emaciated, renew the health of those who have destroyed it, induce continual cheerfulness and equanimity of spirits, and prolong life.

Persons of pale complexion or consumptive habits are restored by the use of a bottle or two to bloom and vigor, changing the skin from a pale, yellow, sickly color to a beautiful florid complexion.

The common expression of those who have used this extract is—I have heard your Cordial highly spoken of, but was one of the incredulous in regard to its merit, having tried various medicines sold for the same purpose without deriving any benefit. I had almost given up all hopes of deriving any relief, and when I purchased some of your Cordial, I had no faith whatever of its benefitting me, but it has.

Church, on the "Island," as the isolated southern section of the city was then known. The pallbearers were old friends and neighbors: B. B. French, late clerk of the House but risen to the presidency of the telegraph line operating between the Capital and New York; J. W. Nairn, druggist; John McDuell, census clerk; P. S. Hooe, unidentified; Ezra Williams, unidentified; Charles W. C. Dunnington, principal policeman at the Capitol. She was buried in an unmarked grave in the Congressional Cemetery.

Anne Royall would have liked what one Washington newspaper said of her. "She was a woman of considerable literary attainments and benevolence, and of strict integrity." [19]

NOTES

Chapter I

1. Alexander S. Guffey, "The First Courts of Western Pennsylvania," *Western Pennsylvania Historical Magazine*, July 1924, VII, No. 3, 174.

2. George Washington to Joseph Reed, April 25, 1781, *Pennsylvania Archives*, Ser. I, Vol. 9, 102.

3. Guffey, *op. cit.;* Court of Quarter Sessions, Westmoreland County, Docket, Greensburgh, Pennsylvania (1773 to   ), 17.

4. The account of the destruction of Hanna's Town is drawn for the most part from George Dallas Albert, *History of Westmoreland County* (1882); Sherman Day, *Historical Collections of the State of Pennsylvania* (1843); *Pennsylvania Magazine of History and Biography* (1877), I, No. 1; John N. Boucher, *History of Westmoreland County* (1906); *Washington-Irvine Correspondence*, arranged and annotated by Consul Willshire Butterfield (1882); John F. Watson, *Annals of Philadelphia* and *Pennsylvania in the Olden Time* (1850); Edgar W. Hassler, *Old Westmoreland* (1900).

5. James McSherry, *History of Maryland from its First Settlement in 1634 to the Year 1848* (1852), 176.

6. The possibility that William Newport was an illegitimate Calvert was first suggested by Sarah Harvey Porter in a biography, *The Life and Times of Anne Royall* (1908). To Miss Porter belongs the credit for assembling the first book-length biography of Mrs. Royall. It was no easy task. One point which stumped her was William Newport's origin. On page 19 of *The Life*, the following appears:

> The early Maryland archives mention but one William Newport. In a letter to Governor Sharpe, dated 1767, Lord Baltimore wrote from London:
>
> . . . "An absurd report, I am informed, has been spread through the Province that My late uncle, Mr. Calvert's son, was doubted to be Legitimate and consequently I had settled the Province on him after my death. Whereas Mr. Calvert who has appointed me by his will his Guardian and Executor, expressly declares him *not* Legitimate and before his death gott me to give him an annuity by the name he goes by of Mr. Newport, son of Judith, I forgett her name. . . ."

Though the given name of "Mr. Newport" is not mentioned in the quote above, further research by Miss Porter turned up a list of persons receiving annuities from the Maryland proprietors. The list recorded one payment of "Four Hundred pounds of tobacco to William Newport." (*The Life*, 19.) Miss Porter suspected a connection between Anne Newport's father and William Newport of the annuity. When she could establish none she supplied the reader with food for thought and left him to draw his own conclusions. On page 26 of *The Life* we read:

> Very likely the little girl [Anne Newport Royall] . . . was of neither Calvert nor of Stuart lineage. But she might well have been of both, for the lords of Baltimore were all men of brains. . . .
> [This] recalls the eagerness for reading—as described by Lord Harrington—of Elizabeth, the little Stuart Princess later famous in history as the unfortunate "Winter Queen." . . . The mental resemblance of Anne Royall to Elizabeth's daughter, Sophia, electress of Hanover, and mother of George I of England, is absolutely startling to one who has studied both women. Many of Sophia's reflective but energetic letters might have been written by Mrs. Royall, while many of the latter's fearless acts might easily have been performed by the indomitable electress.

These lines have produced unfortunate results. Later writers have transformed Miss Porter's conjectures into fact. See George Stuyvesant Jackson, *Uncommon Scold* (1937), 17; Richardson L. Wright, *Forgotten Ladies* (1928), 304; *Dictionary of American Biography* (1930), XVI, 204.

Though I can offer no new material about Anne Newport's paternity, I have at least identified "My late uncle" and his bastard son "Mr. Newport," alluded to by Lord Baltimore, and thus can dispose of the fantastic confusion of Mrs. Royall's illegitimate connection with the Calvert family.

For a number of pages preceding Lord Baltimore's letter in the *Maryland Archives*, XIV, Part 3, are various communications from his secretary in England, Caecilius Calvert, to Governor Sharpe at Annapolis, conveying his Lordship's wishes for administering his province. Caecilius' letters abruptly ceased in 1765 and thereafter Lord Baltimore personally carried on the correspondence with Sharpe. This suggested that Caecilius Calvert, because of his name, might have been "My late uncle," and that his death could explain why no more of his letters appear in the *Archives*.

Thanks to Mrs. Russell Hastings of New York, who had made a study of Calvert genealogy, I received a sketchy note taken from the English records.

"His [Caecilius's] will . . . bequeaths to 'Caecilius Newport an infant born at my house I rent in Charles Street, Westminster about 20 Aug. 1755, all personal estate etc.'"

As Caecilius was not in line for the title, Mrs. Hastings had paid him scant attention. She did not remember where she had seen his will. After tedious search it was located at the Prerogative Court of Canterbury (Folio Rush-worth, 403). It confirmed his identity as "My late uncle." Two days before his death, on November 8, 1765, Caecilius had signed the will naming "My Nephew Frederick Lord Baron of Baltimore of Ireland" executor of his estate and guardian of his son Caecilius Newport. Judith, the mother whose name Caecilius Calvert could not recall, was not mentioned. So that rules out "Mr. Newport," born in 1755 in London, as the precocious father of Anne Newport, born June 11, 1769 in Baltimore. The William Newport who received the tobacco annuity remains a man of mystery.

7. I have found no evidence to support the tale that William Newport was a Tory and British spy unless the tobacco annuity is key to his involvement. William Newport was the name of the father of Anne Newport, we learn from his daughter who, strange to say, only briefly mentioned her sire three times in the hundreds of thousands of words she wrote and published. In contrast, her mother, sister, stepbrother and neighbors on several frontiers are given detailed attention. Anne said her father taught her the letters of the alphabet from a Bible and so she was old enough to have remembered more about him. Inattention from her pen has helped to keep alive suspicion that William Newport was not a father she cared to boast about. One can develop further suspicions if the remote location of the Westmoreland County cabin to which Newport took his family is considered. Cautious settlers lived close to blockhouses. William Newport went off on long trips, his daughter wrote, leaving his family with no more protection than the lock on the door. (Anne Royall, *Letters from Alabama* (1830), 85.) Could he have been assured that they were safe from Indian attack? Of course, Newport may simply have been a trader, but this had become a very risky business in western Pennsylvania on the eve of the outbreak of the Revolutionary War.

8. The 1748 date of Mary Newport's birth is from the commissioner's decision handed down in May 1819, at Greenbrier Courthouse, Virginia (now West Virginia), in the case of Ann Royal vs. Newton Gardner. The later dates are from Anne Royall, *Southern Tour*, III (1831), 235. Miss Porter, in *The Life*, page 18, wrote that Mary Newport was a connection of the Andersons of Middle River, Virginia. I do not think she was. Chapter II of this book should make clear why not. Mrs. Royall wrote that her mother came from Annapolis (Anne Royall, *Black Book*, I (1828), 308). At the Maryland capital I searched records of a prodigious number of Ander-sons—births, marriages, deaths, wills, rents, tax rolls, *Maryland Gazette*—without results. The same research was fruitlessly carried out in Baltimore, in case Mary had been married there.

Anne Royall confused me with the statement that she was "also a de-scendant of noble blood, viz: on one side, from the Butler family, Duke of Ormand of Ireland, and on the other, from the Newport (Sir John) family same country." (*Paul Pry*, April 5, 1834). My guess is that the lady, having

been handed a most unpleasant snub was trying to impress someone by un-
furling a noble ancestry. Butler, of course, was the name of her stepfather.

9. Anne Royall, *Pennsylvania* II (1829), 206 *et seq.; Letters from Alabama*,
85 *et seq.*

No deed apparently has been recorded showing that William Newport
owned land in Westmoreland County. And this is odd. Why should he
have abandoned Baltimore for the Pennsylvania frontier, if not to acquire
land? Like other settlers, Newport may have been slow to register his deed.
The first sale of land near him was not recorded at the county seat until
sixteen years after the property changed hands. Delay was due to the long
drawn-out quarrel between Virginia and Pennsylvania over their boundaries.
A landholder felt little purpose would be served by a trip to Robert Hanna's
tavern-court when Virginia threatened to seize the courthouse and disregard
all previous real estate transactions in the disputed territory. (Lewis C.
Walkinshaw, "Seventy-Five Years Before New Alexandria," *New Alexandria* (Pennsylvania) *Press*, February 2, 1934.) A point in favor of Newport's
ownership is that when Anne Newport (Royall) visited the neighborhood
many years afterwards her sister Mary Newport (Cowan) was residing on
the Mount Pisgah land in a home her husband had built. Perhaps the land
was her inheritance.

10. I am going out on a limb for Patrick Butler, though not without good
reasons. The name of Patrick Butler appears on various petitions originating
at Fort Shields during the time the Newports lived at Denniston's Town.
Colonel John Shields commanded a troop of frontier rangers. Patrick was
the only Butler of record then living thereabouts. In the *Pennsylvania
Archives* Patrick Butler is listed frequently, sometimes as a militiaman but
more often as a frontier ranger, in the company of Dennistons, Parrs,
Irvins, Moores, Blanes, Jacks, Manns and Craigs, all neighbors about whom
Anne Royall wrote. See *Pennsylvania Archives,* Series 3, XXIII, 283, 315;
Series 5, IV, 431; Series 6, II, 353. In Albert's *History of Westmoreland
County,* page 69, is a list of names attached to a petition dated 1774. Nearly
every male residing near the county seat signed. Patrick Butler, the sole
Butler, is among the signers at Fort Shields. A similar petition, dated 1780,
from Fort Shields appears in the *History of Western Pennsylvania, and of
the West and of Western Expeditions and Campaigns* by a Gentleman of the
Bar, Appendix XXVII (1847), 258. Patrick Butler signed it, along with the
same neighbors named above, all of which, I trust, is not mere coincidence.

No marriage license for Patrick Butler and Mary Newport has been
found, which is understandable with the county in turmoil and traveling
clergymen often at great inconvenience to report the bonds they tied.
Neither is there a birth certificate for their son James. That lack is also
understandable; more than likely there was no doctor present.

11. Albert, 119.

12. Royall, *Letters from Alabama,* 154.

13. Albert, 138.

14. Royall, *Letters from Alabama*, 154. Because this biographical history contains so many quotes from Anne Royall's books and newspapers, I have not used the customary dots to indicate words dropped from her text. Editing has not altered what she originally wrote.

15. Hassler, 176.

CHAPTER II

1. Joseph A. Waddell, *Annals of Augusta County, Virginia* (1902), 98.

2. *Ibid.*, 332. Employment by the Anderson family on Middle River is probably what started the rumor that the maiden name of Mrs. Butler was Anderson.

3. Royall, *Letters from Alabama*, 99.

4. George R. Gilmer, *Sketches of Some of the First Settlers of Upper Georgia, of the Cherokees, and the Author* (1926), 27 *et seq.*

5. Delia Agnes McCulloch, "The Pioneer John Lewis and His Illustrious Family," *West Virginia Historical Magazine Quarterly*, Vol. 4, No. 2, 82 *et seq.*; J. Lewis Peyton, *History of Augusta County, Virginia* (1882), 112.

6. Anne Royall, *Sketches of History, Life and Manners in the United States* (1826), 88 *et seq.* Hereafter the long title of this book will be given simply as *Sketches*.

7. James K. Paulding, *Letters from the South Written During an Excursion in the Summer of 1816*, I (1817), 112; Waddell, 27; Royall, *Letters from Alabama*, 21.

8. Charles A. Beard and Mary R. Beard, *The Rise of American Civilization*, I (1935), 266.

9. Royall, *Sketches*, 87. Writing in 1823, Mrs. Royall said she "left Augusta thirty-six years ago." The statement appears to fix her departure from the Anderson farm in the year 1787. Description of Anne Royall is from the (Providence, Rhode Island) *Literary Subaltern*, reprinted in the (Charleston, Virginia, later West Virginia) *Western Register*, August 14, 1830. The editor of the *Subaltern*, a friend of Mrs. Royall, saw her many times and published numerous articles about her. A Baltimore editor, John H. Hewitt, in his book *Shadows on the Wall* (1877), 23, described Mrs. Royall as "squatty, round-faced, sharp-nosed, thin-lipped." Anne once described herself as "a little old woman" and another time as "wee." (W. E. Beard, "Mrs. Anne Royall," *American Historical Magazine*, Vol. 9, 343.) Anne Royall, *Black Book*, III (1829), 113. Description of Mrs. Royall as "tall and angular" which appeared in "Washington in Literature," a paper by Ainsworth Rand Spofford, published in *Records of Columbia Historical Society*, Vol. 6, 49, is probably inaccurate. Mr. Spofford was too young to have known Mrs. Royall personally.

10. Porter, 34. The account was sent Miss Porter by Mrs. Eva Grant

Maloney of Craig City, Virginia, who quoted her aunt Mrs. Sarah Hamilton.

11. Paulding, I, 177; Royall, *Sketches*, 83; D. Henry Ruffner, "Dennis Calaghan," *West Virginia Historical Magazine Quarterly*, Vol. 4, No. 4, 328. One finds the innkeeper's name spelled various ways. I have used the version of Mr. and Mrs. Perceval Reniers, of White Sulphur Springs, West Virginia, authorities on the history of this section of the United States.

12. Perceval Reniers, *The Springs of Virginia* (1941), 42; Oren F. Morton, *A History of Monroe County, West Virginia* (1916), 202.

13. Description of the location of William Royall's plantation is from a notice announcing auction of the property on June 30, 1813: File Box 235, Circuit Clerk's Office, Augusta County Courthouse, Staunton, Virginia. In succeeding chapters reference in the notes to this source, a veritable Pandora's treasure, will be designated simply as File Box 235, *op. cit.* In this file of legal papers Anne Royall's name is invariably written Ann.

14. Royall, *Sketches*, 40.

15. John Royall Harris, "The Colonial Royalls of Virginia," *Virginia Magazine of History and Biography*, XXXII and XXXIII, *passim;* Eva Turner Clark, *Francis Epes* (1942), *passim;* various papers in suit of James Roane and wife Elizabeth vs. Ann Royall *et al.* File Box 235, *op. cit.* I have given Richard Royall two sons, whereas Doctor Harris states that he had "at least three sons." (*Op. cit.* XXXIII, 105.) My source is William Royall's niece who, in the action brought to declare her uncle's will a forgery, swore that she was the "only daughter of an only brother" of William Royall. (James Roane and wife Elizabeth vs. Ann Royall *et als.*, James Roane's Bill of Complaint, File Box 235, *op. cit.*) Description of the Hundred Neck from will of Elizabeth Royall, Amelia County Courthouse, Will Book, No. 2, 340; Chesterfield County Courthouse, Virginia, Deed Book No. 7, 361.

16. Chesterfield County Courthouse, Virginia, Court Order Book, No. 1, 107 *et seq.; ibid.*, 390; Clark, 238.

17. Amelia County Courthouse, Virginia, Deed Book No. 10, 29; *ibid.*, No. 20, 285.

18. *Ibid.*, Will Book No. 253, 340.

19. *Huntress* (Washington, D.C.), February 4, 1843; *ibid.*, July 14, 1838; William Wirt Henry, *Patrick Henry, Life and Correspondence* (1891), I, 277, 282.

20. *Paul Pry*, August 18, 1832; *Huntress*, April 22, 1854; Porter, 39; Harris, XXXIII, 107; *Paul Pry*, November 3, 1832.

21. Morton, 130; James Truslow Adams, *The March of Democracy* (1932), 211.

22. Porter, 34.

23. Earl G. Swem and John W. Williams, *Register of the General Assembly of Virginia* 1776–1918 (1918), 13; *ibid.*, 220.

24. *Journal of the House of Delegates for the Commonwealth of Virginia* (1781–86), 61 *et seq.*

25. James Roane and wife Elizabeth vs. Ann Royall *et al.*, deposition of John Lewis, File Box 235, *op. cit.*
26. (Staunton, Virginia) *Weekly Register*, March 14, 1807; Royall, *Southern Tour*, III, 224–236.
27. *Ibid., Letters from Alabama*, 88.
28. *Ibid., Black Book*, II, 13; *ibid., Southern Tour*, III, 14.
29. Morton, 201.
30. Lewis Preston Summers, *Annals of Southwest Virginia*, 1769–1800 (1929), 450; Monroe County Courthouse, Union, West Virginia, Order Book Sweet Springs District Court 1789–1805, 109 and *passim*. The name of Colonel John Stuart is sometimes written Stewart. I have followed the spelling in the colonel's memoir, published in the *West Virginia Historical Quarterly*, V, No. 2, 128 *et seq.*
31. James Roane and wife Elizabeth vs. Ann Royall *et al.*, James Roane's Bill of Complaint, File Box 235, *op. cit.*; Ann Royall's Bill of Complaint, *ibid.*
32. Summers, 552. Record of the marriage of William Royall to Anne Newport is quoted from the copy filed by Mrs. Royall when she applied for a pension: Pension Claim, Folio W8566, Veteran's Administration, Washington. The only clue I have as to the age of William Royall indicates he was born somewhere around 1740. Visiting City Point in 1827, Anne Royall remarked that her husband had "spent his childhood [there], some 80 years since." (Royall, *Black Book*, I, 250.)

CHAPTER III

1. James Roane and wife Elizabeth vs. Ann Royall, *et als.*, Separate answer of James Wylie, File Box 235, *op. cit.* Reference to this cache of papers appeared in the notes of Chapter II. Because Chapter III leans so heavily on File Box 235 for material, I have delayed until now to tell about this find. The papers have never before been used. It was known, from statements made by Mrs. Royall, that her in-laws had succeeded in breaking the will of William Royall, but the whereabouts of the records of the litigation was a mystery. And no wonder! One would expect to find them at the courthouse in Union, seat of Monroe County, where the will of William Royall was probated. There was nothing at Union other than the recorded will. Nearby Lewisburg, Greenbrier county seat, yielded no information and should not have, though in bygone days when courts were distant from the action, county lines were sometimes crossed to accommodate litigants. There was left Fincastle, but that seemed an unlikely prospect because the Sweet Springs had been taken out of Botetourt County and handed over to Monroe County more than a decade before the will was probated. Records at Fincastle, however, contained a number of tantalizing references to the case of Roane vs. Ann Royall *et als.* But there was no collection of papers telling about a trial. Finally an entry in the record book mentioned that the case

had been sent to Chancery Court at Staunton on appeal. Here was a new county—Augusta—involved.

In Staunton record books indicated the appeal had never been heard. And still no papers. Credit for eventually flushing File Box 235 belongs to General E. W. Opie, editor of the Staunton, Virginia, *News-Leader*. All the material pertaining to the will contest had been stashed away in File Box 235 on a shelf in the circuit clerk's office. I am most grateful to General Opie; and also to Blanche Humphreys of Ronceverte, West Virginia, who copied the contents of File Box 235 for me.

Besides the Roane suit, File Box 235 also contains the papers pertaining to two more suits: Ann Royall vs. Newton Gardner and his wife Anna. R. M., and the two Gardners vs. the Roanes and Mrs. Royall. These papers have been most helpful in filling out Anne Royall's years at Sweet Springs which, up to now, have been a blank.

2. Royall, *Sketches*, 69, 60; John Stuart, *Memorandum*—1798, July 15th, *West Virginia Historical Magazine Quarterly*, V, No. 2, 128. Mrs. Royall gave the names of the long hunters as "Carver" and "Suel." Sewell's name is spelled several different ways in local histories. I have corrected Mrs. Royall's spelling to conform with that used by Perceval and Ashton Reniers. Mrs. Royall wrote the name of Lewisburg's first lady as Welsh. This, too, I have changed because I found it written Welch more frequently in old documents.

3. John P. Hale, *Trans-Allegheny Pioneers* (1931), 202; Stuart, 132.

4. Royall, *Sketches*, 68, 69.

5. *Ibid.*, 61 *et seq.*; "John Ewing and the Clendenin Massacre," *West Virginia Magazine Quarterly*, IV, No. 2, 203 *et seq.* Mrs. Royall spelled the name Clendening. I have lopped off the "g" in favor of the more prevalent spelling of western writers.

6. Royall, *Sketches*, 72.

7. Waddell, 217; *The Life and Adventures of Robert Bailey* . . . , written by himself (1822), 64.

8. Morton, 203–205.

9. Military Certificates, 1811–1876, Book No. 3, 28, State Land Office, Virginia State Capital, Richmond; *Dictionary of American History*, V, 379; *Huntress*, April 18 and 25, 1840. James Marcus Brumbaugh, *Revolutionary War Records* (1936), II, 112, *et seq.* Scattered through the last volume, which is devoted to Virginia records, are listed numerous assignments to Benjamin W. Ladd, indicating that he was a heavy collector of the certificates.

10. Land grants to William Royall in the vicinity of Charleston were: on Elk River near mouth, 195 acres; on Coal River, 1556 acres; on Coal River, in partnership with William Neel, 1000 acres. [Morgan Homer] Dyer's *Index to Land Grants in West Virginia* (1896), 660, 673, 674. In official documents of Virginia, Clendenin's Station, as the West knew it, appears under the name Fort Lee, honoring "Lighthorse Harry" Lee. It was, of

course, one of a string of forts the state maintained on the frontier as defense against Indian raids. Roy Bird Cook, *The Annals of Fort Lee* (1935), 1, 18.

11. Royall, *Letters from Alabama*, 33.

12. James Roane and wife Elizabeth vs. Ann Royall *et als.*, Separate answer to Bill of Complaint, File Box 235, *op. cit.*

13. Royall, *Sketches*, 20.

14. *Ibid., Black Book*, I, 251.

15. James Roane and wife Elizabeth vs. Ann Royall *et als.*, Answer of Anna Cowan Gardner to Bill of Complaint, File Box 235, *op. cit.* This affidavit, submitted by Newton Gardner, husband of Anne Malvina, revealed the age of Mrs. Royall's niece at the time of her arrival at Sweet Springs. The same information is repeated by Gardner in his "answer" in the suit of Ann Royall vs. Newton Gardner and Anna R. M., File Box 235, *op. cit.*

16. Royall, *Southern Tour*, III, 224; Anne Royall to Messrs. Carey & Lea, June 1824, *Notable American Women*, case 7, box 20, Pennsylvania Historical Society, Philadelphia.

17. James Roane and wife Elizabeth vs. Ann Royall *et als.*, Separate answer of Ann Royall and Anna Cowan Gardner to Bill of Complaint, File Box 235, *op. cit.* Here I have followed the spelling of Wiley's name as it appears in Mrs. Royall's Answer. Wiley testified he had changed the spelling in 1809 to Wylie. If it is written thus in the court record I am currently using, then I follow the record.

18. Deed Book No. 55, 77, Charles City County Courthouse, Virginia.

19. James Roane and wife Elizabeth vs. Ann Royall *et als.*, Answer of Anna Cowan Gardner to Bill of Complaint, File Box 235, *op. cit.*; Will Book, 1799–1817, 222, Monroe County Courthouse, Union, West Virginia.

20. Deed Book No. 4, 405, Charles City County Courthouse, Virginia; *ibid.*, Deed Book No. 15, 247; Deed Book No. 55, 77, Chesterfield County Courthouse, Virginia.

21. James Roane and wife Elizabeth vs. Ann Royall *et als.*, Answer of Anne Cowan Gardner to Bill of Complaint and Separate Answer of James Wylie, File Box 235, *op. cit.* Proof of the Royalls' long-standing friendship with Matthew Dunbar is substantiated by references made by Anne Royall in *Letters from Alabama* to "Dear Matt" to whom *The Letters* were addressed.

22. James Roane and wife Elizabeth vs. Ann Royall *et als.*, Separate Answers of Anne Royall and James Wylie to Bill of Complaint, File Box 235, *op. cit.*

23. *Ibid.*, Depositions of Charles Shawver and Charles Dew, File Box 235, *op. cit.*

24. *Ibid.*, Depositions of Dr. Charles W. Lewis, John Lewis, James Thompson and John Shawver, File Box 235, *op. cit.*

25. *Ibid.*, Affidavit of William R. Roane, File Box 235, *op. cit.*

26. *Ibid.*, Separate answer of James Wylie, File Box 235, *op. cit.*

27. *Ibid.*, Deposition of Charles Dew, File Box 235, *op. cit.*

28. *Ibid.*, Separate Answers of Ann Royall, Ann Cowan Gardner, and James Wylie to Bill of Complaint, File Box 235, *op. cit.*

29. *Huntress*, May 1, 1841; James Roane and wife Elizabeth vs. Ann Royall *et als.*, Separate Answer of Ann Royall to Bill of Complaint, File Box 235, *op. cit.*

Chapter IV

1. James Roane and wife Elizabeth vs. Ann Royall *et als.*, Affidavit of James R. Roane, File Box 235, *op. cit.*

2. Separate Answer of Ann Royall to Bill of Complaint; Deposition of Isaac Hutchinson, *ibid.*

3. Will Book, 1799–1817, 222, 269, Monroe County Courthouse, Charleston, West Virginia; Deed Book D, 500, 171, Kanawha County Courthouse, Charleston.

4. Royall, *Letters from Alabama*, 33.

5. James Roane and wife Elizabeth vs. Ann Royall *et als.*, Deposition of Andrew Beirne, File Box 235, *op. cit.*

6. John P. Hale, *Trans-Allegheny Pioneers* (1931), Chapter XXXVII, *passim*; Royall, *Sketches*, 44 *et seq.*; Doctor W. H. Ruffner, "The Ruffners," *West Virginia Historical Quarterly*, I, no. 4, 44; George W. Atkinson, *History of Kanawha County* (1876), 198.

7. Deed Book D, August 14, 1813, Kanawha County Courthouse, *op. cit.*

8. Court Order Book, 1814–1819, 56, *ibid.*

9. Deed Book D, August 9 and 10, 1813, *ibid.*

10. Ann Royall vs. Jacob Smith, Circuit Court Record, October 31, 1814, Greenbrier County Courthouse, Lewisburg, West Virginia.

11. James Roane and wife Elizabeth vs. Ann Royall *et als.*, Deposition of Andrew Beirne; Separate Answer of James Wylie vs. James Roane and wife Elizabeth and Ann Royall, Depositions of William Herbert and of Andrew Burns (sic), File Box 235, *op. cit.*

12. James Roane and wife Elizabeth vs. Ann Royall *et als.*, James Roane's Bill of Complaint, *ibid.*

13. Deed Book D, 273, Kanawha County Courthouse, *op. cit.*

14. James Roane and wife Elizabeth vs. Ann Royall *et als.*, Depositions of Newton Gardner, William R. Cox, Isaac Noyes and Charles Brown, File Box 235, *op. cit.*

15. Ann Royall vs. Newton Gardner and Anna R. M., his wife, observations on exceptions taken by plaintiff's counsel, *ibid.*

16. Various papers, *ibid.*

17. Ann Royall vs. Newton Gardner and Anna R. M., his wife, Deposition of Frances Slaughter; James Roane and wife Elizabeth vs. Ann Royall, *et als.*, Deposition of Newton Gardner, *ibid.*

18. Royall, *Letters from Alabama*, 70.

19. Royall, *Sketches*, 38; Ann Royall vs. Newton Gardner and Anna R. M., his wife, Deposition of Frances Slaughter, File Box 235, *op. cit.*; Deed Book D, 541, Kanawha County Courthouse, *op. cit.*

20. Common Law Order Book, 1800 to 1823, 261, Botetourt County Courthouse, Fincastle, Virginia.

21. James Roane and wife Elizabeth vs. Ann Royall *et als.*, various papers, File Box 235, *op. cit.*

22. Common Law Order Book, 1800 to 1823, 262, Botetourt County Courthouse, *op. cit.*

23. James Roane and wife Elizabeth vs. Ann Royall *et als.*, Affidavit of James Roane, Richmond, Virginia, May 29, 1817, File Box 235, *op. cit.*

CHAPTER V

1. Ann Royall vs. Newton Gardner and his wife Anna Malvina, affidavit of Matthew Dunbar, May 22, 1820; Ann Royall, Bill of Complaint, May 27, 1818, File Box 235, *op. cit.*

2. Jackson, 43; Porter, 45; Atkinson, 198; Anne Royall to Carey & Lea, June 1824, *op. cit.*

3. Reverend George Bryce, D.D., *Makers of Canada* (1909), 115 *et seq.*; Royall, *Letters from Alabama*, 7–8.

4. *Ibid.*, 9, 41.

5. *Ibid.*, 20, 48.

6. *Ibid.*, 39.

7. *Ibid.*, 45.

8. *Ibid.*, 41–49; Thomas P. Abernathy, "The Formative Period in Alabama," *Alabama State Historical Society*, Historical and Patriotic Series No. 6, 27.

9. Royall, *Letters from Alabama*, 54–56.

10. *Ibid.*, 77–80.

11. *Ibid.*, 61.

12. *Ibid.*, 69–75.

13. *Ibid.*, 66; *ibid.*, *Southern Tour*, I, 39; *ibid.*, III, 97.

14. James Roane and wife Elizabeth vs. Ann Royall *et als.*, File Box 235, *op. cit.*; Common Law Order Book, 1800–1823, 301, Botetourt County Courthouse, Fincastle, Virginia; *ibid.*, 313–336.

15. *Ibid.*, 334–336; James Roane and wife Elizabeth vs. Ann Royall *et als.*, Decree 1819, File Box 235, *op. cit.*; Royall, *Southern Tour*, I, 39; *ibid.*, III, 107; *Huntress*, April 25, 1840.

16. Ann Royall vs. Newton Gardner and wife Anna Malvina, various papers, File Box 235, *op. cit.*

17. Newton Gardner vs. Ann Royall, various folios, particularly folio 139, No. 3, Superior Court, Kanawha County Courthouse.

18. Marriage Records, 1816–1843, *ibid.;* Royall, *Letters from Alabama,* 114.

19. Nina Leftwich, *Two Hundred Years of Muscle Shoals* (1935), 36.

20. Royall, *Letters from Alabama,* 105.

21. *Ibid.,* 137–151; Thomas McAdory Owen, *History of Alabama* (1921), I, 427; *ibid.,* II, 1056; James Edward Saunders, *Early Settlers of Alabama* (1899), 199.

22. Leftwich, 38; A. P. Whittaker, "The Muscle Shoals Speculation," 1723–1789, *Mississippi Historical Review,* XIII, No. 3, 366; Royall, *Letters from Alabama,* 145, *et seq.*

23. *Ibid.,* 155–157.

24. *Ibid.,* 165.

25. *Ibid.,* 88, 92, 97.

26. Superior Court, folio no. 3, 139, Kanawha County Courthouse; Royall, *Letters from Alabama,* 144.

27. *Ibid.,* 141; Anne Royall to Mathew Carey, February 12, 1824, *op. cit.;* (Albany, New York) *Daily Advertiser,* February 12, 1825.

28. Anne Royall to Carey & Lea, June 1824, *op. cit.;* Royall, *Sketches,* 14. The Pope mansion is still standing and it is a beauty. In the 1830's the property was acquired by Doctor Charles Hayes Patton who married a daughter of Colonel Beirne, thus reinforcing the old mercantile partnership of Beirne & Patton. The house remains in the possession of a descendant of the family. (Publication of Huntsville branch, American Association of University Women, *Glimpses into Ante-Bellum Homes,* 5.)

CHAPTER VI

1. Hale, 276; *Huntress,* September 28, 1839; Royall, *Southern Tour,* III, 219–236.

2. *Ibid.,* I, Appendix, 6–7; *Ibid.,* III, 237.

3. Royall, *Sketches,* 49–50; Oren R. Morton, *Centennial History of Allegheny County, Virginia* (1923), 103; Mrs. James R. Hopley, "Anne Sargeant Bailey," *Ohio State Archeological Society Quarterly,* XVI, 340 *et seq.*

4. Anne Royall to Mathew Carey, February 12, 1824, *op. cit.;* Anne Royall to Messrs. Carey & Lea, June 1824, *op. cit.*

5. Victor W. Von Hagen, *Maya Explorer: John Lloyd Stephens and the Lost Cities of Central America and Yucatan* (1947), 66; J Howard Payne to George Watterston, August 26, 1840, George Watterston Papers, Library of Congress, Washington. American authors began to be taken up by American publishers in the late 1830's. "The *Booksellers Advertiser* pointed out that whereas only ten American novels were printed in 1834, thirty-one appeared in 1835:" David Kaser, *Messrs. Carey & Lea of Philadelphia* (1957, 70.)

6. F. J. Maier, "Mathew Carey, Publicist and Politician," *Records of the American Catholic Historical Society of Philadelphia*, XXXIX, No. 2, 125; Charles Morris, editor, *Makers of Philadelphia* (1894), 22; *Huntress*, November 23, 1839.

7. Ellis P. Oberholtzer, *The Literary History of Philadelphia* (1906), 343; *Biographies of Successful Philadelphia Merchants*, published by James K. Simon (1864), 17–18.

8. Royall, *Black Book* I, 313. There is surely more to be told about Mrs. Royall's departure from western Virginia than I am able to put down here. According to Mason Campbell, editor of the (Charleston) *Western Virginian and Kanawha County Gazette*, September 20, 1826, Anne Royall was confined for debt "for the greater part of a year in the Greenbrier County jail," and, upon being "released by the indulgence of her creditor," immediately fled Lewisburg. Roy Bird Cook, Charleston historian, wrote me that Campbell was wont to dip "his pen in vitriol," and clippings from the *Western Virginian* that I have read confirm the truth of his statement. Campbell also was not always an accurate reporter. At the courthouse in Lewisburg I found the record of a judgment for debt handed down against Anne Royall at the May, 1823 court term, when she was still in Alabama. The plaintiff was John Brahan who was awarded $135 plus interest, and $8.43 costs. (Law Order Book No. 2, 277.) No particulars of the litigation are given, and I do not know that Mr. Brahan was the kindhearted creditor Mr. Campbell had in mind. The fact is that Anne Royall did not arrive in Lewisburg until September or October, 1823, and left for Washington around December 5. A new version of how Anne Royall managed her trip to Alexandria, Virginia, came to my attention in a collection of short biographies entitled *The Square Pegs*, by Irving Wallace. The author wrote that "she found her food in garbage behind tavern kitchens and slept in the open" (p. 252). The statement is undocumented and I can find no evidence to support it. Garbage did not lie about in those days. Pigs ate it. Mrs. Royall was always her own best reporter and, once she had a little success, did not mind admitting to all the hardships suffered to achieve it. I feel sure that if she had foraged in this fashion she would have told us. I think the documented sources of this present chapter make clear that Anne Royall made her way to Alexandria on the reputation of her husband as a soldier and a Mason.

9. Royall, *Sketches*, 83–99.

10. *Ibid., Black Book,* I, 141; Mary G. Powell, *The History of Old Alexandria* (1928), 273.

11. Royall, *Black Book*, III, 224.

12. Anne Royall to Mathew Carey, February 12, 1823. Royall, *Sketches*, 200.

13. Anne Royall to Messrs. Carey & Lea, June, 1824, *op. cit.*

14. Royall, *Sketches*, 112–113.

15. Powell, 272; Royall, *Sketches*, 101.

16. *Huntress*, February 4, 1843; *ibid.*, June 6, 1840.

17. Royall, *Southern Tour*, III, 6; *ibid.*, *Black Book*, I, 410; *ibid.*, III, 228.

18. *Ibid.*, *Sketches*, 117.

19. *Ibid.*, *Black Book*, I, 142–144.

20. *Ibid.*, *Sketches*, 119.

21. *Ibid.*, 121; *ibid.*, *Black Book*, I, 149–150.

22. *Ibid.*, *Sketches*, 156, 130–133.

23. *Huntress*, December 16, 1843; New Orleans *Daily Picayune*, August 6, 1842; Royall, *Black Book*, III, 110. Another version of the meeting with Sally Dorret presents Anne Royall as

> wearied and heart-sick . . . one severely stormy day wandering through the streets in search of a gentleman to whom she had a letter of introduction, and applying at a house for information. A little girl who answered her inquiry, ran to tell her mother that a lady dripping with wet and looking very sick, was standing in the hall. Before the girl's return Mrs. R. had fainted and fallen to the floor, from sheer exhaustion. She was at once taken to bed, and owing to exposure, &c., a raging fever set in, through which she was nursed by the girl. . . . That little girl was "Sally," well-known wherever Mrs. R. has visited as her inseparable companion, which she continued to this day. (*New York Express*, March 4, 1843.)

The above was written by one of the friendly Brooks brothers—James or Erastus—editors of the *New York Express*, who spelled each other as Washington correspondent of their newspaper during most of the years Anne Royall was a resident of the Capital. The story is given here simply to show how legends grow up around famous people and soon become gospel truth. Anne Royall never knew Sally's parents; they had died before she arrived in the Capital. "Little girl" Sally married about a year after Anne first met her.

24. *Huntress*, April 18, 1840; 19th Congress, 2nd Session, *Register of Debates*, III, 655–656, 663, 667, 686–687; Royall, *Pennsylvania*, I, 88; *ibid.*, *Black Book* II, 117.

25. Anne Royall to Henry Carey, April 26, 1824. This letter appeared on "List Number Twenty-Four," a collection of autographs offered for sale by Robert K. Black, Upper Montclair, New Jersey.

26. Royall, *Sketches*, 174–175, 159.

27. *Ibid.*, 158–161.

28. Margaret Bayard Smith, *The First Forty Years of Washington Society* (1906), 95; Royall, *Southern Tour*, I, 117; *ibid.*, *Letters from Alabama*, Appendix, 187, 188; Henry Adams, *John Randolph* (1882), 23.

29. 19th Congress, 2nd Session, *Register of Debates*, 686; *Paul Pry*, March 31, 1832; Royall, *Black Book*, III, 112.

30. *Paul Pry*, December 3, 1831.

31. Royall, *Sketches*, 171.

32. *Ibid., Black Book*, III, 130.

33. *Ibid., Sketches*, 140; *ibid., Black Book*, III, 215; *ibid., Sketches*, 170.

34. Benjamin Perley Poore, *Reminiscences of Sixty Years in the National Metropolis* (1886), I, 157–158; Royall, *Black Book*, I, 138–139.

35. *Ibid., Sketches*, 182; *Huntress*, December 16, 1843; Royall, *Black Book*, I, 110; Mary Frances Anderson, "The Old Brick Capitol, Washington, D.C.," *American Historical Society, Inc.*, XXIII, No. 2, 162 *et seq.;* Royall, *Letters from Alabama*, Appendix, 200.

36. *Ibid., Sketches*, 140–166.

37. *Ibid.*, 130; William Dawson Johnston, *History of the Library of Congress* (1904), I, 74; Royall, *Sketches*, 150.

38. *Ibid.*, 121–125; *ibid., Black Book*, I, 236.

39. *Ibid.*, 110; *ibid., Sketches*, 166.

40. *Huntress*, March 4, 1848; Royall, *Sketches*, 166, 169.

41. *Ibid.*, 165, 162, 156; Timothy Flint, *Recollections of the Last Ten Years, Passed in Occasional Residences and Journeyings in the Valley of the Mississippi* (1826), 386.

42. *Dictionary of American Biography* (1937), VII, 101; Allen C. Clark, "Joseph Gales, Junior, Editor and Mayor," *Records of the Columbia Historical Society*, XXIII, 127–128; Royall, *Sketches*, 153. In *Paul Pry*, March 24, 1832, Anne Royall explained how she happened to select her nicknames for Joseph Gales: "A neighbor of ours had four sons whom she called John-ee, Sam-ee, Jim-ee and Jo-ee, and sometimes the latter Josey. So we make free with Brother Joe, all in good nature and good fellowship."

43. Wilhelmus Bogart Bryan, *History of the National Capital* (1914), II, 45 note, 60; Royall, *Sketches*, 175–178; W. E. Woodward, *Lafayette* (1938), 426.

44. Harris, *op. cit.* XXXIII, 107; Royall, *Black Book* III, 215; *ibid., Letters from Alabama*, Appendix, 188. Besides the above, Mrs. Royall made other references in her books to the letter Lafayette gave her.

CHAPTER VII

1. A. Levasseur, *Lafayette in America in 1824 and 1825* (1829), I, 173; Royall, *Sketches*, 186.

2. *Ibid.*, 188–202. Between these page numbers, Mrs. Royall relates of her first visit to Baltimore. She does not tell all, and additional memoirs crop up in her other travel books. See *Southern Tour*, I, 8, and *Pennsylvania*, I, II.

3. Reese D. James, editor, *Old Drury of Philadelphia* (1932), 158; Clayton Coleman Hall, editor, *Baltimore Its History and Its People* (1912), 652; J. Thomas Scharf, *History of Baltimore City and County* (1881), 687.

4. George W. Howard, *The Monumental City, Its Past and Present Resources* (1873), 469.

5. Royall, *Sketches*, 205–234, incidents of Mrs. Royall's visit to Philadelphia.

6. *Ibid., Black Book*, I, 97.

7. *Ibid., Pennsylvania*, I, 86–87.

8. Hughes Oliphant Gibbons, *A History of Old Pine Street* (1905), 185–189.

9. Royall, *Pennsylvania*, I, 89.

10. Ellis Paxson Oberholtzer, *Philadelphia, A History of the City and Its People* (1912), II, 46.

11. Royall, *Pennsylvania*, I, 90, 85; *Dictionary of American Biography* (1937), V, 73.

12. Royall, *Pennsylvania*, I, 90.

13. *Ibid., Sketches*, 237; Charles M. Haswell, *Reminiscences of an Octogenarian* (1895), 170.

14. Royall, *Sketches*, 240; *ibid., Black Book*, I, 315.

15. *Ibid., Sketches*, 245–255; advertisement in (New York) *National Advocate*, November 17, 1824, gave route, schedule, and other details about the *Legislator*.

16. Royall, *Sketches*, 256.

17. *Ibid., Sketches*, 264–267.

18. *Ibid.*, 266; Henry Walcott Boynton, *Annals of American Bookselling* 1638–1850 (1932), 16; (Fremont) *Rider's New York City* (1823), 346.

19. Royall, *Black Book*, II, 6; *ibid., Black Book*, I, 3; Boynton, 163.

20. *Paul Pry*, March 3, 1832, reprinted from the *Morning Courier and New York Enquirer*; Isaac Goldberg, *Major Noah* (1937), 155.

21. Royall, *Black Book*, II, 3; *ibid.*, 8.

22. George C. D. Odell, *Annals of the New York Stage* (1927), III, 121 *et seq.*; Oscar Weglin, "Micah Hawkins and the Saw-Mill," *Magazine of History*, XXXII, No. 3, 13–16; Royall, *Sketches*, 267.

23. *New York American*, February 28, 1825; *New York Daily Advertiser*, February 28, 1825.

24. *New York Mirror*, May 25, 1824.

25. Royall, *Black Book*, II, 11.

CHAPTER VIII

1. Royall, *Sketches*, 270.

2. (Albany) *Daily Advertiser*, February 12, 1825.

3. Manuscript Diary of DeWitt Clinton, March 15, 1825 and March 25, 1825, *New York Historical Society*, New York City.

4. Royall, *Sketches*, 284; *ibid., Black Book*, I, 12.

5. *Ibid., Sketches*, 282; Marquis James, *Andrew Jackson: Portrait of a President* (1937), 127.

6. *New York Commercial Advertiser*, June 7, 1826; *New York, A Guide to the Empire State*, compiled by the Works Progress Administration (1940), 182; Royall, *Sketches*, 282.

7. *Ibid.*, 279; Madeline S. Waggoner, *The Long Haul West* (1959), *passim*; Marvin A. Rapp, *Canawl Water and Whiskey* (a pamphlet, no dates, no page numbers); Samuel Hopkins Adams to the author.

8. Royall, *Sketches*, 286.

9. *Ibid.*, 292; Charles Wells Chapin, *Sketches of the Old Inhabitants of Old Springfield* (1893), 22.

10. Royall, *Sketches*, 296–299.

11. *Ibid.*, 300; Louise J. R. Chapman, "A Visit to Mrs. Sigourney," *Connecticut Quarterly*, January–March, 1895, 47.

12. Royall, *Sketches*, 308–347.

13. *Ibid.*, 333–334; Esther Forbes, *Paul Revere and the World He Lived In* (1942), Chapter VII.

14. Cleveland Amory, *The Proper Bostonians* (1947), 143–144; Royall, *Sketches*, 348–349.

15. *Dictionary of American Biography* (1937), I, 61; Van Wyck Brooks, *The Flowering of New England* (1936), 121; Royall, *Sketches*, 337–349.

16. *Hallowell* (Maine) *Gazette*, September 12, 1827, quoted from the *Ipswich* (Masachusetts) *Journal*.

17. Royall, *Sketches*, 337; Anne Royall to Jared Sparks, June 30, 1826, Houghton Library, Harvard College Library; Royall, *Black Book*, II, 113.

18. *Ibid.*, 114; *Hallowell Gazette*, September 12, 1827, reprinted from the *Boston Commercial Gazette*.

19. Royall, *Sketches*, 372.

20. *Ibid.*, *Black Book*, II, 8.

21. Wentworth Hamilton Eaton, *The Famous Mather Byles* 1707–1781 (1914), 174, 217, 223; (New Haven) *Cennecticut Herald*, June 26, 1826; Royall, *Sketches*, 334–335.

22. *Ibid.*, *Black Book*, I, 3; Edward A. Atwater, ed., *History of New Haven to the Present Time* (1887), 391; Royall, *Pennsylvania*, II, 33 (note).

23. Mary Hewitt Mitchell, *History of New Haven County* (1930), I, 132; Royall, *Black Book*, I, 6.

24. *Ibid.*, *Sketches*, 388; H. R. Warfel, *Noah Webster: Schoolmaster to America* (1936), 421–422; Anne Royall to Jared Sparks, June 30, 1826, *op. cit.*

25. Royall, *Sketches*, 387–388.

26. *Ibid.*, *Black Book*, I, 3, 7.

CHAPTER IX

1. *Paul Pry*, March 3, 1832, reprinted from the *Morning Courier and New York Enquirer; National Advocate*, June 1, 1826; Royall, *Black Book*, I, 280.

2. *New York Daily Advertiser*, June 20, 1826.

3. Royall, *Black Book*, I, 7–8.

4. (New Haven) *Connecticut Herald*, June 20, 1826, reprinted from *Boston Commercial Gazette*.

5. (Boston) *Columbian Centinel*, July 5, 1826.

6. Royall, *Black Book*, I, 8; (Worcester) *National Aegis*, June 21, 1826; (Salem) *Essex Register*, June 26, 1826; *National Aegis*, June 28, 1826.

7. (Springfield) *Hampden Journal*, July 12, 1826.

8. Charles McCarthy, "The Antimasonic Party: A Study of Political Antimasonry in the United States 1827–1840," *Annual Report of the American Historical Association*, I–VI, 515, 541–543.

9. John C. Palmer, *The Morgan Affair and Anti-Masonry* (1924), 36.

10. A. J. G. Perkins, *Frances Wright: Free Enquirer* (1939), 209; *New York Missionary Magazine*, III, 363.

11. *Dictionary of American Biography* (1937), XIV, 127.

12. Royall, *Black Book*, III, 110; second part of quote from letter of Anne Royall to Mordecai M. Noah, (Lexington) *Kentucky Gazette*, June 26, 1829, reprinted from the *New York Enquirer*. The *Enquirer* was a new daily begun by Major Noah in April, 1826. He still published the *National Advocate*. In 1829 the *Enquirer* was merged with the *Morning Courier* and renamed the *Morning Courier and New York Enquirer* which we have already begun to cite in the notes.

13. Royall, *Black Book*, I, 13.

14. *Ibid.*, 13–16; *Saratoga Sentinel*, July 18 and July 25, 1826.

15. "The Private Journal of Nicholas Biddle," Introduction and notes by Edward Biddle, *Pennsylvania Magazine of History and Biography*, IV, No. 3, 208; "Our Country and Its People," prepared under the auspices of *The Saratogan* (1899), 392; Royall, *Black Book*, I, 17–18; Achille Murat, *Moral and Political Sketch of the United States* (1832), 358.

16. Royall, *Black Book*, I, 35, 36, 30.

17. Palmer, 38; Royall, *Black Book*, I, 25–26; *New York Daily Advertiser*, July 28, 1826; *Utica Intelligencer*, August 1, 1826; *New York Commercial Advertiser*, August 7, 1826; Royall, *Black Book*, I, 41.

18. *Ibid.*, 47–57.

19. (Rochester) *Monroe Republican*, August 8, 1826; *New York Commercial Advertiser*, September 1, 1826.

20. Royall, *Black Book*, I, 26, 61–75.

21. Mrs. H. S. Colvin's (Washington) *Weekly Messenger*, September 30, 1826, reprinted from the *New York Enquirer*.

22. Anne Royall to Durrie & Peck, September 27, 1826, manuscript division, Library of Congress, Washington.

23. Royall, *Black Book*, I, 91; *Dictionary of American Biography* (1937), III, 97.

24. (Charleston) *Western Virginia* and *Kanąwha County Gazette,* August 2, and September 20, 1826; *ibid.,* October 31, 1826, reprinted from the (Woodstock, Virginia) *Sentinel of the Valley.* Copies of the *Gazette* are rare, probably because it had a short life. I consulted an incomplete file in the Department of Archives and History, Charleston, West Virginia. I found no copies anywhere of the *Sentinel of the Valley.*

25. Royall, *Black Book,* I, 97; *Baltimore Patriot,* October 17, 1826, reprinted from the (Philadelphia) *Freeman's Journal.*

26. *New York Enquirer,* September 6, 1828; Royall, *Black Book,* I, 96; Mrs. Royall's letter, dated April 4, 1829, was originally published in the *New York Enquirer.* I have been unable to find a copy of the newspaper for this date. Fortunately the letter was reprinted by the (Lexington) *Kentucky Gazette* from which I extracted my quote. Royall, *Pennsylvania,* I, 93; (Charleston, South Carolina) *City Gazette,* March 25, 1830.

27. Royall, *Black Book,* I, 100–106.

CHAPTER X

1. John W. Forney, *Anecdotes of Public Men* (1873–81) (1881), I, 115; Royall, *Black Book,* I, 126; (Washington) *United States Telegraph and Commercial Herald,* February 27, 1827.

2. Royall, *Black Book,* I, 127; W. W. Story, editor, *Life and Letters of Joseph Story* (1851), I, 517.

3. (Providence) *Literary Cadet and Rhode Island Statesman,* August 8, 1827.

4. Royall, *Black Book,* I, 260.

5. *Boston Lyceum,* I, No. 3, 160; Mrs. A. S. Colvin's (Washington) *Weekly Messenger,* March 3, 1827; Royall, *Black Book,* I, 112.

6. Anne Royall to Colonel Freeman, March 8, 1827, quoted in Catalogue No. 8, The Book Farm, Hattiesburg, Mississippi.

7. *New York Enquirer,* March 1, 1827; Royall, *Black Book,* I, 141, 144; *ibid.,* II, 195.

8. *Hampden Journal,* July 18, 1827; (Northampton) *Old-Hampshire Post,* July 21, 1827; (Middletown) *Middlesex Gazette,* reprinted in the *Literary Cadet and Rhode Island Statesman,* July 28, 1827; (Newport) *Rhode Island Republican,* August 2, 1827; *Boston Statesman,* August 3, 1827.

9. Haswell, 187.

10. Royall, *Black Book,* I, 155; *ibid.,* II, 11–13; *ibid.,* I, 163.

11. McCarthy, 540; *New York Observer and Chronicle,* November 18, 1826.

12. Royall, *Black Book,* I, 152–153.

13. *Ibid.,* 249–251.

14. *Ibid.,* 303; *ibid., Southern Tour,* I, 215; *ibid., Pennsylvania,* I, 71.

15. *Ibid.*, *Black Book*, I, 318; Adolph B. Benson, "Catherine Potter Stith and Her Meeting With Lord Byron," *South Atlantic Quarterly*, XXII, 10–22.

16. A pamphlet, reprint of Doctor Ely's "Discourse Delivered on the Fourth of July, 1827."

17. (Harrisburg, Pennsylvania) *Chronicle*, March 10, 1828, which quoted the Third Annual Report of the Sunday School Union, written by Doctor Ely.

18. Royall, *Black Book*, I, 163.

19. *Ibid.*, 236; *New York Observer and Chronicle*, November 18, 1826; Royall, *Black Book*, I, 326.

20. *Kentucky Gazette*, June 26, 1829, reprinted from the *New York Enquirer*; Royall, *Black Book*, II, 3; McCarthy, 549; John Bach McMaster, *A History of the People of the United States* (1883–1924), V, 274.

21. Royall, *Black Book*, II, 6; *ibid.*, III, 221–222; *New York Enquirer*, June 15, 1827; *ibid.*, June 8, 1827; Royall, *Black Book*, II, 22.

22. *Ibid.*, 5.

23. McCarthy, 504 *et seq.*

24. Royall, *Black Book*, I, 327.

CHAPTER XI

1. *Huntress*, April 6, 1844; Royall, *Black Book*, II, 28–29; *Huntress*, February 11, 1843.

2. Royall, *Black Book*, II, 43–49.

3. *Ibid.*, 64–66; *ibid.*, 91.

4. *Ibid.*, 111–112.

5. *Ibid.*, 125–129; Charles Francis Adams, editor, *Memoirs of John Quincy Adams comprising portions of his Diary from 1795 to 1849* (1875), VII, 321.

6. *Catalogus Medicinae in Universitate Harvardiana* (1827), Widener Library, Harvard College, Cambridge. Only five catalogues were issued—in 1821, 1824, 1827, 1830, 1833. After Czar Alexander's present, which the college had to acknowledge without letting the monarch know he was the victim of a joke, the Harvard College Fac. disbanded the Med Fac.

7. The letter, dated November 15, 1831, was published in *Paul Fry*, December 3, 1831.

8. (Salem) *Essex Register*, August 20, 1827; *Salem Gazette*, August 21, 1827.

9. Royall, *Black Book*, II, 159–161; Mrs. E. Vale Smith, *History of Newburyport* (1854), 349.

10. Royall, *Black Book*, II, 180–189.

11. *Ibid.*, 190–194, 196, 205, 208; George Augustus Wheeler, *History of Brunswick, Topsham and Harpswell* (1878), 730.

12. Royall, *Black Book*, II, 317; *Hallowell* (Maine) *Gazette*, September 12, 1827; *ibid.*, October 3, 1827; (Hallowell) *American Advocate; Hallowell Gazette*, October 3, 1827.

13. Royall, *Black Book*, II, 256–260.

14. *Ibid.*, 267, 284, 322.

15. *Hallowell Gazette*, September 12, 1827, reprinted from the *Portland Argus*.

16. Royall, *Black Book*, II, 217.

17. *Ibid.*, 347; *ibid.*, III, 4.

18. *Ibid.*, 29–56; Abby Maria Hemenway, editor, *Vermont Historical Quarterly Gazeteer*, V, 599.

19. (Worcester) *National Aegis*, February 6, 1828, reprinted from the (Providence) *Literary Cadet and Rhode Island Statesman;* (Boston) *New England Galaxy*, January 25, 1828.

20. Royall, *Black Book*, III, 91–99.

21. *Huntress*, December 16, 1843; Bryan, I, 536; Royall, *Black Book*, III, 110, 140.

22. *The Marylander*, September 24, 1828; *New York Enquirer*, May 23, 1828; Royal, *Black Book*, III, 110.

23. *Ibid.*, 124, 113, 114; Thomas Hart Benton, *Thirty Years View* (1854), I, 95; *Huntress*, November 12, 1842; *ibid.*, February 6, 1847; *Paul Pry*, January 5, 1833; James A. Padgett, editor, "The Leters of Colonel Richard M. Johnson of Kentucky," *Register of the Kentucky State Historical Society*, Vol. 38, No. 123, 188.

24. Royall, *Black Book*, III, 131–140.

25. *Ibid.*, 146–172; Constance McLaughlin Green, *Washington: Village and Capital*, 1800–1878 (1962), 104.

26. *Huntress*, November 23, 1839; Ben Perley Poore, *Perley's Reminiscences* (1886), I, 43; *Huntress*, November 30, 1839.

27. Margaret Bayard Smith, *Forty Years of Washington Society* (1906), 212; Claude G. Bowers, *The Party Battles of the Jackson Period* (1922), 34; Royall *Black Book*, III, 150–170. Mrs. Royall's estimate of Colonel Brearley's relations with the Creeks is not borne out by correspondence and papers on file at the Indian Bureau, Washington. Two years after she talked with the colonel, the Creeks petitioned President Jackson to remove Brearley. Their charges against the agent are summarized by Marquis James in *The Raven* (1929), 111–112.

28. Royal, *Black Book*, III, 171–184.

CHAPTER XII

1. McCarthy, 439, quoted from (Harrisburg) *Pennsylvania Reporter and Democratic Herald*, October 28, 1831.

2. McCarthy, 428; Royall, *Pennsylvania*, I, 4.

3. *Ibid.*, *Black Book*, I, 305; *ibid.*, *Pensylvania*, I, 30. The Maryland Historical Society, Baltimore, own copies of both Chase books. The earliest, in two volumes, is entitled *Extracts in Prose and Verse by a Lady of Maryland, together with a Collection of Original Pieces of Prose and Verse Con-*

sisting Principally of Pieces of Moral Instruction, Descriptions of Fine Scenery, Delineations of Distinguished Characters, etc. The latter volume includes a number of poems signed Edgar, which was Miss Chase's pseudonym.

4. Royall, *Pennsylvania,* I, 32, 36, 60; *Pennsylvania Reporter and Democratic Herald,* February 19, 1828.

5. Royall, *Pennsylvania,* I, 61, 62; Bowers, 32–34; Royall, *Pennsylvania,* I, 80.

6. *Ibid.,* 66; *Scharf & Westcott,* III, 1869; Royall, *Pennsylvania,* I, 82.

7. *Ibid.,* 100, 102; Reverend Uzal W. Condit, A.M., *The History of Eaton, Penn'a* (1889), 36; Royall, *Pennsylvania,* I, 132–140; American Guide Series, *Pennsylvania* (1947), 504.

8. J. Bennett Nolan, *Early Narratives of Berks County* (1927), 176; Royall, *Pennsylvania,* I, 149–150; *Scharf & Westcott,* III, 2337.

9. Royall, *Pennsylvania,* I, 158, 162–164, 172; Hubert H. Beck and William Frederic Worner, "Horse-Racing in Lancaster County," *Lancaster County Historical Society Quarterly,* XXXVII, No. 3, 55; William Frederic Worner, *Old Lancaster* (1927), 162, quoted from the *Lancaster Intelligencer,* November 4, 1828, and from the *Lancaster Journal,* October 31, 1828; Royall, *Pennsylvania,* I, 168–169, 164; H. J. M. Klein, editor, *Lancaster County, Pennsylvania, A History* (1924), II, 879.

10. Royall, *Pennsylvania,* I, 188; *Harrisburg Argus,* November 8, 1828.

11. Royall, *Pennsylvania,* I, 190, 193, 219, 218, 200; *Bedford* (Pennsylvania) *Gazette,* November 28, 1828, reprinted from the *Carlisle Gazette.*

12. Royall, *Pennsylvania,* I, 249; *Bedford Gazette,* November 28, 1828.

13. Royall, *Pennsylvania,* II, 40–42, 76, 55, 90; American Guide Series, *Pennsylvania, op. cit.,* 79; Royall, *Pennsylvania,* II, 102, 112–125, 66.

14. *Ibid.,* 151–163.

15. *Dictionary of American Biography, op. cit.,* XX, 550; Royall, *Pennsylvania,* II, 164; *Huntress,* November 3, 1838.

16. Royall, *Pennsylvania,* II, 201–222.

17. *Ibid.,* 245–246; *Western Virginian,* February 11, 1829; Royall, *Pennsylvania,* II, 268.

CHAPTER XIII

1. Arthur M. Schlesinger, junior, *The Age of Jackson* (Menton Abridged Edition, 1949), 2.

2. Royall, *Letters from Alabama,* 171; Poore, I, 92, *et seq.*

3. Royall, *Letters from Alabama,* 173–178; Leon G. Tyler, *Letters and Times of the Tylers* (1884), I, 550.

4. Royall, *Letters from Alabama,* 182–224; James Truslow Adams, *The March of Democracy* (1932), 297; Smith, 296.

5. Royall, *Letters from Alabama,* 212.

6. *Ibid., Pennsylvania*, I, 216; *ibid., Black Book*, II, 394; *ibid., Pennsylvania*, I, 216; *ibid., Black Book*, III, 210; *ibid.*, II, 194.

7. George Watterston to Edward Everett, January 26, 1829, Papers of George Watterston, I, 1815–1835, Manuscript Division, Library of Congress, Washington; Henry Clay to George Watterston, July 21, 1829, *ibid.;* William Dawson Johnston, *History of the Library of Congress* (1905), I, 190–192.

8. Royall, *Black Book*, III, 203; *ibid., Pennsylvania*, II, Appendix, 6; *ibid.*, 12; *ibid.*, 4.

9. William Cranch, *Reports of Cases Civil and Criminal in the United States Circuit Court of the District of Columbia from 1801 to 1841* (1842), III, 618–619; *Boston Columbian Centinel*, July 15, 1829; *Morning Courier and New York Enquirer*, July 29, 1829; *ibid.*, July 17 and July 3, 1829; Royall, *Pennsylvania*, II, Appendix, 7; *New York Commercial Advertiser*, July 6, 1829; *ibid.*, July 31, 1829; *Niles' Register*, July 18, 1829; Thomas J. Kirkland and Robert M. Kennedy, *Historical Camden* (1905), II, 344; *New York Observer*, July 11, 1829; *Bedford* (Pennsylvania) *Gazette*, July 24, 1829.

10. Cranch, *op. cit.*, 619, 620, 626.

11. (Boston) *New England Galaxy*, July 31, 1829; *New York Spectator*, July 24, 1829, reprinted from the *New York Commercial Advertiser; Niles' Register*, August 8, 1829; *National Intelligencer*, July 31, 1829, reprinted from the *National Journal;* Porter, 137; Royall, *Black Book*, III, 211.

12. *Morning Courier and New York Enquirer*, July 17, 1829; Royall, *Pennsylvania*, II, 189; *ibid.*, Appendix, 22; *Morning Courier and New York Enquirer*, July 16, 1829; *New England Galaxy*, July 31, 1829.

13. (Harrisburg) *Intelligencer*, August 4, 1829, reprinted from the *New York Commercial Advertiser*.

14. *Ibid.*

15. *Worcester National Aegis*, August 26, 1829; *New York Spectator*, August 7, 1829; Allan C. Clark, "Joseph Gales, Junior," *Records of the Columbia Historical Society*, XXIII, 110; Royall, *Black Book*, II, 395; *ibid., Southern Tour*, III, 217.

Chapter XIV

1. Royall, *Southern Tour*, I, 20; Poore, I, 99; Anne Leakin Sioussat, *Old Baltimore* (1931), 314; Royall, *Southern Tour*, I, 6.

2. *Ibid.*, 17, 16; *ibid.*, III, 59.

3. *Ibid.*, 19–24.

4. W. S. Laidley, "Philip Doddridge," *West Virginia Historical Magazine*, January, 1902, 64; Royall, *Southern Tour*, I, 35–38; Hugh Blair Grigsby, "The Virginia Convention of 1829–30," *Virginia Historical Society Publication* (1854), 42–43, 77.

5. Royall, *Southern Tour*, I 38–43.

6. *Ibid.*, 40; *ibid.*, *Black Book*, I, 300; Margaret Couch Anthony Cabell, *Sketches of Lynchburg* (1858), 103 *et seq.* I am most grateful to the Virginia State Library, the Valentine Museum at Richmond, and the Jones Memorial Library at Lynchburg, for sending me information on Harvey Mitchell. Unfortunately our researches have not brought to light the Royall miniature. I am especially grateful, too, to Miss J. M. Campbell, librarian of Jones Memorial, who troubled to get in touch with owners of family portraits from the brush of Harvey Mitchell, in the hope of turning up something that might be helpful. Wilmer L. Hall, then state librarian of Virginia, called my attention to the fact that "in the Washington and Georgetown directory of 1860 Harvey Mitchell is listed as a clerk in the Land Office and lived at 436 North N Street; of 1863, he was a draughtsman in the Land Office and lived at N North cor of 13th St." This information I joined with an interview in the Edward V. Valentine Collection, which Mr. Valentine had with Robert T. Craighill, of Lynchburg. The veteran Craighill said that Mitchell had "died during the War, aged about 65 years." A search of District newspapers for the period 1863–1866 failed to turn up an obituary. A search also of deaths and wills registered in the same period likewise brought no results. This note is given at length in the hope that some little detail will be helpful to someone in locating the miniature of Anne Royall.

7. Royall, *Southern Tour*, I, Appendix, 24; *Paul Pry*, March 31, 1832; Royall, *Southern Tour*, I, 53.

8. *Ibid.*, 58–64, 68, 75, 77.

9. *Ibid.*, 86–92.

10. *Ibid.*, 116–188.

11. *Ibid.*, 120–121. Another version of the meeting is given by Powhatan Bouldin in *Home Reminiscences of John Randolph of Roanoke* (1878), 76. According to Mr. Bouldin, Randolph "was driving out one morning in his coach . . . when he met the stage in which Mr. John C. Calhoun happened to be traveling from the South on his way to Congress. . . .

> The two great statesmen had no sooner recognized each other than Mrs. Royal [sic] put her head out the window, saying at the top of her voice, "Good morning, Mr. Randolph."
> She had scarce uttered the salutation ere Mr. Randolph clapped his fingers to his nose, making a sound, which indicated he smelt an insufferable stench, told the driver to drive on, and thus left Mr. Calhoun to reflect upon the eccentric nature of the man from Roanoke.

I believe that if Anne Royall had traveled with John C. Calhoun—Vice-President Calhoun he was then—she would have reported the journey in detail, including the Randolph gesture directed at her. I have quoted Mr. Bouldin simply to present one more example of the inaccurate legends which Anne Royall attracted. Here timing disproves the Bouldin tale. Congress had not adjourned when Mrs. Royall left Washington and there the Vice-President should have been, presiding over the Senate, instead of "traveling *from* the South." Mrs. Royall, of course, was traveling *to* the South.

12. Royall, *Southern Tour*, I, 137, 139, 164; *Raleigh Star and North Carolina Gazette*, March 4, 1830.

13. Royall, *Southern Tour*, II, 3–32. These pages tell about Mrs. Royall's Charleston experiences. In addition, for this note, other sources are (Charleston) *Southern Patriot*, March 15, 1830; for Doctor Holbrook, *Dictionary of American Biography*, IX, 129. Sad to relate, most of the Holbrook Library, collections, notebooks, etc., were destroyed during the Civil War. By that time the doctor had won an international reputation, but he was too old to start over again. Nowadays his surviving publications, when they turn up, bring high prices from collectors.

14. *Southern Patriot*, April 12, 1830, reprinted from the *Morning Courier and New York Enquirer;* Barnett A. Elzas, *Leaves from My Historical Scrap Book*, second series (1908), 3; *Southern Patriot*, March 19, 1830.

15. Royall, *Southern Tour*, II, 40–63; *Camden Journal*, March 27, 1830, quoted from Thomas J. Kirkland and Robert M. Kennedy, *From Historical Camden* (1905), II, 345.

16. Royall, *Southern Tour*, II, 63–75; (Augusta) *Chronicle and Advertiser*, March 31, 1830.

17. Royall, *Southern Tour*, II, 76–81.

18. *Ibid.*, 96.

19. *Ibid.*, 140, 147.

20. *Ibid.*, 184, 191; Una Pope-Hennessey, *The Aristocratic Journey* (1931), 6.

21. *Ibid.*, 108; Royall, *Southern Tour*, II, 199.

22. *Ibid.*, 201; *ibid.*, III, 7–8, 47–48, 75, 34.

23. *Ibid.*, 19–23; the Levy business condensed from pp. 57–73.

24. *Ibid.*, 27–46.

25. *Ibid.*, 30.

26. *Ibid.*, 66–67.

27. *Ibid.*, 38–39.

28. *Ibid.*, 60–61.

CHAPTER XV

1. Royall, *Southern Tour*, III, 130–136; *Dictionary of American History* (1940), II, 181.

2. Royall, *Southern Tour*, III, 142; Bernard DeVoto, *Across the Wide Missouri* (1947), 14; Royall, *Southern Tour*, III, 148, 161.

3. *St. Louis Beacon*, June 17, 1830; Royall, *Southern Tour*, III, 154, 155.

4. *Ibid.*, 148, 162.

5. *Ibid.*, 163, 168.

6. W. E. Beard, "Mrs. Anne Royal," *American Historical Magazine*, IX, 348; *Nashville Republican and State Gazette*, July 14, 1830, reprinted from the *Murfreesboro* (Tennessee) *Courier*.

7. Royall, *Southern Tour*, III, 202.

8. *Ibid.*, 204–214.

9. *Ibid.*, 219–221; 223–225.

10. (Connersville, Indiana) *Political Clarion*, August 7, 1830.

11. Royall, *Southern Tour*, III, 226–228; *Biographical and Genealogical History of Wayne, Fayette and Franklin Counties, Indiana* (1899), II, 752.

12. Royall, *Southern Tour*, III, 230–235.

13. *Ibid.*, 236–237. Anne Royall's statement that her mother was in her 78th year in 1830 is at variance with an earlier documentation of Mrs. Butler's age. In the litigation, Ann Royall vs. Newton Gardner and wife, *op. cit.*, the Decision of the Commissioner said that Mary Butler at the time of taking her testimony, November 4, 1818, was seventy years old. If this date is accepted then, when her daughter saw her in Indiana the mother was about eighty-two years old.

14. Royall, *Southern Tour*, III, 238; Frances Trollope, *Domestic Manners of the Americans* (1827), 74; Royall, *Southern Tour*, III, 240; Vernon Louis Parrington, *Main Currents in American Thought*, II (1927), 163; Royall, *Southern Tour*, III, 241.

15. Trollope, condensation of pp. 60–67; Royall, *Southern Tour*, III, 240; James Truslow Adams, *The March of Democracy* (1932), 272.

16. Royall, *Southern Tour*, III, 239, 242, 244 *et seq.*

17. *United States Telegraph*, November 9, 1830; *Pittsburgh Statesman*, November 3, 1830.

18. Allegheny County Courthouse, Pittsburgh, Quarter Session Minutes, October, 1829 to June 1832, V, 85; Royall, *Southern Tour*, I, Appendix, 10.

CHAPTER XVI

1. Anne Royall to James Butler, March 23, 1831, letter published in the (Connersville, Indiana) *Political Clarion*, April 16, 1831.

2. American Guide Series, *North Carolina* (1939), 197; *Niles' Register*, June 25, 1831; Royall, *Southern Tour*, I, 147.

3. *Paul Pry*, July 30, 1836; Margaret L. Coit, *John C. Calhoun* (1950), 200; Richard B. Morris, ed. *Encyclopedia of American History* (1953), 171; *Paul Pry*, December 3, 1831.

4. *Ibid.*, November 23, 1833; Goldberg, 233; Ralph C. H. Catterall, *Second Bank of the United States* (1903), 171; *Paul Pry*, May 5, 1832; *ibid.*, January 21, 1832; *ibid.*, May 5, 1832.

5. *Boston Traveller*, November 15, 1831; Anne Royall to James Butler, letter printed in *Paul Pry*, December 10, 1831; *Paul Pry*, December 3, 1831; Poore, I, 105; *Paul Pry*, November 19, 1836.

6. *Ibid.*, December 3, 1831. Prior to the birth of *Paul Pry*, Anne Royall had used quoted interviews in her travel books. The anti-Mason interview would seem to disprove the following statement from Robert W. Jones, *Journalism in the United States* (1947), 270: "The interview story was one of Greeley's contributions to newspaper style and enterprise. Before Greeley's day an interview was not told between quotation marks, but indirectly, in the English manner, the writer giving his version and impressions of what was said." Jones cited an interview that the *New York Tribune* editor had with Brigham Young in 1859 as the first quoted newspaper interview, but pointed out that, "in the *Journalism Quarterly* of September, 1936, Professor George Turnbull of the University of Oregon School of Journalism" credited James Gordon Bennett the elder with "creation of the newswriting vehicle known as the interview." The Bennett interview was with Martin Van Buren in January, 1839. In the column report appeared two direct quotes: "How do you do, Mr. Bennett." "Pretty well, I thank you." *(Ibid.*, 271) Bennett may very well have been the originator of the quoted interview, and he probably wrote such interviews earlier than 1839. Anne Royall, his admirer, simply picked up his style.

7. *Paul Pry*, December 3, 1831, reprinted from the *Camden* (South Carolina) *Journal;* (Hartford, Connecticut) *New England Weekly Review,* April 16, 1832; James Kay to Anne Royall, July 18, 1833, letter printed in *Paul Pry*, July 27, 1833.

8. Frances Trollope, *Domestic Manners of the Americans* (1927 edition), 145; *Paul Pry*, June 16, 1832; *ibid.*, July 20, 1833.

9. *Ibid.*, February 4, 1832; *ibid.*, September 15, 1832; *ibid.*, August 31, 1833; *Huntress*, February 22, 1840.

10. Julia Francescia's *Letter to General Jackson* (1831), 18; *Paul Pry*, December 10, 1831; Schlesinger, junior, 41; *Paul Pry*, December 31, 1831; *ibid.*, December 22, 1832; *ibid.*, August 4, 1832; *Register of Debates in Congress, 1st session*, Friday, July 13, 1832, 1204.

11. *Paul Pry*, August 4, 1832; *ibid.*, September 8, 1832; *Huntress*, June 19, 1841; Montgomery newspaper quoted in the *National Young Democrat,* November, 1936; *Paul Pry*, August 4, 1832.

12. *Morning Courier and New York Enquirer*, February 8, 1832; *Paul Pry*, February 18, 1832.

13. *Ibid.*, June 30, 1832; Bryan, II, 239.

14. *Paul Pry*, February 18, 1822; James Truslow Adams, *The March of Democracy* (1932), 299; Marquis James, *Andrew Jackson*, II (1937), 313; Schlesinger, junior, 44; *Paul Pry*, January 19, 1833.

15. *Ibid.*, March 23, 1833; *ibid.*, April 21, 1832; *ibid.*, March 9, 1833; *ibid.*, March 16, 1833; *ibid.*, February 9, 1836; *ibid.*, February 13, 1836; *Huntress*, March 18, 1837; *Daily Intelligencer*, March 2, 1839; Bryan, II, 543; *Huntress*, March 16, 1839.

16. Bowers, 173, 371 *et seq.; Paul Pry*, December 3, 1831; *ibid.*, July 20, 1833; Royall, *Southern Tour*, II, 217.

17. William Stickney, ed., *Autobiography of Amos Kendall* (1872), 306, 307; *Paul Pry*, June 27, 1835.

18. *Ibid.*, August 10, 1833; *ibid.*, August 24, 1833; *ibid.*, March 19, 1836; *ibid.*, August 22, 1835.

19. *Ibid.*, July 6, 1833; *ibid.*, April 6, 1833; *ibid.*, April 26, 1834; *ibid.*, March 28, 1835; *ibid.*, June 20, 1835; *ibid.*, July 9, 1836.

20. *Ibid.*, November 2, 1833; *ibid.*, April 18, 1835; *ibid.*, April 25, 1835; *Huntress*, January 14, 1837; *ibid.*, May 13, 1837.

21. *Ibid.*, May 20, 1837; *ibid.*, May 12, 1838; *Paul Pry*, May 16, 1835; *Huntress*, June 30, 1838; *Paul Pry*, June 13, 1835.

22. *Huntress*, July 28, 1838; *ibid.*, August 11, 1838; *ibid.*, April 4, 1841; *ibid.*, November 17, 1838; *ibid.*, September 8, 1836.

23. *Register of Debates in Congress* (1834), XII, part 2, 1936; *Paul Pry*, September 20, 1834; *ibid.*, November 1, 1834.

24. *Ibid.*, January 21, 1832; *ibid.*, February 4, 1832; *ibid.*, November 1, 1834; *Scharf & Westcott*, III, 2183; *Paul Pry*, November 1, 1834.

25. *Ibid.;* Haswell, 275; W. Harrison Bayle, *Old Taverns of New York* (1915), 475; *New York Sun*, October 13, 1834.

26. *Paul Pry*, November 1, 1834; Edward Irving Carlyle, *William Cobbett* (1904), 214; William Cobbett, *Andrew Jackson* (1834), 162; *Paul Pry*, December 27, 1834.

Chapter XVII

1. *Paul Pry*, April 25, 1835; *ibid.*, August 22, 1835.

2. The account of Barnum's visit was put together from the 1855 edition of his autobiography, *The Life of P. T. Barnum*, 163–165; a later edition entitled *Struggles and Triumphs* (1869), 78; and the 1870 edition, 66–67.

3. *Paul Pry*, October 10, 1835; Leftwich, 24; H. R. Howard, *History of Virgil A. Stewart and His Adventure* (1836), *passim;* A. G. Walton, *History of the Detection, Conviction, Life and Designs of John A. Murrell* (1835).

4. *Huntress*, March 3, 1838; *ibid.*, October 1, 1843; *ibid.*, July 10, 1852.

5. *Dictionary of American Biography*, II, 197; *New York Herald*, August 17, 1836; *ibid.*, August 19, 1836; *ibid.*, August 26, 1836; *Paul Pry*, November 19, 1836; *Huntress*, January 21, 1843.

6. *Paul Pry*, November 19, 1836.

7. *Huntress*, March 11, 1837; *ibid.*, May 6, 1837; *Paul Pry*, May 6, 1836.

8. *Ibid.*, June 28, 1834; *Huntress*, May 13, 1837; *ibid.*, November 3, 1838; *ibid.*, January 20, 1838; *ibid.*, September 4, 1841.

9. *Ibid.*, October 28, 1837; *New York Sun*, October 13, 1834; *Paul Pry*, September 1, 1832; *ibid.*, August 11, 1832; *Dictionary of American History*, I, 352; *Paul Pry*, June 11, 1836; *ibid.*, June 30, 1836.

10. *Huntress*, January 12, 1839; *ibid.*, April 14, 1838; *ibid.*, December 4, 1841; *ibid.*, August 24, 1839.

11. Morris, 182; Samuel Eliot Morrison, *Oxford History of the American People* (1965), 456; John Bartlett, *Familiar Quotations* (1951), 404 *note;* Poore, I, 233; *Huntress*, June 20, 1840; *ibid.*, December 26, 1840.

12. *Ibid.*, May 18, 1844; *ibid.*, July 18, 1840; *ibid.*, November 14, 1840; *ibid.*, December 5, 1840, reprinted from the *Pittsburgh Manufacturer; Paul Pry*, June 25, 1836; *Huntress*, February 27, 1841; Coit, 348.

13. *Huntress*, August 7, 1841; *ibid.*, June 17, 1841; *ibid.*, June 26, 1841; *ibid.*, August 7, 1841; *ibid.*, March 5, 1842; *ibid.*, June 1, 1844.

14. *Ibid.*, January 11, 1845; *ibid.*, February 22, 1845.

15. *Ibid.*, November 6, 1841; November 27, 1841.

16. (Richmond, Virginia) *Daily Star and Transcript*, January 25, 1841; *Huntress*, December 31, 1842; *ibid.*, February 6, 1841; *Huntress*, October 9, 1841; *ibid.*, December 25, 1841, January 11, 1845, June 28, 1845, November 8, 1845. The Streeter story has been pieced together mostly from items reprinted by *The Huntress*. Not all items were used, but above we give dates where others can be found. Only a few copies of the *Star and Transcript* are in library collections: Henry E. Huntington Library, two issues; Library of Congress, five; American Antiquarian Society, one; University of Virginia, one.

17. *Huntress*, May 20, 1843; Haswell, 331; *Huntress*, March 17, 1849.

18. *Ibid.*, January 11, 1845, reprinted from the *Baltimore Sun; ibid.*, May 4, 1850, reprinted from the (Bellow Falls) *Gazette; ibid.*, June 28, 1851; *ibid.*, September 10, 1842.

19. *Ibid.*, April 1, 1843; *ibid.*, May 20, 1843; *ibid.*, August 3, 1839.

20. *Paul Pry*, February 27, 1836; *ibid.*, May 21, 1836; *ibid.*, May 28, 1836; *Huntress*, April 21, 1838; *ibid.*, February 22, 1845; *ibid.*, July 11, 1846.

21. *Ibid.*, February 22, 1845; *ibid.*, March 9, 1844; George Ticknor Curtis, *Life of Daniel Webster* (1870), II, 342, Daniel Webster to Hiram Ketchum, July 21, 1848; *Huntress*, August 21, 1848.

CHAPTER XVIII

1. *Huntress*, November 29, 1845; *ibid.*, June 7, 1845; *ibid.*, September 20, 1845, reprinted from the *Picayune; Huntress*, May 22, 1847.

2. *Ibid.*, April 28, 1848; *ibid.*, May 17, 1845.

3. *Ibid.*, June 13, 1846; *ibid.*, March 15, 1845; *ibid.*, May 8, 1847.

4. *Ibid.*, November 3, 1844; *ibid.*, June 2, 1849.

5. *Logansport* (Indiana) *Telegraph*, October 18, 1845; *Logansport Pharos*, January 31, 1878, reprinted from the (Indianapolis) *Sentinel*, January 21, 1878; Kathleen Laird, librarian, Iowa State Historical Library, to the writer, March 25, 1958; *Huntress*, September 17, 1853; *ibid.*, February 18, 1854.

6. *Ibid.*, March 8, 1851; (Union, West Virginia) *Monroe Watchman*, September 26, 1935; *Huntress*, January 18, 1851; *ibid.*, October 26, 1839, quoted from the *Picayune; Huntress*, February 24, 1849; *ibid.*, December 25, 1847.

7. Department of Interior, Bureau of Pensions, Washington, District of Columbia Roll, Act July 29, 1848; *Huntress*, November 30, 1844; *ibid.*, July 10, 1852; *Congressional Globe*, Appendix, 32nd Congress, Session 1, Vol. 25, 28; Poore, I, 173.

8. Anne Royall to J. Q. Adams, December 30, 1839, Department of Interior, Bureau of Pensions, Washington, Folio W. 8566; *Huntress*, March 4, 1848; *ibid.*, August 1, 1840.

9. *Ibid.*, March 17, 1849; *ibid.*, March. 15, 1845; *ibid.*, March 16, 1850 and May 22, 1847: two quotes combined for pen portrait of Webster the orator.

10. Rufus Rockwell Wilson, *Washington, the Capital City* (1901), I, 306; *Huntress*, October 21, 1843; *ibid.*, November 24, 1849; *ibid.*, December 8, 1849; *ibid.*, June 14, 1851; *ibid.*, July 25, 1840; *ibid.*, November 13, 1852.

11. *Ibid.*, August 4, 1849; *ibid.*, November 16, 1850; *ibid.*, October 2, 1847. After a few years the Reverend Dr. Ely was brought back from Missouri to take over the pastorate of an obscure Philadelphia church where he worked with dedication, but avoided public controversy. In 1851 his career was abruptly ended with a paralysis. (*Scharf & Westcott*, II, 1298.) *Huntress*, December 1, 1849.

12. *Ibid.*, October 12, 1850; *ibid.*, January 27 and February 3, 1849, two editorials quoted and combined.

13. *Ibid.*, January 8, 1853; *ibid.*, November 6, 1852; *ibid.*, November 27, 1852, quoted from the *American Courier;* Paxton Hibben, *Henry Ward Beecher: An American Portrait* (1927), 345.

14. *Huntress,* July 27, 1850; *ibid.*, November 22, 1845; *ibid.*, October 19, 1850; *ibid.*, February 21, 1852; Ainsworth P. Spofford, *Eminent and Representative Men of Virginia and the District of Columbia of the Nineteenth Century* (1893), 85.

15. *Huntress*, September 4, 1844; *ibid.*, August 5, 1843; *ibid.*, February 28, 1846; *ibid.*, September 7, 1844; Royall, *Southern Tour*, II, 208.

16. *Huntress*, October 9, 1852; *ibid.*, March 8, 1845; *ibid.*, July 31, 1847; *ibid.*, October 9, 1852; *ibid.*, June 22, 1844; *ibid.*, June 11, 1853; *ibid.*, February 11, 1854; *ibid.*, April 23, 1853; *ibid.*, December 2, 1853.

17. *Ibid.*, June 11, 1853; *ibid.*, August 21, 1853; *ibid.*, December 31, 1853; *ibid.*, April 29, 1854; *ibid.*, May 27, 1854.

18. *Ibid.*, April 8, 1854; *ibid.*, June 24, 1854; *ibid.*, July 1, 1854; *ibid.*, July 24, 1854.

19. *Washington Sentinel*, October 5, 1854; (Washington) *Evening Star*, October 3, 1854. Thanks to the interest aroused by Mrs. Porter's biography, a small monument was placed on Anne Royall's grave on May 12, 1914.

INDEX

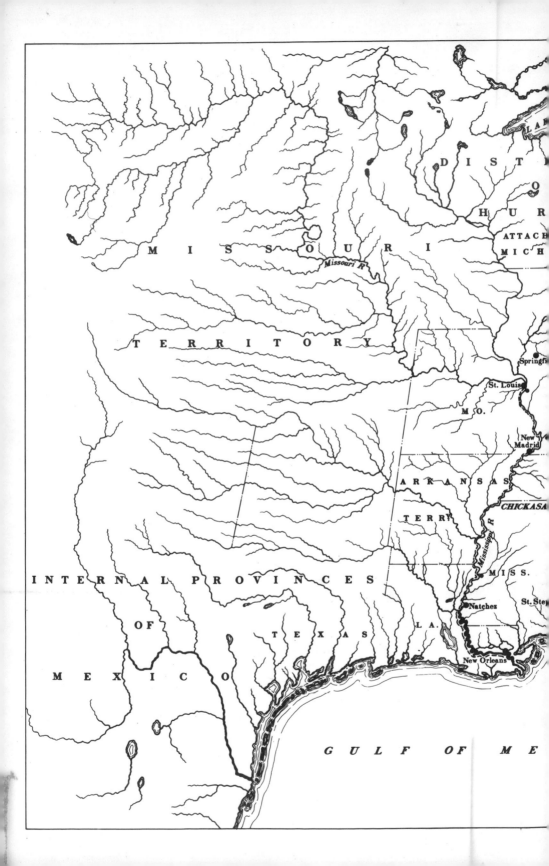